Latinos in the United States

Para la memoria de mi abuelito José Uresti y mi abuelita María Figueroa Uresti y para Mijitos de mí vida: Daniel, Joseph, y Jesse.
[To the memory of my grandfather José Uresti and my grandmother María Figueroa Uresti and to my beloved sons: Daniel, Joseph, and Jesse.]
[Rogelio Sáenz]

Para mis padres Maria y Oscar Morales por todos los sacrificios que hicieron por mí.
To Brian, Brianna, and Joaquin for teaching me the true joy of life.
[To my parents Maria and Oscar Morales for all of the sacrifices that they made for me.]
[Maria Cristina Morales]

Latinos in the United States

Diversity and Change

ROGELIO SÁENZ AND
MARIA CRISTINA MORALES

polity

Copyright © Rogelio Sáenz and Maria Cristina Morales 2015

The right of Rogelio Sáenz and Maria Cristina Morales to be identified as Author of this Work has been asserted in accordance with the UK Copyright, Designs and Patents Act 1988.

First published in 2015 by Polity Press

Polity Press
65 Bridge Street
Cambridge CB2 1UR, UK

Polity Press
350 Main Street
Malden, MA 02148, USA

All rights reserved. Except for the quotation of short passages for the purpose of criticism and review, no part of this publication may be reproduced, stored in a retrieval system, or transmitted, in any form or by any means, electronic, mechanical, photocopying, recording or otherwise, without the prior permission of the publisher.

ISBN-13: 978-0-7456-4271-0
ISBN-13: 978-0-7456-4272-7(pb)

A catalogue record for this book is available from the British Library.

Library of Congress Cataloging-in-Publication Data

Sáenz, Rogelio.
 Latinos in the United States : diversity and change / Rogelio Sáenz, Maria Cristina Morales.
    pages cm
 Includes bibliographical references and index.
 ISBN 978-0-7456-4271-0 (hardcover : alk. paper) -- ISBN 0-7456-4271-3 (hardcover : alk. paper) -- ISBN 978-0-7456-4272-7 (pbk. : alk. paper) -- ISBN 0-7456-4272-1 (pbk. : alk. paper) 1. Hispanic Americans. 2. Hispanic Americans--Social conditions. 3. Hispanic Americans--Economic conditions. 4. Immigrants--United States--Social conditions. 5. Hispanic Americans--Cultural assimilation. I. Morales, Maria Cristina. II. Title.
 E184.S75S228 2015
 973'.0468--dc23
                    2014047149

Typeset in 9.5 on 12 pt Utopia by
Servis Filmsetting Ltd, Stockport, Cheshire

The publisher has used its best endeavours to ensure that the URLs for external websites referred to in this book are correct and active at the time of going to press. However, the publisher has no responsibility for the websites and can make no guarantee that a site will remain live or that the content is or will remain appropriate.

Every effort has been made to trace all copyright holders, but if any have been inadvertently overlooked the publisher will be pleased to include any necessary credits in any subsequent reprint or edition.

For further information on Polity, visit our website: politybooks.com

Contents

Tables and Figures		vi
Prefaces		ix
1	Introduction	1
2	The Diverse Histories of Latinos	7
3	Historical and Contemporary Latino Immigration	24
4	The Demography of Latinos	49
5	Political Engagement	69
6	Education	86
7	Work and Economic Life	100
8	Families	121
9	Religion	139
10	Health and Health Care	158
11	Crime and Victimization	180
12	Mass Media	197
13	Conclusions	218
Appendices		233
	A. List of Occupations Comprising "Latino Immigrant Jobs" by Sex	233
	B. Results of Multiple Regression Analysis Examining the Relationships between Selected Predictors and the Logged Wage and Salary Income by Place of Birth and Sex, 2011	234
References		236
Index		262

Tables and Figures

Tables

1.1	Racial Identification of Seven Largest Latinos Groups, 2011	5
3.1	Persons Obtaining Legal Permanent Resident Status by Region and Period	44
3.2	Ten Latin American Countries with the Most Persons Obtaining Legal Permanent Resident Status by Period	45
3.3	Number of Latino Immigrants in the US and Median Years in the US, Selected Groups, 2010	46
4.1	Demographic Characteristics of Latino Groups, 2011	62
4.2	Latino Population Changes in Latino New-Destination States and Other States, 2000–2010	67
6.1	Percentage of Persons 16 to 24 Years of Age who are Dropouts by Race/Ethnic Group, Sex, and Place of Birth, 2011	92
6.2	Percentage of Persons 25 Years of Age and Older who are High School Graduates by Race/Ethnic Group, Sex, and Place of Birth, 2011	93
6.3	Percentage of Persons 25 Years of Age and Older who are College Graduates by Race/Ethnic Group, Sex, and Place of Birth, 2011	94
7.1	Percentage of Labor Force Employed by Race/Ethnic Group, Place of Birth, and Sex among Persons 25 to 64 Years of Age, 2011	105
7.2	Selected Characteristics Related to Job Quality by Race/Ethnic Group, Place of Birth, and Sex among Persons 25 to 64 Years of Age, 2011	108
7.3	Selected Characteristics Related to Economic Attainment by Race/Ethnic Group, Place of Birth, and Sex among Persons 25 to 64 Years of Age, 2011	111
7.4	Disparities in Wage and Salary Income Obtained by Multiple Regression Analysis for Selected Race/Ethnic Groups Relative to Whites by Place of Birth and Sex, 2011	115
8.1	Marriage and Divorce Characteristics among Persons 25 to 44 Years of Age by Race/Ethnic Group, Sex, and Place of Birth, 2011	126
8.2	In-marriages and Out-marriages among Married Individuals by Race/Ethnic Group, Sex, and Place of Birth, 2011	128
8.3	Heterosexual and Same-Sex Cohabitation Rates by Race/Ethnic Group, Sex, and Place of Birth, 2011	131
8.4	Percentage of Children in Family Households with Female Householders and No Husband Present by Race/Ethnic Group and Place of Birth, 2011	133
8.5	Selected Household Arrangement Characteristics by Race/Ethnic Group, Sex and Place of Birth, 2011	134
9.1	Percentage Distribution of Latino Groups by Religious Affiliation, 2006	152

9.2	Demographic and Socioeconomic Profile of Latinos by Religious Affiliation, 2006	153
9.3	Political Characteristics among Latinos by Religious Affiliation, 2006	153
10.1	Death Rates for Selected Race/Ethnic Groups by Age and Sex, 2010	162
10.2	Age-Adjusted Death Rates for Selected Causes of Death by Race/Ethnic Group, 2010	164
10.3	Causes of Death for which Latinos Have Higher Age-Adjusted Death Rates Compared to Whites, 2010	166
10.4	Percentage of Students in Grades 9 to 12 Engaging in a Series of Health Risk Behaviors by Race/Ethnic Group and Sex, 2011	168
10.5	Percentage of Persons Obese by Race/Ethnic Group, Age, and Sex, 2007–2010	169
10.6	Percentage of Persons Without a Usual Source of Health Care by Race/Ethnic Group and Age, 2010–2011	172
10.7	Percentage of Persons without Health Care Insurance by Race/Ethnic Group, Age, and Place of Birth, 2011	175
11.1	Degree of Concern Regarding Deportations of Self, Relatives, or Friends by Place of Birth (%)	190

Figures

4.1	Latino Population in the US, 1980–2010	50
4.2	Percentage Change in the Latino and US Populations by Period	50
4.3	Percentage of US Population Growth Due to Latino Population Growth by Period	51
4.4	Percentage Share of Latinos in the US Population, 1980–2010	52
4.5	Age-Sex Pyramid for Latinos and Whites in the US, 2011	53
4.6	Percentage Share of Latinos and Whites by Age Group in (a) the US, (b) California, and (c) Texas Populations, 2011	55
4.7	Total Fertility Rate of Latina and White Women in the US, 2010	56
4.8	Infant Mortality Rate of Latinos and Whites in the US, 2008	58
4.9	Life Expectancy of Latinos and Whites in the US by Sex, 2008	58
4.10	Number of Births and Deaths among Latinos and Whites in the US, 2006–2010	59
4.11	Population Projections (in 1,000s) for Latinos and Whites, 2010–2060	60
4.12	Projected Percentage Share of Latinos and Whites in the US Population, 2010–2060	61
4.13	Indices of Dissimilarity Representing Differences between Latino Groups and the US Population in States of Residence, 2010	64
4.14	Latino New-Destination States	66
5.1	Perception of Which Political Party is More Concerned about Latinos, by Latino Group, 2011 (%)	78
5.2	Level of Approval of President Obama, by Latino Group, 2011 (%)	79
5.3	Percentage of Latinos Satisfied with How Things are Going in the US, by Latino Group, 2011	79
5.4	Percentage of Latinos who Believe Situation for Latinos Has Improved Compared to Last Year, by Latino Group, 2011	80

5.5	Las Vegas Student Activists	83
6.1	Academic and Socioeconomic Profile of Bowie High School in Comparison to the El Paso Independent School District and the State of Texas, 2010	96
7.1	Percentage of Latino Workers Foreign-Born, 1980–2010	117
7.2	Percentage of Latino Teenagers 16 to 19 Years of Age Unemployed by Poverty Status, 1980–2010	118
7.3	Percentages of Latino Workers who are Women and Latino Couples with Women Contributing More Income than Men, 1980–2010	119
9.1	Percentage Distribution of Latinos by Religious Affiliation, 2006	151
10.1	Ratio of Latino-to-White Death Rates by Age and Sex, 2010	163
10.2	Life Expectancy at Birth for Selected Race/Ethnic Groups by Sex, 2010	163
10.3	Percentage of Persons with a Disability by Race/Ethnic Group, Age, and Sex, 2011	170
10.4	Percentage of Persons with a Disability among Native-Born Latinos, Foreign-Born Latinos, and Whites by Age and Sex, 2011	171
10.5	Percentage of Persons without Health Care Insurance by Race/Ethnic Group, Age, and Place of Birth/Citizenship Status, 2011	173
10.6	Percentage of Persons in Poverty without Health Care Insurance by Race/Ethnic Group and State of Residence, 2011	176
11.1	Percentage of Latinos who Perceive that Immigration Enforcement Should be the Responsibility of the Federal Government and Not Local Police	188
11.2	Percentage of Latinos Stopped by Police and Asked About Immigration Status, by Latino Group	189
11.3	Percentage of Youth who Have Had a Knife/Gun Pulled on Them in the Past Year, by Race/Ethnic Group and Place of Birth	191
11.4	Percentage of Youth who Saw a Shooting or Stabbing at Least Once in the Past Year, by Race/Ethnic Group and Place of Birth	192
11.5	Percentage of Youth who Do Not Feel Safe in Their Neighborhood, by Race/Ethnic Group and Place of Birth	193
12.1	Average Annual Number of Articles in *The New York Times* Containing "Latino" or "Hispanic", 1980–2013	214
12.2	Percentage of Articles in *The New York Times* Containing "Latino" or "Hispanic" that Also Contain "Immigration" or "Immigrant", 1980–2013	214

Prefaces

Ever since I discovered sociology back in the late 1970s as an undergraduate at Pan American University, I have used the sociological framework to make sense of the world and to seek ways to improve the lives of people on the margins of society. While I have written on a wide variety of topics, the major constancy of my writing has been a focus on Latinos. I have used my writing to call attention to major problems that confront Latinos and to try to find ways to improve the conditions of *nuestra raza*.

For long I have had a dream of writing a book on Latinos – one that tells the story of the history of the different groups that form the Latino population, their experiences in the United States, and what the future holds for us as a people. I was fortunate that Emma Longstaff at Polity Press contacted me about writing such a book. After signing the contract, her colleague, Jonathan Skerrett, has worked closely with me. The writing of the book has taken a longer time than I expected, but it has truly been a labor of love. I was also fortunate to be able to call on the talents of Maria Cristina Morales, a colleague and a former student of mine, to collaborate with me on writing the book. We have had fun doing this.

I am very thankful to Emma for her confidence in me. I am likewise very grateful to Jonathan for his guidance, encouragement, and his electronic elbow all the way from Cambridge, UK that kept the book project moving along. I have been lucky to have great colleagues and friends at Texas A&M University, the University of Texas at San Antonio, and far beyond. I have also been quite fortunate to have wonderful friends in San Antonio who support me, nourish me intellectually and artistically, and who keep me laughing. Also, I thank my beautiful sons – Daniel, Joseph, and Jesse – for their constant love, for being wonderful individuals, and for their many great accomplishments which constantly make me proud of them. Finally, I thank Janie Valadez for the beautiful journey we have started.

Rogelio Sáenz
San Antonio, Texas

When I think of how my interest in the sociology of Latinos developed I can trace it to my own childhood. I grew up in El Paso, Texas, a majority Latino and impoverished city along the US–Mexico border. I lived the border life straddling two cultures and not being fully incorporated into either one. The complexity of living along the US–Mexico border challenges me and is the source of my sociological imagination. This is the place that I call home, today as an associate professor of sociology at the University of Texas at El Paso (UTEP).

It is a great privilege to be writing this book with my mentor and friend Rogelio Sáenz. Rogelio was my thesis and dissertation chair. At the time when I started the sociology graduate program I was only one of two Latina/o students at Texas A&M

University. As a Latina I can testify to the sense of isolation that students like me underwent as they attained their PhDs, yet I was very fortunate to have Rogelio's mentorship.

Sitting in my office at UTEP I can see, and at times even hear, Anapra, one of the most impoverished neighborhoods in Juárez. I look to Juárez with both fondness and sadness as I see a city trying to recuperate from violence. Yet, I also look at it with gratitude and acknowledgement of the sacrifices that my parents, Maria and Oscar, made for me and my siblings Cindy and Oscar as they settled in the US. Without all of their support, and the love of my grandmother Aurora, I would not be where I am today. I am also fortunate to have my nephew Noah and nieces Ale, Andrea, and Bella and my brother-in-law Andres and sister-in-law Lyllian in my life. I am also grateful for my academic friends who have strengthened me emotionally and intellectually throughout the years, in particular, Lorena Murga, Cynthia Bejarano, Sara Grineski, Tim Collins, and Leisy Abrego. Mostly I am grateful to my immediate family. My husband Brian Roebuck who selflessly puts me first and is the most positive person, my son Joaquin whose joy is infectious, and my daughter Brianna who lives her life bravely without boundaries.

Maria Cristina Morales
El Paso, Texas

1 Introduction

Despite common perceptions that Latinos are newcomers to the US, they have a long presence in this nation extending back nearly two centuries. Over this long period of time, countless numbers of Latinos have been born in the US while others continue to make their way to this country. Over their long history in the US, Latinos have made important contributions to this nation. In particular, Mexicans were initially incorporated into this country more than one and a half centuries ago, with Puerto Ricans becoming associated with the US more than a century ago. The US, especially in the Southwest, bears profound Latino – particularly Mexican – roots. Indeed, much of the land in the Southwest belonged to Mexico until 1848 with the signing of the Treaty of Guadalupe Hidalgo at the end of the Mexican-American War. As a result of this treaty, Mexico lost about 55 percent of its land to the US. Latinos living in the Southwest, then, exist in land that once was part of Mexico.

Over the last several decades, Latinos have played an important role in the changing demography of the US. The increasing prominence of Latinos makes them the engine of population growth in the US. The growing presence of Latinos in the US is having an impact on the nation's culture and institutions. Population projections indicate that Latinos will increasingly drive the nation's demography and future throughout the twenty-first century. Already we see the important role that Latinos played in the reelection of President Obama in November 2012. It is estimated that the Latino electorate will double by 2030 (Taylor et al. 2012a). This book provides a sociological overview of Latinos to help readers better understand the past, present, and future of the diverse groups that comprise the Latino population in the US. In the following section we will identify some of the major influences of Latinos on the US in the realms of history, culture, language, and cuisine.

The Deep Roots and Influences of Latinos on the US

The influence of Latinos on the US reaches far back in history. A testament to this historical presence are the many cities across the Southwest that bear Spanish names, including Casa Grande, Guadalupe, Mesa, Nogales, Sierra Vista in Arizona; Chula Vista, Fresno, Los Angeles, Merced, San Diego, San Francisco in California; Aguilar, Alma, Blanca, Dolores, Las Animas, and Pueblo in Colorado; Belen, Española, Las Cruces, Las Vegas, Raton, and Santa Fe in New Mexico; and Amarillo, Del Rio, El Paso, La Feria, San Antonio, and Zapata in Texas. In addition, the influence of Latinos on the US can be seen in the English language, as many Spanish words have come into use in the English language through the ranching past of Mexicans in the Southwest. The litany of Spanish words that are part of the English language includes arroyo, avocado, barbeque, buckaroo, burro, chaparral, conquistador, corral, desperado, dolly welter, junta, lariat, lasso, mesa, mesquite, patio, pimento, rodeo, salsa, savanna, sierra, tango, ten-gallon hat, tomato, and vanilla (Wikipedia 2013). Over the last several decades Spanish language instruction has increased dramatically in the US and became the most popular language studied by American students at the university level in the mid-1990s (Gearing 2010). For example, according to a study of college enrollment in foreign languages in 2009 by the Modern Language Association (Furman et al. 2010), 864,986 students in the US were enrolled in a Spanish language course, while the second most popular foreign language, French, had only a quarter of the enrollment of Spanish. In 2010 Spanish was the most common language among persons 5 years of age and older who spoke a language other than English at home in the US, with nearly 37 million persons speaking Spanish (US Census Bureau 2013b). Furthermore, approximately 2.7 million non-Latino individuals – three quarters of these being whites – spoke Spanish in 2010 (US Census Bureau 2013b) with the number nearly doubling between 1980 and 2010 (Ruggles et al. 2010).

The influence of Latinos – especially of Mexicans – can also be seen in the food that Americans consume. Indeed, the three most popular ethnic cuisines in the US are Italian, Mexican, and Chinese. A recent Mintel survey indicated that 70 percent of persons prepared an Italian dish within the last month, with 63 percent making a Mexican dish, and 46 percent a Chinese meal (Full-Service Restaurants 2012). These three cuisines in the same order were also the most popular among menu items in 2011 according to the Mintel Menu Insights (Full-Service Restaurants 2012). Moreover, Mexican/Latino foods accounted for 55 percent of the overall ethnic food market, which approximated $3 billion in 2011 (Meszaros 2012). The dethroning of ketchup by salsa for the title of the most popular condiment in 1991 is emblematic of the rising popularity of Mexican food in the US (O'Neill 1992). What's more, tortillas outsold sliced sandwich bread in 2008.

Mexican businesses have also made important inroads into the US market. Bimbo is the largest baker, Cemex the top cement supplier, and Cinéplex is the most rapidly growing luxury movie theater chain in the US (O'Neil 2013).

In the world of music, *Rolling Stone* began a section on Latino music in late 2012 (Newman 2012). A significant number of Latino musicians have gained popularity as "crossover" artists who rank highly in Spanish and English language music charts. Historically, the list of leading Latino crossover performers has grown to include Marc Anthony, Raymond Ayala (aka Daddy Yankee), Celia Cruz, Gloria Estefan, Jose Feliciano, Enrique Iglesias, Ricky Martin, Carlos Santana, Selena, Shakira, and Richie Valens (DeVitt 2011).

The Diversity of Latinos

Before continuing, it is important to understand the population changes Latinos have experienced over the last half century. In the early 1960s, the Latino population largely comprised persons of Mexican origin alongside a relatively small Puerto Rican and an even smaller Cuban population with the vast majority (approximately 85 percent) being born in the US. A half century later the Latino population is much more diverse. While Mexicans still account for nearly two-thirds of the Latino population, Latinos today originate from the Caribbean, Central and South America, as well as Spain, with close to two-fifths born outside of the US.

The combination of an established population that has been in the US for many generations alongside newcomers contributes to a diverse Latino population. Latinos also differ significantly on the basis of language, physical attributes (e.g. skin color), families and household formation, socioeconomic status, among many other variations. Furthermore, as elaborated in chapter 2, Latino subgroups differ significantly in their histories and particularly in the ways that they were initially incorporated into the US. Mexicans and Puerto Ricans were initially incorporated into the US through warfare in the nineteenth century. In contrast, Cubans were embraced as "golden exiles" and granted refugee status when they began immigrating to the US in 1959 as they were fleeing communism and Fidel Castro. Dominicans were initially allowed to immigrate to the US as a form of safety valve guarding against the rise of dissension in the Dominican Republic in the 1960s. Salvadorans and Guatemalans came to the US in large numbers beginning in the late 1970s to escape the ravages of vicious civil wars in their countries, but their pleas for refugee status were largely rejected despite fleeing brutal governments supported by the US. Finally, Colombians began immigrating to the US in the 1980s as they sought haven from the brutal cartel wars that devastated the country and its people. These varying histories of incorporation into the US led to diverse paths of inclusion with some groups enjoying easier paths than others. This leads us to ask, how can groups with varying histories and migratory trajectories at different time periods and disparate conditions all be labeled as "Latinos"?

The Making of Latinos in the US

The US government through its Office of Management and Budget (OMB) which oversees the Census Bureau has historically had difficulty in identifying Latinos. For example, in the 1930 census during the period surrounding the Great Depression and the Repatriation Program seeking to return persons of Mexican origin to Mexico, Mexicans were treated as a racial category – for the only time ever in the history of the US census. As the Latino population grew during the 1940s and 1950s, the Census Bureau tried to identify this population by defining people as "persons of Spanish surname" and "persons of Spanish language," along with national origin and ancestry. Toward the end of the 1970s, the US government came up with the term "Hispanic" to identify the Latino population, although the 1980 census used the category "person of Spanish origin." The mass media celebrated and glorified the "Hispanic" term during the 1980s. For example, *Time* featured a story on the Latino population and dubbed the 1980s as the "decade of Hispanics" with Hispanic Heritage Month initiated in 1988 (Dávila 2001). Nonetheless, certain Latinos were critical of the Hispanic term because they felt that it was imposed by the national government and that it celebrated Spanish rather than indigenous roots. By the 1990s, the Latino term began to be used increasingly in the mass media. Yet, some still expressed disapproval of this term because these individuals see it as neglecting their Spanish ancestry.

We use the term Latino in this book. It should be understood that the terms Latino and Hispanic represent the same people, though people differ in their preference for the labels. For instance, a national survey of Latinos/Hispanics found that half of the sample did not have a preference for one label over the other; however, of those that favored one identity, Hispanic was more popular (Taylor et al. 2012b).

While Latino and Hispanic represent "pan-ethnic" labels, being umbrella terms that are made up of various subgroups, Latinos tend to prefer labels that describe their national origin, i.e., Mexican, Puerto Rican, Cuban, etc. Indeed, slightly more than half of Latinos picked a national-origin label over the pan-ethnic Latino or Hispanic term (Taylor et al. 2012b). This is particularly the case for migrants from Latin America and Spain who view themselves not as Latino or Hispanic but as Mexican, Puerto Rican, Cuban, Guatemalan, Bolivian, or Spanish. Indeed, people in, say, Colombia regard themselves as *Colombianos* or Colombians rather than Latino or Hispanic, as the latter terms are not even appropriate pan-ethnic terms in their home countries – that is, they are labels constructed in the US. Nevertheless, regardless of their own preference, when immigrants come to the US they become recipients of the Latino or Hispanic pan-ethnic identities. While gradually they may come to adopt the "Latino" or "Hispanic" labels, the preference for the national-origin labels remains.

Similarly, social constructions of race vary tremendously between Latin American countries and the US. For example, Latin American countries use a variety of designations along the racial color line and there is a common saying in Latin America that "money whitens," suggesting that persons who are economically prosperous are treated as white. In contrast, the US has consistently featured a black/white racial dichotomy in which a single drop of black blood results in a person being considered and treated as black. Thus, dark-skin individuals who may be viewed as white in their home country are treated as black in the US. For example, people in the Dominican Republic, despite their historical ties to Africa, deny their African ancestry in favor of their Spanish and indigenous roots. Dark-skinned Dominican immigrants are surprised to learn that they are black in the US.

Racial Matters

While social scientists view race as a social construction, it is real in its consequences. Although there is greater variation in the genetic structure within racial categories than across racial categories, societies continue to place individuals into racial categories on the basis of physical features, namely skin color. Racial groups are then stratified on the basis of race along a variety of social, economic, and political dimensions. Given the long history of white privilege, persons who are white are at the top of the stratification system, while those with the darkest skin are situated at the bottom. Latinos vary widely on the skin-color spectrum. As such, some Latinos are dark while others are characterized by light skin. People who have populated Latin America as well as Spain have a wide array of features associated with different racial categories. The mixture of racial features stems from African, Arab, Asian, European, and indigenous roots.

According to the OMB and the US Census Bureau, Latinos represent an ethnic group rather than a racial category. Nonetheless, on census-related forms, Latinos are asked to classify themselves racially. Data from the 2011 American Community Survey can be used to assess the racial distribution of Latinos and to examine variations across specific Latino groups. Overall, nearly two-thirds of Latinos identified themselves as white with more than a quarter considering themselves "other" (table 1.1). Only 4 percent classified themselves as multiracial and 2 percent selected the black racial category.

Table 1.1 *Racial Identification of Seven Largest Latino Groups, 2011*

Latino Group	White	Black	American Indian/ Alaska Native	Asian/ Pacific Islander	Other	Multiracial
Mexican	67.6	0.7	1.0	0.3	26.9	3.6
Puerto Rican	57.3	7.0	0.5	0.6	27.3	7.3
Cuban	87.8	3.8	0.1	0.3	5.5	2.6
Salvadoran	52.0	0.9	0.5	0.2	42.7	3.7
Dominican	33.8	11.8	0.4	0.4	45.9	7.7
Guatemalan	50.5	1.1	1.7	0.7	40.9	5.0
Colombian	75.5	1.6	0.4	0.4	17.8	4.4
Other Central American	58.1	6.6	0.8	0.3	28.5	5.8
Other South American	67.9	0.9	0.5	0.4	25.1	5.2
Other Latino	63.0	1.7	1.6	1.9	22.7	9.2
Total Latino	65.1	2.0	0.9	0.4	27.3	4.4

Source: 2011 American Community Survey Public-Use File (Ruggles et al. 2010).

Latino groups vary greatly on their members' racial identities. For instance, Cubans (87.8%) and Colombians (75.5%) identified themselves solidly as white as did two-thirds of other South Americans (excluding Colombians) and Mexicans. In contrast, Dominicans were the least likely to categorize themselves as white with only one-third doing so. Upwards of 40 percent of Dominicans (45.9%), Salvadorans (42.7%), and Guatemalans (40.9%) labeled themselves racially as "other." Three groups (Other Latinos, 9.2%; Dominicans, 7.7%, and Puerto Ricans, 7.3%) were the most likely to consider themselves as multiracial. Similarly, three groups (Dominicans, 11.8%; Puerto Ricans, 7.0%; and Other Central Americans [excluding Guatemalans and Salvadorans], 6.6%) identified themselves as black.

In general, native-born Latinos are more likely than their foreign-born counterparts to classify themselves racially as white (data not shown here). Cubans deviate from this pattern with a greater portion of foreign-born individuals (90.4%) viewing themselves as white compared to native-born persons (84.4%). Overall, foreign-born persons had a greater tendency to identify themselves as "other" compared to their native-born counterparts.

The racial designation of Latinos in 2011 differs greatly compared to racial preferences expressed in the 2000 decennial census. In particular, Latinos, across all groups, were more likely to classify themselves as white and less likely to identify themselves as "other" in 2011 than in 2000. This change does not necessarily mean that Latinos have become more assimilated or that they are now much more likely to view themselves as white. Instead, in an effort to get Latinos to commit themselves to a racial category aside from "other," the Census Bureau on the 2010 census and the subsequent ACS questionnaires specifically informed Latinos that they were to answer both the Latino/Hispanic question as well as the race question and, furthermore, instructed them that "Latino/Hispanic" was not considered a race. Yet, even though an increasing share of Latinos view themselves as white, non-Hispanic whites do not support this perception (Feagin 2010). In a study of 151 white college students, Feagin and Dirks (2005) found that the large majority of students viewed Latinos, including Mexican Americans, Puerto Ricans, and Cubans, as non-white. Thus, even when adopting the white racial identity, Latinos are generally not perceived as such.

This book will examine the varying groups that constitute the Latino population as well as how they vary across different social, economic, political, and demographic dimensions. Data will be presented to illustrate the heterogeneity of the Latino population by considering variations in national origin, place of birth, and sex. Moreover, the book will engage readers through highlighting the major issues and trends that Latinos face in the various aspects of their lives. We will raise several issues of critical concern that are affecting the lives of Latinos today and ultimately impact their future.

Structure of the Book

The book consists of 13 chapters. The book begins with an introduction (this chapter) to Latinos, with the following chapter providing a historical overview of the largest Latino groups in the US. Subsequently, the next two chapters of the book provide an examination of the Latinos' immigration experience (chapter 3) and demography (chapter 4). The book then proceeds to overview the institutional experiences of Latinos, including the areas of political engagement (chapter 5); education (chapter 6); work and economic life (chapter 7); family (chapter 8); religion (chapter 9); health and health care (chapter 10); crime and victimization (chapter 11); and mass media (chapter 12). The chapters on the status of Latinos within several institutions begins with a discussion of relevant theoretical perspectives. We then illustrate the patterns of Latinos across selected characteristics associated with the institution using several data sources. Subsequently, the chapters highlight important issues and questions that need to be monitored to improve the lives of Latinos. Lastly, a concluding chapter (chapter 13) provides an overview of the major patterns associated with Latinos and offers a portrait of what the future is likely to hold for Latinos in the US.

To better understand the diversity of the Latino population and the various modes into which they initially arrived in the United States and the ways they have been incorporated into this country, it is useful to examine in the next chapter the historical origins of the variety of groups that form the Latino population.

2 The Diverse Histories of Latinos

The roots of Latinos in the US today can be traced to Latin America and Spain. These countries, from which Latinos originate, share a common Spanish language, although indigenous languages are also spoken in many Latin American countries. Latin American countries also share an experience of colonization from Spain beginning in the late fifteenth century and independence from Spain starting in the early nineteenth century. Moreover, Latin American countries also are linked to the US extending back to the mid-nineteenth century through a variety of means including warfare, political intervention, economic investment, globalization, and free trade. The linkages between Latin America and the US represent the roots of colonization and migration over nearly two centuries.

Migration theory (see chapter 3) demonstrates that political, economic, and social linkages between developed countries (e.g., US) and developing countries stimulate the movement of people from the latter to the former. In particular, the world system theory developed by Wallerstein (1974) and applied to the field of migration by Massey et al. (1993) helps us understand how developed countries in the core area of the world system enter developing countries on the semi-periphery or periphery of the world system and upset the traditional political, economic, and social patterns. International migration to developed countries then represents one way in which people in affected developing countries respond to their disrupted situations. The US for long has been involved economically, politically, and socially in the activities of countries throughout Latin America as we will illustrate below. The encroachment of the US into these countries includes the exploitation of resources and labor, the protection of US economic interests, and intrusion into the political affairs of countries through the policies of manifest destiny, gunboat diplomacy, and the propping up of right-wing dictatorships and dismantling of left-wing administrations.

Because space does not allow us to provide a historical overview of each country that Latinos originate from and how these countries are linked to the US, we will focus on doing this for seven Latin American countries with the largest populations in the US, namely Mexico, Puerto Rico, Cuba, the Dominican Republic, El Salvador, Guatemala, and Colombia. This group of countries provides us great diversity with respect to types of linkages with, timing of initial immigration to, modes of incorporation into, and the subsequent experiences of immigrants in, the US.

Historical Linkages between Latin American Countries and the US

Immigration does not happen in a vacuum. Rather a wide set of factors influence whether or not people contemplate uprooting themselves and their families and heading out to a foreign land. As we will see below, the US, through its political actions and economic interests, has played an important role in spurring Latin Americans to move to the US over nearly two centuries. González (2000) provides a fitting description of the process involving the entrance of US interests, the exploitation of resources, the support for right-wing governments, the uprooting of the poor, and the eventual immigration of many to the US. González (2000) notes that:

> [A] series of military occupations in the century . . . allowed US banks and corporations to gain control over key industries in every country. Latin American ventures sprang up on Wall Street overnight as sugar, fruit, railroad, mining, gas, and electric company executives raced south on the heels of the marines. Thanks to the aid of pliant local elites and of US diplomats or military commanders who often ended up as partners or managers of the new firms, the newcomers quickly corralled lucrative concessions while the host countries fell deeper into debt and dependence. Whenever conflict erupted with a recalcitrant nationalist leader, the foreign companies simply called on Washington to intervene. The pretext was usually saving US citizens or preventing anarchy near our borders. To justify those interventions, our diplomats told people back home the Latin Americans were incapable of responsible government . . . They fashioned and perpetuated the image of El Jefe, the swarthy, ruthless dictator with slick black hair, scarcely literate broken-English accent, dark sunglasses and sadistic personality, who ruled by fiat over a corrupt banana republic. Yet even as they propagated that image, our bankers and politicians kept peddling unsound loans at usurious rates to those very dictators. Critical details of how the dictators rose to power and terrorized their people with Washington's help, or how regimes provided a "friendly" business climate for North American firms, remained hidden deep in diplomatic correspondences. As US-owned plantations spread rapidly into Mexico, Cuba, Puerto Rico, the Dominican Republic, Honduras, and Guatemala, millions of peasants were forced from their lands . . . [B]eginning with World War II, which shut down the supply of European labor, North American industrialists initiated massive contracting of Latin Americans for the domestic labor front. Thus began a migration process whose long-term results would transform twentieth-century America. (pp. 59–60)

Below we highlight the historical context involving the encroachment of the US into the political and economic affairs of the seven countries listed above and the subsequent movement of people to the US.

Mexico

The first direct link between the US and a Latin American country involved conflict between the US and Mexico. As soon as Mexico gained its independence from Spain in 1821, the US already had its Manifest-Destiny-colored glasses clearly focused on Mexico (Alvarez 1973). Trying to avert US plans to take Mexican land, the Mexican government opened up its northern frontier region (Texas) to foreign settlement from the US. In a short period, white settlers from the US outnumbered Mexicans by a ratio of five to one (Alvarez 1973). Tensions mounted as settlers did not abide by two requirements: pledging allegiance to Mexico and converting to Catholicism (Alvarez 1973). Hostilities heightened after Mexico abolished slavery – most of the settlers were from the South and owned slaves – and halted immigration. Finally, tensions were heightened by internal conflicts within Mexico between the centralists forces – which included Santa Ana, who presided over Mexico – and the federalist forces – which included the Texas outpost including Mexicans living in the region.

With Texas a stronghold of federalism and stirrings of a revolt in the air, Santa Ana marched his troops to quell the rebellion forces in Texas, an event culminating in March 6, 1836 when the Mexican army defeated the Texans at the Alamo in San Antonio. Approximately six weeks later, Texas troops caught Santa Ana and his army off guard in the Battle of San Jacinto. Santa Ana surrendered Texas, at which time Texas became an independent nation.

Nonetheless, the nationhood of Texas was short-lived. Within a decade, the US had annexed Texas. Mexico considered this a slap on the face. Yet, there was still a major dispute between Mexico and the US regarding the boundary between Texas and Mexico. Mexico considered the Nueces River as the boundary, while the US regarded the Rio Grande as the border (Alvarez 1973). The disputed territory between the two boundary lines represented a "no man's land." When General Zachary Taylor marched his troops into the area in 1846, Mexico considered this an invasion, marking the beginning of the Mexican–American War (Alvarez 1973). The war did not last long, as it terminated with the signing of the Treaty of Guadalupe Hidalgo on February 2, 1848. With the signing of the Treaty, Mexico ceded approximately half of its land to the US. In addition, Mexicans who lived on their land and who were now on US soil were given a year to decide on whether to head south to Mexico or to remain on their land and become US citizens. Most of these Mexicans opted to become US citizens. Moreover, the Treaty stipulated that the culture, language, and religion of Mexicans who became US citizens would be respected.

Thus, the Treaty of Guadalupe Hidalgo marked the creation of the Mexican American population – what Rodolfo Alvarez (1973) described as "Mexicans" by birth and "Americans" by the might of arms. The initial incorporation of Mexicans into the US was through warfare, portending barriers that Mexican Americans would experience in their new country. Indeed, when incorporation is not voluntary – that is, when people do not voluntarily choose to move to a new country – members of the host society do not readily accept the newcomers and may treat them as less than human and members of the incorporated group may also resent members of the host society. Despite their US citizenship status and guarantees that their culture, language, and religion would be respected, Mexican Americans largely became a landless proletariat as they lost their land through both legal and extralegal means (Acuña 1972; Alvarez 1973; Montejano 1987).

Over time, the links between the US and Mexico would intensify. As we will see in chapter 3, US growers lobbied to ensure that they continued to have access to cheap Mexican immigrant labor, while Congress sought to drastically curb immigration from Southern and Eastern Europe. In addition, the US and Mexico governments established the Bracero Program, a guest-worker program that brought approximately 4.8 million Mexicans to work as contract laborers to assist the US during its labor shortage associated with World War II. US corporations also took advantage of Mexico's Border Industrialization Program which began in 1965 and which gave the US access to cheap Mexican labor along the US–Mexico border. The establishment of the North American Free Trade Agreement formalized the economic bonds between the US, Canada, and Mexico. These linkages between the US and Mexico have been associated not only with the movement of capital and goods but also the flow of Mexicans to the US.

More recently, we have witnessed an exodus from Mexico to the US as a consequence of the drug war and economic displacement (Morales et al. 2013a). It is estimated that 71,804 people have lost their lives in the drug war between 2006 and 2011 (Morales et al. 2013a). Large-scale violence and economic displacement have uprooted many Mexicans who have moved to the US (Morales et al. 2013a). Yet only a very small proportion (1.6%) of political asylum seekers have been granted this status between 2006 and 2011 (Morales et al. 2013a).

While Mexicans have been in the US for many generations, more than 150 years after the signing of the Treaty of Guadalupe Hidalgo, they continue to occupy the bottom structures of the US stratification system. As we will see in later chapters, even US-born Mexicans continue to lag behind whites and other Latino groups in such areas as educational attainment, occupational attainment, and income. Racial and ethnic groups that were initially incorporated into the US through non-voluntary modes, such as Mexican Americans, have been seen as colonized groups (Barrera 1979; Blauner 1972).

Cuba

Toward the end of the nineteenth century, as Cuba sought to gain its independence from Spain, the US sought to serve as a mediator between Spain and Cuba, an offer that Spain rejected. President McKinley sent the USS Maine to Havana to protect its interests and people in Cuba in January 1898. About three weeks after its arrival, the Maine suffered an explosion in which 260 crew members lost their lives (Cavendish 1998). Although the cause of the explosion was not fully determined, rabid sentiments fomenting in the American press pushed for laying blame on Spain resulting in the US going to war against Spain. The war was relatively short-lived, lasting less than four months. At the conclusion of the war, the Treaty of Paris was signed on December 10, 1898. With the signing of the treaty, Spain gave independence to Cuba, ceded Puerto Rico and Guam, which became US territories, and allowed the US to purchase the Philippines for $20 million (Cavendish 1998). The passage of the Teller Amendment earlier in 1898 assured that the US would not have permanent control over Cuba, other than in a transitional stage.

Consistent with the stipulations of the Teller Act of 1898, the US exercised control over Cuba for only a few years as Cuba transitioned to a state of independence and US occupation of Cuba ended in 1902 (González 2000). Cuba's first Congress began governing the country on May 20, 1902 and Thomas Estrada Palma became the first president of the nation (González 2000). Nonetheless, the US did not disappear entirely as it had significant economic and political interests in Cuba. Thus, following the provisions of the Teller Act, the US established a provisional government following a revolutionary uprising within the country in 1906 and pulled out in 1909 (González 2000).

A couple of decades later, Fulencio Batista emerged as a powerful kingpin who governed the country directly as president himself, and indirectly through his handpicking of presidents (Argote-Freyre 2006). Batista led the Revolt of the Sergeants and took over the government on September 4, 1933 (Argote-Freyre 2006). Batista's rule was supported by the US, who saw him as a stabilizing force to counter liberal forces (González 2000). Batista ruled Cuba with a strong hand for approximately 25 years. Under Batista's rule, corruption flourished with drug and gambling interests making their way into Cuba (English 2009). Using government funds, Batista built luxurious hotels that enriched him and his cronies, including US mafia kingpins (English 2009). Havana was dubbed the "Latin Las Vegas" (Sierra 2014). Batista quelled opposition with violence against his opponents. Nonetheless, forces led by a young lawyer named Fidel Castro began forming with the aim of overthrowing Batista.

As Fidel Castro assumed political power on January 1, 1959, many middle- and upper-class Cubans fled Cuba as they stood to lose their property and wealth as the nation became a communist stronghold. Unlike their Mexican and Puerto Rican counterparts who made their way to the US mainland with limited resources, the first wave of Cuban immigrants – commonly referred to as "golden exiles" – were drawn from the elite of Cuban society. Because they were fleeing a US communist enemy, Cubans fleeing Castro were allowed to enter the US as political refugees and were granted social and economic services to help them settle and adjust to life in the US. Given their own social, economic, and political capital that they arrived with along with the generous treatment that they received in the US as political refugees, in a relatively short period of time Cubans were able to become integrated into the US, more specifically in the Miami area where they formed successful ethnic enclaves where their businesses thrived (Portes and Bach 1985).

A couple of decades later another wave of Cuban immigrants was allowed to enter the US. In April 1980, faced with a weakening economy, Castro encouraged Cubans whom he labeled as "anti-social elements" to leave Cuba (Powell 2005, p. 185). Over a period from April to October in 1980, approximately 125,000 Cubans were transported to the US from Mariel Bay in Cuba, leading to these individuals being referred to as "Marielitos." The group included 24,000 with a criminal record (Powell 2005). While Marielitos were originally allowed to enter the US as refugees, their swelling numbers caused a change in policy in June 1980 when sanctions were leveled against persons transporting Cubans, and the classification of these immigrants was changed from "refugees" to "entrants (status pending)," placing them in the same category as Haitian immigrants (Powell 2005, p. 185). Marielitos included more individuals with limited resources as well as persons with darker skin compared to the earlier wave of Cuban immigrants. While Marielitos faced greater problems adjusting than the earlier wave of Cuban immigrants (Aguirre et al. 1997), they were readily absorbed into the ethnic enclave economies of Miami, thus benefitting from the favorable economic position of the established Cuban community (Card 1990).

Puerto Rico

Puerto Ricans share a colonized group status with Mexican Americans. The initial incorporation of Puerto Ricans into the US also involved warfare, this time in the form of the Spanish–American War. As noted above, the terms of the Treaty of Paris meant that Spain gave independence to Cuba and ceded Puerto Rico and Guam, which became US territories.

In contrast to US involvement in Cuba, US control over Puerto Rico in one fashion or another has been more longstanding. There have been three phases associated with the relationship between the US and Puerto Rico. Immediately after Puerto Rico became a commonwealth of the US, Americans were faced with the question of what to do with a territory that was not white. The choice was to keep it as a commonwealth rather than to make it a US state. The Foraker Act of 1900 pretty much established Puerto Rico as a colony of the US (González 2000). The Act's provisions included the stipulation that Puerto Ricans would be citizens of Puerto Rico and not the US; the US president would appoint Puerto Rico's governor and Supreme Court; and the US Congress had veto power on any laws in Puerto Rico. It was obvious that the US was calling the shots while Puerto Ricans had no say over their own affairs. In fact, under the Foraker Act, Puerto Rico enjoyed a lower degree of self-governance compared to when it was under Spanish rule (González 2000). To make matters worse, a provision of the Foraker Act allowed for the devaluation of the Puerto Rico peso, which allowed US sugar companies to amass vast amounts of land, readily transforming coffee farmers into an agricultural proletariat (González 2000). It is estimated that approximately 5,000 Puerto Ricans left the island as contract workers to toil in the sugar plantations of the Hawaii Sugar Planters Association (González 2000).

The second phase of US and Puerto Rican relations took effect with the signing of the Jones Act in 1917. The stipulations of the Act included the provision that Puerto Ricans be granted US citizenship and be allowed to freely travel between the island and the mainland, thus opening a migration route to New York (Aranda 2007). However, the US president retained the power to appoint the governor, the Supreme Court, and other top officials. Thus, there were some gains for the Puerto Rican population, but the US government was still in charge (González 2000).

The third phase of US and Puerto Rican relations began when the Jones Act was amended by the US Congress in 1947 through the passage of the Elective Governors Act. The act allowed Puerto Ricans to elect their own governor. In 1948, Luis Muñoz Marin became the first governor of Puerto Rico to be elected by its own people.

A year earlier, Marin had instituted Operation Bootstrap, a program designed to industrialize Puerto Rico through foreign investment – mostly US corporations – by "offering them low wages, a tax-free environment to set up their factories, and duty-free export to the mainland" (González 2000, p. 63). The program resulted in a "massive displacement of agricultural workers and urbanization" (Aranda 2007, p. 16). Puerto Rico's excess labor made its way from rural areas to urban areas of the island as well as to the US mainland (Aranda 2007).

The inequity between Puerto Rico vis-à-vis other states in the US mainland are readily apparent. For example, no other state – excluding Nevada – has sent more soldiers on a per capita basis to Iraq or Afghanistan as has Puerto Rico (Lakshmanan 2008). However, while Puerto Ricans can participate in the presidential primaries (having 63 delegates), they are not allowed to cast their vote in the final presidential elections in November (Lakshmanan 2008).

Puerto Rico has held four plebiscites on the island's status – to remain a commonwealth of the US, become a US state, or gain independence from the US. These elections have occurred in 1967, 1993, 1998, and 2012. The vote has shifted with the majority favoring commonwealth status in 1967 (60%) and 1993 (49%), the majority favoring "none of the above" (50%) followed by statehood status (47%) in 1998, and the majority (61%) preferring statehood in 2012 (Wikipedia 2014).

Like Mexican Americans – the other Latino group considered a colonized minority – Puerto Ricans in the US mainland occupy the lowest levels of the social and economic stratification system in the US. The group's low status occurs despite the fact that almost all Puerto Ricans are US citizens and the group has been in the US mainland since first gaining US citizenship in 1917. Indeed, Puerto Rican newcomers to the mainland have tended to occupy the same low social and economic status of their predecessors who have been in the US for generations.

Dominican Republic

Another Caribbean country – the Dominican Republic – for long attracted the attention of the US. In particular, the US attraction to the Dominican Republic centered on its protection of US economic interests as well as to deter communism in the Caribbean region. Great political instability characterized the country from the time of its independence in 1844 to the early 1930s, a period that witnessed 123 political rulers there (Crandall 2006). The US, nonetheless, viewed the Dominican Republic as a strategic location that could serve as a coaling station for warships and in 1869 the US sought to annex the country into the US (Crandall 2006). While Dominicans overwhelmingly supported the vote to become part of the US under the strong arm pressure of then-president Buenadventura Báez, the annexation treaty was not supported by the US senate (Crandall 2006).

For the next several decades the Dominican Republic continued to exist in a state of political and economic instability, much of this under the despotic leadership of General Ulisés Heureaux who ruled with great brutality between 1882 and 1899 when he was assassinated (Crandall 2006). His assassination was followed by heightened instability as various rebel groups fought for control of the country. In order to bring some order, some groups called for US protectorate status while still others sought a reconsideration of US annexation (Crandall 2006). While the US hesitated to enter militarily at this time, it did take actions to protect US financial interests in order to collect debt from the Dominican government (Crandall 2006).

The country established some political stability with the presidency of Ramón Cáceres in 1906, but this was short-lived as his assassination in 1911 ushered in magnified political turmoil (Crandall 2006). Within five years, the country found itself in another civil war, which resulted in President Wilson sending in US troops to occupy the Dominican Republic (Crandall 2006). The US occupation lasted eight years until November 1924 leaving behind "an elected government, a professional police force, a stronger financial position, and seeming internal stability" (Crandall 2006, p. 44). Nonetheless, the calm and stability proved deceptive, as significant changes and turmoil were on the near horizon.

A Dominican soldier, Rafael Trujillo, quickly ascended the scale of the military hierarchy during the period of US occupation. As the US ended its occupation of the country, Trujillo became president of the Dominican Republic in 1930 (Crandall 2006). Trujillo would go on to rule and terrorize the country as a brutal dictator for three decades. Still, because of his staunch opposition to fascism and communism, the US government supported his presidency (Crandall 2006). Trujillo bolstered US support by spending luxuriously on political lobbyists in Washington, DC, and entertaining congressional delegations that visited his country (Crandall 2006). Trujillo squashed an invasion by Cuban forces shortly after Castro gained political control of Cuba, thus demonstrating his importance to the US as a useful force deterring communism in the region (Crandall 2006).

Nonetheless, President Kennedy began to distance the US government from Trujillo as he feared an uprising by communist forces in the Dominican Republic. On May 30, 1960, with the support of the US Central Intelligence Agency (CIA), Trujillo was assassinated outside of Santo Domingo (Crandall 2006). The death of Trujillo did not end his dictatorship as members of his family, especially his son Ramfis, continued to rule indirectly over the country during Joaquín Balaguer's presidential administration (Crandall 2006). Political instability followed with the overthrow of Balaguer by General Rafael Echevarría in 1962, who, with pressure from the US government, was promptly arrested and exiled, only to be replaced by Captain Elías Wessin y Wessin (Crandall 2006). The death of Trujillo and the political instability resulted in the start of a massive wave of immigration to the US beginning in 1962, as migration had been virtually impossible under Trujillo's reign (Hernández 2004). The US government facilitated this immigration as a way to defuse political opposition (Grasmuck and Grosfoguel 1997; Riosmena 2010).

The presidential elections in December 1962 resulted in the election of Juan Bosch, who had returned to the island after being in exile for 25 years (Crandall 2006). The US government was uneasy with Bosch's leadership as he was viewed as an ineffective leader who was too lenient on local communist forces (Crandall 2006). With the US government refusing to provide defense to Bosch as opposition forces nipped at his heels, the Dominican army overthrew Bosch in 1963 with a three-person civilian junta, led by Donald Reid Cabral, assuming leadership until elections took place in 1965 (Crandall 2006). Yet, in several months following the 1963 coup, Cabral would become president of the junta as two of the original members stepped down (Crandall 2006). Economic problems and austerity measures imposed by the International Monetary Fund (IMF) intensified political instability in the country. As Cabral sought to postpone the presidential election until September 1965, he was overthrown in a coup on April 24, 1965.

This overthrow led to complete bedlam as the military and civilians openly revolted. The instability and violence resulted in President Johnson sending in 1,700 Marines on April 27, 1965 to evacuate Americans from Santo Domingo (Crandall 2006). Yet, it was clear that Johnson feared a communist uprising through the return to power of Bosch and after a short period of time he dispatched an escalating number of troops in efforts to deter communism. The number of US troops nearly quadrupled from 6,200 on May 1 to 23,000 ten days later (Crandall 2006).

As order was restored, the presidential election took place in June 1966. The US government directed funds to support the campaign of Balaguer whose primary opposition was Bosch. Balaguer, the US-supported candidate, won the presidency with the majority of the vote (Crandall 2006). The Balaguer administration had two major goals, as Hernández (2004) points out: economic development and political stability. Economic development was promoted through the increase of investments from the US alongside the expansion of industrial production, commercial trade, and finance (Hernández 2004). While these measures served to create significant economic development, unemployment rose due to industrial intensification (Grasmuck and Grosfoguel 1997; Hernández 2004). Political stability was pursued through iron-fist rule involving political repression, murder, and incarceration, with approximately 3,000 killed during Balaguer's first two presidential terms (Hernández 2004). In addition, political stability was also advanced through the emigration of political discontents. Indeed, through a tacit agreement with the US government, political dissidents of the government found easy passage to the US (Hernández 2002, 2004). As Hernández (2004) observes, in 1959, prior to Trujillo's assassination, 19,631 Dominicans requested a passport with only 1,805 granted; in contrast, a decade later, each of the 63,595 petitioning for a passport was granted one.

Though Dominicans were not incorporated as colonized minorities into the US, in many respects their socioeconomic standing in the US has resembled the position of Mexicans and Puerto Ricans. The low socioeconomic position of Dominicans is likely to be related to their racial characteristics. Recall from chapter 1 that Dominicans are the Latino group with the greatest share viewing themselves racially as black. A significant amount of research has shown that people with darker skin tend to fare worse socioeconomically compared to persons with lighter skin (Gómez 2000; Morales 2008a; Murguia and Telles 1996; Telles and Ortiz 2008).

El Salvador

In some ways, historically, the US has not been as directly involved in the political, economic, and social affairs of El Salvador as has been the case with the four countries that we have examined thus far (White 2009). Indeed, much of the conflict that El Salvador has experienced throughout its history has involved hostility with the other countries forming Central America: Costa Rica, Guatemala, Honduras, and Nicaragua, with animosity being particularly acute with Guatemala. Yet, while the influence of the US over El Salvador has historically been more sporadic than those of the other countries, the US strongly supported the right-wing dictatorship during the country's civil war which occurred between 1980 and 1992. The roots of the civil war, however, originated almost a century earlier.

After a tumultuous period of nation building during the half century from 1821 to 1871, El Salvador entered a new era in 1871 as it experienced a dramatic shift in its major crop from indigo to coffee (Menjívar 2000; White 2009). This transformation resulted in the rise of an oligarchy composed of the "Fourteen Families" that dominated the coffee industry (White 2009, p. 66). The emergence of the coffee oligarchy seriously reshaped political, economic, and social relations in the country. White (2009) points out that during the 1871–1932 period associated with the establishment of the coffee oligarchy:

> El Salvador became more liberal economically, yet less democratic, more militarized, and thus more violent. At the same time, there were reformers, but they tended toward increasing the consolidation of power into the hands of the elite and away from the majority of the population. (p. 65)

The 60-year period between 1871 and 1932 saw the consolidation of lands from indigenous peasants to the coffee oligarchy. Indeed, in 1882 a law was established that outlawed communal land holdings (Menjívar 2000). Further, the military, as protectors of the interests of the coffee oligarchy, suppressed and unleashed violence against peasants. The US government had a hand in this violence. White (2009) observes that the Military History Museum located in San Salvador features 100 US-made weapons with the earliest one originating in 1872. While indigenous peasants revolted against the military in protest against their loss of land and suppression, such insurgency was consistently quelled.

El Salvador's coffee product flourished on the world market during the second half of the nineteenth century. White (2009) illustrates the burgeoning sales of coffee by noting that "in 1855, a population of 394,000 exported a total of 765,324 pesos worth of goods, while in 1892, 703,000 people exported close to 7 million pesos worth of goods" (p. 67).

The beginning of the twentieth century saw the continuation of the oligarchy amassing lands, with coffee increasingly grown on large coffee plantations. The loss of land and the continued transformation of coffee production led to peasants working on such large-scale operations. White (2009) describes the conditions under which peasants worked:

> A typical coffee plantation well into the twentieth century consisted of a poor work environment for the peasant who labored all day for an owner who provided only two meals plus a meager wage. Unions were strictly prohibited through most of the country . . . which severely limited the peasantry's ability to improve their lot. This occurred due to the power of the elites within politics . . . [B]etween 1898 . . . and 1931 every president was a coffee grower. (p. 72)

The coffee oligarchy continued to flourish economically throughout the first several decades peaking in the 1920s (Menjívar 2000; White 2009). This prosperity was associated with a shift toward more favorable conditions for workers. Menjívar (2000) indicates that "at this time the government allowed a wide range of openness and reform, including relaxed labor policies, such as the creation of a ministerial-level workers advocate, the right to unionize and the eight-hour workday" (p. 39). Furthermore, a communist party emerged alongside other political parties and in 1931 El Salvador carried out its first free presidential election with Arturo Araujo winning the presidency (Menjívar 2000).

Yet, this political shift was short-lived with worsening economic conditions associated with the Great Depression. Araujo was overthrown after serving only a few months as president, with his vice president, General Maximiliano Hernández Martínez, assuming the reins of power, thus signifying the return of the military presidency (Menjívar 2000).

As in earlier times, peasants prepared to revolt against their oppressors. The uprisings were not successful as the military, as protectors of the coffee oligarchy, simply had too much power. The worst carnage occurred in 1932 with the massive crushing of a revolt against the government in western El Salvador. This event, known as *La Matanza* (the Massacre), resulted in the killing of an estimated 30,000 people, many Pipil, an indigenous group (González 2000; Menjívar 2000). For indigenous peasants, this event resulted in "a heightened culture of fear of the government forces that lasted until 1992" (White 2009, p. 75). In addition, *La Matanza* led to a crushing of their spirit and suppression of their ways of life. As White (2009) observes:

> Many of the surviving Indians resolved to eschew or hide their traditional culture in order to protect themselves from future persecution, indicating yet another level of destruction accomplished by the military. They knew that the

government had targeted their fellow Pipils especially and therefore chose to blend in more as a result. (p. 75)

The massacre served to provide calm and tranquility for the oligarchy "free of unions and organizations . . . to implement economic policies in their own interests" (Menjívar 2000, p. 40).

In response to this violence along with the usurpation of land, many peasants moved from their areas of origin during this period. Many relocated to other parts of the country, while others immigrated to neighboring Honduras which featured more favorable employment opportunities, especially in its banana industry (Menjívar 2000). Estimates suggest that Salvadorans accounted for approximately half of the residents of some communities located in the northern portion of Honduras (Menjívar 2000). Furthermore, the volume of Salvadorans immigrating to Honduras continued to rise, with the number quadrupling from roughly 25,000 in the 1930s to 100,000 in the 1940s (LaFeber 1984; Menjívar 2000). Such movement took a heavy toll on rural communities from where these migrants originated.

Over the period between 1950 and 1980, the government generally promoted industrial development, specifically import-substitution industrialization (Menjívar 2000). These policies led to the development of a small middle class alongside a working class in urban areas. However, the large number of peasants who migrated to urban areas lived on the margins economically. Thus, there was great unrest among the poor countered by immense repression on the part of the military which was supported by the US (Menjívar 2000).

In the early 1960s, economic policies shifted toward the encouragement of export-based industry, which tended to further attract investments from the US (Menjívar 2000). El Salvador's economy thrived during this period with the country boasting the largest number of small manufacturing firms in Central America during the mid-1960s (Menjívar 2000). However, economic prosperity was not evenly distributed, as the poor continued to lag further behind economically. Menjívar (2000) relates that:

> Profits continued to leave the country, more land evictions occurred, and the mechanization of production contributed to an increase in unemployment among rural and urban workers. Commercial agriculture grew at the expense of subsistence agriculture. (pp. 43–4)

Economic pressures on the poor were exacerbated during the mid-1960s when coffee prices dropped in the global market, disease took a toll on cotton production, and private investments fell (Menjívar 2000; Montgomery 1982). Unemployment increased four-fold from 5 percent in 1961 to 20 percent in 1971 (Menjívar 2000; Montes 1987). The continued usurpation of land by the coffee oligarchy further drove peasants off their land with the number of landless peasants quadrupling between 1961 and 1975 (González 2000). Governmental budget cuts, rising unemployment, and enhanced movement of peasants into urban areas further devastated the lot of the country's poor (Menjívar 2000). Nonetheless, military spending rose during this period. Unrest fomented in urban areas assisted by the growth of revolutionary guerrilla groups that had emerged in these places (Menjívar 2000). Many Catholic priests, who had long been supporters of the coffee oligarchy, dominated by liberation theology thought, turned their attention to the plight of the poor (González 2000). The military reacted with force and "paramilitary networks of informers such as ORDEN

(Nationalist Democratic Organization)," which were charged with conducting surveillance for the government (Menjívar 2000, p. 44). The network of informers had a devastating effect on people as they could easily be accused of being a guerrilla sympathizer which subjected them to harsh violence, including kidnapping and murder (Menjívar 2000).

Political and economic conditions in El Salvador plummeted by the late 1970s. As Menjívar (2000, p. 48) notes, "[b]y the end of that decade [1970s], the two main stabilizing forces that held the Salvadoran economy together – a solid demand for Salvadoran exports in the international market and easy access to foreign credit – had collapsed." In this context, wages were cut drastically for workers in urban and rural areas alike and, as the political situation declined alongside economic instability, multinational corporations left the country (Menjívar 2000). Rising levels of political repression against voices calling for social justice resulted in escalating levels of organization on the part of oppositional forces. In the 1977 elections, characterized by large-scale fraud, General Carlos Humberto Romero gained power. As a stalwart defender of the oligarchy, Romero sought to control the oppositional forces who were calling for social justice with increased levels of repression (Menjívar 2000). He ruled with an iron fist between 1977 and 1979, when he was overthrown by a military-civilian junta (Menjívar 2000). While the new government sought to make progressive changes, it met resistance from the extreme right and extreme left (Menjívar 2000). The extreme right opposed the progressive changes and viewed the new government as communist, while the extreme left accused it of merely being a puppet for the military (Menjívar 2000).

Political changes in the US fomented further political discord in El Salvador. In light of overt political repression of the Romero administration, President Carter terminated military support for the government (Menjívar 2000). However, President Reagan, fearing the takeover by communists, reversed this decision in a strong fashion. As Menjívar (2000, p. 50) observes "by 1982 Washington was sending approximately $1.5 million a day to keep the Salvadoran economy afloat." Indeed, approximately 70 percent of the $3.7 billion that the US gave to El Salvador went to weapons and related war assistance between 1981 and 1989 (González 2000). Greater US involvement resulted in greater opposition on the part of the right and left opposition forces toward the government, with armed warfare taking a dramatic toll on the Salvadoran people for a dozen years (Menjívar 2000). Menjívar (2000) aptly describes the horrendous violence that the Salvadoran people experienced being caught between the government and the oppositional forces:

> The low-intensity warfare project in El Salvador involved direct armed confrontation and undercover paramilitary operations against all sectors of society that supported or were suspected of supporting or even sympathizing with the guerilla combatants ... It also involved terror tactics such as death squad operations and attacks against civilian populations (mainly in rural areas), including massacres of entire villages believed to be sympathetic to the guerillas. Landless peasants and the unemployed were frequently suspected of involvement with oppositional organizations. But potentially anyone who was disliked or had an enemy who could point a finger could be branded a guerilla sympathizer. To demand justice in this environment would have meant an act of resistance, and consequently a threat to existence ... But the use of intimidation and violence to retain political and economic power in El

Salvador was not novel. What was new ... was the use of systematic terrorism based on the organized use of murder, kidnapping, and destructive violence by extremist groups as a means to obstruct the political process. The implacable opposition of the organized left and the extreme right unleashed a spiral of violence that affected ... all sectors of Salvadoran society. The report by the United Nations Truth Commission ... attributes culpability to both the government and guerilla forces for the violence that ravaged the country during the war years. (pp. 50–1)

In the end, the 12-year war resulted in more than 75,000 deaths and an untold number of persons disappeared (United Nations 1993).

The bloodshed uprooted Salvadorans to other parts of the country, Central American countries, Mexico, and the US (Menjívar 2000). The movement of Salvadorans to the US skyrocketed, doubling between the 1960–9 and 1970–9 period and rising nearly five-fold from 29,428 in 1970–9 to 137,418 in 1980–9. The numbers would double again between 1980–9 and 1990–9 (US Department of Homeland Security 2012). Furthermore, the population of Salvadorans living in the US rose eight-fold from 94,000 in 1980 to 701,000 in 1990 (González 2000). The increasing movement of Salvadorans to the US during the war was facilitated by "vital social, cultural, and historical linkages established over many years of US influence in [El Salvador]" (Menjívar 2000, p. 56).

However, unlike Cubans who fled communism, Salvadorans were overwhelmingly turned down as political refugees. While it was clear that Salvadorans were fleeing vicious violence, this bloodshed was at the hands of the US-supported government. Indeed, the US Immigration and Naturalization Service (INS) only approved 2.6 percent of petitions for political asylum on the part of Salvadorans between 1983 and 1990; in contrast, during the same period INS authorized 25.2 percent of political refugee requests of Nicaraguans, a group that was fleeing a left-wing government that the US was seeking to overthrow (González 2000). Thus, Salvadorans have by and large lived a life in limbo and uncertainty in the US. This instability along with the lack of US citizenship for many resulted in difficult economic, social, and political conditions in the US. Nonetheless, the US Department of Justice in the fall of 1990 granted temporary protected status (TPS) to Salvadorans who had entered the country on or prior to September 19, 1990 (Menjívar 2000). The TPS program expired in December 1994. Despite the temporary protected status alongside other events, including the ruling in the *American Baptist Churches* v. *Thornburgh* case, which resulted in the decision that INS policy toward Salvadorans was discriminatory, and the 1997 Nicaraguan Adjustment and Central American Relief Act (NACARA), the majority of Salvadorans remain undocumented in the US (Menjívar 2000).

Guatemala

El Salvador's history has much in common with that of its neighboring country of Guatemala. As in the case of El Salvador, the interest of a particular industry dominated the economic and political affairs in Guatemala which resulted in the appropriation of land and the making of a landless peasantry. In the case of Guatemala, the dominating industry is the banana. However, unlike El Salvador where a coffee oligarchy consisting of 14 Salvadoran families dominated the industry, in Guatemala it was the United Fruit Company (UFCO), a US corporation. Yet another difference between El Salvador and Guatemala is that the civil war of the former lasted 12 years (1979–92), whereas the Guatemalan civil war endured over a period of more than four decades (1954–96).

As González (2000) points out, Guatemalan presidents over the first several decades of the twentieth century served to promote and support the interests of UFCO. UFCO particularly benefitted through the presidency of Jorge Ubico who presided over Guatemala between 1931 and 1944. By the end of his administration, UFCO boasted over a million acres of banana plantations throughout Central America (González 2000). UFCO and one of its affiliates, International Railways of Central America (IRCA), were the two largest employers in Guatemala. The nation's poor, composed primarily of Mayan peasants, suffered greatly during the Ubico administration. For example, they were forced to work on government projects. In addition, vagrancy laws and the requirement that Mayan peasants needed to carry passbooks tied them to UFCO and other large landowners (González 2000). Ubico ruled the country with an iron fist.

Yet, in 1944 a voice for democracy emerged at the hands of a "coalition of middle-class professionals, teachers, and junior officers, many of them inspired by Franklin D. Roosevelt's New Deal liberalism" (González 2000, p. 136). The coalition gained momentous support including the nation's trade unions and eventually succeeded in forcing Ubico to resign (González 2000).

The following year, Guatemala had its first democratic election resulting in Juan José Arévalo, an academician who had lived in exile, becoming president (González 2000). Arévalo instituted a variety of progressive changes. González (2000) notes that Arévalo "abolished Ubico's hated vagrancy laws, recognized labor rights, established the country's first social security and rural education programs, and offered government loans to small farmers" (p. 136). Such policies upset UFCO and the country's upper class. Nonetheless, through the support of communist groups alongside that of trade unions, Arévalo's policies gained public support.

In the next election in 1951, Arévalo's disciple, Jacobo Arbenz Guzmán, a military officer, became Guatemala's new president (González 2000). Arbenz sought to distribute land more equitably, as "only 2 percent of the landholders owned 72 percent of the arable land, and only a tiny part of their holdings was under cultivation" (González 2000, p. 136). In 1952, the Guatemalan congress enacted Decree 900, which expropriated lands of 600 acres or more not under use (González 2000). As part of the decree, landowners would be compensated for the assessed value of their property and peasants would be granted low-interest loans to allow them to pay for their land. While the law affected mostly large landowners, UFCO was particularly impacted. González (2000) notes that the expropriated land "covered the vast holdings of the United Fruit Company, which owned some 600,000 acres – most of it unused" (p. 137). UFCO additionally complained about the sum of money – $1.2 million – that it would receive from the government, a figure derived from UFCO's own accountants' assessments of their property values prior to the decree being enacted (González 2000). UFCO and the US State Department requested a sum of $16 million, which the Guatemalan government did not accept (González 2000).

The powerful Dulles brothers – Secretary of State John Foster Dulles and CIA director Allen Dulles – convinced President Eisenhower to launch the CIA-directed "Operation Success" to overthrow Arbenz (González 2000). As an aside, the Dulles brothers were "former partners of United Fruit's main law firm in Washington" (González 2000, p. 137). After the successful coup, the leader of the operation, Colonel Carlos Castillo Armas, was appointed president of Guatemala, with his administration quickly receiving US recognition and financial support. Castillo promptly took the country to the pre-democracy era. As González (2000) observes "he quickly outlawed more than five hundred trade unions and returned more than 1.5 million acres to United Fruit and the country's other big landowners" (p. 137).

González describes the violent bloodshed that Guatemalans endured "over the next four decades, its people suffered from government terror without equal in the modern history of Latin America" (p. 137). González (2000) notes that, with US assistance, by the mid-1970s a total of 20,000 people had been killed with the number of murdered and disappeared reaching 75,000 a decade later.

Guatemalans, like their Salvadoran counterparts, began fleeing to the US by the late 1970s and early 1980s seeking refuge against the massive violence. The number of Guatemalans immigrating to the US legally more than doubled from 23,837 in 1970–9 to 58,847 in 1980–9 (US Department of Homeland Security 2012). Nonetheless, in the US, Guatemalans met the same fate that Salvadorans experienced. Over the period of 1983 to 1990, of all Guatemalans seeking refugee status in the US only a mere 1.8 percent received approval (González 2000). As was the case with Salvadoran immigrants, Guatemalan immigrants were fleeing from a vicious government supported by the US. In the US, Guatemalans lived a life in limbo and uncertainty aggravated by the undocumented status of many.

Colombia

South Americans have increasingly immigrated to the US beginning in the 1980s and 1990s. Colombia has led the pack in this movement to the US and Colombians now represent the seventh largest Latino group in the US. In many ways, Colombians differ from other Latino groups that have immigrated recently to the US. For example, the major factor that propelled Colombians to move to the US was the drug cartel violence that claimed so many lives during the 1980s and 1990s, although its own bloody civil war had occurred decades earlier – a vicious civil war that lasted nearly a decade beginning in 1948. In addition, in general the earliest waves of Colombians tended to possess relatively high levels of education and light skin, traits that are useful in gaining a foothold into the US mainstream. As such, Colombians tend to resemble the earliest waves of Cuban immigrants who relocated to the US after Fidel Castro took power in Cuba in 1959.

Stemming back to its formation as a nation when it became independent from Spain under the name of Gran Colombia (its name changed to New Granada in 1830 and finally to Colombia in 1863), for long there was tension between conservative and liberal forces. The former wanted a centralized government linked to the church while the latter called for a decentralized government separate from the church. Relative peace was maintained through an agreement that the two parties would alternate power with each holding the presidency for a given period of time. At the turn of the century (1899–1902), tension heightened between the Conservative and Liberal parties, which resulted in a bloody civil war that claimed the lives of approximately 100,000 people. Civil war reemerged in the period from 1948 to 1957 as a result of the assassination of Jorge Eliecer Gaitan, the leader of the Liberal Party (González 2000). His killing led to a massive riot in Bogota with approximately 2,000 persons killed. The riot led to a decade-long vicious bloody civil war that claimed an estimated 180,000–200,000 lives (González 2000). Due to its vicious nature and the toll of lost lives, the civil war became known as *La Violencia* (the Violence). The war not only split families but also uprooted many persons from rural areas who resettled in urban areas (González 2000). The civil war came to a close in 1957 when negotiators agreed to the two parties alternating power, as was the case earlier (González 2000).

Nonetheless, the conclusion of the war spurred the emergence of guerilla groups that dominated urban (M-19) and rural (Fuerzas Armadas Revolucionarias de Colombia, FARC – Armed Forces of the Colombian Revolution) areas (González 2000). The guerilla groups exerted much violence throughout the country. Yet, opportunities arose for many marginalized guerrilla-trained youth when warfare broke out in the cities of Cali and Medellín between drug cartels competing for control of the global cocaine market (González 2000). The youths were recruited as drug couriers and as assassins (González 2000). Murder and terrorism became rampant in the midst of the cartel wars. González (2000) observes that a Bogota newspaper in 1987 reported that "43 people were killed on the streets of Bogotá, Cali, and Medellín, the three largest cities, assassinated by armed hoodlums who indiscriminately gunned down women, children, beggars, and garbage collectors for fun and target practice" (p. 158). González (2000) points out that in 1997, 31,000 persons were killed in the country. Meanwhile, violence continued in rural areas as soldiers and right-wing paramilitary groups wreaked havoc and murdered people accused of supporting left-wing guerrillas (González 2000). Colombia became one of the deadliest countries in the world.

This violence prompted many Colombians, especially those from the educated segment of the population, to immigrate to the US. In fact, the flow of Colombians had actually started at the height of *La Violencia* with the number of Colombians immigrating legally to the US increasing from 3,454 in 1940–9 to 15,567 in 1950–9 and to 68,371 in 1960–9 (US Department of Homeland Security 2012). Still, the violence of the cartel wars was associated with increasing numbers of Colombian immigrants to the US: 71,265 in 1970–9; 105,494 in 1980–9; 137,985 in 1990–9; and 236,570 in 2000–9 (US Department of Homeland Security 2012). González (2000) points out that the earliest waves of Colombians became well established and integrated economically in New York City, where they are predominantly located. Nonetheless, González (2000) notes that the later waves have created schisms as a certain share of Colombian immigrants have included people associated with drug cartels, thus creating tension between the earlier and more recent arrivals.

Summary

We examined in this chapter the histories of the seven largest Latino groups. These seven Latino groups differ in their pasts, modes of incorporation into the US, and the time frame in which people began immigrating to the US. Yet, there are some similarities as well. For example, the groups are bound together by their conquest and eventual independence from Spain as well as their common Spanish language. People originating from these seven countries as well as from throughout Latin

America and Spain became Latino or Hispanic in the US. Furthermore, the seven countries had a variety of ties to the US involving warfare as well as the US intervening in the political affairs of countries and providing military and financial support to prop right-wing governments that ruled with an iron fist, often protecting US business and political interests. The establishment of such links between the US and many Latin American countries, intensified more recently through free-trade agreements, has served to promote immigration of Latin Americans to the US. Finally, as noted earlier, the initial mode of incorporation of Latinos in the US has woven a path toward integration with some groups, such as Mexicans and Puerto Ricans, experiencing hardships, while others, such as Cubans and Colombians, enjoying easier upward mobility and integration into the US.

The next chapter provides an overview of the migration perspectives that have been used to explain international migration as well as US immigration policies and practices that have affected the flow of immigration to the United States.

3 Historical and Contemporary Latino Immigration

Throughout US history millions of people have come to the US from all around the world. An array of factors has propelled their movement to this country. In addition, an assortment of US immigration policies and programs have impacted the ease or difficulty associated with their entry into this country. Over time, the face of immigration has shifted dramatically. In the twentieth century, we have seen the source of immigration shift from Europe at the onset of the century to Latin America and Asia beginning in the mid-1960s and increasingly so toward the close of the century.

This chapter provides an overview of the historical and contemporary Latino immigration. We begin with an examination of theoretical perspectives that have been developed to understand the international movement in order for readers to gain a framework for making sense of the sustained Latino immigration over the last century. These theoretical perspectives remind us that the movement of people across international borders does not occur in a vacuum; rather, they are driven by economic, global, historical, and structural forces. Subsequently, we provide a discussion of policies that have shaped and affected Latino immigration and, concomitantly, describe the changing volume of immigration associated with such policies. Furthermore, we review the historical and contemporary shifts in immigration to the US with particular emphasis on the expanding immigration from Latin America beginning in the 1960s and intensifying over subsequent decades. Finally, we outline the major and most pressing issues related to Latino immigration in the US.

Theoretical Perspectives

Over the last half century, demographers, economists, and sociologists have developed theoretical frameworks to understand the movement of people. In general, these perspectives have focused on the internal migration of people within countries, the push and pull factors that drive the movement, and the economic factors that propel people to move (Greenwood 1985; Lee 1966). In the last several decades, theoretical perspectives have been advanced to capture the broader context in which international migration occurs. In particular, these theoretical frameworks have called attention to the role that labor markets, households, globalization, historical forces, and social networks play in the movement of people across international boundaries. We draw below on the inventory and assessment of immigration theoretical perspectives undertaken by Massey and his colleagues (Massey et al. 1993; see also Massey and Espinosa 1997; Massey et al. 2005).

Initiation of International Migration

Neoclassical economics

Economics push-pull perspectives have a long tradition in efforts to understand human migration. The neoclassical economics perspective draws on assumptions that humans are rational, seeking to increase their net economic benefits, and that they have complete information regarding conditions across labor markets. The neoclassical economics framework features two forms – macro and micro – based on the level of unit of analysis (e.g., labor markets, individual, etc.).

The macro variety of the neoclassical economics perspective focuses on the disequilibrium of the supply and demand for labor across labor markets. On the international stage, there are some countries, such as the US, that have favorable economic conditions characterized by low levels of unemployment and high wages, reflecting a high demand for labor. On the other hand, other countries, such as Mexico, are characterized by high levels of unemployment and low wages, evincing a high supply of labor. The labor saturation is especially evident in light of high fertility levels and large shares of young people entering the labor market. The neoclassical economics perspective suggests that flows of labor will be directed from countries with excess labor to those with labor needs, such as the movement of workers from many countries in Latin America to the US. The theory proposes that the movement of workers across labor markets is a response to disequilibrium across labor markets and that eventually equilibrium is restored when the supply and demand for labor is in balance across labor markets. Certainly, the excess labor in many Latin American countries and labor needs in the US has been associated with the movement of people to the US. More recently, however, the flow of immigrants from Latin America, especially from Mexico, has slowed dramatically (Passel et al. 2012). Among a variety of factors that have been associated with this decline has been the dramatic drop in the fertility rate in Mexico and Latin America, which has resulted in a smaller labor force (Cave 2013).

The micro form of the neoclassical economics perspective spotlights the decision making that potential migrants conduct as they evaluate costs and benefits associated with the potential place(s) of destination and site of origin. Benefits related to the place of destination include favorable labor market conditions, such as high wages, low unemployment, and the possibility of job advancement. Costs associated with the movement include the monetary cost of relocation, money foregone in the job search, as well as psychic expenditures related to cutting ties with family and friends in one's place of origin. The theory proposes that the likelihood of movement is enhanced when the benefits of the movement outweigh costs related to the relocation. The theory suggests that people are rational and that they have complete information about varying labor markets. However, in the case of international migration, especially of people with limited resources, we will see below that they rely on social networks and social capital to navigate movement. As such, the individual form of the neoclassical economics perspective is relevant to understanding Latin American immigration to the US, but as part of a larger framework that incorporates reliance on social networks and social capital (see below).

The new economics of migration
While the new economics of migration, similarly, highlights economic factors, it is broader than the neoclassical economics perspective in a few respects. For example, the center of attention is not individuals or labor markets, but households where members are mobilized to maximize household resources. In addition, the framework broadens the context to account for the various ways in which households survive economically in light of financial and environmental uncertainty. People in many developing countries have limited options at their disposal to protect themselves against a variety of risks that can devastate their economic well-being. For example, in Mexico small-scale farmers are vulnerable to unexpected downturns in the economy, the weather, and other related events. Thus, a significant drop in the value of the peso as well as the absence of rain can affect tremendously the livelihood of the country's poor. In addition, the poor do not have access to financial and insurance institutions that can protect them against such calamities.

As a strategy for protection against such distress, household members perform a diverse set of activities to minimize risks. Accordingly, households behave in a similar fashion as smart investors that diversify their investment portfolios. For instance, in the case of households engaged in small-scale farming, certain household members may tend to the raising of crops, others may take off-farm employment in the local or surrounding area, and still others may immigrate to the US from where they can send remittances to the household. As such, immigration represents a strategy that allows the household to minimize the risks of uncertainty while amassing resources from the business of migration. Historically, remittances have been a major part of the economy of Mexico and other Latin American countries (Massey and Parrado 1994; Orozco 2002). It is estimated that nearly $69.3 billion in remittances flowed to Latin America in 2011, with $22.7 billion directed to Mexico alone (Orozco 2012).

Dual labor market theory
The neoclassical and new economics of migration perspectives focus primarily on decisions that individuals and households make to maximize income or minimize risks. The dual labor market perspective shifts attention to the links between labor market demands in developed countries and the movement of labor from developing countries (Massey et al. 1993; Piore 1979).

As opposed to international migration driven by push factors in the country of origin and pull factors in the country of destination, the dual labor market perspective argues that the movement is due simply to the latter factors. As such, the structure of labor markets makes international migrants an essential component of the economies of developed countries (Massey et al. 1993). Four attributes of the economies of developed countries, such as the US, are particularly important to understanding the inherent demand for migrant labor. First, developed countries face situations involving large demand alongside a small supply among their native populations for low-skill jobs. In order to make such jobs attractive to native-born workers, employers would need to raise wages. However, the boosting of wages for low-skill jobs would put pressures on employers to elevate the wages for jobs slightly higher in the hierarchy of occupational prestige, with the raising of such wages leading to further pressures to increase wages at still higher levels of the echelon of occupational prestige – a situation referred to as "structural inflation." Thus, developed countries have a need for immigrant labor that takes jobs at such low levels, thus ensuring the smooth operation of the economy without having to raise wages across the board.

Second, occupational hierarchies are essential for the motivation of workers, who can earn status for holding certain jobs as well as seeking to climb higher in the job echelon (Massey et al. 1993). Dead-end jobs at the bottom of the occupational structure are devoid of status and provide little upward mobility, thus not being attractive to native-born workers. The elimination of the bottommost jobs would simply result in the next tier of workers becoming the new basement level jobs. Hence, employers are attracted to low-wage immigrant labor that is primarily concerned with obtaining income rather than job status. Indeed, the low wages that immigrants receive for dead-end jobs are higher than those that they receive in their home country. In fact, as many immigrant newcomers continue to see themselves as part of their home country, they also derive status through remitting money to their family back home.

Third, due to the duality of capital which is fixed and labor which is flexible, labor markets are segmented into the primary sector and the secondary sector (Massey et al. 1993). The primary sector consists of capital-intensive labor in which employers invest heavily through training and education. Because employers invest in primary-sector workers, employers seek to retain them. As such, primary-sector workers receive favorable wages and benefits, and have an opportunity for upward mobility within the organization. In contrast, the secondary sector is characterized by a labor-intensive workforce that is largely expendable, as employers let go of this segment of the labor force when they are not needed or the economy is not doing well. Thus, workers in this sector of the labor force receive low wages, limited benefits, at best, and have little opportunity for upward mobility. Again, native-born workers are not attracted to this segment of the labor force, with immigrant laborers filling this labor niche.

Fourth, the need for immigrant labor to fill low-wage, dead-end jobs has been exacerbated by the decline of two segments of the labor force whose supply has dwindled due to demographic forces. In particular, in the past, women and teenagers filled such jobs. However, over the last several decades, women have experienced increasing levels of labor force participation and divorce rates, both of which cemented their status as income earners, and they have experienced significant declines in their fertility, which has limited the labor supply of teenage workers. The decline of women and teenagers as occupants of low-wage, dead-end jobs has made immigrant labor even more attractive to employers.

In sum, the dual labor market perspective illustrates the forces that made low-wage immigrant labor a necessary part of the labor force of developed countries. Simply put, the economies of developed countries, such as the US, depend very heavily on immigrant labor originating from developing countries, such as Mexico and other Latin American countries.

World system theory
The world system perspective for understanding the initiation of international migration stems from the theoretical insights of Wallerstein (1974). This framework focuses

on the development and expansion of the structure of the world market with roots in the sixteenth century (Massey et al. 1993). According to this perspective, the penetration of capitalists from developed countries and multinational corporations into the economic markets of developing countries sets the emergence of international migration from developing countries to developed countries. In particular, the entrance of capitalist interests into the economies of developing countries is associated with disruptions and dislocations to the traditional labor markets of those countries. Furthermore, in order to protect the economic interests of their capitalist corporations, developed countries often intervene in the political affairs of developing countries, as illustrated in chapter 2, thus setting off added forces stimulating immigration.

As capital interests enter developed countries, land becomes an increasingly valuable commodity. Capitalist farmers in developed countries usurp land from the hands of subsistent farmers and other small-scale operators and turn to high-yield seeds, expensive fertilizers, and mechanized production. Recall earlier the case of El Salvador's coffee oligarchy who wrested land from subsistent farmers. The lives of small-scale operators who cede their land are transformed dramatically, as they lose their livelihood. Some of these individuals work for the increasingly large plantations, others move to urban areas, and still others immigrate to developed countries.

The penetration of capital affects other industries aside from agriculture. For instance, capitalists from developed countries and multinational corporations enter developed countries to take advantage of their cheap labor through the formation of assembly plants under the guise of helping the country industrialize. The US has a long history of such programs in Latin America, most notably in the form of Operation Bootstrap in Puerto Rico in 1947 and the Border Industrialization Program (BIP) in Mexico in 1965, which was the precursor of the North American Free Trade Agreement (NAFTA). Such industrialization efforts sever relations and transpose peasants into laborers making them increasingly mobile and subject to migration (Massey et al. 1993). As was the case in Puerto Rico and Mexico involving the industrialization programs noted above, many laborers working in assembly plants eventually sought to improve their fortunes in the mainland US.

Moreover, transportation routes are established between the developed country and the developing country to ship products. Such transportation paths serve to not only move capital and products but also people, who immigrate to the developed country to pursue economic opportunities or join family members.

The set of theories just reviewed provide us an understanding of how international migration is initiated. The theoretical perspectives point to the importance of labor market forces involving the imbalance between labor supply and labor demand as well as the economic-related calculations that migrants undertake to decide whether or not to migrate, the survival strategies that households use to maximize economic resources and minimize economic risks, the structural labor market forces involving developed countries needing low-wage labor from developed countries, and the dislocation of workers when capitalist enterprises enter developing countries. We now turn to a discussion of the theoretical perspectives that provide insights into how immigration is sustained.

Perpetuation of International Migration

Network theory

International migration is not a solitary act. Rather, people rely on their social networks to facilitate movement across international borders. Massey et al. (1993) define migrant networks as "sets of interpersonal ties that connect migrants, former migrants, and nonmigrants in origin and destination areas through ties of kinship, friendship, and shared community origin" (p. 448). In particular, networks represent a form of social capital that people can tap into in order to facilitate international migration and secure employment in the place of destination (Massey et al. 1993). A valuable and instrumental feature of social networks is that information derived from one's social networks serves to reduce the costs and risks associated with immigration.

Potential migrants draw on the stock of knowledge accumulated by members of the community, including relatives and friends, to gain important information as they seek to immigrate and subsequently look for employment in the place of destination. Once the potential migrant, himself or herself, engages in migration and settles in the place of destination, he or she becomes another potential link to other potential migrants contemplating an international move. Thus, we can imagine a particular rural community in Mexico that initially did not have anyone who had immigrated to the US. Given the lack of a stock of knowledge of immigration in the community, the first person moving to the US would find it difficult and costly to set out abroad and would also face hardships in locating employment and assistance. The difficulties would be slightly less for the second person moving to the US because he/she could draw on the experience and information of the earliest immigrant. Hence, the difficulty, cost, and risk of migration decline as increasingly more people engage in immigration and obtain important information that can be shared with other potential immigrants. As Massey et al. (1993) point out: "Once the number of migrants reaches a critical threshold, the expansion of networks reduces the costs and risks of movement, which causes the probability of migration to rise, which causes additional movement, which further expands the networks, and so on" (pp. 448–9). Moreover, while originally the immigration flow consists of a selective population, such as young men, over time the immigration stream includes a broader segment of the population (Massey et al. 1993).

Institutional theory

As the flow of immigration emerges for one country to another, private institutions and voluntary, non-profit organizations arise to meet the imbalance between the large number of people who seek to enter a developed country, such as the US, and the limited number of slots available to accommodate people's desire to immigrate (Massey et al. 1993). As the country of destination erects barriers and obstacles, including policies, to bar persons from entering the country without proper authorization, entrepreneurs and institutions arise to provide goods and services to immigrants to enhance their probabilities of entering the country. For the most part, these are underground activities that assist immigrants, such as human smugglers (e.g., *coyotes* in the case of human smugglers, who provide their services to assist immigrants to enter the US from Mexico), businesses providing fraudulent documents (e.g., social security cards, passports, etc.) and arranged marriages between US citizens and immigrants, contract laborers who arrange for employment of unauthorized labor, as well as people and businesses who cater to the food and lodging needs of immigrants (Massey et al. 1993). Furthermore, voluntary, non-profit humanitarian organizations also emerge to assist immigrants. Such organizations assist immigrants through the provision of water and food during their journey, social services, counseling, as well as protecting them from human rights and related abuses (Massey et al. 1993).

As these individuals, businesses, institutions, and organizations providing goods and services to immigrants become firmly established and known to immigrants, they become part of the stock of knowledge and social capital that immigrants draw on to navigate immigration and facilitate settlement in the country of destination. As such, these entities serve to ensure the continuation of immigration.

Cumulative causation
Immigration is sustained in yet another way. In this case, immigration itself alters the social context in which other persons in the sending community make decisions regarding whether or not to engage in international migration (Massey et al. 1993). Thus, each episode of immigration makes subsequent immigration more likely because the act of immigration increasingly alters the environment of the community of origin, resulting in other individuals being more likely to immigrate as well. This is a process known as cumulative causation which stems from the work of Gunnar Myrdal (1957).

There are various ways in which immigration alters the social context which leads to ensuing immigration being more likely. These alterations involve the distribution of income, the distribution of land, the organization of agrarian production, the culture of migration, the regional distribution of human capital, and social labeling (Massey et al. 1993). For example, as people start moving from the sending community, immigration widens income inequality in the community. Immigrants attain more income from their jobs abroad which they remit back home. Other individuals in the community experience relative deprivation as their own income lags behind those of migrants, leading to greater probabilities of others immigrating to earn higher income levels. In addition, with their remittances, immigrants purchase land which they typically take out of production with the long-range plan for returning or retiring to live in a home built on the land. As more immigrants make similar purchases of land and take it out of production, there is a declining need for agricultural labor, which stimulates these individuals to immigrate in search of employment. Furthermore, in cases where immigrants purchase land to farm, due to their favorable economic position, they are able to engage in more capital-intensive forms of agriculture than is typical of the sending community, again leading to a decline in the need for agricultural laborers, who seek better economic opportunities abroad. Moreover, immigration alters immigrants themselves, along with their tastes, preferences, and lifestyles. As such, in order to satisfy the newly-acquired lifestyles, immigrants are more likely to continue engaging in immigration as well as to stimulate others to seek such pursuits through the vehicle of immigration. Hence, the culture of migration becomes deeply entrenched in people's behavior, leading increasingly to an expectation that people will immigrate. Additionally, as immigration becomes more widespread in the community of origin, the home community experiences a significant loss of its human capital which negatively affects the need for labor locally, further stimulating people to immigrate in pursuit of better economic opportunities. Finally, as immigrants are drawn to certain low-paying jobs in the country of destination, those positions become known as "immigrant jobs," which reduces the likelihood that native workers will take such employment.

In sum, we have provided an overview of the different theoretical approaches that help us understand how immigration is initiated and how it is sustained over time. These perspectives can be used to comprehend the movement of people from Latin America to the US over the course of more than a century. Below we discuss US policies and programs over the last century which at times have facilitated the movement of people from Latin America, especially from Mexico, and at other times made it increasingly difficult for individuals from this region to immigrate to the US.

US Immigration Policies and Programs

The US has established a variety of policies and programs, at times in conjunction with Mexico, over the last century which have impacted the flow of immigrants from Mexico and the rest of Latin America to the US. To a certain extent, these actions have at times welcomed Mexican and other Latin American immigrants and at other times have shunned these individuals.

Over the course of the nineteenth century and into the first couple of decades of the twentieth century, US immigration policy toward Mexico and Latin America was mute (LoBreglio 2004). Indeed, during this period the movement of Mexicans across the US–Mexico border was fairly unregulated. This situation contrasted sharply from the major US immigration policies and programs that sought to limit immigration of certain groups including Chinese with the creation of the Chinese Exclusion Acts of 1882 and 1892, Japanese with the signing of the Gentlemen's Agreement in 1907, and Southern and Eastern Europeans with the passage of the Immigration Acts of 1917, 1921, and 1924. In fact, while many Americans rabidly called for policy to curtail or eliminate immigration from Southern and Eastern Europe which led to the establishment of immigration policy between 1917 and 1924, US agriculturalists from the Southwest argued vociferously to exempt Mexicans from the literacy requirement and head tax imposed by the Immigration Act of 1917 and from the quota system that limited the number of people allowed to immigrate from specific countries which was stipulated by the Immigration Acts of 1921 and 1924 (LoBreglio 2004). This incident almost a century ago illustrates the long and established dependence of US employers on cheap labor from Mexico and subsequently from other parts of Latin America.

The Establishment of the Border Patrol

As a compromise for Mexico being exempted from immigration quotas constituted by the Immigration Act of 1924, the US established the US Border Patrol in 1924 as part of the US Department of Labor with the passage of the Labor Appropriation Act of 1924. While surveillance efforts targeted the flows of undocumented Chinese, it also prevented the entry of undocumented Mexicans along the US–Mexico border.

Indeed, the creation of the Border Patrol marked the criminalization of the Mexican immigrant in the US, although it was not illegal for an employer to hire undocumented laborers (Bustamante 1972). Border Patrol agents are referred to as *"la migra"* by Mexicans on both sides of the border.

The Repatriation Program

The Great Depression ushered in a new economic era which displaced people from their jobs and placed them on breadlines. As such, despite efforts to curtail immigration legislatively at the beginning of the 1920s, by the end of the decade the flow of immigration to the US came to a halt due to the Great Depression. In efforts to protect the handful of jobs available, the US sought to eliminate foreign job competition. Due to the proximity of Mexico along with the deep-seated racism against Mexicans in the US, Mexicans became a convenient scapegoat. Quickly President Hoover authorized the Mexican Repatriation Program in 1929 and his successor, President Franklin Delano Roosevelt, prolonged the program until 1939. Balderrama and Rodríguez (2006) illustrate the context in which the US government fervently sent Mexicans back home:

> Americans, reeling from the economic disorientation of the depression, sought a convenient scapegoat. They found it in the Mexican community. In a frenzy of anti-Mexican hysteria, wholesale punitive measures were proposed and undertaken by government officials at the federal, state, and local levels. Immigration and deportation laws were enacted to restrict emigration and hasten the departure of those already here. Contributing to the brutalizing experience were the mass deportation roundups and repatriation drives. Violence and "scare-head" tactics were utilized to get rid of the burdensome and unwanted horde. An incessant cry of "get rid of the Mexicans" swept the country. (p. 1)

Countless numbers of Mexicans, along with persons born in the US, were deported or coerced into voluntarily returning to Mexico with estimates ranging from 400,000 to 2,000,000 individuals (Sáenz and Murga 2011). The most commonly cited figure of 500,000 (Hoffman 1974) suggests that approximately one-third of Mexicans counted in the 1930 US census were returned to Mexico. This repatriation program illustrates the way in which the US government has tended to view Mexican immigrants, as a workforce that is welcome when needed but an easily disposable labor pool and convenient scapegoat during economic downturns.

Bracero Program

Within a few years from the termination of the Mexican Repatriation Program, the US took to the warfront in World War II. As young men went off to war, women picked up the job slack as they joined the labor force. However, there were still major labor shortages, particularly in agriculture. Mexicans now represented a much-needed and welcome source of labor. The US established the Bracero Program in an accord with Mexico in 1942 with "bracero" referring to the Spanish term for manual labor or someone who works with his arms. The program allowed Mexico to send contract laborers to the US to work for a specific amount of time. US employers found the program very attractive, so much so that the Bracero Program was extended way beyond the end of World War II with the initial extension occurring in 1951 with the signing of Public Law 78.

Most academics simply think of the Bracero Program as an effort that mutually helped Mexico and the US. Mexico profited through a portion of its population working in the US; the US benefitted from a cheap source of labor that the country desperately needed. However, we need to understand the context in Mexico in which the Bracero Program was developed. At the time, Mexico was undergoing an industrialization of its agricultural industry (Hernández 2006). As outlined above with the cumulative causation theoretical perspective, Mexican workers were being uprooted at the time through the privatization of land, the mechanization of agriculture, and a focus on the export of agricultural production (Hernández 2006). Still, Mexico, especially in the case of large agricultural growers, had an eye on its own low-wage labor as being an essential part of the country's effort to industrialize its rural areas (Hernández 2006).

Consequently, there was a certain level of opposition in Mexico to the Bracero Program with fears that Mexican laborers would seek better opportunities in the US either through the Bracero Program or as undocumented migrants. Mexico could regulate the flow of its laborers who went to the US as braceros, a task that is much more difficult in the case of undocumented migration (Hernández 2006). As an incentive for braceros to return to Mexico, the Mexican government withheld 10 percent of their wages and held those funds in Mexican banks, money that they would supposedly receive upon their return migration. Years later, the Mexican government did not return the funds, which was the impetus for the Bracero Movement in 2004. As they began to enter retirement, the braceros began mobilizations to recover the 10 percent of the wages that had been withheld. To curtail the flow of undocumented migration to the US, Mexico negotiated with the US to police its southern border to prevent undocumented immigration. Hernández (2006) points out that "beneath the [Bracero Program] agreement to import *braceros* were commitments to prevent Mexican laborers from surreptitiously crossing into the US and to aggressively detect and deport those who had successfully affected illegal entry" (p. 423). The US and Mexican governments worked bi-nationally to prevent Mexicans from entering the US without proper documentation.

Nonetheless, as soon as Mexican laborers found out about the initiation of the Bracero Program, many ventured to the Bracero recruitment center in Mexico. Upon arriving, however, many discovered that they were ineligible as "(o)nly healthy young men with agricultural experience, but without land, who had secured a written recommendation from local authorities verifying that their labor was not locally needed, were eligible for *bracero* contracts" (Hernández 2006, p. 425). Consequently, these prohibitive conditions stimulated a large number of individuals to migrate to the US in search of employment without the blessing of the Mexican and US governments.

The outflow of Mexican laborers as undocumented immigrants resulted in an uproar among agribusiness employers who complained about the decimation of the local labor force. Indeed, Mexican President Manuel Ávila Camacho received significant grievances from landholders in such states as Baja California, Jalisco, and Tamaulipas who demanded a stop to the outpouring of Mexican laborers (Hernández 2006). Bracero workers, too, leveled complaints against the large flow of undocumented immigrants who they reasoned brought down wages and worsened labor conditions in general (Hernández 2006).

By 1943, the US increased dramatically the US Border Patrol's budget and border patrol personnel along its southern border (Hernández 2006). When the enhanced border patrol resources did not lead to a rise in deportations, the Mexican government even pressed the US to stop the Bracero Program given that its own economy was suffering due to labor needs associated with out-migration (Hernández 2006). In response, Hernández (2006) observes that the chief supervisor of the US Border Patrol, W.F. Kelly, "launched an 'intensive drive on Mexican aliens' by deploying 'Special Mexican Deportation Parties' throughout the country" (p. 428). These efforts were successful in increasing the number of apprehensions of Mexican immigrants with the sum more than doubling from 11,775 in 1943 to 28,173 in 1944 (Hernández 2006). Furthermore, the concentration of Border Patrol efforts on the US southern border and on Mexican immigrants resulted in almost exclusively Mexican apprehensions accounting for an average of 90 percent of all persons detained annually between 1943 and 1954 (Hernández 2006).

The US and Mexican governments made adjustments to make it more difficult for undocumented immigrants to return to the US after deportation. Traditionally, unauthorized immigrants were deported at the US–Mexico border, facilitating re-entry. By April 1945, however, Mexican immigrants were routed to the interior and rural places in need of agricultural laborers, thus making return migration to the US more difficult (Hernández 2006). Mexico also placed its own border patrol agents along its northern border, in such places as Tamaulipas, to discourage undocumented migration to the US, as well as to arrest those that tried to cross back into Mexico (Hernández 2006). Furthermore, as entry of undocumented immigrants shifted toward California, the US Border Patrol erected chain-link fences to deter immigration, thus sending immigrants toward more dangerous routes that placed them at risk for dehydration and hypothermia (Hernández 2006), hazards that continue today.

Nonetheless, despite the concerted efforts by the US and Mexico governments to curtail undocumented immigration, the volume of apprehensions continued climbing in the early 1950s. For instance, the number of apprehensions of Mexican undocumented immigrants by US Border Patrol agents along the Mexican border increased 80 percent from 279,379 in 1949 to 501,713 in 1951 (Hernández 2006). Yet, one needs to keep in mind that the apprehensions represent episodes of apprehensions rather than individuals. Thus, a given individual could be apprehended five times in a month, with the five apprehensions – instead of the one individual – tallied in the summation of apprehensions. It is estimated that by the end of the 1940s, one-third of apprehended individuals were "repeat offenders," i.e., they had been apprehended multiple times (US Immigration and Naturalization Service 1948; see also Hernández 2006).

Early in the 1950s, the US Border Patrol shifted its tactics toward an all-out attack on apprehending and deporting undocumented immigrants, a strategy that would serve as a model for Operation Wetback which would be introduced shortly. Hernández (2006) describes this heightened approach:

> In February of 1950, US Border Patrol Inspector Albert Quillin of South Texas launched a new strategy that would soon form the core of US Border Patrol activities.

"At 5 am, Tuesday, February 11, 1950, Quillin convened a detail of twelve border patrolmen with 'two buses, one plane, one truck, a carryall and . . . nine automobiles' at a point four miles east of Rio Hondo, Texas." There, the officers set up a miniature immigration station and split into two teams. Each team was given maps of the area and instructions to apprehend as many undocumented immigrants as possible, quickly process them through the temporary immigration station, and then place them on one of the waiting buses that would take deportees directly to the border. That day, about 100 undocumented Mexicans were deported from the Rio Hondo area. The next day, this same detail moved on to Crossroads Gin near Los Fresnos, Texas, and raided farms. By the end of the second day, an additional 561 undocumented Mexicans had been deported. On the third and fourth days, this detail moved into San Benito, Texas, from where they deported 398 Mexicans. Altogether, Quillin's detail apprehended over 1,000 undocumented laborers in four days of work. Word quickly spread regarding Quillin's accomplishments and within two weeks his model was being applied throughout South Texas. (pp. 440–1)

Quillin's model was dubbed "Operation Wetback." It was highly lauded and became a part of the operations of Border Patrol agents across the Southwest. US Border Patrol apprehensions nearly doubled from 459,289 in 1950 to 827,440 in 1953 (Hernández 2006). While the volume of apprehensions was inflated by repeat "offenders," the general public in the US and Mexico associated the rising numbers with a crisis (Hernández 2006).

Operation Wetback
In response to the increasing public concern, the US government officially launched Operation Wetback in May 1954. President Eisenhower picked retired Army general Joseph Swing as commissioner of the Immigration and Naturalization Service to lead the operation (Hernández 2006). Operation Wetback continued the practice established by Quillin along with the cooperation of the Mexican government which, as before, relocated deportees in areas within Mexico that had labor shortages. As Hernández (2006) notes, despite the lack of novelty with the official Operation Program compared to Quillin's model, Swing boasted about the success of the program which netted nearly 1.1 million apprehensions. This figure, however, truly overestimated the impact of the official Operation Wetback program as it reflects the number of apprehensions during Fiscal Year 1954 which terminated on June 30, 1954 (Hernández 2006). As such, the existence of the official Operation Wetback program occupied only the last two weeks of Fiscal Year 1954 (Hernández 2006). The following fiscal year (1955), which contained the largest segment of Operation Wetback, resulted in only approximately 254,000 apprehensions (Hernández 2006). Operation Wetback officially was terminated in the late 1950s coinciding with the end of the Eisenhower administration. The Immigration and Naturalization Service estimates that approximately 1.3 million apprehensions occurred during the course of the program, although some suggest that this figure is inflated (Koestler 2013). Yet, Operation Wetback failed to stop the flow of Mexican undocumented immigrants whose labor continued to be welcome by US growers (Ngai 2004). Still, in both its official and unofficial forms, Operation Wetback resulted in the apprehension and deportation of countless undocumented Mexican immigrants through the collaborative efforts of the US and Mexican governments. It also reflects variations

in the way the US government has viewed Mexican immigrants in which the country welcomes them when they are needed and the economy is favorable and shuns them when they are unwanted and the economy is suffering.

The Bracero Program would go on to outlive Operation Wetback. Due to its popularity with US growers, the program survived significantly past the end of World War II. The Bracero Program finally came to a close in 1964. Approximately 4.8 million Mexicans came as contract workers as part of the Bracero Program (Gamboa 2000). It is important to understand that the Bracero experience was quite instrumental in the development of social capital and social networks on the part of *braceros*. Indeed, persons participating in the labor contract program gained a significant amount of information regarding different parts of the US and labor conditions, knowledge that helped people navigate the immigration route and that they could share with relatives and friends contemplating migration to the US. Such knowledge is essential for building and sustaining immigration ties between Mexico and the US, as illustrated by the network and cumulative causation theoretical perspectives above.

There is a postscript to the termination of the Bracero Program that needs to be told here, even though it does not involve US-based policy. The end of the Bracero Program brought a significant amount of concern to community leaders and public officials along Mexico's northern border. It was feared that once the program ended, *braceros* would remain in Mexican border communities rather than return to their homes in the interior of Mexico, thus exacerbating the already high unemployment rates along the border. To avert such problems, the Mexican government established the Border Industrialization Program (BIP) in 1965 as a way to stimulate foreign investment and develop its northern border region. The program stipulated that foreign corporations establish "twin plants," one on the Mexican side and the other on the US side. The plants were referred to as *maquiladoras*, reflecting the Spanish term signifying the portion of the product that the miller retains after grinding the stock. Videla (2008) notes the factors that BIP capitalized on in establishing the program: "proximity to the US; use of favorable articles of the US Tariff Code, which permits firms to import goods manufactured abroad with US components to reenter the US, paying duty only on the value-added, cheap labor; and a Mexican government friendly to investors" (p. 592). Videla (2008) intimates that BIP translated into "tax incentives for foreign firms, lax enforcement of environmental laws, and a blind eye to the breaking of labor laws" (p. 592).

From the beginning of BIP, US firms have taken advantage of the program incentives and Mexico's cheap labor force. *Maquiladora* operations soared after its implementation and were an especially bright economic spot in the Mexican economy during the 1980s when the country experienced a major economic crisis which saw the peso plummet significantly (O'Neil 2013). There are now approximately 3,000 *maquiladoras* which employ about 1.3 million workers along the northern Mexican border (Bacon 2011). The geographic and economic impact of *maquiladoras* expanded dramatically with the passage of the North American Free Trade Agreement (NAFTA) in 1994.

Again, the BIP and, as we will see later below, NAFTA, represent routes through which the US made inroads into the Mexican economy in search of labor and consumer markets. As such, consistent with the world system theory, the movement of capital and products across international borders begets the immigration of people as well.

While the mid-1960s saw the termination of the movement of contract labor from Mexico to the US as part of the Bracero Program, it would result in a major shift in immigration policy that led to a significant change in the source of immigrants to the US.

Immigration and Nationality Act of 1965 (Hart-Celler Act)

The 1960s represented an era of social change in the US. In particular, groups that had been historically marginalized, most notably blacks, called for their inclusion in all societal institutions. The Civil Rights Act of 1964 ushered in significant policies that sought to do just that in the areas of education, housing, employment, and voting. It was in this era that marked changes took place in immigration policy in the US. Recall that up to this point, immigration quotas favoring some groups, most notably northern and western Europeans, and limiting or completely excluding others (e.g., southern and eastern Europeans and Asians) were still in place. The Immigration and Nationality Act of 1965, also referred to as the Hart-Celler Act, ended the immigration quota system. In signing the bill, President Lyndon B. Johnson observed that the policy will "repair a very deep and painful flaw in the fabric of American justice. It corrects a cruel and enduring wrong in the conduct of the American Nation ... And this measure that we will sign today will really make us truer to ourselves both as a country and as a people" (1965, p. 1).

The Immigration and Nationality Act of 1965 additionally included two major provisions. First, the Act created two broad categories – exempted immediate relatives and a preference system based on other family relations and occupation and skills. US citizens could petition to have three categories of immediate relatives gain entry into the US. The three immediate-relative categories included spouses of US citizens, children under 21 years of age of US citizens, and parents of US citizens (Liu et al. 1991). Individuals entering as immediate relatives were excluded from the hemisphere and country numerical limits of immigrants (see below). The preference system included six categories based on preferences: first preference: unmarried children (over 21 years of age) of US citizens (not more than 20% of total); second preference, spouses and children of permanent residents (26%, plus any slots not used for the first preference); third preference, professionals and scientists or artists of exceptional ability (not more than 10%); fourth preference, married children of US citizens (10%, plus any slots not allocated in the first three preferences); fifth preference, brothers and sisters of US citizens (24%, plus any slots not allocated in the first four preferences); and sixth preference, skilled and unskilled workers in occupations for which labor is in short supply in the US (not more than 10%) (Liu et al. 1991). Second, the Act placed numerical limits on immigration, excluding exempted immediate family relative immigrants, based on hemisphere (170,000 for eastern hemisphere with a maximum of 20,000 for a given country in this hemisphere and 120,000 for western hemisphere with no limit imposed on any country in this hemisphere) (Reimers 1983).

There is a romanticized interpretation of the Immigration Act of 1965 as a policy that corrected a temporary lapse of the equitable and democratic American character (see, for example, Glazer 1987). However, as Luibheid (1997) argues, the Immigration and Nationality Act of 1965 was meant as rhetoric rather than to open the doors for non-white groups such as Asians, Africans, and Latin Americans. In fact at the time that the bill was signed, President Johnson (1965) indicated that the policy was "not a revolutionary bill" and that it would "not affect the lives of millions" (p. 1). Many supporters of the bill argued that few Asians would immigrate to the US following the signing of the bill given that there were relatively few Asian immigrants in the country due to the Asia-Pacific Triangle which barred immigration from Asia. For example, Attorney General Robert Kennedy noted at most 5,000 Asians would enter the US the first year with the number virtually disappearing afterward (Center for Immigration Studies 1995). Similarly, Senator Edward Kennedy expressed assurance that immigrants, especially those from Africa and Asia, would not flood into the US and thus would not affect the current racial/ethnic composition of the country (Center for Immigration Studies 1995). Further, Senator Hiram Fong asserted that the bill would not change the culture of the US (Center for Immigration Studies 1995). Indeed, the bill was meant to erase the racist blemish associated with restrictive quotas and to alleviate the immigration of southern and eastern Europeans into the US (Reimers 1983). It was believed that because there were few Asians in the country, they would not benefit greatly from the new immigration policy. Similarly, Mexicans would now be subjected to immigration limits due to the ceiling of 120,000 for the western hemisphere.

In reality, the Immigration and Nationality Act of 1965 dramatically transformed the source of immigration from Europe to Latin America and Asia. The policy's focus on family benefitted Mexicans tremendously as US citizens were able to petition for close relatives to gain entry into the US and undocumented immigration from Mexico rose with approximately one million undocumented immigrants apprehended along the US–Mexico border by the end of the 1970s (Reimers 1983). In addition, Cubans also benefitted through provisions which allowed them to immigrate to the US as refugees (Reimers 1983). In addition, Asians were able to enter the US in large numbers through occupational and skill preferences with subsequent family sponsorship once the newcomers had obtained US citizenship alongside the admission of refugees from Indochina – from Vietnam, Cambodia, and Laos – into the US following the end of the Vietnam War (Liu et al. 1991; Reimers 1983). In the end, Reimers (1983) observes that "Clearly they [US policymakers] did not see how the new law would work, nor could they predict the fairly generous response to the US to the post 1965 refugee crisis, both of which have brought about a fundamental shift in historic immigration patterns to the US" (p. 25). Indeed, from the 1960s to the present, immigrants originating from Latin America have constituted at least two-fifths of all immigrants admitted to the US with Asians accounting for at least an additional one-third, with the percentage of immigrants from Europe ranging from 10 percent (1981–90) to 18 percent (1971–80) (Sáenz and Murga 2011).

Immigration Reform and Control Act of 1986 (Simpson-Mazzoli Act of 1986)
By the mid to late 1970s, as undocumented immigration, particularly hailing from Mexico, rose significantly, many Americans were calling for major changes in immigration policy. After much debate, President Ronald Reagan signed into law the Immigration Reform and Control Act (IRCA) of 1986, also known as the Simpson-Mazzoli Act of 1986. IRCA consisted of four major provisions: (1) amnesty for individuals who could document that they had been living in the US continuously since January 1, 1982 (persons who could prove that they had worked at least 90 days

in agriculture within the past year); (2) employer sanctions for persons who had knowingly hired undocumented workers; (3) an assurance that there would be an adequate amount of seasonal and replacement agricultural workers for agricultural employers; and (4) an increase in funds to bolster enforcement at the US–Mexico border. Approximately three million persons received permanent residence status through IRCA with approximately three quarters of these being Mexican (Massey et al. 2002).

IRCA had a significant impact on the structure of immigration in several ways. For example, immigrants gaining legal status through IRCA saw their wages increase (Amuedo-Dorantes and Bansak 2011), though other research shows the opposite trend (Donato and Sisk 2012; Durand and Massey 2003). In addition, the attainment of legal status through IRCA freed immigrants to move in search of employment beyond traditional areas, resulting in the increasing movement of immigrants to new destination areas, primarily in the South and Midwest (Hernández-León and Zúñiga 2000). Furthermore, US employers adapted to employer sanctions by using subcontractors to obtain workers, hence not having to worry about whether or not their employees were documented (Phillips and Massey 1999; Taylor et al. 1997). Thus, employers are not liable given that they do not directly hire undocumented workers and the subcontractors benefit by retaining a portion of workers' wages for the provision of the legal buffer (Durand and Massey 2003).

North American Free Trade Agreement (NAFTA)

On the heels of the establishment of the European Union (EU) on February 7, 1992, the US, Canada, and Mexico signed the North American Free Trade Agreement (NAFTA) in December 1992, with President Clinton signing NAFTA into law in the US in December 1993 and the program going into effect in 1994. In many ways, NAFTA formally marked the long economic association between, in particular, the US and Mexico. Indeed, Mexico opened its doors for business to the US extending back to the mid-nineteenth century under the Benito Juárez presidency and intensified under the 27-year Porfirio Díaz regime commonly known as the Porfiriato (O'Neil 2013). American economic moguls such as William Randolph Hearst along with the likes of the Guggenheims and Rockefellers invested heavily in Mexico and reaped massive wealth at that time (O'Neil 2013). More recently, as noted above, the Border Industrialization Program (BIP), beginning in 1965 after the termination of the Bracero Program, opened up Mexico's northern border to foreign businesses, especially American ones. Unlike the EU agreement which saw stronger countries propping up weaker countries, such as Spain and Portugal, and opening up borders not only for capital and goods but for workers as well, NAFTA maintained the unequal relationship between Mexico and its northern neighbors and only allowed the movement of capital and products but not workers.

As the world system perspective suggests, the implementation of NAFTA led to major transformations in the Mexican economy including the uprooting of workers in some industrial sectors that could not compete with American producers. As NAFTA went into effect on January 1, 1994, the Zapatista Nationalist Liberation Army, under the direction of Subcomandante Marcos, rose to protest NAFTA and the anticipated negative economic impact on the population in Mexico's poorest regions, such as Chiapas. Corn producers were especially hurt economically by NAFTA as they were unable to compete with American corn producers who enjoyed government subsidies. As O'Neil (2013) notes, "some of the biggest aggregate losers from NAFTA were Mexico's small farmers, and rural poverty increased in the years following the passage of the free trade agreement" (p. 97). Not coincidentally, following the inception of NAFTA, Mexican emigration increased significantly in corn-producing states with large indigenous populations, notably Chiapas, which had traditionally not engaged in migration to the US (Batalova and Terrazas 2010). Thus, just as we saw global forces affecting the meat-packing industries in the late 1970s and 1980s with the ensuing development of Latino new-destination areas in the US Midwest and South regions, so too do we see international elements creating new-sending areas in Mexico (Batalova and Terrazas 2010).

NAFTA now has been in place for nearly two decades. Many observers argue that the accord has been a win-win situation for Canada, Mexico, and the US. O'Neil (2013) points out that while it is difficult to pinpoint success or failure associated directly with NAFTA due to major economic changes over the period since it came into existence, she notes that the following are general patterns:

> In the years after NAFTA's signing, the economies of all three countries grew faster than the OECD average. Trade between the partners, too, increased much faster than overall world levels. Mexico's exports to the US grew fivefold and US exports to Mexico quadrupled, bringing the annual trade total to approximately US$460 billion in 2011. While the US was already Mexico's most important export market, it is now even more so, and Mexico has become the second most important destination for US exports in the world (following Canada). (pp. 95-6)

In addition, poverty has dropped significantly since the mid-1990s. For example, the percentage of people classified as poor under Mexico's governmental measures dropped from 70 percent to nearly 40 percent today (O'Neil 2013). Concurrently, there has been an expansion of Mexico's middle class. O'Neil (2013) observes that "In the last fifteen years, Mexico's middle [class] has blossomed. An open and diversifying economy, expanding home ownership and credit, new schools, new products, and new opportunities have all worked in its favor" (p. 106).

The Militarization of the Border

While the US opened its borders to the movement of capital and products into and out of Mexico with the establishment of NAFTA, the US sealed its southern border with the creation of a series of programs designed to make it more difficult for immigrants to gain entry into the country at the most popular entry points. In September 1993, about three months before President Clinton signed NAFTA into law, the US Immigration and Naturalization Service (INS, whose name was changed to Department of Homeland Security in 2001) established Operation Blockade (later becoming Operation Hold the Line) in El Paso, Texas. Roughly a year later, in October 1994, INS launched Operation Gatekeeper in San Diego. Operation Safeguard was also mounted in Nogales, Arizona, in October 1994 and then again in 1999 as the flow of undocumented immigrants made their way into Arizona once the southern California entry point had been blockaded. Moreover, Operation Rio Grande was launched in August 1997 along the south Texas border (Brownville and McAllen).

These operations have militarized the border and have made it very difficult to gain entry into the US through traditional entry routes (Dunn 2009). As conventional routes were sealed off, undocumented immigrants circumvented the blockages by taking dangerous and inhospitable routes through mountains and deserts. As such, the launching of operations to seal off the border at common entry points has resulted in significant increases in deaths among immigrants attempting to enter the US (Eschbach et al. 1999; Santos and Zemansky 2013). For example, the number of deaths associated with border crossing more than doubled between 1995 and 2006 in the Border Patrol's Tucson sector, which includes much of the Arizona desert (US Government Accountability Office 2006). Over the last few years, as immigrant entry points have moved to South Texas, there has been a significant increase in immigrant deaths in this region (MacCormack 2012). The irony, of course, is that while the NAFTA accord opened borders to the exchange of capital and products between countries, labor was not allowed to freely move across borders.

The Criminalization of Immigrants

These efforts to make it increasingly difficult for immigrants to gain entry into the US through its southern border represented a harbinger of policies that criminalized immigrants. Two laws that President Clinton signed into law in 1996 set the stage for the criminalization of immigrants: Anti-Terrorism and Effective Death Penalty Act (AEDPA) and the Illegal Immigration Reform and Immigrant Responsibility Act (IIRIRA). Together, these policies further empowered the INS to apprehend, detain, and deport undocumented immigrants and minimized the rights of immigrants to appeal decisions affecting their deportation (Douglas and Sáenz 2013). AEDPA allowed for the deportation of unauthorized immigrants who committed any of a litany of crimes without any review (Douglas and Sáenz 2013; Verdeja 2002). The policy allowed immigrants to be deported for misdemeanors and offenses considered retroactively, e.g., they could be subject to deportation for committing crimes for which they had already served their time (Douglas and Sáenz 2013).

The IIRIRA policy further added a series of additional measures that criminalized unauthorized immigrants. In particular, IIRIRA "authorized the construction of a fourteen-mile fence along the US–Mexico border; doubled the force of border patrol agents; allowed for summary exclusion of immigrants (for example, immigration officials were granted the authority to summarily deport individuals apprehended within one hundred miles of the border); expanded the grounds for deportation; reduced the allowable documents to satisfy I-9 requirements; and prohibited legal immigrants from federal welfare provisions for the first five years of their US residency" (Douglas and Sáenz 2013, p. 205). Furthermore, IIRIRA "required the detention of all immigrants, including permanent residents, facing deportation for most criminal violations until the final resolution of the case" (Hines 2006, p. 17; see also Douglas and Sáenz 2013). In addition, IIRIRA's section 287(g) established authorized federal immigration officials to sign a memorandum of agreement (MOA) with state and local law enforcement officials which allowed the latter to execute federal immigration law enforcement activities (Douglas and Sáenz 2013).

Policy measures that criminalized immigrants were intensified immediately after the terrorist attacks of 9/11. A month after the strikes, President George W. Bush established the Department of Homeland Security which incorporated the Immigration and Naturalization Service (INS). Furthermore, in late October 2001, he signed into law the USA PATRIOT (Uniting and Strengthening America by Providing Appropriate Tools Required to Intercept and Obstruct Terrorism) Act of 2001. This Act "significantly increased the budget for immigration enforcement and tripled the number of Border Patrol agents on the northern border; ... expanded the government's ability to detain and deport terrorists, however defined; ... instituted a 'Special Registration' program [that] ... required men aged 16 to 45 from Arab and Muslim countries in residence in the US to register with the Department of Homeland Security and answer questions" [this provision ended in May 2003] (Douglas and Sáenz 2013, p. 206).

The three programs outlined above (AEDPA, IIRIRA, and USA PATRIOT) have led to a massive increase in immigrant detainees held in detention centers, many operated by the private sector (e.g., Corrections Corporation of America and the GEO group) (Douglas and Sáenz 2013). The average daily immigrant detainee population skyrocketed from 6,785 in 1994 to 33,330 in 2011 (Douglas and Sáenz 2013; Siskin 2007, 2012). The immigration detention business is quite lucrative and has been characterized as an immigration-industrial complex which benefits individuals with ties to the corporate, governmental, and criminal justice sectors (Douglas and Sáenz 2013; Fernandez 2007; Golash-Boza 2009). Deportations have also increased noticeably over the last several years during the Obama administration. Indeed, the number of immigrant deportations reached an all-time high during the 2012 fiscal year (October 1, 2011 to September 30, 2012) at 409,849, 11 percent higher than the 369,221 immigrants deported during the 2008 fiscal year under the George W. Bush administration (Dinan 2012).

As can be seen, over the last century there have been major changes in immigration policy. At certain periods, immigration policies and associated programs have been favorable toward Latin American immigration – particularly originating from Mexico – while at other times these have sought to deport or halt immigration to the US. One thing is certain – immigration policies have changed the face of immigrants in the US.

Historical Latin American Immigration to the US

It is difficult to obtain the data necessary to directly enumerate the volume of immigration. This is particularly the case when we try to enumerate the flow of immigration over time. We draw here on historical immigration data from the US Department of Homeland Security (2013) on the volume of persons obtaining legal permanent resident status extending back to 1820. A few caveats are in order. First, the data represent a proxy for the level of immigration from a given region in the world for a certain time period given that the statistics enumerate the number of persons obtaining legal permanent resident status – as such they could have lived in the US for any period of time prior to being granted this status. Second, the immigration statistics do not account for all other immigrants who arrived during a given period through other routes including, for example, those who arrived as visitors or undocumented immigrants. Third, the data are based on the country of last residence rather than country of birth. Finally, the data presented here are aggregated across Latin

America and, thus, include some groups living in certain parts of Latin America such as the Caribbean (e.g., Haitians and Jamaicans), Central America (e.g., Belizeans), and South America (e.g., Brazilians, Guyanese, and Surinamese) that are not classified as Latino.

Historically, nearly 78.5 million immigrants have obtained legal resident status in the US between 1920 and 2012. Of these, the country of last residence is known for close to 72.8 million individuals with approximately 55 percent originating from Europe. Latin Americans account for a quarter of all immigrants who have secured legal permanent residence status and whose last country of residence is known. A significant number of Latin American immigrants, largely originating from Mexico, have attained legal permanent residence status since the beginning of the twentieth century (table 3.1). For example, in the two decades (1910s and 1920s) surrounding the Mexican Revolution and its aftermath, Latin Americans accounted for approximately one-ninth of all immigrants who received legal permanent resident status in the US at that time.

Nonetheless, the passage of the Immigration Act of 1965 (Hart-Celler Act) represented a watershed event for Latin American immigrants. They have constituted the largest segment of all immigrants who attained legal permanent residence status between the decades of the 1960s and that of the 2000s, with the peak taking place during the 1990s when they comprised about 52 percent of this total. The percentage of Asians has also grown since the 1960s when they made up 13 percent of immigrants that obtained legal permanent resident status at that time to a high of more than two-fifths in the 1980-9 and 2000-12 periods. In fact, Asians outnumbered Latin Americans for the first time with respect to the number of immigrants securing legal permanent resident status during the 2010-13 period, coinciding with the noticeable decline in Mexican immigration over the last few years (Passel et al. 2012). For Latin American and Asian immigrants, the decade of the 1990s represented each group's pinnacle with respect to the number of persons becoming legalized with 4.9 million Latinos and nearly 2.9 million Asians becoming legal permanent residents at that time.

In contrast to the overall expansion of Latin Americans and Asians since the 1960s, the share of US immigrants attaining legal permanent resident status that are European has dropped from 32 percent in the 1960s to a low of 7 percent in the 2010-12 period. The peak level of Europeans receiving legalized status occurred more than a century ago when close to 7.6 million Europeans obtained legalization in the 1900-9 decade.

Ten countries accounted for slightly more than three quarters of all Latin American immigrants receiving legal permanent resident status between 1820 and 2012 (table 3.2). However, Mexicans stand out in this field. Indeed, nearly 8.1 million Mexican immigrants have obtained legal permanent residence status between 1820 and 2012, accounting for about 45 percent of all Latin Americans who have received legalized status historically. In the post-1960 period the share of Mexican representation among Latin Americans receiving legal permanent resident status peaked in the 1980s (56%) but the portion has declined progressively to a low of close to 36 percent in the 2010-12 period.

The peak period of the attainment of legalized status has occurred in the last couple of decades. For example, the largest number of persons obtaining legal permanent resident status occurred in the 1990-9 period for people moving from

Table 3.1 Persons Obtaining Legal Permanent Resident Status by Region and Period

Period	Latin America	Europe	Asia	Africa	Oceania	Other America	Not Specified	Total
1820-9	7,358	99,618	34	19	2	2,298	19,173	128,502
1830-9	20,030	422,853	55	66	1	11,881	83,495	538,381
1840-9	16,231	1,369,423	121	67	3	34,296	7,196	1,427,337
1850-9	19,974	2,622,617	36,080	104	110	64,227	71,442	2,814,554
1860-9	12,372	1,880,389	54,408	458	107	118,055	15,472	2,081,261
1870-9	21,036	2,252,050	134,071	441	9,094	324,853	592	2,742,137
1880-9	32,318	4,638,684	71,152	768	7,341	497,527	778	5,248,568
1890-9	34,682	3,576,411	61,304	432	3,279	4,074	14,112	3,694,294
1900-9	154,742	7,572,569	300,441	6,326	11,677	123,140	33,493	8,202,388
1910-19	361,824	4,985,411	269,736	8,867	12,339	708,715	488	6,347,380
1920-9	641,963	2,560,340	126,740	6,362	9,860	949,315	930	4,295,510
1930-9	67,591	444,404	19,292	2,120	3,240	162,728	0	699,375
1940-9	142,240	472,524	34,532	6,720	14,262	186,195	135	856,608
1950-9	508,335	1,404,973	135,844	13,016	11,319	413,309	12,472	2,499,268
1960-9	1,218,990	1,133,443	358,563	23,780	23,659	455,204	119	3,213,758
1970-9	1,723,766	826,327	1,406,526	71,405	39,983	179,870	326	4,248,203
1980-9	2,538,108	669,694	2,391,356	141,987	41,432	156,396	305,406	6,244,379
1990-9	4,942,317	1,349,219	2,859,899	346,410	56,800	194,825	25,928	9,775,398
2000-9	4,205,161	1,349,609	3,470,835	759,734	65,793	236,368	211,930	10,299,430
2010-12	1,200,783	273,097	1,265,277	299,360	17,344	59,139	21,296	3,136,296
Total	17,869,821	39,903,655	12,996,266	1,688,442	327,645	4,882,415	824,783	78,493,027

Source: US Department of Homeland Security (2013).

Table 3.2 *Ten Latin American Countries with the Most Persons Obtaining Legal Permanent Resident Status by Period*

Country	1820–2012	1960–9	1970–9	1980–9	1990–9	2000–9	2010–12
Mexico	8,067,025	441,824	621,218	1,009,586	2,757,418	1,704,166	426,866
Cuba	1,302,577	202,030	256,497	132,552	159,037	271,742	102,184
Dominican Republic	1,253,310	83,552	139,249	221,552	359,818	291,492	141,461
El Salvador	769,104	14,405	29,428	137,418	273,017	251,237	52,898
Colombia	706,262	68,371	71,265	105,494	137,985	236,570	64,263
Guatemala	417,146	14,357	23,837	58,847	126,043	156,992	30,915
Peru	391,075	19,783	25,311	49,958	110,117	137,614	40,313
Ecuador	361,891	34,107	47,464	48,015	81,358	107,977	31,815
Honduras	233,433	15,087	15,653	39,071	72,880	63,513	19,207
Nicaragua	225,364	10,383	10,911	31,102	80,446	70,015	9,733
Latin America	17,869,821	1,218,990	1,723,766	2,538,108	4,942,317	4,205,161	1,200,783

Source: US Department of Homeland Security (2013).

Mexico, the Dominican Republic, El Salvador, Honduras, and Nicaragua, while the peak decade of legalization took place in the 2000–9 period for people migrating from Cuba, Colombia, Guatemala, Peru, and Ecuador.

The increasing diversity of Latin Americans gaining legalized status is reflected in the rising prevalence of particular groups of immigrants. For instance, three Latin American countries (Colombia, Cuba, and the Dominican Republic) made up slightly more than a quarter of Latin American immigrants legalized during the 2010–12 period. While information on legal permanent residents in the country is useful for gaining an understanding of historical trends on the volume of people who have obtained this status, it is important to remember that these individuals did not necessarily immigrate at the same time that they attained their legalized status.

We can obtain an estimate of the number of Latino immigrants that were in the US in 2010 through the examination of data from the 2010 American Community Survey Public-Use File (Ruggles et al. 2010). While the data are not historical, they do have a few advantages over the US Department of Homeland Security (2013) data used in the analysis described above. In particular, the data are based on foreign-born persons who identified themselves as Latino and who immigrated to the US regardless of their method of entry as well as their current legal status.

In 2010 there were approximately 18.8 million Latinos who immigrated at some time to the US (table 3.3). Mexicans account for more than three-fifths (62.2%) of Latino immigrants in the US. Five other groups (Salvadorans, Cubans, Dominicans, Guatemalans, and Colombians), each with more than half a million immigrants, make up close to another quarter of Latino immigrants in the country. The groups vary widely in the median amount of time that immigrants have lived in the US, with a range from 10 to 25 years. The groups with the greatest longevity in the US include Panamanians (25), Spaniards (24), and Nicaraguans (21), while those with the

Table 3.3 *Number of Latino Immigrants in the US and Median Years in the US, Selected Groups, 2010*

Latino Group	Number of Immigrants	Median Years in US
Mexican	11,707,590	15
Salvadoran	1,139,510	15
Cuban	1,108,369	19
Dominican	853,276	17
Guatemalan	741,011	11
Colombian	630,477	14
Honduran	486,685	10
Ecuadorian	432,393	14
Peruvian	405,662	13
Nicaraguan	236,497	21
Venezuelan	164,330	10
Argentinean	149,232	13
Spaniard	91,494	24
Chilean	83,451	19
Panamanian	76,736	25
Bolivian	71,140	15
Costa Rican	66,056	18
Puerto Rican	57,002	19
Uruguayan	48,149	10
Paraguayan	15,077	13
Other	252,968	17
Total	18,817,105	15

Source: 2010 American Community Survey Public-Use File (Ruggles et al. 2010).

shortest stay in this country include Hondurans (10), Uruguayans (10), Venezuelans (10), and Guatemalans (11).

New Immigration Patterns from Mexico and Latin America

Despite the major increases in the volume of immigration from Latin America during the twentieth century, as shown in the analysis above, there has been a noticeable slowdown in Latin American immigration to this country. Thus, the volume of Asian immigration for the first time surpassed that of Latin American immigration in 2012–13. In addition, it has been observed that the number of unauthorized immigrants in the US, the majority (58%) of whom are from Mexico, peaked at 12 million in 2007 and has fallen to 11.1 million over the period from 2009 to 2011 (Passel and Cohn 2012; Pew Research Center's Hispanic Trends Project 2013). Moreover, demographic analysis has shown that after four decades of ongoing net migration from Mexico to the US, the flow has reversed during the 2005–10 period when 1.39 million Mexicans moved from the US to Mexico compared to 1.37 million Mexicans who migrated from Mexico to the US (Passel et al. 2012). The decline of immigration from Mexico to the

US has been attributed to a variety of factors including a worsening US economy, an increasingly favorable economic situation in Mexico, enhanced border security, high levels of violence in Mexico, and a significant decline in Mexico's fertility level (Passel et al. 2012). The major question is whether the recent declines in immigration from Mexico to the US are short- or long-term trends.

Questions Related to Latino Immigration in the Future

The movement of people from throughout Latin America to the US has occurred over a sustained time period. This is particularly the case among Mexicans. Mexican immigration to the US has been unique in various ways, for no other group immigrating to the US from the rest of the world has the experience of Mexican immigrants. For example, Mexican immigrants coming to the US are moving to land that once belonged to their country. Through the Treaty of Guadalupe Hidalgo in 1848 at the conclusion of the Mexican–American War, Mexico ceded more than half of its territory to the US, much of the southwestern portion of the US today. In addition, substantial immigration from Mexico to the US has occurred virtually unaltered for a century. Furthermore, the proximity of Mexico to the US has historically allowed Mexicans to move back and forth relatively easily, although the militarization of the border after 9/11 has made this more difficult.

Immigration has been important in other ways besides altering the demography of the Latino population. The constant flow of immigrants from Latin America has served to reinforce and enrich the Spanish language and cultures stemming from the countries of origin. Immigrants bring with them their Spanish language (and increasingly indigenous languages) and their cultural values and practices. As such, the perpetual arrival of newcomers strengthens the Spanish language and cultures of the Latino community in the US. In addition, as noted in chapter 1, with the growth of the Latino population we have also seen the increase of Spanish-language instruction as well as the rising popularity of Latino foods and music.

Yet, as the Latino population has expanded in the US, there has been a backlash against the group, with immigrants becoming a primary target of those that want to halt immigration. Over the last several decades there has been continual debate over the economic and social impact of Latino immigrants – especially Mexican immigrants – on the US. One of the most recent treatises warning against the detrimental impact of Latino immigrants on the country's cultural fabric is Samuel Huntington's (2004) book titled *Who Are We? The Challenges to America's National Identity*. He contends that the values of Mexicans clash with those of the puritanical and British values that form the foundation of the US. There has also been a rise of anti-immigrant sentiment against Latinos, immigrants and native-born alike, through the formation of vigilante groups, hate speak, and local policies targeting Latino immigrants. At the same time, however, there are opposing forces, most notably the business community, that recognize the value of Latino immigrants, particularly in the domain of the economy. Latino immigrants represent the bedrock of many industries that depend on them heavily as the primary labor force, in such areas as the agriculture, construction, homecare, hotel, landscape, and restaurant sectors. Severe cuts in the availability of Latino immigrant labor in these industries would have a tremendous effect on these sectors of the economy and would drive up consumer costs significantly.

Summary

In this chapter, we provided an overview of theoretical perspectives that have been used to explain international migration. We also overviewed policies and programs that have been associated with shifts in immigration to the United States. In addition, we examined the changing source of immigration to the United States from Europe to Latin America and Asia over the last half century. One major change over the last few years has been the decline in immigration from Mexico – whether this is a short- or long-term situation remains to be seen. In the next chapter we provide an overview of the demography of the Latino population and the important role that immigration has played.

4 The Demography of Latinos

The Latino population has changed tremendously over the last half century and has grown dramatically during this period. In 1965 it was largely composed of Mexicans with a small Puerto Rican population and an even smaller Cuban population. In addition, at that time only about 15 percent of Latinos were born outside of the US. A half century later, the Latino population is much more diverse, encompassing groups from throughout Latin America as well as Spain. Moreover, this change has occurred through the increasing immigration from throughout Latin America, with approximately 40 percent of Latinos today born outside of the US.

With the increasing demographic prominence of the Latino population over the last several decades, Latinos have become the engine of the US population. Today, Latinos account for approximately 55 percent of the overall population growth of the US. If it was not for Latinos, the US would be a tremendously different country demographically. Indeed, it would resemble many European countries and selected Asian countries that are characterized by minute population growth or even declining populations brought about through a significant aging of the population alongside very low levels of fertility. Instead, the US is growing faster than all but a handful of European countries today (Population Reference Bureau 2010), largely due to the demographic influence of its Latino population.

This chapter describes the major population growth of the Latino population over the recent past. It highlights the various factors that have produced this growth, including the group's young age structure, high fertility, low mortality, and high immigration. The chapter underscores the significant variations across Latino subgroups. The chapter closes with a discussion of population projections which point to the increasing presence of Latinos in the US population over the coming decades.

Latino Population Trends

We can examine the population trends in the US over the last four decades to illustrate the increasing importance of Latinos to the demographics of the US population. Over the last four decennial censuses the Latino population has increased rapidly from 14.6 million in 1980 to 22.4 million in 1990 to 35.3 million in 2000 and to 50.5 million in 2010 (figure 4.1). Hence, the Latino population increased 3.5 times during the last 30 years. In fact, if the US Latino population were a country in 2010, it would be the 25th largest country in the world (Population Reference Bureau 2010).

The Latino population has expanded at a relatively rapid rate over the last three decades. The growth was especially fast during the 1990–2000 period when the Latino population increased by 58 percent, while the percentage change has been the slowest at 43 percent during the last decade (2000–10) (figure 4.2). The slower growth in

50 THE DEMOGRAPHY OF LATINOS

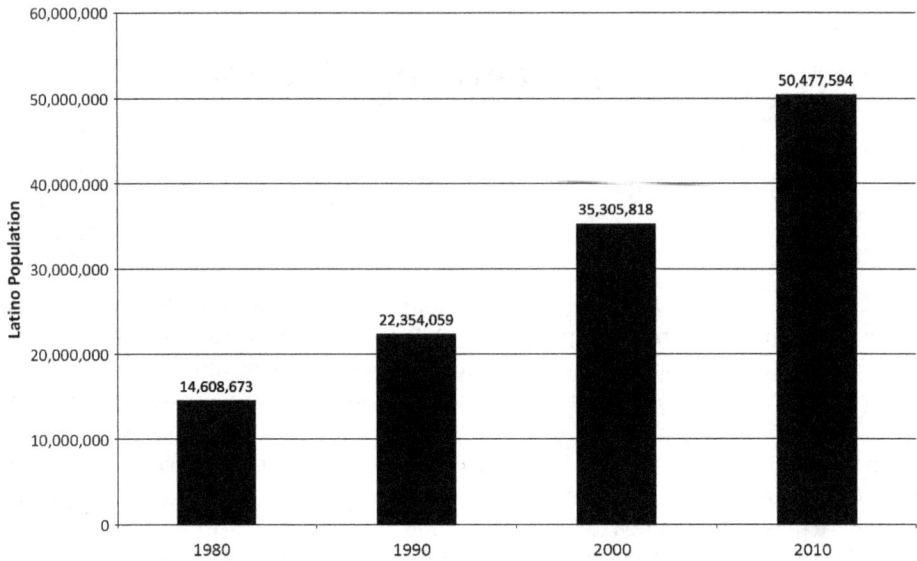

Figure 4.1 Latino Population in the US, 1980–2010
Sources: Hobbs and Stoops (2002) and US Census Bureau (2013c).

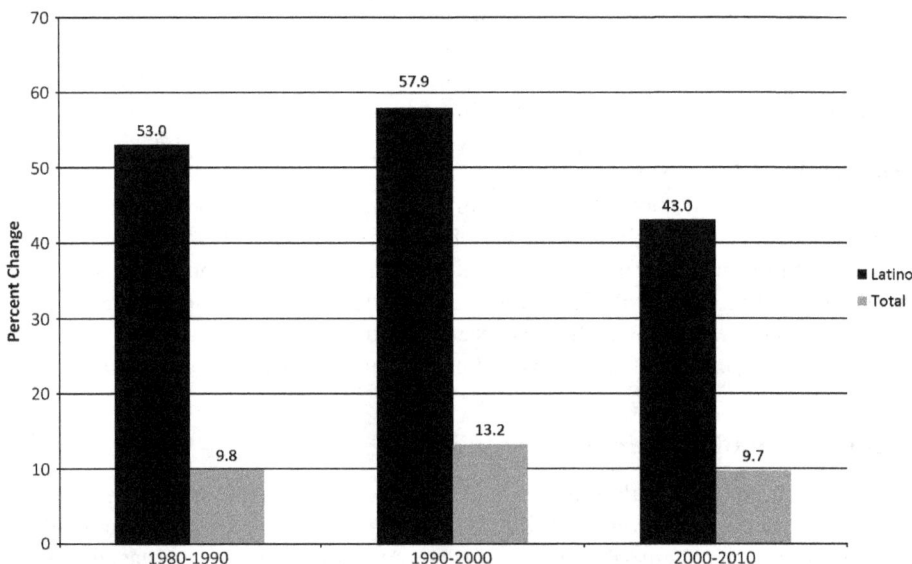

Figure 4.2 Percentage Change in the Latino and US Populations by Period
Sources: Hobbs and Stoops (2002) and US Census Bureau (2013c).

the last decade reflects the significant decline in immigration from Mexico during the last several years (Passel et al. 2012). Still, the Latino population has grown much more rapidly compared to the nation's overall population, increasing 5.4 times more rapidly in 1980–90 and 4.4 times more rapidly in each of the last two decades (1990–2000 and 2000–10).

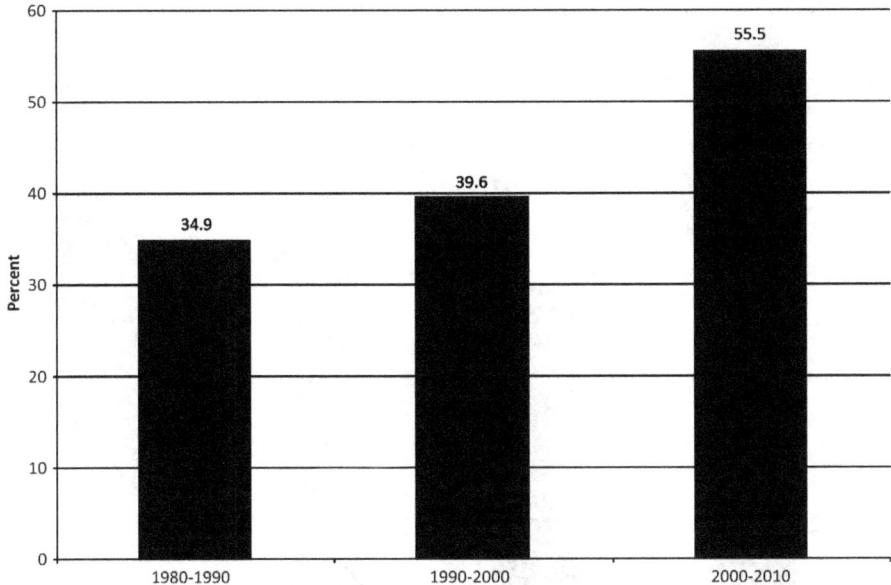

Figure 4.3 Percentage of US Population Growth Due to Latino Population Growth by Period
Sources: Hobbs and Stoops (2002) and US Census Bureau (2013c).

Over the last three decades the Latino population has increased its share of the US overall population growth occurring each decade. For example, despite its relatively small population size in 1980 (14.6 million), Latinos accounted for more than one-third (34.9%) of the nation's total population growth with the share expanding to approximately two-fifths (39.6%) in the 1990–2000 period and to more than half (55.5%) in the 2000–10 period (figure 4.3). These trends support the notion that Latinos represent the engine of the US population.

Illustratively, the Latino population has expanded its share of the overall US population rapidly over the last four decades. Latinos comprised one in every 16 (6.4%) persons in the US in 1980 with its share magnifying to one in every 11 persons in 1990 to one in every eight persons in 2000 and to one in every six individuals in 2010 (figure 4.4).

Why has the Latino population grown so rapidly compared to other segments of the US population? There are four demographic factors that account for the swift growth of the Latino population – youthful age structure, relatively high levels of immigration, relatively high rates of fertility, and low levels of mortality. Each of these factors is illustrated below to understand the dynamics behind the rapid growth of the Latino population.

Age Structure

The disparate growth of Latinos and whites in the US is driven significantly by the distinctions in the age structures of these groups. In particular, Latinos represent the youngest racial or ethnic group in the US with a median age of 27 in 2000, while whites are much older with a median age of 42.

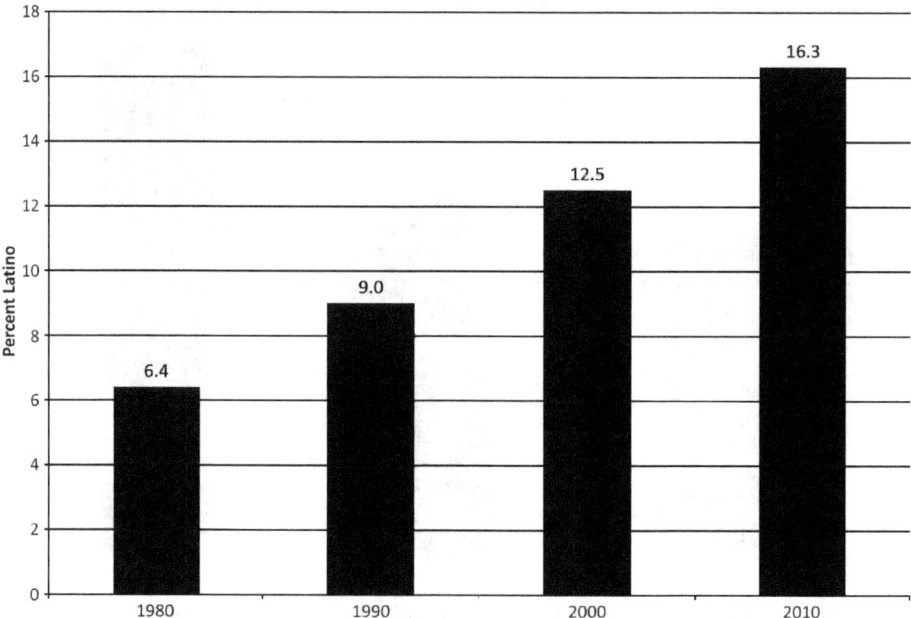

Figure 4.4 Percentage Share of Latinos in the US Population, 1980–2010

Sources: Hobbs and Stoops (2002) and US Census Bureau (2013c).

The differences in age structure can be viewed graphically by examining the age-sex pyramid of the two groups (figure 4.5). Demographers use the age-sex pyramid to depict how youthful or old a given population is as well as the relative presence of males and females across age groups. The age-sex pyramid consists of a vertical axis of five-year age groups while the horizontal axis provides an indication of the percentage of males or females in each age group as a percentage of the entire Latino population of interest. To illustrate, an examination of the Latino age-sex pyramid in figure 4.5 shows that boys 0 to 4 years of age constitute 5.0 percent of the entire Latino population. A comparison of the Latino and white age-sex pyramids clearly displays the youthfulness of the Latino population as evidenced by a wide base at the younger ages indicating a large presence of youngsters in the Latino population. In addition, the needle-like shape associated with the older ages signifies relatively few older people among Latinos. In contrast, the age-sex pyramid of whites deviates quite a bit from that of Latinos. In particular, the white age-sex pyramid is dominated by baby boomers – persons between the ages of 45 and 64. The base is much narrower compared to that of Latinos, indicating that youth comprise a relatively small share of the white population while the top of the pyramid has wider bars than that of Latinos showing that older persons constitute a larger portion of the white population.

The distinction in the age structure between whites and Latinos can be illustrated by examining the ratios of youths (0 to 14) to elderly (65 and older) in each of these populations. In the Latino population, there are five persons less than 15 years of age per one individual 65 and older. In contrast, the ratio is even among whites, i.e., there is one person less than 15 years of age for each individual 65 and older. The disparities

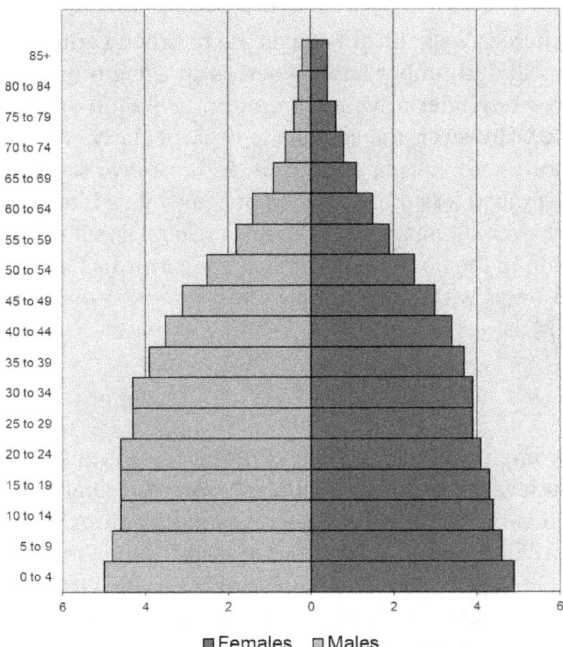

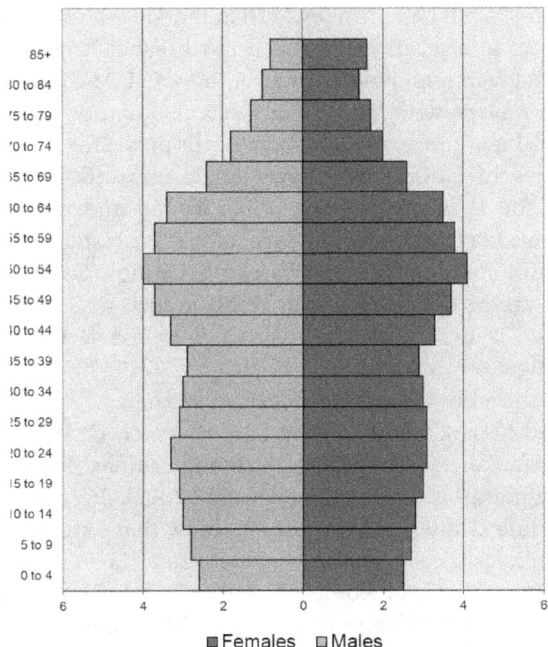

Figure 4.5 Age-Sex Pyramid for Latinos and Whites in the US, 2011

Source: 2011 American Community Survey Public-Use File (Ruggles et al. 2010).

in the age structures of Latinos and whites have major implications for future growth favoring Latinos.

Furthermore, there is a significant age divide between Latinos and whites. In the US, while whites still outnumber Latinos across all age groups, the share of whites falls progressively from older to younger groups, while the opposite is the case for Latinos (figure 4.6). However, the age divide is particularly acute in the two largest states in the country – California and Texas. In these two states, Latinos outnumber whites in age groups less than 40 years of age while whites have the numerical advantage in ages over 40. Again, these trends portend significant alterations to the nation's population in the near future. In fact, Latino births outnumber white births in California and Texas with this pattern expected to be replicated soon in Arizona and Nevada (see Martin et al. 2012).

Fertility

For long, Latina women have had relatively high levels of fertility, much of this associated with their low level of education. Figure 4.7 shows the total fertility rates of Latina and white women along with those of selected Latina groups. The total fertility rate (TFR) is a measure of the average number of births that women have as they pass through their fertility-age years (15–44) conforming to the fertility levels as they age from one age group to the next. Overall, Latina women average 2.35 births compared to white women with 1.79 births, with the fertility level of Latinas being about 30 percent higher than that of white women. The fertility rates of Latinas, however, vary significantly across groups. For example, Cuban women have a very low fertility rate averaging 1.29 births, a full half birth lower than that of whites. Puerto Rican women also are below the 2.1 total fertility level that is the threshold representing the average births needed for a given population to reproduce itself. Mexican women (2.26) are slightly above the replacement level. In contrast, women originating from Central and South America have approximately three births on average.

The fertility rates of Latinas have dropped significantly over the last couple of years. Indeed, the fertility rates of Latinas overall and those of Mexican and Cuban women are today at the lowest level since the National Center for Health Statistics began producing fertility measures for Latinos. Over the last five years, the total fertility rate of Latinas fell from 2.86 in 2006 to 2.35 in 2010. However, this drop in births is driven by the major fall in the fertility rate of Mexican women descending from 3.00 in 2006 to 2.26 in 2010. In a matter of only five years, the average number of births to Mexican women fell by 0.75 births. Further analysis conducted by researchers at the Pew Research Center's Hispanic Trends Project indicates that the fertility decline among Latinas has been most prominent among immigrants (Livingston and Cohn 2012). It is speculated that this major fertility decline is due to the economic blow that Latinos have experienced during the economic crisis over the last several years (Livingston and Cohn 2012). The low fertility rate of Mexican women (2.26) is nearly as low as that of women in Mexico where the total fertility rate was 2.2 in 2010 (Population Reference Bureau 2010; for a discussion of the rapid drop in fertility in Mexico, see Frank and Heuveline 2005).

Fertility, like migration, has always played a prominent role in the growth of the

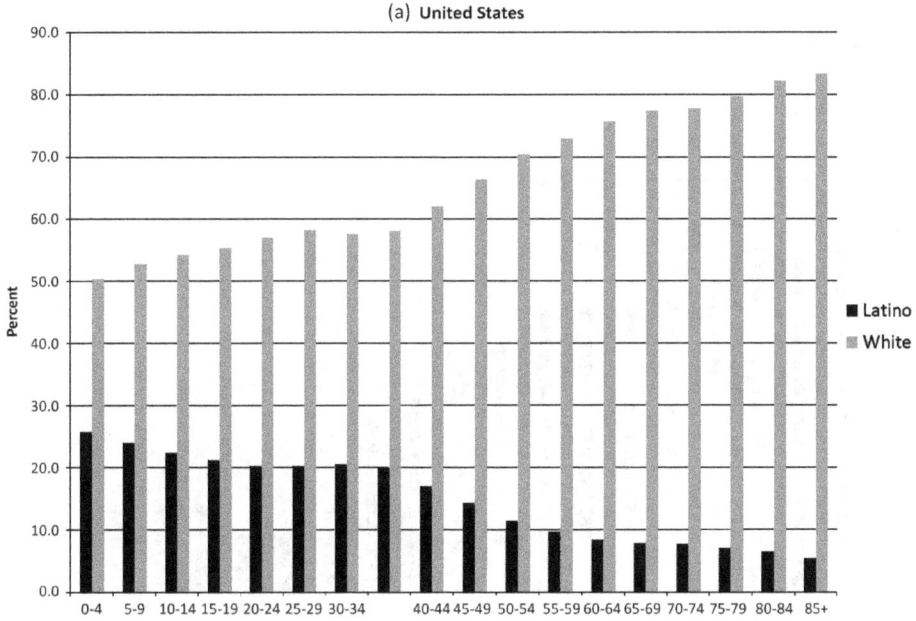
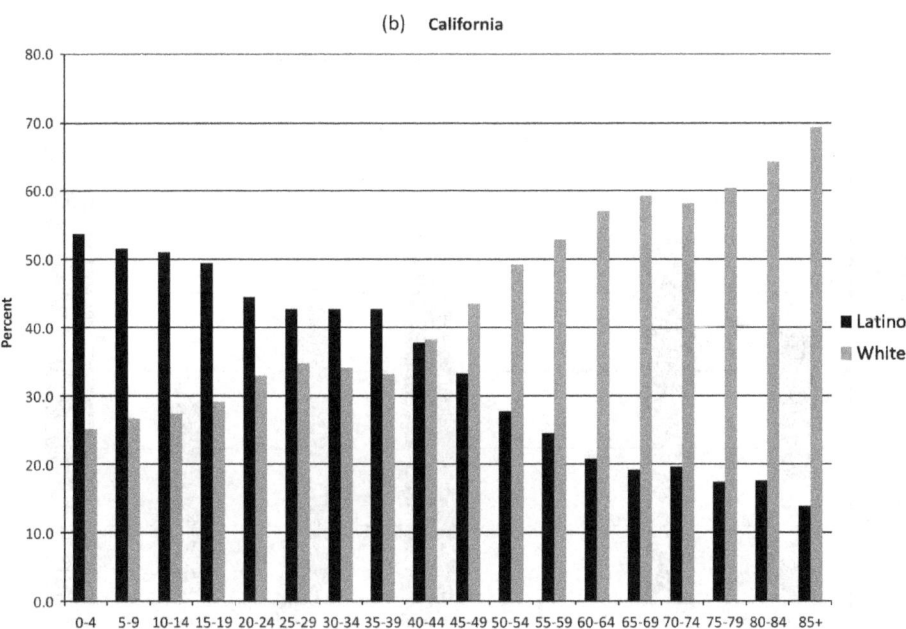

Figure 4.6 Percentage Share of Latinos and Whites by Age Group in (a) the US, (b) California, and (c) Texas Populations, 2011

Source: 2011 American Community Survey Public-Use File (Ruggles et al. 2010).

56   THE DEMOGRAPHY OF LATINOS

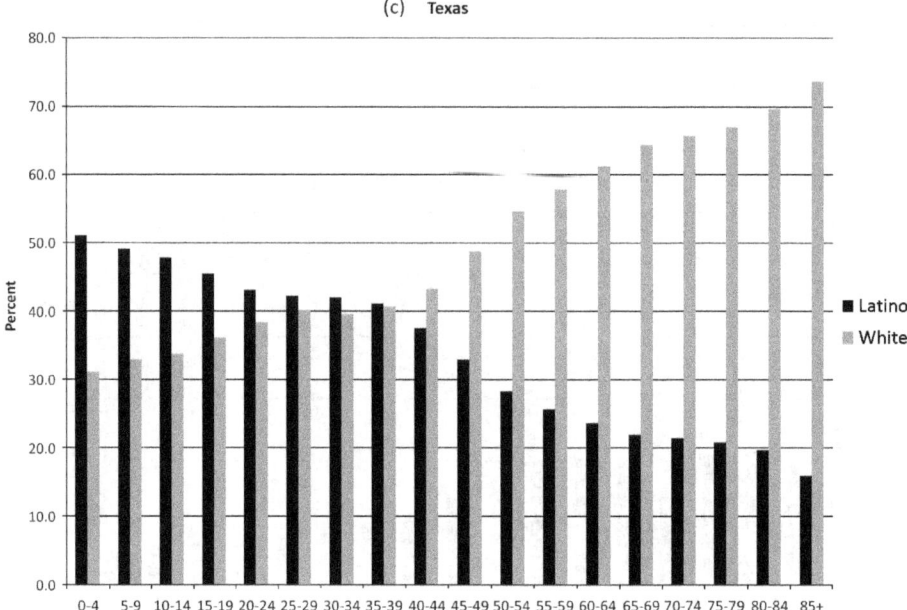

Figure 4.6 (Continued)

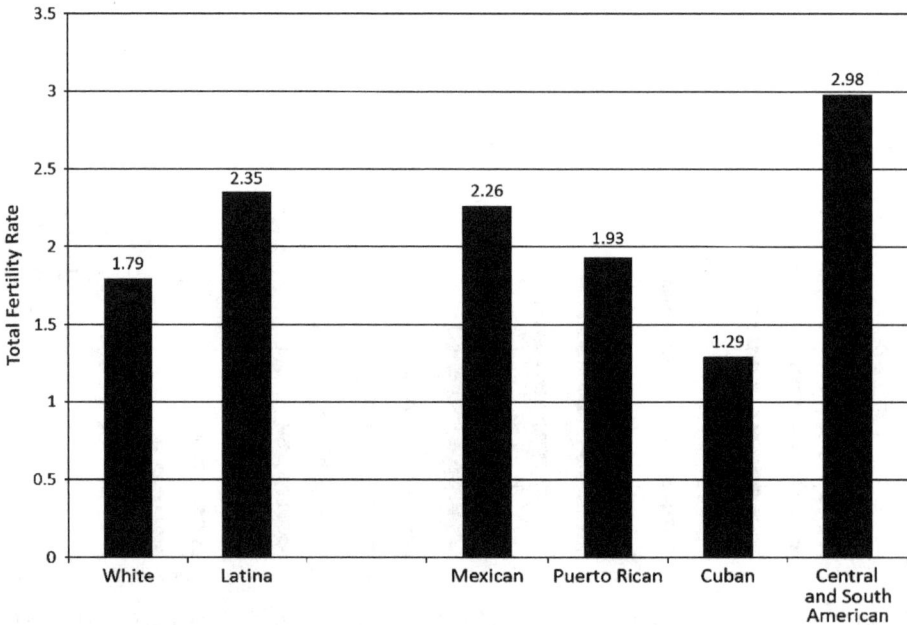

Figure 4.7 Total Fertility Rate of Latina and White Women in the US, 2010
Source: Compiled with data from Martin et al. (2012).

Latino population. The declining fertility and migration levels suggest that the rate of increase of the Latino population is likely to slow a bit, though it will undoubtedly continue to grow much faster than that of the white population due to the youthfulness of the Latino population. The major question is whether the fertility rates among Latinas will remain low or whether they will rebound when the economy improves.

Mortality

Sociologists and demographers have for long observed that individuals with low socioeconomic standing tend to die at higher rates and live shorter lives compared to people of higher socioeconomic levels (Kitagawa and Hauser 1973). Latinos possess a bundle of characteristics that place them at risk for high levels of mortality and truncated lives. These include low levels of education, high rates of poverty, high prevalence in dangerous jobs, low levels of health insurance coverage, and high rates of obesity and diabetes. However, in actuality, despite this configuration of risk factors, Latinos have lower mortality rates and live longer than whites. This unexpected phenomenon has baffled demographers and epidemiologists and bears the name "the epidemiological paradox" (Markides and Coreil 1986; Sáenz and Morales 2012). The epidemiological paradox along with the explanations that have been proposed to account for the paradox will be covered in greater detail in chapter 10.

Here we provide an illustration of the mortality and life expectancy advantage that Latinos enjoy over whites. Mortality data from the National Center for Health Statistics for 2009 show age-specific mortality rates across 19 age categories. These data show that Latinos have lower mortality rates compared to whites in 16 of the 19 age categories (the exceptions being age groups 10–14, 15–19, and 20–24 for males and 1–4, 5–9, and 10–14 for females) (Kochanek et al. 2011).

Similar patterns are observed when we examine infant mortality rates, which refers to the number of infants who die in a given year before reaching their first birthday per 1,000 live births during the year. Overall, Latino (5.66) and white (5.63) babies die at comparatively similar levels, reflecting the epidemiological paradox due to the low level of infant mortality rate of Latinos despite their low socioeconomic characteristics (figure 4.8). Latino groups vary on their infant mortality rates with Central American and South American (3.13) and Cuban (4.73) babies having lower infant mortality rates than whites, while Puerto Rican (7.88) babies are at the greatest risk of not surviving to see their first birthday.

The latest life tables containing information on the Latino population provide additional evidence for the existence of the epidemiological paradox. Life tables represent the most versatile tool of demographers as they can be used for many applications. The life table, which can be broken down by race/ethnicity and sex, starts off with a cohort of 100,000 babies who are subjected to probabilities of death (derived from current mortality rates) at each age until the entire cohort dies off (Poston and Bouvier 2010). One of the most useful functions of the life table is to determine the life expectancy of a population given the existing mortality rates. The latest life tables based on mortality rates in 2008 show that Latino baby boys born in 2008 are expected to live, on average, 2.5 more years than white baby boys, while Latina baby girls born that year are expected to outlive white baby girls by 2.6 years (figure 4.9).

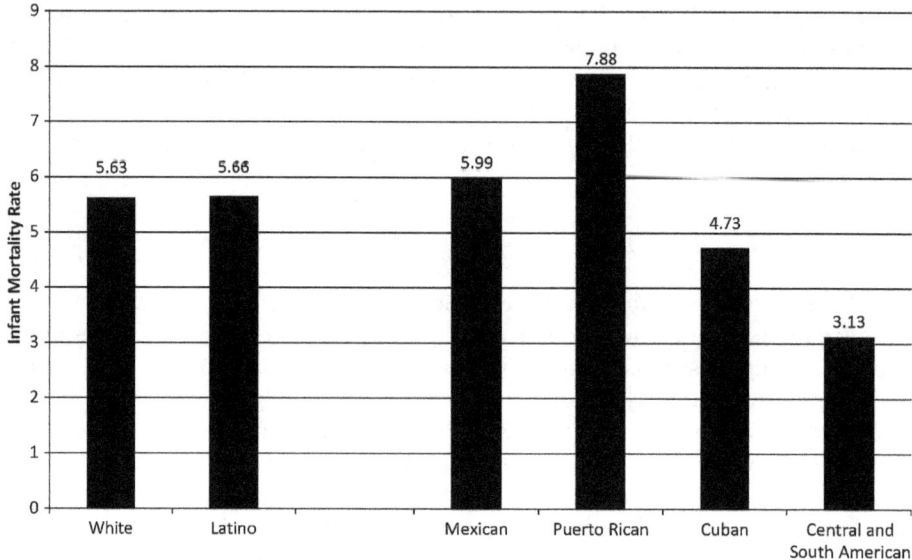

Figure 4.8 Infant Mortality Rate of Latinos and Whites in the US, 2008
Source: Compiled with data from Miniño et al. (2011).

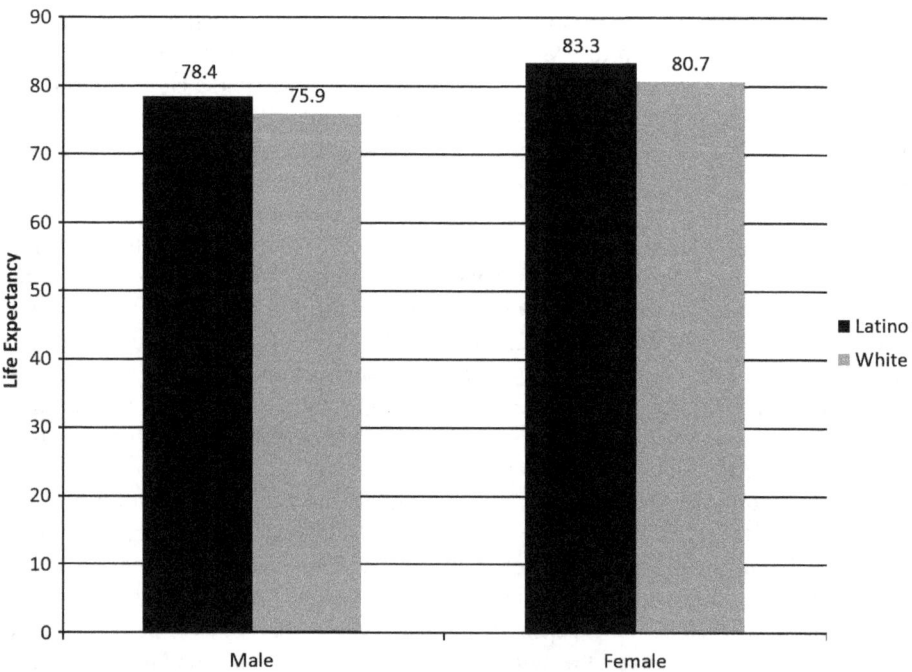

Figure 4.9 Life Expectancy of Latinos and Whites in the US by Sex, 2008
Source: Compiled with data from Arias (2012).

Thus, as a whole, it is clear that the low level of mortality among Latinos relative to whites plays an important role in the comparatively rapid pace at which the Latino population has grown. The impact of mortality is intensified when we take into account the young age structure of Latinos. Indeed, not only do relatively few Latinos die because a large portion of the population is young but the rate at which Latinos die at each age is relatively low as well.

Natural Increase

The age structure differences between Latinos and whites strongly impacts the relative volume of births and deaths within these groups. Demographers use the term natural increase to represent the difference between births and deaths, with natural increase occurring when there are more births than deaths and natural decrease resulting when deaths outnumber births. Figure 4.10 presents the number of births and deaths for Latinos and whites during the 2006–10 period. The two groups vary dramatically in the volume of births and deaths during the five-year period. In particular, whites had slightly more births (11,261,748) than deaths (9,779,779) during the period, while Latinos had a much greater prevalence of births (5,087,823) than deaths (693,830). As such, Latinos had 7.33 births for every one death compared to whites with 1.15 births per one death. This dramatic difference in the birth-to-death ratio reflects the younger age structure of Latinos and the older age structure of whites. Put simply, a youthful population such as that of Latinos produces a large number of births with relatively few people dying. In contrast, an older population such as that of whites generates a

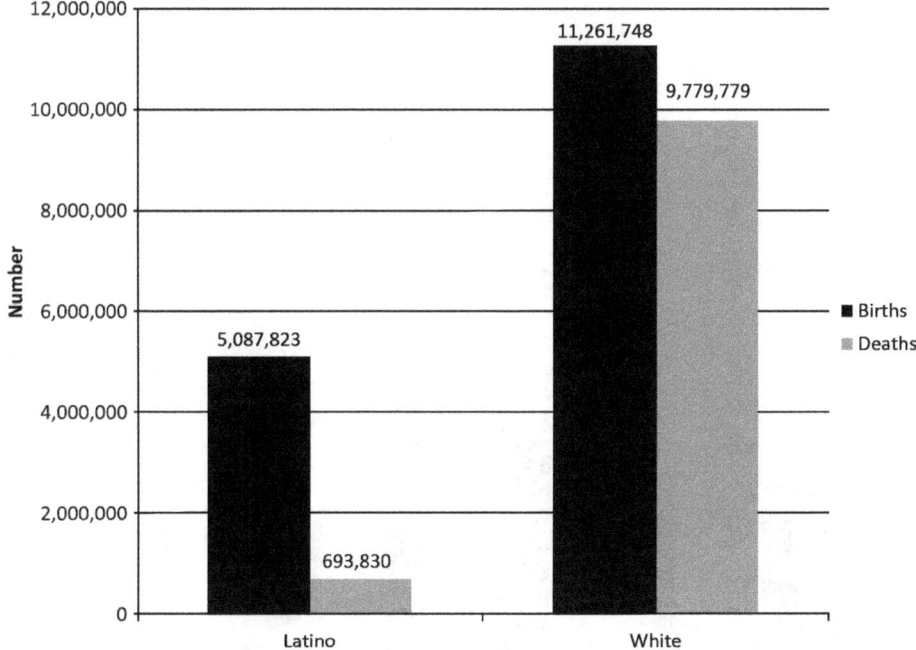

Figure 4.10 Number of Births and Deaths among Latinos and Whites in the US, 2006–2010
Sources: Center for Disease Control and Prevention (2013a, 2013b, 2013c).

large quantity of deaths and limited births. As the white baby boom population (born between 1946 and 1964) gets into the elderly ages (65 and older), a process that started in 2011, it is likely that whites will experience natural decrease, i.e., more deaths than births. The massive differences in the current and expected birth-to-death ratios between Latinos and whites have major implications for the future of the US.

Latinos and the Future US Population

The latest population projections conducted by the US Census Bureau are based on the 2010 decennial census (for a description of the methodology and assumptions used to generate the population projections, see US Census Bureau 2013f). Overall, it is projected that the US population will increase from 308.7 million in 2010 to nearly 420.3 million in 2060. The Latino population is projected to increase from 50.5 million in 2010 to 63.8 million in 2020 to 78.7 million in 2030 to 94.9 million in 2040 to 111.7 million in 2050, and to 128.8 million in 2060 (figure 4.11). Thus, it is expected that the Latino population will expand 2.5-fold between 2010 and 2060. In contrast, the white population is projected to remain fairly stable and begin to experience population decline some time between 2020 and 2030. It is projected that in 2060 whites would have approximately 9 percent fewer persons than the group had in 2010.

Growth in the US population will continue to be driven largely by the expansion of the Latino population with the share of the total growth due to Latinos ranging from 53 percent in the 2010–20 period to 85 percent in the 2040–50 period. As a result, the relative presence of Latinos in the US population is expected to rise from 16 percent

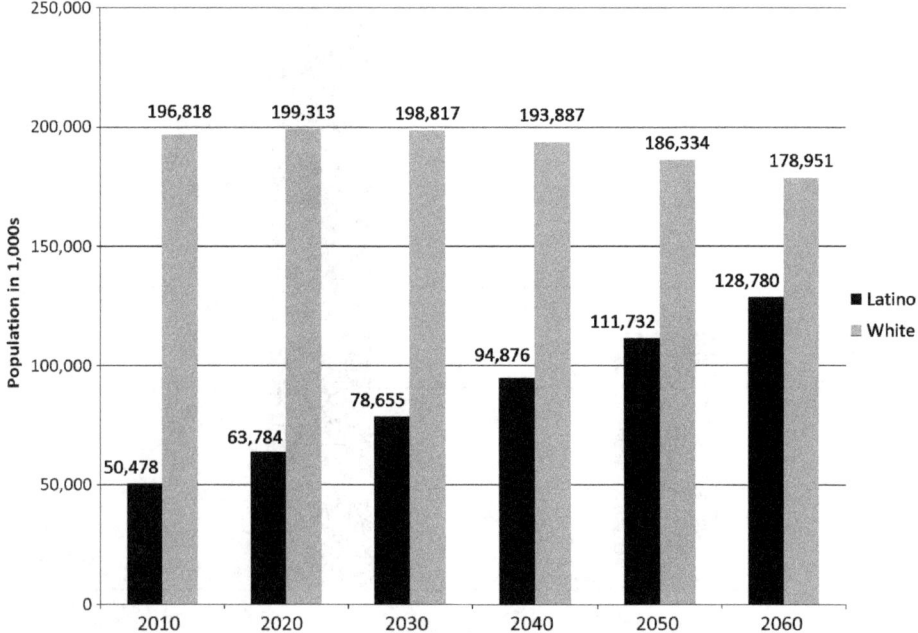

Figure 4.11 Population Projections (in 1,000s) for Latinos and Whites, 2010–2060

Sources: US Census Bureau (2013c, 2013e).

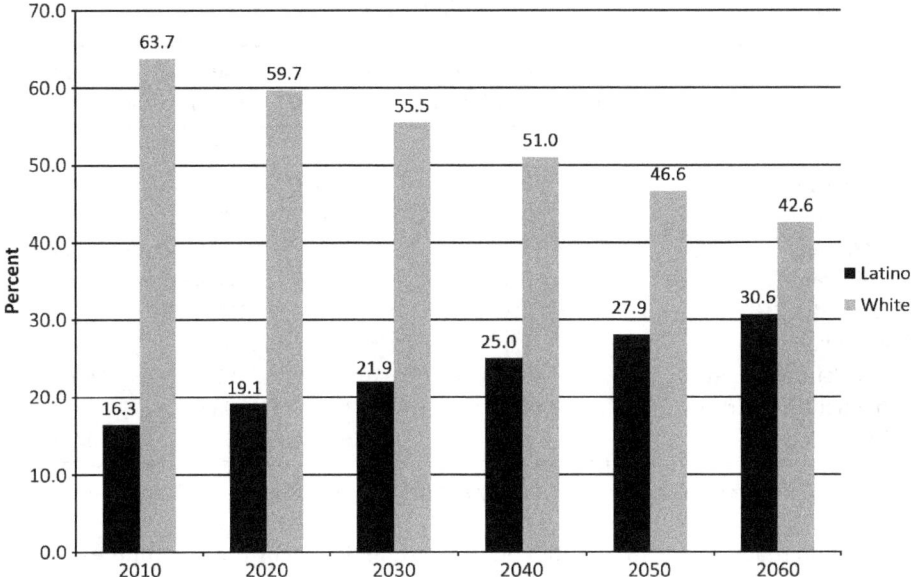

Figure 4.12 Projected Percentage Share of Latinos and Whites in the US Population, 2010–2060

Sources: US Bureau of the Census (2013c, 2013e).

in 2010 to 25 percent by 2040 and to nearly 31 percent by 2060 (figure 4.12). This is an amazing expansion of Latinos in the US population, especially given that in 1980 they accounted for only 6.4 percent of the nation's population. By way of contrast, the share of the white population in the country's population is expected to decline from 64 percent to 51 percent in 2040 and to close to 43 percent by 2060. Again, the differing demographic future of Latinos and whites is driven by the major variations in their age structures today.

We have seen the major growth of the Latino population over the last 30 years as well as its projected increase over the next half century. It is clear that Latinos represent the engine of the US population as the nation's population is largely driven by growth in the Latino population. We now turn to an examination of the demographic variation that exists across groups that comprise the Latino population.

Demographic Variations in Latino Groups

As noted in the earlier chapters, the different groups that comprise the Latino population vary on a variety of dimensions including their demographic characteristics. To a certain extent, these variations are due to the length of time the groups have been in the US, mode of incorporation, and the socioeconomic resources that immigrants bring with them to this country.

Despite the increasing diversity of the Latino population, it continues to be dominated by the Mexican population. Indeed, data from the 2011 American Community Survey indicate that nearly two-thirds (64.6%) of Latinos are Mexican with nearly one-tenth being Puerto Rican (table 4.1). The relatively high share of the Latino

Table 4.1 *Demographic Characteristics of Latino Groups, 2011*

Latino Groups	Percentage of Latino Population	Median Age	Sex Ratio	Percentage Foreign-Born
Mexican	64.6	25.0	105.4	34.7
Puerto Rican	9.5	28.0	96.9	1.0
Cuban	3.6	40.0	99.5	57.6
Salvadoran	3.8	29.0	106.0	59.8
Dominican	2.9	28.0	86.0	56.0
Guatemalan	2.3	27.0	130.9	64.2
Colombian	1.9	34.0	80.3	64.3
Other Central American	2.8	30.0	97.3	59.5
Other South American	4.0	33.0	98.0	64.7
Other Latino	4.6	30.0	99.0	14.9

Source: 2011 American Community Survey Public-Use File (Ruggles et al. 2010).

population that is Mexican is sustained to a certain degree by the youthfulness of the Mexican (median age = 25) population with no other Latino group being younger. On the other hand, the Cuban population is the oldest with a median age of 40, relatively similar to the median age of 42 among whites. South Americans, including Colombians, also are somewhat older than other Latino groups aside from Cubans.

The Latino groups also vary significantly on imbalances between males and females measured commonly using the sex ratio, which represents the number of males per 100 females. Three groups (Guatemalan, Salvadoran, and Mexican) include more males than females with the imbalance being greatest among Guatemalans who have a sex ratio of 131 (table 4.1). In contrast, females are far greater represented than males among Colombians (80.3) and Dominicans (86.0). As we will see in subsequent chapters, imbalances in gender have implications for family structure, living arrangements, and employment.

The Latino groups also differ on the basis of the presence of foreign-born individuals. The relative size of immigrants across groups is related to the length of presence in the US among the Latino groups. Obviously, because persons born in Puerto Rico are automatically US citizens, few Puerto Ricans (1.0%) are foreign-born (table 4.1). The residual group (Other Latino) also has a relatively low level of immigrants with about 15 percent being born outside of the US, although it is difficult to depict the group due to its diversity. Mexicans, the group that has been in the US the longest while still having high levels of immigration, have more than one-third (34.7%) of their members who are foreign-born. On the other hand, all other groups have been in the US for a shorter period of time with each having the majority of their members who are foreign-born. Nearly two-thirds of Other South Americans (64.7%), Colombians (64.3%), and Guatemalans (64.2%) were born outside of the US.

The Geography of Latinos

While Latinos increasingly span across the US, they continue to be concentrated in particular states. Specifically, as is the case with other racial and ethnic groups,

Latinos tend to reside at a close proximity to those who are similar to them in national origin. This form of residence is helpful when people have limited resources and must rely on kin and friends and their social networks for various types of assistance, including social support, financial assistance, housing accommodation, assistance locating employment, and so forth.

Compared to the overall US population Latinos are concentrated in a handful of states. For example, at least half (50.9%) of the overall US population lived in nine states in 2010 (data not shown here). California had the largest share of the US population with approximately one in eight persons living in that state. In contrast, nearly 55 percent of Latinos overall are clustered in three states (California, Texas, and Florida). In fact, Latinos are more than twice as likely as the country's overall population to be living in California (27.8% versus 12.1%) and Texas (18.7% versus 8.1%).

Similarly, the groups that comprise the Latino population are also concentrated in a few states (data not shown here). The most extreme case is among Cubans with more than two-thirds (68%) living in only one state (Florida). In addition, slightly more than three-fifths of Dominicans and Mexicans are concentrated in two states (Dominicans: New York and New Jersey; Mexicans: California and Texas). Furthermore, half or more of four other groups are clustered in three states: Colombians (Florida, New York, and New Jersey), Salvadorans (California, Texas, and New York), Other South Americans (Florida, New York, and California), and Puerto Ricans (New York, Florida, and New Jersey). The other three Latino groups (Guatemalan, Other Central Americans, and Other Latinos) are aggregated in four states. In general, Puerto Ricans and Dominicans tend to be clustered in the northeast (New York and New Jersey); Central Americans in the southwest (California and Texas), Florida, and New York; South Americans in the northeast (New York and New Jersey), Florida, and California.

We can also assess the degree to which the distribution of state residences of the different Latino groups compares to the distribution of the overall US population. To do this, we compute the index of dissimilarity (D) for each of the Latino groups (see Poston and Bouvier 2010). D ranges from 0 (the two groups being compared have the identical distribution across geographic units, e.g., states) to 100 (the comparison groups do not share common residence across the geographic units). The index represents the percentage of members of a given group being compared (say, Mexicans) to another group (say, the overall US population) that would have to move to another state in order for the two groups to have the same distributions across states. Compared to the overall US population, Dominicans (67) and Cubans (64) are the most dissimilar on the states where they live (figure 4.13). Three other groups (Puerto Ricans, Mexicans, and Colombians) exhibit relatively high levels of variation from the overall national population on their states of residence with Ds above 45. On the other hand, Guatemalans (30.7) exhibit the greatest degree of similarity to the overall US population with respect to the distribution of the population across states.

Nonetheless, over the last few decades, the Latino population has increasingly fanned out to areas beyond where they have been traditionally concentrated. The Mexican population epitomizes this movement to new areas where Latinos have historically not inhabited. We computed indices of dissimilarity based on data

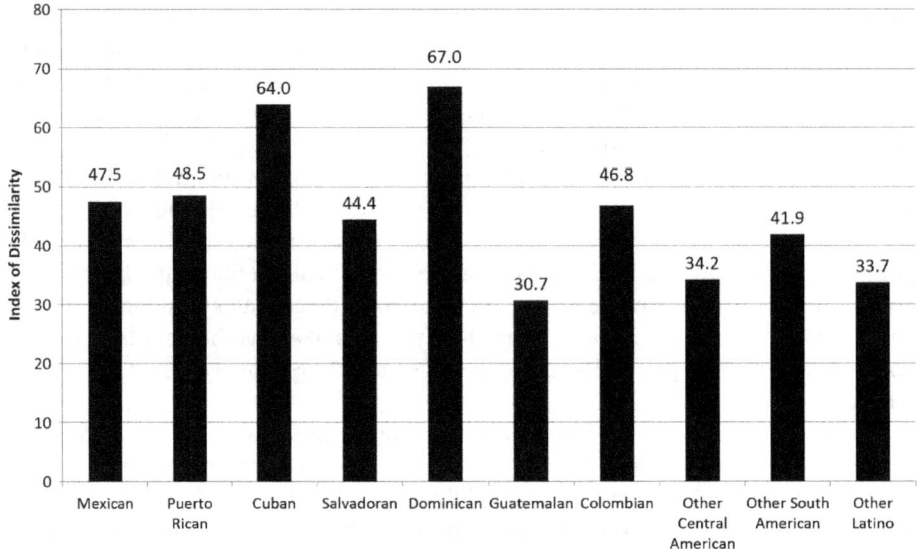

Figure 4.13 Indices of Dissimilarity Representing Differences between Latino Groups and the US Population in States of Residence, 2010[a]

[a] The index of dissimilarity is a measure that ranges from 0 to 100 and represents the percentage of members of a particular group being compared (e.g., Mexican population versus US total population) that would have to relocate to other states in order for the two groups to have the same state distribution. A value of 0 would indicate that the two groups have the same state distribution while a value of 100 would show that the two groups do not share residence in any state.

Source: Compiled with data from US Census Bureau (2013c).

obtained from the 2000 and 2010 Summary File 1 (US Census Bureau 2013a, 2013c) and the 1980 and 1990 5% Public-Use Microdata Samples (PUMS) (Ruggles et al. 2010). The index of dissimilarity comparing the state distributions of Mexicans and the total population has declined significantly from 62.9 in 1980 to 61.4 in 1990 to 52.8 in 2000 and to 47.5 in 2010. Similarly, the proportion of Mexicans living in California and Texas has dropped from approximately three quarters in 1980 (73.1%) and 1990 (74.3%), to two-thirds (65.5%) in 2000, and to three-fifths (60.9%) in 2000. The movement into new areas among Mexicans and Latinos in general illustrates how the Latino population is changing and having an impact on areas that have not traditionally had members of this group. These areas have been referred to as Latino new-destination areas.

Latino New-Destination Areas

Latino new-destination states have experienced significant transformations of their populations, characterized by a historical absence of Latinos along with a rapid growth of this population over the course of the last few decades. In many of these places, the growth of the Latino population has been associated with transformations in the meat and poultry processing industry beginning in the 1970s (Kandel and

Parrado 2005). At that time, due to increasingly global competition, meat and poultry packer executives sought to cut labor costs (Gouveia and Sáenz 2000; Sáenz 2012b). They did this through the movement of meat and poultry operations from urban areas to rural areas located largely in the Midwest and South (Zúñiga and Hernández-León 2006). These rural communities were hungry for economic growth, provided lucrative incentives to lure business, and were not friendly environments to labor unions. As a result, the well-paying jobs in packing houses turned into low-wage jobs with limited benefits and even more dangerous working conditions due to increasing speeds on the production line (Gouveia and Sáenz 2000; Sáenz 2012b). Accordingly, few workers in such localities were eager to take such jobs. Latino immigrants represented a sought-after labor pool. Recruitment of Latino immigrants took place in southwestern states, especially California and Texas, as well as in Mexico (Cohen 1998).

We use a procedure here to identify Latino new-destination states. In particular, we use the following criteria to classify new-destination states: (a) are in the continental US, (b) were not among the 20 states with the most Latinos in 1980, (c) in 1980 Latinos represented less than 3.2 percent of the state's overall population (i.e., half of the 6.4% value at the national level), and (d) had at least a 245 percent growth in the Latino population between 1980 and 2010 (i.e., the same level of growth at the national level). This approach leads to the identification of 20 states as Latino new-destination states (Alabama, Arkansas, Delaware, Georgia, Iowa, Kansas, Kentucky, Maryland, Minnesota, Missouri, Nebraska, New Hampshire, North Carolina, North Dakota, Oklahoma, Rhode Island, South Carolina, South Dakota, Tennessee, and Wisconsin). As shown in figure 4.14 most of these states are located in the Midwest and South.

The Latino new-destination states share the commonalities that they had relatively few Latinos in 1980 and have experienced dramatic increases in the Latino population since then. Georgia and North Carolina represent the quintessential Latino new-destination states. In 1980, Georgia was ranked 24th with respect to its size of the Latino population with a population of 61,260, while North Carolina was 27th with a population of 56,667, and Latinos represented 1 percent of the population of each state. By 2010, Georgia had the 10th largest Latino population with a population of 853,689, while North Carolina was ranked 11th with a population of 800,120, the Latino population grew approximately 14-fold, and Latinos now represent more than 8 percent of the population of each state. Although less dramatic, the experience of the other 18 states show similar trends.

The Latino population grew substantially in Latino new-destination states. For example, the Latino population nearly doubled in new-destination states from nearly 2.7 million in 2000 to close to 5.2 million in 2010 (table 4.2). By contrast, the white population across the 20 new-destination states increased by merely 3.5 percent during the decade. Overall, new-destination states contained one-tenth of the nation's Latino population. Eight new-destination states experienced more than a doubling of its Latino population between 2000 and 2010 led by South Carolina (147.9%), Alabama (144.8%), Tennessee (134.2%), and Kentucky (121.6%).

The Latino population exerted demographic force in the population change of Latino new-destination areas in the last decade. For instance, even though in 2000 Latinos made up only one in 25 residents of new-destination states, they accounted for one-third of the overall growth of the 20 new-destination states (table 4.2).

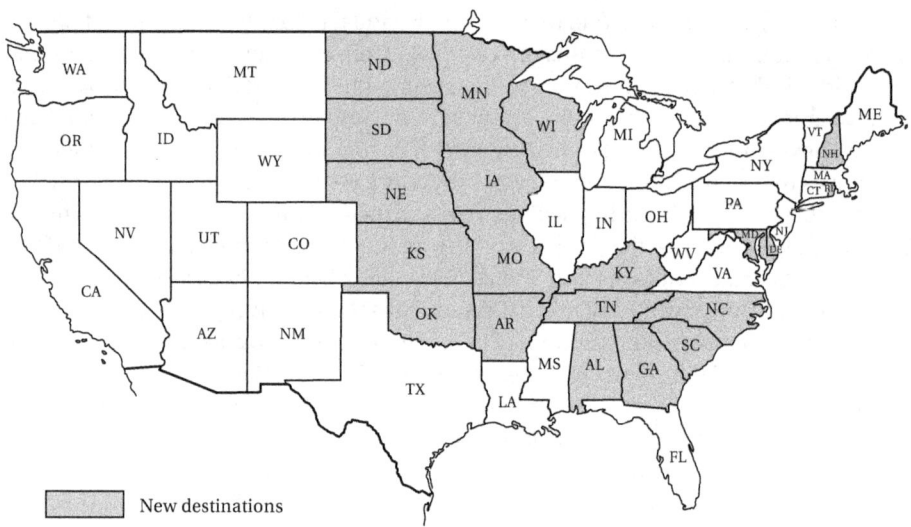

Figure 4.14 Latino New-Destination States[a]

[a] New destination states are defined as those that: (a) are in the continental US, (b) were not among the 20 states with the most Latinos in 1980, (c) in 1980 Latinos represented less than 3.2% of the state's overall population (i.e., half of the 6.4% value at the national level), and (d) had at least 245% growth in the Latino population between 1980 and 2010 (i.e., the same level of growth at the national level).

Noteworthy is that the absolute growth of Latinos (2,530,339) across the 20 new-destination states was greater than that of whites (1,966,621). Latinos in five states were responsible for from half to two-thirds of the growth of these areas (Kansas, 67.9%; Nebraska, 63.4%; Iowa, 57.5%; Maryland, 50.9%; and Oklahoma, 50.8%). Furthermore, in Rhode Island, if it were not for the growth in the Latino population, the state would have lost population between 2000 and 2010, as the state experienced an increase of 4,248 people while the Latino population rose by 39,835 during the decade. In fact, the white population actually declined in Maryland (–128,589), Rhode Island (–54,748), Iowa (–9,221), and Kansas (–3,458), with these declines in the white population offset by the growth of 242,716, 39,835, 69,071, and 111,790 in the Latino population, respectively.

As a result of the rapid growth of the Latino population in new-destination states, their presence grew across all of these states. Overall, in the aggregate, the percentage of Latinos across the 20 states increased from 3.6 percent in 2000 to 6.4 percent in 2010 (table 4.2). Latinos comprised more than 8 percent of the populations of eight states with the highest shares in Rhode Island (12.4%), Kansas (10.5%), and Nebraska (9.2%).

Over the last few decades, Latinos have fanned out across the US with their movement particularly noticeable in Latino new-destination states. While the Latino population is still relatively small especially in some states, it will likely become the engine of the population of new-destination states. The Latino population living in new-destination states possesses demographic characteristics that are

Table 4.2 *Latino Population Changes in Latino New-Destination States and Other States, 2000–2010*

	Latino Population		Latino % Change	% of 2000–10 State Growth Due to Latinos	% of State Population Latino	
States	2000	2010	2000–10		2000	2010
Alabama	75,830	185,602	144.8	33.0	1.7	3.9
Arkansas	86,866	186,050	114.2	40.9	3.2	6.4
Delaware	37,277	73,221	96.4	31.4	4.8	8.2
Georgia	435,227	853,689	96.1	27.9	5.3	8.8
Iowa	82,473	151,544	83.7	57.5	2.8	5.0
Kansas	188,252	300,042	59.4	67.9	7.0	10.5
Kentucky	59,939	132,836	121.6	24.5	1.5	3.1
Maryland	227,916	470,632	106.5	50.9	4.3	8.2
Minnesota	143,382	250,258	74.5	27.8	2.9	4.7
Missouri	118,592	212,470	79.2	23.8	2.1	3.5
Nebraska	94,425	167,405	77.3	63.4	5.5	9.2
New Hampshire	20,489	36,704	79.1	20.1	1.7	2.8
North Carolina	378,963	800,120	111.1	28.3	4.7	8.4
North Dakota	7,786	13,467	73.0	18.7	1.2	2.0
Oklahoma	179,304	332,007	85.2	50.8	5.2	8.9
Rhode Island	90,820	130,655	43.9	937.7[a]	8.7	12.4
South Carolina	95,076	235,682	147.9	22.9	2.4	5.1
South Dakota	10,903	22,119	102.9	18.9	1.4	2.7
Tennessee	123,838	290,059	134.2	25.3	2.2	4.6
Wisconsin	192,921	336,056	74.2	44.3	3.6	5.9
New-Dest. States	2,650,279	5,180,618	95.5	32.9	3.6	6.4
All Other States	32,655,539	45,296,976	38.7	64.4	15.7	19.9
Total	35,305,818	50,477,594	43.0	55.5	12.5	16.3

[a] Due to population loss of non-Latinos, the total population of Rhode Island increased by only 4,248 between 2000 and 2010, while the Latino population grew by 39,835 during this period.

Source: US Census Bureau (2013a, 2013c).

associated with rapid population growth. Indeed, the median age of whites ranges from 40 to 44 across the 20 new-destination states while the median age of Latinos is less than 25 in 16 of the 20 states (US Census Bureau 2013c). Latinos are the youngest in North Dakota (median age of 21.9), Iowa (22.2), South Dakota (22.3), and Nebraska (22.8). Furthermore, only two states (Maryland, 27.1%; and Rhode Island, 29.2%) have Latino populations where youth less than 15 years of age make up less than 30 percent. In contrast, persons less than 15 years of age comprise more than

35 percent of the Latino populations of six states (Iowa, 36.1%; South Dakota, 36.1%; Nebraska, 35.8%; Kansas, 35.1%; Minnesota, 35.1%; and Wisconsin, 35.1%).

Furthermore, new-destination states also have a considerable immigrant population. For example, foreign-born individuals comprise more than 40 percent of the Latino populations of nine of the 20 new-destination states with over half born outside of the US in Maryland (52.5%), Georgia (51.0%), and North Carolina (50.5%) (US Census Bureau 2013d). In addition, as males tend to predominate among Latino immigrants, all of the new-destination states except Rhode Island have more males than females among their Latino populations (US Census Bureau 2013c). Four states have Latino populations in which there are more than 120 males per 100 females: Kentucky (sex ratio of 126.9), Alabama (126.8), South Carolina (125.8), and Tennessee (120.1).

Summary

The demographic journey of the Latino population over the last several decades has been profound. The population is expected to continue its domination of the nation's population growth in the coming decades, although there are signs of declines in fertility and immigration. Thus, the major question is whether fertility and immigration among Latinos will rebound to levels observed prior to the economic crisis.

An additional question to consider is whether the US will implement policies to ensure that Latino youth become key contributors to society. Demographic shifts driven by the growth of Latino youth translates to them being a significant portion of the labor force and that they will work alongside an aging white population. Yet, as we will see in the chapter on education, the social integration of Latino youth is a major challenge.

We now shift our focus over the course of the next eight chapters to examine Latinos within the context of eight institutions involving political engagement (chapter 5), education (chapter 6), work and economic life (chapter 7), family (chapter 8), religion (chapter 9), health and health care (chapter 10), crime and victimization (chapter 11), and mass media (chapter 12). It will be clear that the immigration and demographic patterns of the Latino population are intimately related to the experience of Latinos in each of these institutions.

5 Political Engagement

In this chapter we seek to examine the location and exercise of power of Latinos in the US. We question whether democracy, as a form of government for the people and by the people, is fully extended to Latinos. This concern has existed historically. Indeed, the sentiments of exclusion and fear about "Mexicanization" and "Latinization" that exist today can be rooted back to the nineteenth century in the US–Mexican War and the annexation of northern Mexico in the US (Montejano 1999) as well as to other forms of colonization in the history of Latino incorporation in this country (chapter 2). Rodolfo Acuña's *Occupied America* (1972) referred to the Southwest as an *internal colony* given that Mexican land and people are being controlled by an imperialistic US and that variations of such colonization are still with us today. This is evident in the political alarmists' tones and concerns about cultural retention surrounding the "browning of America" (Montejano 1999; Sáenz et al. 2007b).

The exclusion of Latinos from the benefits of white privilege are legally embedded and determined by the courts in the US. For example, historian George A. Martinez (1997) has traced the legal construction of whiteness as it is applied to the Mexican-origin community. In *Inland Steel Co. v. Barcelona* an Indiana appellate court addressed whether Mexicans are white. The court noted that about one-fifth of Mexico's inhabitants are white, two-fifths are indigenous, and the remainder are mixed-blood blacks, Japanese, and Chinese. As such, the court held that "Mexicans" are not white. Texas courts considered the same question in *In re Rodriguez* (1897) at a time where it was necessary to be "white" in order to naturalize. The outcomes of this case illustrated how racial categories can be constructed in the court's decision that Mexicans are non-white in the anthropological sense but that treaties with Mexico allowed Mexicans to become US citizens. Yet, in 1930 Mexican Americans were considered white in *Independent School District v. Salvatierra*, a desegregation case in Del Rio, Texas, in which the court ruled that Mexican American children cannot be separated from children of "other white races." Note that the court ruling still permitted for the segregation of Mexican Americans on the basis of being limited English proficient. In 1969 in *Lopez Tijerina v. Henry* the court refused to allow for Mexican Americans to define themselves as a group in order to seek a class action to secure equality in local schools. These are just some of the examples of the political contentiousness on defining Mexicans and excluding them from whiteness and by extension white privilege.

An example of the political exclusion of Latinos today concerns the criminalization and marginalization of Latino immigrants. As discussed in chapter 3, Latino immigrants constitute the largest portion of the foreign-born population and the limited and unequal rights they are granted in society questions whether democracy, as the US political model, remains the standard. In particular, although immigrants contribute to society through the taxes that they pay (e.g., sales taxes, property taxes, and salary/wage taxes), through their work, and through largely obeying US laws (see chapter 11), they are not extended the same rights as citizens. With the exception of K-12 education and emergency health care, undocumented immigrants and legally permanent residents (for the first five years) do not qualify for social benefits. Thus, while Latino immigrants contribute to society, they are not granted basic human rights pointing to the weakening of democratic standards in the US (Sáenz et al. 2013).

Another telling example of a barrier towards democracy concerns the court positions on immigrant labor rights. Even though immigrants are legally protected by labor laws, the applicability of those laws becomes problematic in cases where judges prioritize the violation of federal immigration laws over labor violations such as the 1942 case of *Hoffman Plastic Compounds v. National Labor Relations Board (NLRB)* (2002). At the hearing to determine the backpay to Jose Castro who was illegally fired for union organizing activities, Castro admitted to being unauthorized to work. The Court found that Castro could not be granted backpay because of his citizenship status. Thus, the Court sided with the immigration policy, holding that undocumented workers were not entitled to the same remedies as authorized workers. This has become a notable example of competing laws in the US and the prioritizing of immigration policy over any rights extended to immigrants.

However, it is both immigrant and native-born Latinos who are under-represented in political dialogues and political appointments. Sáenz (2012a) argues that one of the reactions from whites to the growing Latino population entails efforts to minimize their political power which places into question democratic principles. Sáenz (2012a) asserts:

> As the nation's demography has shifted dramatically over the last few decades with the disproportionate growth of nonwhites, especially Latinos, the political landscape has shifted ... [A]nti-democracy forces have engineered political warfare against Latinos and African Americans in an effort to minimize the political influence that, in a perfect world, would accompany their growing presence. And there has been no effort to try to mask this erosion of democracy. (p. 5)

Sáenz (2012a, p. 5) notes several ways that democracy has been weakened in response to the increasing numerical representation of groups of color such as Latinos. First, the minimal progress that minority groups gained following Civil Rights legislation has been practically eliminated by the vilification of affirmative action, done under the pretense that this is actually reverse discrimination. Second, the establishment of oppressive drug and immigration policies over the last several decades has led to a massive ballooning of incarceration in this country, with Latinos and African Americans (males in particular) becoming the overwhelming majority of people in jails, prisons, or on parole or probation. Third, as the nation's youth population is increasingly non-white, education has become a declining priority at the federal and state levels. Fourth, states around the country, most notably Texas, have undertaken overt gerrymandering efforts with a variety of subterfuge to dilute the political potential of Latinos and African Americans, whose population growth outpaces that of whites. Fifth, numerous states around the country have passed legislation requiring photo identification for voting. Sáenz (2012a) concludes that contributing to the historical measures used to keep marginalized groups from participating in a democratic society – slavery, Jim Crow laws, and poll taxes along with the presence of Ku Klux Klan and the Texas Rangers that intimidated African American and Latino voters – "Contemporary efforts to shut out Latinos and African Americans and, more widely, the poor, contribute only the latest acid eroding our nation's bedrock of democracy" (p. 5).

In this chapter we discuss theoretical perspectives that help to examine the status of Latino political party identification and group position. We also discuss highlights from the Chicana/o Movement and Latino Civil Rights for bilingual and bicultural education. We then use data from the Pew Research Center's Hispanic Trends Project's 2011 National Survey of Latinos to illustrate Latino political perceptions of which political party is more concerned about Latinos, approval for President Obama, satisfaction with the manner in which things are going in the US, and whether the situation for Latinos is improving in this country. We end with questions related to the political future of Latinos. In particular, we discuss how Latinos are shaping policies through various forms of human agency such as voting behavior and social movements.

Theoretical Frameworks

Elite Model of Power vs. Pluralist Model of Power

The pluralist model of government views political power as being dispersed rather than concentrated. A theoretical example is the government model of representative democracy in the US that is created by and for the people, where the will of the majority prevails, there is equality before the law, and decisions are made to maximize the common good (Eitzen and Baca Zinn 2007). In this form of government, while decisions are made by a few elected individuals, they represent the wishes and concerns of the plurality. Additionally, in a pluralistic society, groups who vote as a cohesive bloc yield the greatest amount of power (Sanchez and Masuoka 2010).

In contrast to pluralist views of political power, C. Wright Mills (1956) developed the elite model of power as a theoretical framework to describe the power structure. This concept uses a pyramid as a tool to illustrate that a small group on top (i.e., corporate rich, the executive branch of the government, and the military) form the power elite that make important decisions and control the masses represented in the rest of the pyramid. This model is useful to explain the many ways in which people in the US are rather powerless as evident in their exclusion from important decision making, being misinformed, the financing of political campaigns through special interest groups, and the nomination process of political candidates by affluent individuals and corporations (Eitzen and Baca Zinn 2007). Moreover, as a testament to the power of the elite model, most of the leaders in this country are from the upper economic stratum (Eitzen and Baca Zinn 2007). Given that Latinos are disproportionately at the bottom strata, this presents barriers for their political leadership and representation.

Latino Political Party Identification and Group Position

It has been established that power relations matter in the study of minority politics (Bishin et al. 2012). To date most of the literature has examined black-white political power differentials and the near unanimity of blacks' support for the Democratic Party (Dawson 1994). Black party loyalty is attributed to a sense of group consciousness or "linked fate" sustained by blacks' marginalization by dominant whites (Dawson 1994). According to this perspective, those who hold strong perceptions of "linked fate" believe that their individual fate is connected to their racial/ethnic group (Sanchez and Masuoka 2010). As such, "linked fate" is a theoretical construct to help explain why members of a minority group may prioritize the needs of their racial/ethnic group rather than simply their self-interest when making political decisions.

There is some evidence of the "linked fate" phenomena among Latinos (Evans et al. 2012). For instance, due to their experiences with discrimination, Latinos, aside Cubans, prefer the Democratic Party for its pro-racial equality politics (Hajnal and Lee 2011) in contrast to the Republican anti-immigrant rhetoric and policy proposals (Bowler et al. 2006). Still, rising numbers of Latinos supported the Republican Party in 2000 due to George W. Bush's immigration proposals (Evans et al., 2012). Yet, Evans et al. (2012) found no significant preference for the Democratic Party over Independents after accounting for ethnic concerns among non-Cuban Latinos. As such, the Democrats do not have a strong lock on non-Cuban Latinos.

Given the diversity of the pan-ethnic Latino community and the uncommon history in the US, the "linked fate" phenomenon is not as strong or direct as in the African American case (Jones-Correa and Leal 1996; Kaufmann 2003; Sanchez and Masuoka 2010). Some find that Latinos clearly perceive a linked fate, but the processes of acquiring that "linked fate" vary from the African American case (Sanchez and Masuoka 2010).

There is less of a consensus on the influence of socioeconomic status on party identification among Latinos. Some researchers find that income has no influence on party identification (de la Garza and Cortina 2007) while others find that income is another factor influencing "linked fate," with those among the lower economic strata being more likely to perceive that their fate is linked to other Latinos (Sanchez and Masuoka 2010). Moreover, there is limited consensus on the influence of education on political party identification among Latinos. For instance, some find that a higher level of education is associated with stronger identification with the Republican Party (Bowler et al. 2006; Hajnal and Lee 2011), while others find no differences across educational levels (de la Garza and Cortina 2007), still others find a weak but positive association with Republican identification (Alvarez and Garcia Bedolla 2003), and yet others find a positive association with Democratic party identification (Hajnal and Lee 2011).

Other factors that contribute to the heterogeneity of Latinos that influences pan-ethnic political party identification, likely affecting the probability of Latinos voting as a bloc, are perceptions concerning immigration and national origin. In contrast to a collective identity, Latino partisan divisions are attributed to variations in political attitudes and struggles such as those associated with immigration status (Alvarez and Garcia Bedolla 2003). In terms of national origin, while Cubans prefer the Republican Party, other Latinos are more likely to identify as Democrats (Alvarez and Garcia Bedolla 2003; de la Garza and Cortina 2007; Evans et al. 2012). Indeed, Sanchez and Masuoka (2010) question the formation of Latino pan-ethnic group consciousness formation given that linked fate is more pronounced at the national origin identity level. In particular, at the national-origin level linked fate is greater among those who believe it is important to maintain some aspect of Latino culture and those who believe that Latinos can improve their status by working hard.

Latinos vary considerably along lines of acculturation to US norms and structures which has implication for the formation of a pan-ethnic political group consciousness. For instance, being native-born and increasing generational status are associated with identification with the Democratic Party among Latinos, aside Cubans, due to their increased exposure to the political system (Alvarez and Garcia Bedolla 2003; Hajnal and Lee 2011). Spanish speakers have the greatest amount of linked fate, thus signaling that linguistic cultural retention helps to construct Latino group consciousness (Padilla 1985; Ricourt and Danta 2003; Sanchez and Masuoka 2010). Some argue that social integration is more important than pan-ethnicity in the development or retention of a sense of "linked fate" among Latinos. In particular, Sanchez and Masuoka (2010) conclude that "any notion of a 'Brown-utility heuristic' is based not on race or common history but on social integration to American society for the panethnic Latino population" (p. 528).

Additionally, there are subgroup variations in the degree of political subordination at the local level that influence the Latino group position thesis (Bishin et al. 2012). For example, Bishin et al. (2012) compared Latino attitudes and political behavior in two contexts – the conflict condition where the dominant Latino group, in this case Cubans, control local resources and the marginalized group perceives it as unfair; and the no-conflict condition reflecting the absence of intra-Latino competition over power. Supporting the group-position thesis, US policies that favor Cuban immigrants create resentment among non-Cuban Latinos. It is suggested that local dynamics that pit Latino newcomers against other groups, especially against those groups that have been historically subordinated, may also play a role in political dynamics (Bishin et al. 2012).

Rights Claiming: Chicano/Latino Civil Rights and Beyond

As discussed in chapter 2, the history of Latinos – in the case of Mexicans and Puerto Ricans – in the US involves forced incorporation through annexation and colonization. Thus, the question of citizenship rights has always been at the center of the political incorporation of Latinos. The most common understanding of citizenship refers to a legal recognition in the nation-state as in the case of a person who is native-born or naturalized. Legal status distinguishes members of society that are entitled to rights from a society as opposed to those who are non-members or non-citizens. There are approximately 11.1 million undocumented immigrants (mostly of Mexican origin) residing in the US (Passel and Cohn 2012) who are largely not extended the same rights as citizens. However, even for Latinos who are US citizens, the question remains about the degree to which legal citizenship translates to full social incorporation (Morales 2008b). Social citizenship refers to being fully assimilated in a particular nation-state. As such, while native-born and naturalized Latinos may have legal citizenship, this does not translate into equity with the white majority group in terms of their political rights. Indeed, social citizenship has been seriously disputed historically and still today. The US Constitution declared that all citizens are equal, yet at the time of its implementation only white male property owners were declared citizens. One of the paradoxes of citizenship is that its denial occurred in a republic committed to political equality and where a significant portion of its citizens believe they live in a free and just society.

Even beyond rights bounded by nation-states (i.e., citizenship rights) is the question of Latino human rights (Sáenz et al. 2013). The current hostile environment against Latinos, regardless of citizenship status, has impinged on their basic human rights. Particularly telling are the cases of Mexicans and Puerto Ricans who have continued to be viewed as an invading threat despite their long history in the US (Chavez 2008). The antagonism against Latinos is driven by racism fueled by a fear that Latinos are encroaching on the safe space that whites have created and sustained where they have thrived and benefitted from their white status (Sáenz et al. 2013).

Largely attributed to this unequal treatment, Latinos have responded through various forms of rights claiming. To theoretically conceptualize Latino social movements, Rosaldo (1994) coined the concept of "cultural citizenship" to stress the importance of culture for marginalized groups as a tool to claim citizenship rights in a given society. Through this theoretical apparatus, the dynamics of social change have focused on the processes of contestations and affirmation of cultural production occurring within Latino and other "minority" communities.

There are many important and notable forms of resistance among Latinos in the US that deserve our attention – from rebellions against daily forms of micro-aggressions to large-scale social movements. We turn our attention to a discussion of the Chicano Movement of the Civil Rights Era and Latino struggles for linguistic rights.

Chicano Movement

An integral component of the US civil rights struggle is the Chicano Movement of the 1960s and 1970s (Montejano 1999). Although Rodolfo Acuña (1972, 2014), a noted Chicano scholar, has documented that Mexicans and Chicanos have been responding to injustices since the US wars on Texas and the Southwest, the radicalization of Mexican-origin youngsters characteristic of the Chicano Movement occurred from 1965 to 1975 (Cuéllar 1974; Montejano 1999). Chicano activists embraced what was then a label signifying lower status – Chicano and Chicana – and transformed it into a powerful political identity (Montejano 1999).

A catalyst for the movement was the farmworker strikes in California and Texas (1965-6) that ignited broad civil rights mobilizations among all social classes of Mexican Americans – street youth, high school and college students, factory workers, and professionals (Montejano 1999, 2010). The farmworker strikes also gave the Chicano Movement a national leader – César Chávez (1927-93). Chávez, born in Yuma, Arizona, had spent his childhood as a migrant worker and emerged as a central figure in the strike (Acuña 2014). Prior to the strike in 1962 César Chávez and Dolores Huerta established the United Farm Workers (UFW) union that played a central role in publicizing nationally the struggles of Mexican Americans (Gutiérrez 1995). Although the farmworkers movement began as a collective, bargaining rights for Mexican American and Filipino farmworkers in California, through his nonviolent tactics and ethnic symbolism, Chávez galvanized Mexican Americans nationally (Gutiérrez 1995).

The Chicano Movement played a key role in raising public and governmental awareness about the plight of Mexican Americans, even though there were disagreements among Mexican Americans about the militant style of the movement (Gutiérrez 1995) and the marginalization of women within the movement (Montoya 1994). Despite these internal struggles the Chicano Movement saw several defining legal triumphs. In 1965 the California Agricultural Labor Relations Act extended labor rights to farmworkers and brought some closure to the events that helped ignite the movement (Montejano 1999). That same year the Voting Rights Act extended rights to linguistic citizen minorities (Montejano 1999). In 1971 the US District Court ruled in the landmark *Cisneros v. Corpus Christi Independent School District* case that Mexican Americans were considered an identifiable minority group entitled to special federal assistance (Gutiérrez 1995). Other important political transformations credited to the Chicano Movement included winning a number of rural counties and town governments in Texas spearheaded by José Ángel Gutiérrez, as well as a land reclamation movement in New Mexico led by Reies López Tijerina (Montejano 1999).

The Chicano Movement also channeled cultural projects and community organizing throughout the Southwest. This movement encouraged the establishment of advocacy organizations – e.g., the Mexican American Legal Defense and Educational Fund (MALDEF), the Southwest Voter Registration and Education Project (SVREP), and the National Council of La Raza (NCLR) – that sought to dismantle segregationist practices and institutions (Montejano 1999). Moreover, the Chicano Movement fought for Chicanos to have access to colleges and universities (Montejano 1999).

Struggles for Linguistic Rights

A political issue that is central to the well-being of Latinos involves civil rights struggles for linguistic equity. Latinos, and other linguistic minorities, have been battling against English-only policies since the formation of the US. Despite not having an official language at the federal level, there have been numerous attempts over more than a century to implement English-only policies in our educational institutions and in all levels of government.

In the first half of the 1900s we see how several states used English-only policies as a form of segregation and discrimination against Latinos. In Texas the Nationality Act of 1906 legitimized linguistic discrimination by requiring immigrants to speak English in order to naturalize. In 1923 *Meyer v. Nebraska* ruled that the forbidding of instruction in a language other than English in schools violated the 14th Amendment. An exception to the linguistic exclusionary practices of the states named above is the case of New Mexico that joined the union as an official bilingual state authorizing the usage of both Spanish and English for voting and education. During this timeframe, we also see the formation of civil rights groups that are concerned with Latino civil rights at the local level such as San Antonio's *Orden Hijos de America* (Order of the Sons of America) and more widely as in the case of the League of United Latin American Citizens (LULAC), both of which raised awareness about Latino civil rights issues including education. In 1945 Mexican American parents won a very important court battle against several California school districts that challenged *Mendez v. Westminster*, arguing that segregation violates children's constitutional rights which provided the foundation for *Brown v. Board of Education.*

From 1960 to 1975 the influence of the Civil Rights Act of 1964 is evident. Even though a bilingual education program had already been offered in Miami, the Civil

Rights Act of 1964 was the catalyst for bilingual education more widely. Indeed, a few years afterwards the first bilingual-bicultural federal education program was established through the Bilingual Education Act (BEA) Title VII of the Elementary and Secondary Education Act of 1965. However, the struggles for linguistic equity and equality in the schools continued as we learned in the Latino student walkouts in Los Angeles a few years later. Also during this time the Mexican American Legal Defense and Education Fund (MALDEF) was established to protect the civil rights of Mexican Americans. Considerations for linguistic minorities continued with a federal memorandum stressing that students cannot be denied education for having limited English proficiency (LEP). The federal government also relaxed the economic requirements for BEA and formalized accountability mechanisms. Moreover, a couple of important court cases occurred during this period – *Lau v. Nichols*, which barred discrimination of students on account of their race or national origin and *Serna v. Portales Municipal Schools*, which provided a relief program for Spanish-surnamed children. A testament to the social change toward bilingualism is the passage of the Equal Education Opportunity Act of 1974 that made bilingual education more widely available.

Yet, over the period between the 1980s and 2006, English-only politics gained force once again. At the federal level, Senator S.I. Hayakawa even introduced a constitutional amendment to make English the sole official language of the US. Furthermore, debates surrounded No Child Left Behind, questioning whether this policy benefits non-native English speakers. At the state level several states introduced English-only policies – e.g., Propositions 227 and 187 in California, Proposition 203 in Arizona, and Colorado's English for Children Initiative.

From 2005 to the present we have witnessed struggles to protect one of the most important policies of civil rights legislation – the 1965 Voting Rights Act (VRA). This Act closely followed the language of the 15th Amendment, prohibiting the denial of the vote on the basis of literacy and protection against racial and linguistic minority citizen discrimination, at the federal, state, and local levels. The VRA was passed after a century of deliberation and the denial of the vote to African Americans in the South and Latinos in the Southwest and an electoral system that excluded citizens with limited English proficiencies (The Leadership Conference 2014). Indeed, from their forced incorporation into US society, Mexicans have been perceived as a political threat, thus experiencing numerous attempts to dilute or remove their voting rights. Montejano (1999, p. xvi) cited Paul S. Taylor who noted the deep roots of Mexican American struggles for voting rights when in the 1845 Texas Constitutional Convention fears of "*la reconquista*" (the reconquest) arose when stating "Silently they will come moving in; they will come back in thousands . . . and what will be the consequence? Ten, twenty, thirty, forty, fifty thousand may come in here, and vanquish you at the ballot box though you are invincible in arms" (Montejano 1999, p. 232). In 1992 the Congressional Hispanic Caucus successfully pushed for the passage of the Voting Rights Language Assistance Act over the objections of Republicans and English-only advocates signaling that Latinos can influence significant legislation (Montejano 1999). In 2005, English-only proponents pushed for the dismantling of the Voting Rights Act but President Bush reinstated the Act for the fourth time in 2006, allowing for language assistance at the polls. In 2009, the US Supreme Court ruled in *Northwest Austin Municipal Utility District No. 1 v. Holder* that individual jurisdictions should have the opportunity to avoid provisions of the Voting Rights

Act that require preclearance for changes in election procedures. On June 25, 2013 in *Shelby County v. Holder*, the US Supreme Court determined that Section 4(b) of the Voting Rights Act, which identified the states and political subdivisions that have a history of discriminatory voting practices to be subjected to Section 5 that required those jurisdictions to get advanced approval from the federal government before changing their election laws, was deemed unconstitutional. The American Civil Liberties Union (2014) cited a congressional report stating that without Section 5 "racial and language minority citizens will be deprived of the opportunity to exercise their right to vote, or will have their votes diluted, undermining the significant gains made by minorities in the last 40 years."

The English-only initiatives, such as the ones seeking to dismantle VRA, threaten linguistic equity for significant portions of the Latino population. According to estimates from the American Community Survey of 2012, only 26 percent of Latinos speak only English. Most Latinos are bilinguals and about 13 percent of Latinos do not speak English well and 7 percent do not speak English at all. Thus, close to 20 percent of Latinos in the US do not have command of English. Although it is important to keep in mind that contrary to fears that the American way of life is being threatened with the "browning of America," there are clear indications that Latinos do learn English the longer they reside in the US (Sáenz et al. 2007b).

Trends on Latino Political Perceptions

In this section we use data from the Pew Research Center's Hispanic Trends Project's 2011 National Survey of Latinos collected between January 2011 and December 2011 to assess the political perceptions of Latinos who are US citizens. The data are restricted to the perceptions of citizen Latinos in order to get a sense of how these opinions may influence voting behavior. In particular, the data are based on naturalized citizens from various subgroups of Latinos (Mexicans, Puerto Ricans, Cubans, Dominicans, Salvadorans, Other Central Americans, and South Americans). The only groups with sufficient numbers of native-born citizens are Mexicans and Puerto Ricans.

Figure 5.1 illustrates perceptions among Latino subgroups concerning which political party is most concerned for Latinos. Overall, Latino citizens perceive that the Democratic Party is more concerned for Latinos. Specifically, approximately 50 percent or more of several subgroups – Mexicans (naturalized and US-born), Puerto Ricans, Dominicans, and South Americans – perceive that Democrats care more about Latinos. Particularly striking is that over 80 percent of Dominicans believe that the Democratic Party is the most concerned with Latinos. Yet, there are also significant numbers of Latinos that believe there is no difference among the political parties in terms of concerns for Latinos. For instance, over 55 percent of Salvadorans and Other Central Americans feel there is no difference between political parties in terms of who has more concern for Latinos, followed by Mexicans (naturalized and US-born) and Puerto Ricans with 35 percent to 42 percent, and lastly Cubans and Dominicans with less than 20 percent. This signifies that if Latinos' voting behavior is reflective of the linked fate thesis, where they vote as a bloc according to what is best for their group, a significant portion of Latinos are undecided in terms of party affiliation.

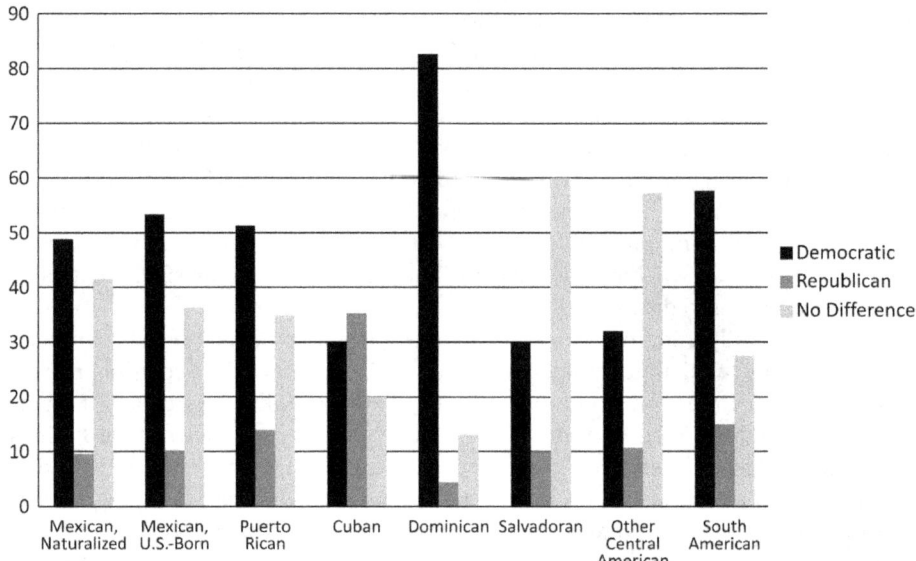

Figure 5.1 Perception of Which Political Party is More Concerned about Latinos, by Latino Group, 2011 (%)

Source: Compiled with data from the 2011 National Survey of Latinos (Pew Research Center's Hispanic Trends Project 2011).

Figure 5.2 shows the percentage of Latinos on the basis of their level of approval regarding how President Obama is handling his job. Overall, all Latino subgroups have over 50 percent approval of President Obama. According to the Pew data, the groups with the highest level of approval for the way in which President Obama is conducting his job are Dominicans (80%) and Salvadorans (70%). The groups more likely to disapprove of President Obama's performance are naturalized Mexicans (43%) followed by US-born Mexicans (37.5%), and South Americans (37.5%).

Figure 5.3 shows the percentage of Latinos who are satisfied with the way things are going in this country today. The only group with over 50 percent satisfaction with how things are going in the US are Cubans. Several groups have percentages of satisfaction that are in the 40 percent range – Dominicans (48%), naturalized Mexicans (45.4%), Salvadorans (42%), and Other Central Americans (41.4%). The groups with the lowest satisfaction are US-born Mexicans (35%), Puerto Ricans (34%), and South Americans (30.8%).

Figure 5.4 shows the percentage of Latinos that believe that the situation for Latinos in the US is improving compared to a year ago. Note that the data collection occurred at the end of 2011. Several Latino subgroups show similar patterns in regards to perceptions of the standing of Latinos in the country. In particular, among all the groups, with the exception of Salvadorans, most believe that the conditions for Latinos have worsened or remained the same. Naturalized Mexicans represent the group that most strongly perceives that conditions have declined for Latinos in the US. Indeed, nearly 50 percent of naturalized Mexicans believe that the situation for Latinos has worsened from the previous year. Similarly, over 40 percent of Other Central Americans believe that conditions have worsened. These patterns among

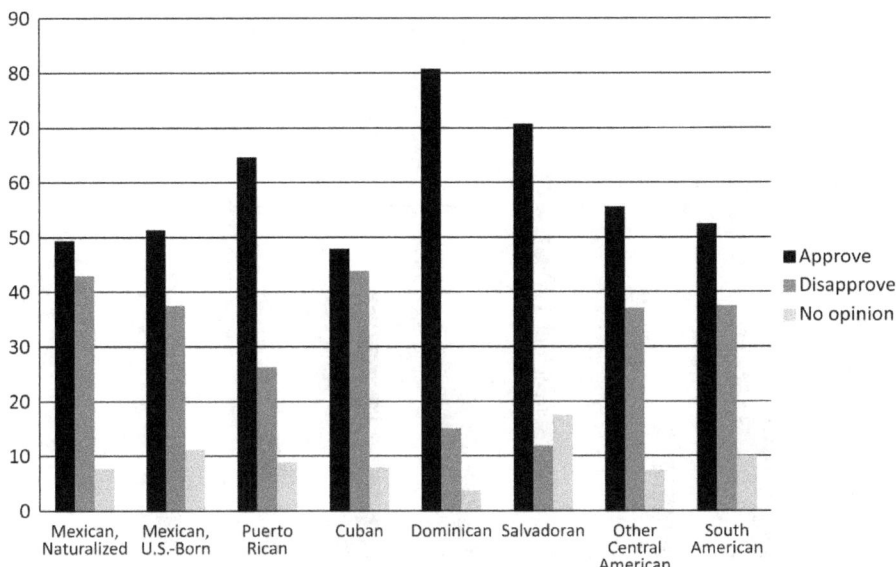

Figure 5.2 Level of Approval of President Obama, by Latino Group, 2011 (%)

Source: Compiled with data from the 2011 National Survey of Latinos (Pew Research Center's Hispanic Trends Project 2011).

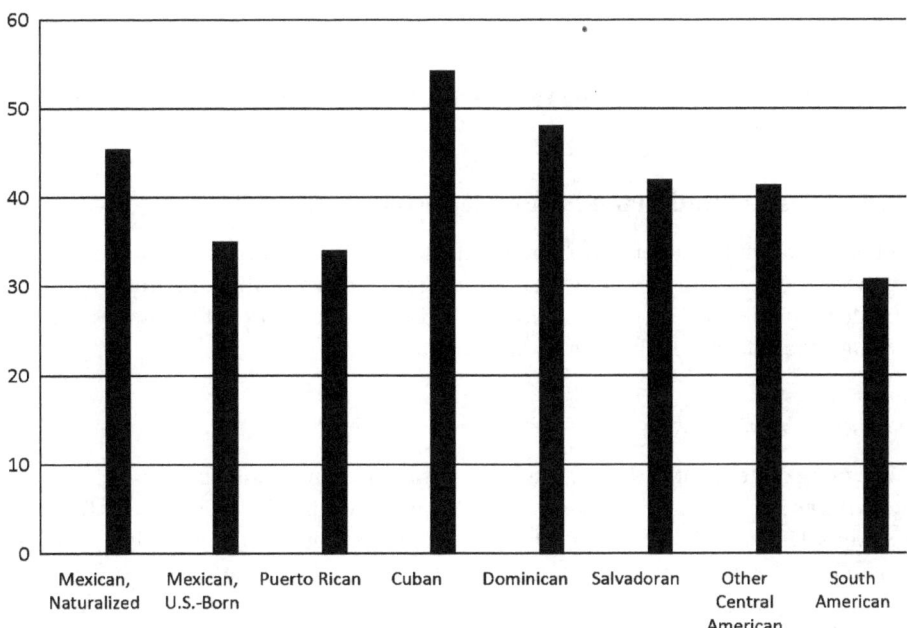

Figure 5.3 Percentage of Latinos Satisfied with How Things are Going in the US, by Latino Group, 2011

Source: Compiled with data from the 2011 National Survey of Latinos (Pew Research Center's Hispanic Trends Project 2011).

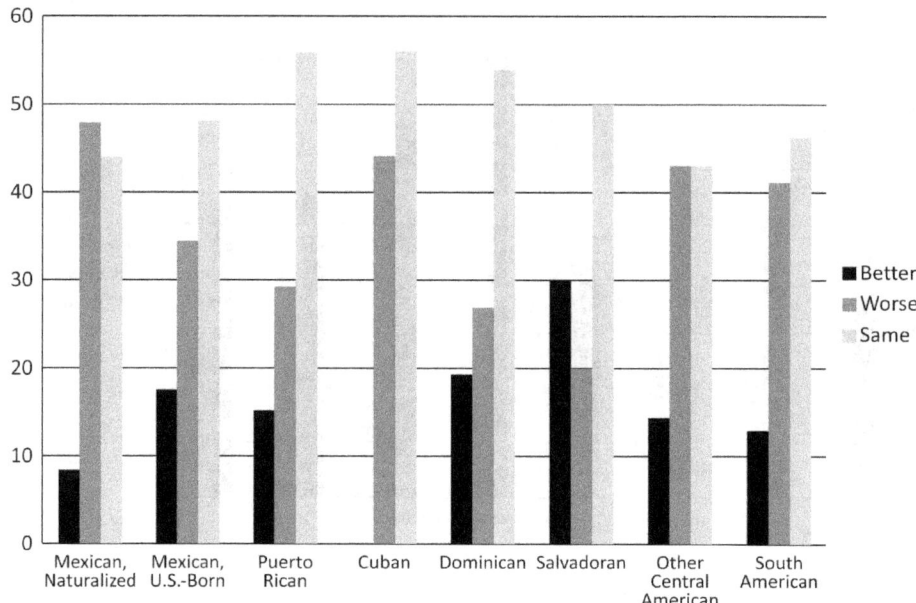

Figure 5.4 Percentage of Latinos who Believe Situation for Latinos Has Improved Compared to Last Year, by Latino Group, 2011

Source: Compiled with data from the 2011 National Survey of Latinos (Pew Research Center's Hispanic Trends Project 2011).

naturalized Mexicans and Other Central Americans may be attributed to their higher susceptibility to deportation.

Questions Related to the Future of Latino Political Power

Having obtained an overview of how Latinos perceive a variety of political-related matters in the country, we now address a couple of issues that are quite important in affecting political engagement among Latinos in the future. These issues concern voting behavior and the Immigrant Rights Movement.

Voting Behavior

The voting patterns of Latinos represent a testament concerning their restricted political power in the US. In regards to the 2012 presidential election the Pew Research Center's Hispanic Trends Project highlighted the impact of the Latino vote, but post-election data from the US Census Bureau showed that the Latino voter turnout rate (48%) remained below that of whites (64.1%) and blacks (66.2%) (Lopez and Gonzalez-Barrera 2013c). Indeed, the Latino voter turnout rate in 2012 is below the rate in 2008 (49.9%). According to census data, while the number of Latinos eligible to vote increased from 2008 to 2012, the percentage who decided not to vote rose even more (Lopez and Gonzalez-Barrera 2013c). The proportion of Latino voter participation in congressional elections is even more dismal, with only a quarter of those who are of voter age choosing to participate (Michelson 2005). These trends have also surfaced in other surveys that show that Latinos and Asians are the least likely to vote regularly (39%), followed by blacks (52%), and whites (59%) (Ramakrishnan and Baldasarre 2003; cited in Michelson 2006).

Demographic patterns, however, predict that Latinos can become a political force in the near future. One of the reasons for Latinos' low voting rates is attributed to their youthfulness (Michelson 2005). While having a young population may hamper the number of Latinos who can currently vote, in the future this demographic pattern suggests a vast increase in the number of eligible voters among Latinos. Indeed, an estimated 800,000 Latinos will turn 18 each year (Lopez and Gonzalez-Barrera 2013c) increasing the number of possible Latino voters. Thus, the Pew Research Center's Hispanic Trends Project projects a doubling of Latino voters by 2030, a gain which is attributed not only to their aging, but also increases in the rate of naturalization (Taylor et al. 2012a). In order for this doubling in voting behavior to occur, Latinos would need to increase their low voter participation and naturalization rates (Taylor et al. 2012a). Moreover, what remains disconcerting are the 11.2 million Latinos who did *not* vote – 5.4 million legal permanent residents and 7.1 million unauthorized immigrants – because they were not eligible to vote in 2012 (Taylor et al. 2012a).

In addition to demographic attributes and socioeconomic status, disparities in voter mobilization among Latinos by political parties and candidates also contribute to their political subordination (Michelson 2005). Survey-based studies find that voter mobilization can increase Latino voter turnout (Michelson 2005), yet they are largely excluded from get-out-the-vote efforts from political parties (Hero et al. 2000; Michelson 2005). Based on four field experiments on Latino voter mobilization in several communities in California – Dos Palos in 2001, Fresno in 2002 and 2003, and Maricopa in 2003 – Michelson (2005) concluded that Latinos are not targeted by voter mobilization campaigns because they do not vote, although they are very receptive to voter mobilization campaigns. Specifically, Latino voter mobilization efforts do not require large budgets or special "Latino" approaches.

The heterogeneity of Latinos can also influence their power as a voting bloc. Illustrating the complexities involved in pan-ethnic coalitions and status inequalities, Bishin et al. (2012) examined the voting behavior of Cubans and non-Cubans in two counties in Florida. They find that pan-ethnicity pulls Latinos from diverse national-origin backgrounds into the ballot box coalitions, yet there are also factors that push Latino voters apart that are rooted in power struggles and status inequality.

Immigrant Rights Movement

While Latino immigrants are not eligible to vote, this does not indicate that they are politically apathetic. On the contrary, they are very politically active. Perhaps the most prevalent example of this is seen in the contemporary immigrant movement (2003–present) in the US. While some politicians may erroneously perceive Latino immigrants as politically powerless due to their ineligibility to vote, immigrant Latinos are political leaders and mobilizers. Indeed, Latino immigrants are educating and mobilizing the industries where they are the preferred laborers, their neighbors, and entire communities about not only immigration reform but the status of Latinos in the country more generally (Morales 2011). More directly, according to the

National Council of La Raza (2009), a significant portion of Latinos, about 62 percent, reside in mixed-status households, thus living with family members who are eligible to vote, a vote that is likely impacted by undocumented household members.

Arguably the contemporary immigrant movement began in 2003 when the Hotel Employees & Restaurant Employees International Union (HERE) spearheaded the Immigrant Workers Freedom Ride (IWFR), an attempt to replicate the 1961 Freedom Rides of the Civil Rights Movement. Approximately 1,000 immigrants and 125,000 union and community organizers were bused from cities throughout the US to Washington, DC, where they met with 120 members of Congress (Morales 2008b). IWFR ended with a demonstration in New York City on October 4, 2004 (Morales 2008b). This movement is also a testament to the coalitions formed among unions, non-governmental organizations and religious organizations around the issue of immigrant rights.

In 2005, anti-immigrant rhetoric rose with the anti-immigrant political proposals such as the Border Protection, Anti-terrorism, and Illegal Immigration Control Act of 2005 – otherwise known as HR 4437. The bill, introduced by Republican Representative James Sensenbrenner from Wisconsin, proposed several anti-immigrant measures such as (1) severely restricting the entry of immigrants into the US, (2) the criminalization of undocumented immigrants (and their families) who are residing in the country, (3) the detainment or deportation of millions of undocumented immigrants, and (4) the possible imprisonment of anyone caught harboring a person without legal immigrant status (Morales 2008b).

The growing anti-immigrant social and political climate in the US manifested by legal acts such as HR 4437 ignited a social movement advocating for immigrant rights. Similar to other movements, student mobilization represented the catalyst for the immigrant movements of 2006. In Las Vegas, for instance, despite the presence of a coalition of unions, hometown associations, religious leaders, and non-governmental organizations, the most important events leading up to the national grassroots mobilization events of April 10 and May 1, 2006 were student walkouts to protest HR 4437 (Morales 2008b; Revilla 2006).

The walkouts began on March 21, 2006 and included elementary, junior high, and high school students. Young people mobilized using technology such as text messaging and electronic social media. Figure 5.5 illustrates some of the students involved in three key political protests consisting of approximately 3,000 youth representing 22 Las Vegas schools (Morales 2008b). A fourth student protest was held the following Saturday to debunk media perceptions that students just wanted an excuse to cut class. These protests mirrored the student walkouts in East Los Angeles in 1968 where thousands of students, largely of Mexican descent, walked out of school to protest the unequal treatment they were receiving in the educational system.

The pro-immigration movement gained momentum initially with the National Day of Immigrants (April 10, 2006) followed by National Boycott Day. The mobilizations on the National Day of Immigrants had parallels with the civil rights movement, as the message of the movement went beyond proclaiming the legalization of immigrants but also made references to the struggle for citizenship rights. On May 1, 2006 immigrants and immigrant rights supporters across the US boycotted work in order to demonstrate to the nation how dependent it is on immigrant labor (the El Gran Paro Americano of 2006). Additionally, supporters demonstrated in major US cities,

Figure 5.5 Las Vegas Student Activists

© Maria Cristina Morales

including New York, Las Vegas, Miami, Chicago, Los Angeles, San Francisco, Atlanta, Denver, Phoenix, New Orleans, Milwaukee, and Dallas (Morales et al. 2013b), and even in more rural locations, such as Nebraska (Benjamin-Alvarado et al. 2009). Particularly visible were marches in Chicago and Los Angeles with 300,000 and 400,000 demonstrators, respectively. Although it is likely that local variations existed, both of these political demonstrations reflect the force of local immigrant movements to spearhead a national movement.

While immigrant mobilization has continued since 2006, the level declined after May 1 of that year, but escalated again with the introduction of proposition of SB 1070 in Arizona (see chapter 11). Signed in April 2010, Arizona SB 1070 (Sáenz et al. 2011), later amended as HB 2162, legalized the *intensified* surveillance of Latinos causing more criminal arrests and detentions of Latinos by state and local police (Heyman 2010). Critics of this law argued that it subjects Latinos to racial profiling, thus violating their civil rights (Golash-Boza 2012).

The reaction to this law created a wave of civil unrest (Harris et al. 2010) as hundreds of protesters from various backgrounds and states such as California, Colorado, and Texas marched to the state Capitol after the law was signed to join about 2,500 others in front of the state Capitol (Leavitt and Gonzalez 2010b). Religious leader Reverend Warren Stewart even thanked lawmakers at an interfaith civil rights event after the Capitol rally and claimed "You have awakened the 21st century civil-rights movement" (Leavitt and Gonzalez 2010b). The law even "provoked an international outcry" (González 2012, p. xi). Indeed, the Mexican government issued a formal statement saying it "laments that Arizona lawmakers and the executive branch didn't take into account immigrants' contributions – economically, socially and culturally" (Harris et al. 2010).

Civil unrest also surfaced in the form of economic boycotts of Arizona. Individual and corporate boycotting of Arizona goods, services, and tourism occurred throughout the nation and beyond (Harris et al. 2010; Leavitt and Gonzalez 2010a). Some noticeable examples of economic protests include the California truck drivers that agreed to stop moving loads into or out of Arizona, Mexico's travel alert to Arizona, cancellation of professional conventions (Yu 2010), San Francisco city attorney and Board of Supervisors proposition not to conduct any business with the state of Arizona (Archibold 2010), and a boycott against the Diamondbacks when they play in cities across the nation.

A separate, but related, on-going component of the immigrant movement are mobilizations for the legalization of youth that migrated as children, commonly referred to as The Dreamers. The name arose from proposed legislation referred to as The Dream Act. For years, mostly Latino youth and their supporters have mobilized colleges, universities, and entire communities across the nation around this issue. Given that The Dreamers are largely Americanized, educated, and had no choice to migrate because they were children when they were brought to this country, this is the component of immigration reform that has the most support. Yet, this policy has not been able to be passed because of attached requirements that supporters of the bill find problematic, such as required military service. On June 15, 2012 there was a triumph for The Dreamers when the White House passed the Deferred Action for Childhood Arrivals (DACA). DACA legalized and authorized individuals for employment for two years if they came to the US as children and met other requirements. According to the US Department of Homeland Security (2014), 521,815 people have been approved for DACA between 2012 and 2014, yet the number that qualify is significantly higher. Indeed, the US Census Bureau (2014) estimates that three out of five noncitizens under 35 have been in the US for at least five years or more and that most came before they were 18 years old. Furthermore, it remains to be seen what happens after the two-year expiration.

Summary

This chapter has provided an overview of the study and trends on Latino political power and historical and contemporary mobilizations for civil rights. We provided an overview of the theoretical frameworks on Latino group position or "linked fate" to determine whether Latinos are voting as a bloc according to what is best for their pan-ethnic group. Generally there is a "linked fate" phenomenon among Latinos, although it is not as strong as in the case of African Americans. Moreover, we highlighted Latino struggles for civil rights – e.g. the evolution of the Chicano Movement and struggles in bilingual and bicultural education that continue to date. In addition, data from the National Survey of Latinos (2011) showed certain commonalities as well as differences in political perceptions across Latino groups, which question whether the political power predicted by demographic patterns will prevail. We also raised two important issues affecting the political power of Latinos in the future – voting behavior and the immigrant movements. There is a disturbing pattern associated with low voter participation among Latinos, which is partly attributed to the exclusion of Latinos from voter mobilization campaigns of political parties. However, the significant demonstration activities surrounding struggles for immigrant rights across the country amply demonstrate that Latinos are *not* politically apathetic. As we saw in this chapter, politics and education have long been intimately linked. We now turn to an overview of educational matters concerning Latinos.

6 Education

It is widely acknowledged that whites surpass Latinos on educational achievement and attainment. This chapter will discuss various mechanisms that sustain the Latino–white gap in education. It is essential to place Latino educational disparities in the context of the unequal academic funding that shapes academic racial inequalities. Unequal funding across public schools creates a situation where middle-class children are mostly successfully educated but children living in poor neighborhoods, many of which are disproportionately Latino and African American, are underserved. The Latino–white educational gap, for instance, is in part attributed to Latinos' ethnic and economic segregation (Sharp and Iceland 2013) and the control of public education through local communities. Public schools in the US are funded through three sources – 9 percent federal, about 47 percent from the state (the level varies across states), and approximately 44 percent from property taxes (Eitzen et al. 2013). This means that neighborhoods occupied by low-income residents have lower property taxes, which translates to schools with limited resources.

Unequal funding of public schools negatively impacts the educational outcomes of Latino youth. In fact, as Jonathan Kozol (1991) observes, poor children are hurt by funding shortages in schools. Some of the issues faced by underfunded public schools include: limited access to technology (e.g., computers and other classroom materials); underpaid teachers; more teachers that did not major in the subject area; schools in need of repair, renovations, and modernization; and higher pupil-teacher ratios (Eitzen and Baca Zinn 2007). Furthermore, these disparities do not take into account the school fees that parents have to pay in many school districts which further marginalize poor Latino children. For instance, many school districts charge student fees for participation in music, athletics, drama, transportation, meals, and other costs (Eitzen and Baca Zinn 2007). This has ramifications for future generations given that children underserved by the educational system are more likely to become adults that are unable to provide for their families (Kozol 1991).

Segregation is also racialized so that at every education level, particularly K-12, students tend to attend schools with others who are similar in terms of race/ethnicity. Indeed, whites attend schools that are predominately white (Fry 2006; Lewis 2003), with some estimating that on average white students nationwide attend public schools that are 80 percent white (Eitzen and Baca Zinn 2007). Latino students are also more likely to enroll in schools with a large Latino student body (Fry 2006), high student-teacher ratios, and with high proportions of students who are dependent on financial aid (Fry 2006). These trends in racial segregation matter because economic resources are attached to white students. Thus, Ochoa (2004) found that schools located in working-class Latino neighborhoods had less advanced placement classes and minimal representation on the school boards in comparison to educational institutions located in the racially integrated middle-class neighborhoods. Yet, it is important to recognize that schools with advancement-placement and college-track courses tend to have minimal representation of Latino students (Ayala 2012; Noguera 1995).

Unfortunately the problems of educational access for Latino youth are not restricted to K-12 but higher education as well. Indeed, the majority of Latino students attend colleges and universities with a Latino concentration (Ayala 2012). Furthermore, Latino students are more likely to attend two-year as opposed to four-year institutions of higher education, which minimizes the odds of attaining a bachelor's degree (Ayala 2012).

While access to higher education is a concern for a significant portion of the Latino population, it is particularly a concern for undocumented immigrants. Despite the importance of attaining a college education for labor market integration, Latino undocumented students do not qualify for federal financial aid or in-state tuition (with the exception of 11 states) which blocks their access to higher education. The high out-of-state tuition in combination with the low economic standing of most Latinos means that undocumented Latinos struggle to pay for college more so than other students who are US citizens. To address this issue the Dream Act (Chapter 5), short for The Development Relief and Education for Alien Minors, proposal intended to provide legal residency to undocumented immigrants who are in good moral standing and who arrived in the US as minors, have lived in the US for a continuous period of time, graduated from a US high school, and are/were in the military or an institution of higher learning. Although the specifics of the Act have varied over the years, it has been debated on and off for a decade and has failed to be enacted. Recently, however, President Obama took initiative and introduced the Deferred Action for Childhood Arrivals (DACA) on June 15, 2012 giving "The Dreamers" and undocumented veterans an opportunity to apply for a deferred action that will allow them lawful presence in the US for two years. To qualify for DACA undocumented immigrants must have arrived in the US when they were under the age of 16, be currently in school or have graduated from high school or attained a GED or have been honorably discharged from the US armed forces, not be a risk to public safety or national security, and be under the age of 30. It is important to note that the future of DACA is unknown given that it did not have congressional support and thus was not enacted into law. More importantly, there is uncertainty concerning the status of DACA recipients after the provisional visa expires in two years.

In this chapter we will illustrate the educational disparities among Latinos in the US. We begin with a discussion of the cultural versus structural theoretical perspectives that have been used to explain the Latino–white gap in education. We then present data from the 2011 American Community Survey (ACS) Public-Use Microdata Sample to examine the educational outcomes of school dropouts, high school graduates, and college graduates among Latino subgroups and two comparative groups (whites and blacks). We then highlight issues in the political climate that can hamper academic success for Latinos in the future – corruption in educational institutions that are forcing Latino students out of the classrooms and policies aimed to erase Latino culture and language.

Theoretical Perspectives

Due to the functionalist perspective notion that we live in a meritocratic society in which everyone has an equal opportunity to succeed, individual and cultural factors are often considered the primary causes as to why Latinos lag academically behind whites. The following theoretical frameworks have been used to account for Latino educational attainment: (1) biological determinism, (2) cultural determinism, and (3) structural-environmental explanations (Murguia and Telles 1996; Valdes 1996). Biological determinism is currently the least common framework in academia used to examine the educational outcomes of Latinos. Yet, society at large still considers biological explanations for the educational disparities among Latinos with notions that they are "less intelligent," thus less capable of reaching the educational achievements of whites. Scholars, however, have largely abandoned biological conceptualizations of race for cultural and structural approaches. Below we discuss both of these perspectives.

Cultural Explanations of the Latino–White Gap in Education

Blaming the victim explanations of the Latino–white gap on education have shifted from biological to cultural perspectives. Cultural deficiency theories that attribute the educational gap between Latinos and whites to inadequacies in Latino culture are prevalent in educational institutions, academic research, and governmental policies. Proponents of this view assert that Latino culture is not conducive to educational success. When it comes to academic performance, for the most part research on Latino students falls under the cultural deficiency paradigm (Valdes 1996). For example, some theoretical perspectives claim that the social environment of disadvantaged children slows their intellectual growth (Hunt 1964). More specifically in the case of Latino students, English limitation continues to dominate the debate about why they lag behind whites academically (Valdes 1996). Such theoretical views fall under the umbrella of "blaming the victim" given that they focus on Latino culture, rather than structural conditions, as being responsible for educational disparities.

Yet, caution needs to be taken in adopting a cultural deprivation framework, given that it is sociologically incorrect to assert that any group can be deprived of culture given that it refers to a set of beliefs, values, customs, and ideas that characterize any human group (Hurn 1993). Consequently, attention has turned to frameworks rooted in the *culture of poverty* (Lewis 1966) (see chapter 8) and other similar theoretical perspectives based on assumptions of white middle-class superiority and the devaluation of other cultures. According to such views, the low educational outcomes of Latinos (and other groups of color) are attributed to the group's culture that lacks ambition as evident by their welfare dependency, low work ethic, and irresponsibility (Lewis 1959; Moynihan 1965). According to this framework, Latinos lag behind educationally because the low socioeconomic status of most of its members has constructed a culture where they are disillusioned with the mainstream culture and have developed beliefs and values that indicate that they have given up on succeeding in conventional ways.

Some contemporary theoretical perspectives have arguably built upon the culture of poverty framework to examine educational disparities. Ogbu (1991), for instance, coined the *oppositional culture* perspective that categorized groups into voluntary and involuntary minorities. Voluntary minorities are immigrant minorities who have entered the US more or less on a voluntary basis or who believe their mobility would result in upward mobility (Ogbu 1991). These immigrants usually initially experience difficulty adjusting to school, but with the passage of time these problems lessen and they experience greater educational success. Involuntary minorities, or caste-like minorities, are "people who did not initially choose to become members of the United States society" (Ogbu 1991, p. 437). Their US arrival is marked by negative conditions such as slavery, conquest, and/or colonization. According to Ogbu (1991), Mexican Americans represent involuntary minorities given that their incorporation in this country involved the conquest and annexation of Mexican territory. Although a significant portion of the Mexican-origin population consists of immigrants, Ogbu categorizes all Mexican-origin people as involuntary minorities given that they are usually defined and treated by mainstream society in terms of the status of the conquered group. In the educational realm, involuntary minorities are not matching their educational aspirations with their effort and their resistance toward school is dampening their achievement. We argue that this is a blaming-the-victim perspective, where Latino youth are blamed for their own education subordination.

More recently, Portes and Zhou (1993) developed the *segmented assimilation* perspective that has gained more notoriety. According to this view, second-generation youth follow one of three integration paths into the host society: (1) assimilation into the white middle class, (2) retention of the ethnic group norms, and (3) downward assimilation. The latter path is arguably reminiscent of the culture of poverty perspective where the group's upward mobility is blocked due to members embracing the cultural views of the underclass.

When the oppositional behavior of Latino students is placed into context, the antagonistic practices are rooted in alienation in the educational settings and from school administrators rather than downward assimilation (Morales 2008b; Valenzuela 1999). An example can be seen in the student walkouts that occurred in the spring of 2006. Latino students in Las Vegas walked out of schools not only in support of immigration reform but as a response to xenophobia, homophobia, nativism, classism, sexism, ageism, and racism (Morales 2008b; Revilla 2006). Indeed, the alienation that Latino students experienced in their schools became apparent when many faced suspension, were not given the opportunity to make up standardized tests and other exams, and with some teachers even purposely giving tests on the walkout days to penalize Latino students (Morales 2008b). Even when not displaying any antagonistic behavior, alienation in the classroom is also evident in Latino invisibility. Lewis (2003), for instance, claims that "Latinas expressed their alienation from school as silently as African American boys did loudly. In many ways their silence was just as potent and destructive as the negative attention that blacks got: these girls' needs still were not recognized or addressed" (p. 80).

Some scholars argue that Latino academic problems stem from a mismatch between the culture at home and that in the schools. Even though the involvement of Latino parents is important for their children's academic motivation (Ayala 2012; Plunkett and Bamaca-Gomez 2003; Valenzuela and Dornbusch 1994), their unfamiliarity with the educational system along with being non-native English speakers, having low levels of education, residing in unsafe neighborhoods, and being involved in secondary labor markets compromises their involvement in the schools (Ayala 2012; Plunkett and Bamaca-Gomez 2003; Toldson and Lemmons 2013). Schools need to engage parents from diverse cultural backgrounds, including non-English speakers, in order to communicate about both positive and negative student achievements (Toldson and Lemmons 2013).

Expanding on the cultural mismatch between Latino students and educational institutions, Angela Valenzuela's (1999) *Subtractive Schooling: US-Mexican Youth and the Politics of Caring* highlights how Latino youths' conceptualization of education is downplayed and assimilationists' policies and practices minimize Latino culture. As such, rather than embracing and enhancing the knowledge that Latino students embody, the educational system takes away their cultural gift and knowledge – thus subtracting rather than adding to their education. Moreover, there is evidence that Latino students value education and even have higher educational aspirations than whites (Goldsmith 2004), signaling that the educational system is not doing enough to develop such ambitions. Indeed, the few Latino students that persevere through the kindergarten-to-higher-education pipeline do so in part due to receiving valuable mentorship and capitalizing on funding opportunities from colleges and universities (Rodríguez et al. 2013).

This leads us back to Weber's philosophy on status groups and to the contemporary notion of "cultural capital" coined by Bourdieu (1974). Accordingly, educational systems operate to adapt to the attitudes and aptitudes belonging to the dominant group. By valuing the cultural capital of children from middle- and upper-class families, inequality is reinforced for working-class and poor children in the school system. This in turn hampers the educational attainment of Latino students most of whom are working class.

Structural Explanations of the Latino–White Gap in Education

In addition to the importance of examining the role of educational institutions in the Latino–white educational gap, another nuanced approach entails an analysis of societal structures that hamper Latino educational outcomes. This approach considers not the individual but rather the marginalization of Latinos in society. One of the most important structural factors affecting educational outcomes is socioeconomic status (SES) (Bourdieu 1977; Morales and Sáenz 2007). In the US, social class has a powerful influence on the odds of attaining additional grade levels (Bidwell and Friedkin 1988). Thus, educational attainment is lower for those at the bottom of the socioeconomic hierarchy than for those at the top. This is a concern given that Latinos are disproportionately represented among the working class (see chapter 7).

Although the effects of SES on academic success are widely acknowledged (Hauser et al. 2000; Morales and Sáenz 2007; Vélez 2008), researchers disagree on the magnitude of this association. This is largely due to race, which also positions people in the stratification system, shaping the type and amount of resources that people have access to (Bonilla-Silva 2013; Feagin 2010; Omi and Winant 1994). As such, the benefits of SES on academic achievement may be reduced in the case of Latinos (and other groups of color). For example, Latinos with higher SES may retain their cultural heritage and still face discrimination from the larger society, dampening the positive effects of social class. Thus, not only is class structurally situated in society but so is race/ethnicity. Illustrating this idea is Bonilla-Silva's (1997) concept of *racialized racial systems* which refers to "societies in which economic, political, social, and ideological levels are partially structured by the placement of actors in racial categories or races" (p. 469). This structural racialization is applicable to Latino educational outcomes because it is crucial to keep in mind the position of Latinos in the US racial hierarchy when examining their academic standing.

In order to fully analyze the effects of structural racism on education, it is necessary to consider the extent to which race itself impacts other elements, such as institutional factors and the racial hierarchy, that maintain Latinos in a substandard position in the education system. Indeed, in a review of the literature on Latino educational attainment, Ayala (2012) argues that it is evident that the position of Latinos in the racial hierarchy plays a significant role in their low educational achievement.

Some structural-conflict perspectives accentuate that the educational system serves as a social reproduction mechanism that replicates existing social hierarchies (Sáenz et al. 2007a). Accordingly, society, including the educational institutions, mirrors the social hierarchies where Latino students inherit the socioeconomic status of their family. Due to institutional barriers and lack of socioeconomic resources, Latino parents, especially immigrants, have not had the tradition of scholarship and schooling in the US (Bean and Tienda 1988). This pattern, in turn, becomes problematic when considering the strong relationship between the education of parents, an indicator of SES, and that of their children. Latino students most likely to graduate from high school are those whose parents are more educated or earn higher income (Romo and Falbo 1996). Similarly, some conflict perspectives reveal a hidden curriculum where schools teach students to follow orders, be quiet, and to please people with authority regardless of the situation (Eitzen and Baca Zinn 2007). This type of instruction is more commonly applied to poor children, including Latino students, where they are taught to interact with large bureaucratic institutions and to downplay their leadership (Sjoberg et al. 1966). Therefore, the educational system is prepping Latino students to be a part of the working class rather than for professional positions.

Educational Trends among Latinos

Data from the 2011 American Community Survey (ACS) Public-Use Microdata Sample are used to examine the educational outcomes of Latino groups and two comparative groups (whites and blacks) along three dimensions: dropouts, high school graduates, and college graduates. This analysis – carried out on the basis of national origin, place of birth, and sex – allows us to determine how the various Latino groups are doing along various educational outcomes.

"Pushed-Out" of High School

One of the more pressing issues that points to how the educational system is failing Latinos relates to the high levels of high school dropouts. Table 6.1 presents the percentages of Latinos between the ages of 16 and 24 who did not have a high school diploma and who were not currently enrolled in school – a proxy for being a high school dropout – in 2011. Overall, Latinos have the highest dropout rates (males,

Table 6.1 *Percentage of Persons 16 to 24 Years of Age who are Dropouts by Race/Ethnic Group, Sex, and Place of Birth, 2011*

Race/Ethnic Group	Male			Female		
	Total	Native-Born	Foreign-Born	Total	Native-Born	Foreign-Born
Mexican	18.2	11.4	36.7	12.9	8.7	27.0
Puerto Rican	13.2	13.3	9.0	10.6	10.6	20.9
Cuban	6.8	5.0	10.9	4.5	2.7	8.9
Salvadoran	18.2	6.4	34.6	15.3	7.6	29.8
Dominican	12.7	9.8	18.5	9.0	7.2	11.8
Guatemalan	37.3	11.1	53.7	25.6	9.4	45.0
Colombian	5.8	5.3	6.5	1.4	1.2	1.6
Other Central American	21.3	8.4	37.9	12.5	5.4	23.5
Other South American	6.3	2.7	9.8	3.9	3.9	3.9
Other Latino	10.5	9.4	19.9	5.3	4.7	11.5
Latino	17.0			11.7		
White	5.8			4.3		
Black	11.8			7.3		

Source: 2011 American Community Survey Public-Use File (Ruggles et al. 2010).

17.0%; females, 11.7%) and whites (males, 5.8%; females, 4.3%) have the lowest dropout rates (table 6.1). In fact, Latinos are nearly three times more likely to be dropouts compared to whites.

Some general patterns arise when we examine the prevalence of dropouts across Latino subgroups. First, males are more likely than females to be dropouts. Second, foreign-born Latinos have higher dropout rates compared to their native-born counterparts. Third, the most elevated dropout rates occur among foreign-born Central Americans and Mexicans. In particular, Guatemalan immigrants are the most likely to be dropouts with 54 percent of males and 45 percent of females being dropouts. More than one-third of foreign-born Mexican, Salvadoran, and Other Central American males are dropouts; close to three-tenths of foreign-born Salvadoran and Mexican females are in the same situation. Fourth, Cubans, Colombians, and Other South Americans have very low dropout rates, with native-born persons from these groups having even lower dropout rates than whites; even Cuban, Colombian, and Other South American foreign-born persons have fairly low dropout rates. Fifth, among native-born Latinos, the highest prevalence of not completing high school occurs among Mexicans, Puerto Ricans, and Guatemalans – in fact, native-born members of these groups have higher dropout rates compared to foreign-born Cubans, Colombians, and Other South Americans. It is clear, then, that there is a significant amount of variation in the prevalence of dropping out across the diverse Latino groups.

Table 6.2 *Percentage of Persons 25 Years of Age and Older who are High School Graduates by Race/Ethnic Group, Sex, and Place of Birth, 2011*

Race/Ethnic Group	Male			Female		
	Total	Native-Born	Foreign-Born	Total	Native-Born	Foreign-Born
Mexican	56.5	78.3	40.6	59.0	80.0	41.3
Puerto Rican	74.8	74.9	68.2	75.3	75.6	59.1
Cuban	77.3	91.2	72.5	76.8	93.2	71.3
Salvadoran	48.0	82.6	43.9	47.8	80.5	44.4
Dominican	66.6	83.1	62.4	65.2	85.7	61.0
Guatemalan	42.4	80.3	38.8	47.1	82.5	43.2
Colombian	86.6	91.1	85.7	84.1	93.9	82.6
Other Central American	62.9	86.5	58.3	70.9	93.4	66.6
Other South American	83.7	95.0	81.6	85.1	93.1	83.7
Other Latino	80.2	83.5	67.9	80.5	83.0	72.2
Latino	61.8			64.5		
White	90.6			91.6		
Black	81.3			83.8		

Source: 2011 American Community Survey Public-Use File (Ruggles et al. 2010).

One caveat that we need to point out, however, is that the dropout measure that we use here is not completely applicable to foreign-born individuals. Given that the measure is based on persons 16 to 24 years of age, it is likely that a certain proportion of immigrants came to the US at these ages and never attended school in this country – i.e., they did not "drop in" to US schools (Sáenz and Siordia 2012). As such, the dropout rates for the foreign-born need to be considered with some caution.

High School and College Graduation

We next examine variations across groups regarding high school and college completion. Table 6.2 provides the percentages of persons 25 years and older who are high school graduates broken down by sex and place of birth. Again, Latinos have the lowest rates of high school completion with only 61.8 percent of males and 64.5 percent of females holding a high school diploma and whites have the highest prevalence of high school graduation (males, 90.6%; females, 91.6%).

As observed earlier with the dropout rate, there are some commonalities when we consider all subgroups of Latinos. First, females overall are more likely than males to have a high school diploma, although there are some exceptions. Second, native-born Latinos are more likely than their foreign-born peers to be high school graduates. Third, less than half of foreign-born Mexicans, Salvadorans, and Guatemalans possess a high school diploma, with foreign-born Guatemalan men (38.8%) having the lowest level of high school graduation. Fourth, native-born Cubans, Colombians, and Other South Americans surpass whites with respect to high school graduation rates

Table 6.3 *Percentage of Persons 25 Years of Age and Older who are College Graduates by Race/Ethnic Group, Sex, and Place of Birth, 2011*

Race/Ethnic Group	Male			Female		
	Total	Native-Born	Foreign-Born	Total	Native-Born	Foreign-Born
Mexican	8.7	13.6	5.1	10.7	16.2	6.0
Puerto Rican	14.7	14.8	13.8	17.8	17.9	11.1
Cuban	24.8	36.1	20.9	24.6	37.3	20.3
Salvadoran	7.0	17.0	5.8	7.3	20.7	5.9
Dominican	14.7	17.3	14.1	16.5	28.4	14.0
Guatemalan	6.5	19.0	5.3	7.9	25.0	6.0
Colombian	31.5	37.4	30.3	30.4	46.0	28.0
Other Central American	14.1	26.8	11.6	18.9	38.6	15.1
Other South American	31.2	45.0	28.8	31.8	44.4	29.6
Other Latino	22.1	20.8	27.1	21.6	20.1	26.5
Latino	12.3			14.5		
White	32.7			31.1		
Black	16.5			20.5		

Source: 2011 American Community Survey Public-Use File (Ruggles et al. 2010).

with native-born Other Central American women achieving this feat as well. Fifth, among the foreign-born, Colombians, Other South Americans, and Cubans are the most likely to be high school graduates; among the native-born, Mexicans and Puerto Ricans have the lowest high school completion rates, with these individuals being less likely to have a high school diploma compared to foreign-born Colombians and South Americans.

Table 6.3 shows the percentages of persons 25 years and older who are college graduates. Overall, again, Latinos have the lowest percentages of persons with a college diploma (males, 12.3%; females, 14.5%), with whites (males, 32.7%; females, 31.1%) being the most likely to be college graduates. In fact, white males are nearly three times more likely than Latino men to be college graduates and white women are twice as likely as Latina women to have a college diploma. In contrast to whites, women are more likely than men to be college graduates among Latinos and blacks.

Similar patterns are revealed when we examine the prevalence of college graduates among Latino subgroups. For the most part, the patterns found earlier exist here as well. As such, we will only highlight a few patterns of particular interest. Latina women are more likely to be college graduates compared to Latino men, especially among the native-born. Indeed, the vanishing representation of Latino males from higher education has been a growing concern (Rodríguez et al. 2013) and has been attributed to culture, peers and labor market demands (Sáenz and Ponjuan 2008). Again, native-born Cubans, Colombians, Other South Americans, as well as native-born Other Central American women are more likely to be college graduates than whites. Close to half of native-born Colombian women (46.0%) have a college diploma. On the other hand, among the native-born, Mexicans (male, 13.6%; female,

16.2%) and Puerto Ricans (male, 14.8%; female, 17.9%) are the least likely to be college graduates with their levels being much lower than those of foreign-born Cubans, Colombians, Other South Americans, as well as Other Latinos.

In sum, while Latinos as a group lag behind whites and blacks in educational attainment, this is not true across the board. Instead, Cubans, Colombians, and Other South Americans stand out with the highest educational attainment levels, with native-born members of these groups surpassing the educational standing of whites. On the other hand, native-born Mexicans and Puerto Ricans, groups that have been in the US the longest, lag behind other native-born Latino groups as well as foreign-born Cubans, Colombians, and Other South Americans on educational attainment.

Questions Related to the Future of Latino Education

The educational disparities among Latinos outlined above not only have implications for the Latino community, but for the nation considering the growing presence of this group. Indeed, Latino students represent the majority of the student body in many schools in the country – in the Southwest and beyond. The National Commission on Secondary Schooling argues that the large Latino population is headed towards economic problems if its youth continue along this path of low academic performance (Valverde 1987). This should be a major concern for the nation given that Latinos will represent an increasing share of the nation's labor force in the coming decades (see chapter 7). Therefore, the continual lag in academic achievement among Latinos undoubtedly could dampen their political, social, and economic success, as well as that of the country as a whole. Below we discuss some examples of the racialization in educational politics that impede Latino educational attainment.

A Case of Institutional Corruption and Latino Students

A telling case about how Latinos are marginalized in public schools and its association with ethnic and economic segregation is that of Bowie High School in El Paso, Texas, located right up against the border fence that separates the US and Mexico. Not only is Bowie High School 99 percent Latino, but almost the entire student body is economically disadvantaged (95%). Moreover, compared to the entire state of Texas, Bowie High School has about 27 percent more at-risk students and over twice the percentage of students that are limited English proficient (see figure 6.1).

Understanding the strong association between standardized test scores in reading, writing, and mathematics and poverty and ethnicity (see Morales and Sáenz 2007), the superintendent of the El Paso Independent School District (EPISD) unlawfully removed the Latino limited English proficient students from the classrooms in Bowie High School in order to increase the school's standardized test scores. Indeed, these students were encouraged to drop out of school by administrators or were removed from the classrooms on testing days. Other students, mostly all Spanish speakers, had credits removed from the academic transcripts so that their low test scores would not affect the school's federal funding (Michels 2012). The scheme worked as the school's test scores improved dramatically. Similar manipulations had also been implemented in other schools in the school district (Michels 2012). Adding fraud to this injustice, the former superintendent pleaded guilty to paying himself and others

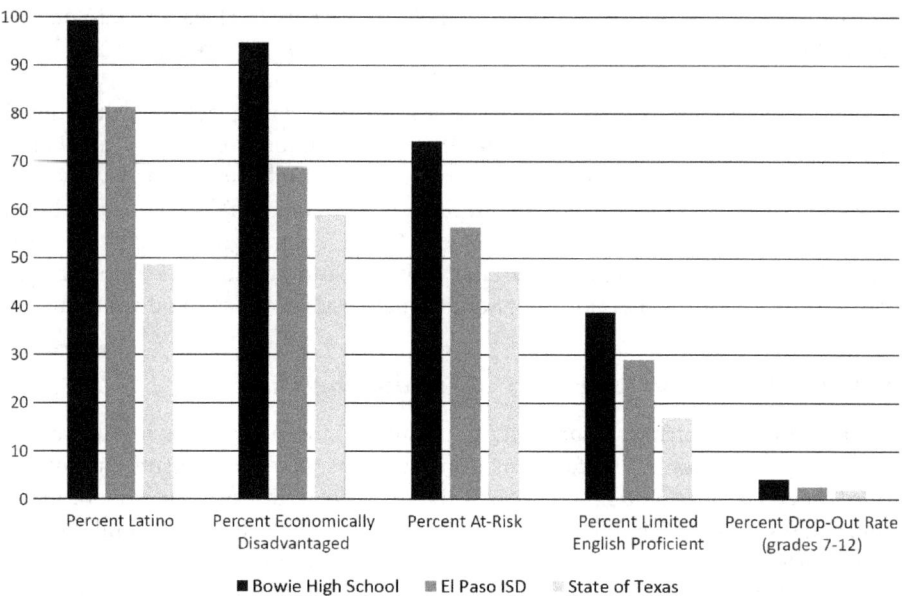

Figure 6.1 Academic and Socioeconomic Profile of Bowie High School in Comparison to the El Paso Independent School District and the State of Texas, 2010

Source: Compiled with data from Public Schools Explorer (The Texas Tribune 2010).

bonuses with federal "No Child Left Behind" funds, procuring $460,000 intended to educate at-risk students. The superintendent is now serving three and a half years in federal prison (Michels 2012).

While this illegal scheme did improve Bowie's test scores, its dropout rate is actually twice as high as that of the state of Texas. The case of Bowie High School illustrates how educational policies aimed to address the low educational achievement of Latino students are blaming individual Latino students rather than examining socio-environmental issues (i.e., low SES) and institutional policies. In the case of Bowie High School, administrative "remedies" encouraged pushing poor Latino youth out of the classroom rather than educating them. This situation, along with the manipulation of federal funds for at-risk youth, called for a civil rights investigation.

Erasure of Latino History and Culture in the Academic Curriculum

Some school districts and governments across the US have been on a mission to erase Latino history and culture from the educational curriculum (Garcia 2001; Leyva 2002). Thus, the educational experiences of Latinos in the US entails struggles to preserve their cultural roots against the endeavors of educational institutions to "Americanize" Latino students by erasing the Spanish language and historical connections to Latin America (Garcia 2001). This leads Vélez (2008) to argue that the historical context of Latino educational experiences in the US "can be summarized under relations of subjugation, colonization, and the specific institutional mechanisms used in different locations to segregate and track Latino students" (p. 129).

An example of state-level initiatives rooted in the viewing of the Latino culture from the deficit model is seen in the case of Arizona's SB 2211. In 2006 the famous Chicana activist Dolores Huerta told an assembly of Tucson High School students that "Republicans hate Latinos" (Lundholm 2011). As a response, the state's superintendent of public instruction began a mission to eliminate K-12 ethnic studies in Arizona on the grounds that it promoted racism, hatred, and politically charged teaching (Lundholm 2011; Rodriguez 2012). In the spring of 2010 the Arizona legislature enacted SB 2211 and Governor Jan Brewer signed it into law in 2011 despite fierce protests (Lacey 2011). SB 2211 did more than discard Mexican American and Chicana/o Studies programs – it also removed curriculum decisions from local school boards (Lundholm 2011) and reduced funding from school districts which fail to comply with the law (Lacey 2011). Educational curricula that promote the overthrow of the US government are explicitly banned which brings into question how US history is going to be taught (Lacey 2011). Such ban erases the struggles and contributions that Latinos and other racial and ethnic groups have made to the US. This is an example of what historian Yolanda Leyva (2002) refers to as an *erasure of memory* that deletes the cultural history of Latinos from US history. Moreover, how can one understand US history without the acknowledgment of subjugation of minority groups and the 200-year-long struggles to overcome injustices (Rodriguez 2012)? Is the curriculum based only on the white majority perspective a form of ethnic studies? Such policy not only robs Latino students of their cultural gift but fails to educate all students about the struggles and accomplishments of all people of color in the US. This has led some to claim that "Arizona banned ethnic studies to protect the reputation of the white majority" (Rodriguez 2012).

The rationale for the enactment of SB 2211 as ethnic studies creating racial hatred should not be a surprise given that this same legislature introduced SB 1070 which legalized the racial profiling of Latinos (see chapter 11). Aligned with SB 1070, the ban, while promoted as targeting all ethnic studies, in practice mostly targeted Latinos and Latino ethnic studies. Indeed, the "Tucson Unified School District's Mexican American program have been declared illegal by the State of Arizona – even while similar programs for black, Asian and American Indian students have been left untouched" (Lacey 2011). The superintendent who pushed the law publicly scrutinized Chicana/o classics such as *The Pedagogy of the Oppressed* and *Occupied America* on the claim that they "inappropriately teach Latino youths that they are being mistreated" and that ethnic study instructors were sometimes unconventional by sprinkling their lessons with Spanish words (Lacey 2011).

Aligned with the issue above are the struggles for bilingual and dual-language education. Similar to the implementation of Arizona's SB 2211 are efforts across the nation to erase the Spanish language. Spanish is often regarded as "the language of foreign immigrants, often undocumented, and blamed for poverty and low level education of US Latinos, Spanish is held in contempt in political and educational circles" (García 2009, p. 109). As a testament to the status of the Spanish language, there is evidence that whites' opposition to bilingual education is rooted in "racial threat" given that opposition is strongest in areas of substantial growth in already sizable Latino populations (Hempel et al. 2013). In chapter 5, we highlighted some of the struggles in Latino civil rights in bilingual and bicultural education – here we only discuss some of the implications of the English-only movement in school districts across the nation.

While the value of learning English is recognized, what is scrutinized is the degree that such endeavors focus on acculturation into white middle-class norms and the erasure of the Latino students' culture. The focus on educational curricula promoting students being monolingual English speakers, writers, and readers is ironic given that globalization rewards people of all races/ethnicities for being multilinguals. Spanish is a global language that is a valuable economic commodity in the US (García 2009). Indeed, Spanish-English bilingual speakers are an asset in the labor market given they perform work duties that matter to the public good (i.e., being multilingual) (Alarcón et al. 2014a), although Spanish bilinguals who speak English very well receive lower average wages than monolingual English speakers (Alarcón et al. 2014b), suggesting a cost associated with Latinos not being fully acculturated. Furthermore, there is a double standard at play in taking Spanish-language classes. Accordingly, white students are often lauded for taking such courses while Latinos are discouraged or ridiculed for enrolling in Spanish-language courses.

Rather than policies aimed at criticizing Latino family values and language, we are in accordance with Valdes (1996) who argues that programs designed to remedy Latino educational disparities should be based on an understanding, appreciation, and respect for Latino students and their families. Administrators need to consider that disrupting the existing Latino culture will have profound costs not only to the culture itself but also to students' educational advancement (see Morales and Sáenz 2007). In sum, educational policies designed to improve the academic outcomes of Latino students need to work in congruence with the Latino family and cultural practices.

Summary

In this chapter we provided an overview of the study and trends on Latino education attainment. We illustrated the culture versus structural theoretical debates in studies of Latino academic outcomes given that explanations of the Latino-white education gap commonly originate from cultural deficit frameworks. Although we believe that culture does play a role, we argue that in addressing the Latino-white education gap, it is important to address the racialized policies and practices that widen the gap and are rooted in "blaming-the-victim" solutions.

We also used data from the 2011 American Community Survey (ACS) to examine variations in educational outcomes across Latino groups and two comparison groups (whites and blacks). The results show that Cubans, Colombians, and Other South Americans have high rates of educational attainment, with native-born persons from these groups surpassing whites on educational attainment levels. In contrast, foreign-born Mexicans and Central Americans have the lowest levels of education. Furthermore, among native-born Latinos, Mexicans and Puerto Ricans lag significantly behind other groups and have lower educational attainment levels than do foreign-born Cubans, Colombians, and Other South Americans.

Lastly, we raised some important issues that are currently affecting the quality of education for Latinos that need to be addressed in order to narrow the Latino-white educational gaps. We highlighted two concerns: (1) institutional corruption and alienation of Latino students in the classroom, and (2) cultural deficiency paradigms that challenge bilingual education and spearhead *erasure of memory* campaigns to eliminate ethnic studies.

We now turn to an overview of the work and economic life of Latinos, patterns that are strongly linked to one's educational attainment.

7 Work and Economic Life

The low educational standing of Latinos is associated with the relatively low economic standing of the Latino population. Yet, historically, certain groups, including segments of the Latino population, have been positioned toward the lower rungs of the economic ladder. In particular, groups that were initially incorporated into the US as colonized or conquered groups – African Americans, Mexican Americans, Native Americans, and Puerto Ricans – continue to have low levels of employment standing, income, alongside high rates of impoverishment.

Geographically, longstanding pockets of poverty have persisted along the US–Mexico border since the federal government began calculating poverty rates (Esparza and Donelson 2008; Sáenz 1997). Moreover, recent evidence has reconfirmed the importance of geographic location on the likelihood of children born in the bottom quintile income category ascending to the top quintile income category (Chetty et al. 2013). For example, children in Memphis (2.6%) and Atlanta (4.0%), regardless of race or ethnicity, have low levels of probability of making this income ascent while those in Bakersfield, California (12.4%), Santa Barbara, California (11.8%), and Salt Lake City (11.5%) are approximately three times as likely to climb to the top one-fifth of income earners.

Historically, Latinos have lagged significantly behind whites on a wide variety of economic measures associated with employment and earnings. The recent economic recession that began in 2007 has impacted Latinos particularly heavily. Indeed, Latinos have experienced a significant drop in household wealth alongside increases in unemployment and poverty since the economic recession started (Taylor et al. 2012c). Nonetheless, recent data point to a turnaround from employment loss to employment gain among Latinos and Asians, a growth not experienced by whites and blacks. For instance, the job growth between 2009 and 2011 among Latinos (6.5%) and Asians (6.8%) was substantially greater than that of whites (1.1%) and blacks (2.2%) (Kochhar 2012a). Moreover, Latinos are projected to account for three quarters of the labor force growth in the US between 2010 and 2020 (Kochhar 2012b). The disproportionate growth of Latinos among the nation's labor force reflects the youthful age structure of Latinos (compared to an aging white population), the relatively high presence of immigrants (who have high rates of labor force participation), and overall high rates of labor force participation (Kochhar 2012b).

This chapter provides an overview of the economic standing of the Latino population. In particular, the chapter begins with a discussion of the various theoretical perspectives that have been put forth to understand the labor market and economic position of people. In addition, the chapter examines the labor market and economic characteristics of selected groups that comprise the Latino population and compares them to whites and blacks. As will become evident, there is a significant amount of variation in the labor market and economic position of Latino subgroups with certain groups faring relatively well while others are not as fortunate. The chapter concludes with a discussion of major trends in the work and economic conditions of Latinos and policies and programs that are needed to improve the overall socioeconomic standing of Latinos.

Theoretical Perspectives

Theoretical perspectives have been developed to understand how individual and structural factors impact the labor market outcomes of individuals. In particular, we can think of labor market outcomes associated with three stages: securing employment, type of job, and reward for work. For the most part, individual and structural factors are related in similar fashion to the three stages of labor market outcomes.

Individual Perspectives

The most basic perspectives developed to understand labor market outcomes are situated at the individual or personal level. As such, individual attributes, such as educational attainment, work experience, English language proficiency, cognitive skills, and soft skills, are seen as factors that contribute to success in the labor market. The human capital perspective is the primary theory that has been used to explain variations in labor market outcomes. Gary Becker (1975), Nobel laureate in economics, developed the human capital theory. The perspective argues that individuals invest in education, skills, and work experience to reap benefits in the labor market. Thus, for example, people pay tuition and related costs in the attainment of a college diploma or a postgraduate degree which assists them in finding more favorable employment as well as greater monetary rewards in the labor market. Similarly, individuals seek out internship and apprenticeship opportunities to enhance their marketability on the job market. Much research has shown a strong positive association between levels of human capital attributes, such as educational attainment, and favorable labor market outcomes including occupational prestige and wage and salary earnings.

Similarly, other personal characteristics are related to labor market outcomes. For example, work experience is generally associated with high wages and salaries. Thus, an extra year of experience is typically related to a bump in the pay of workers. However, as employers have tried to cut labor costs, especially during the latest economic crisis, older workers have had a difficult time finding employment after being laid off. Moreover, given that approximately two-fifths of Latinos are foreign-born, English fluency is another factor that is important in obtaining a job as well as in labor market earnings. Persons who are fluent in English are more competitive in the attainment of jobs that require English language communication with co-workers, clients, or customers. Research has also shown that employers pay a premium for workers who are fluent in English (Hamilton et al. 2008; Mora and Davila 2006a, 2006b; Shin and Alba 2009).

In addition, researchers have increasingly turned their attention to the role that cognitive skills play in labor market outcomes, especially with respect to earnings. Research has demonstrated that people with higher cognitive skills attain higher earnings than those with more limited cognitive skills. Finally, employers often identify "soft skills" as attributes that they look for in employees. Soft skills, according to Moss and Tilly (1996) refer to "skills, abilities, and traits that pertain to personality, attitude, and behavior rather than formal or technical knowledge" (p. 253). These are personal attributes that translate to how well potential workers approximate the mainstream population, i.e., white middle-class standards. Yet, the preference for soft skills extends to jobs where few whites are found. For example, employers seeking to fill positions in low-wage jobs voice a strong preference for Latino immigrant workers over African American workers. They reason that Latinos are hard-working individuals with a strong work ethic. Of course, what is left unsaid is that because many Latino immigrants are undocumented, they tend not to complain about the low wages that they receive and the treacherous work environments that they toil under. As Zamudio and Lichter (2008) observe, employers in the hotel industry in Los Angeles use terms such as "attitude," "motivation," and "work ethic" as code words for "tractability." As such, employers are drawn to the vulnerable status of Latino immigrants, which tends to keep them from complaining against low wages and difficult work conditions.

Individual-level perspectives place the focus directly on workers to understand their labor market outcomes. Thus, if a worker has difficulty finding employment, obtains a job that is not very prestigious, and obtains low wages for the work that he/she does, it is due to their personal characteristics, such as their level of education, work experience, cognitive skills, and soft skills. If they desire more favorable outcomes in the job market, individuals need to invest in attaining higher levels of education and related factors in order to reap more favorable labor market outcomes.

Social Relationships

The influence of factors affecting people's labor market outcomes stem beyond one's own personal attributes. One line of research focuses on the social ties and social networks that people have to others from whom they can draw valuable information and insights to gain entry into particular jobs (McDonald et al. 2009). Due to the limited human capital resources of many Latinos, especially immigrants, such social connections are important in obtaining information regarding the availability of jobs as well as in securing sponsorship from someone who can vouch for job applicants (Pfeffer and Parra 2009). We have seen earlier in the discussion of migration theories the significance of social networks in facilitating the immigration journey as well as in adjusting to life in the areas of destination. Hence, Latinos who are well connected to social networks are likely to be in a better position to obtain employment as well as to receive more favorable earnings compared to their counterparts who lack such social connections (Pfeffer and Parra 2009).

Despite the value of social networks in labor markets, we need to pay attention to the particular forms of social networks. Indeed, one of the earliest observations on the value of such ties is the classic work of Granovetter (1973) highlighting the strength of weak ties. Intuitively, we would think that individuals benefit most favorably from their strong ties and connections to people who are close to them and with whom they maintain regular interactions. However, given the principle of propinquity, we tend to be relatively similar to persons with whom we share strong ties along the lines of socioeconomic status, race and ethnicity, and so forth. As such, we are likely to hold similar information that can help us navigate entry into jobs as those people who are close to us and with whom we come into contact most frequently. In contrast, people with whom we have weak ties are more different than us along a variety of dimensions including socioeconomic status, residence, and race and ethnicity. Hence, people who are a friend of a friend, with whom we are not close, and with whom we do not interact with regularly, are likely to be different from us, interact in social settings that are different than the social circles we run in, and, as such, have information that is distinct from that which we possess. Information drawn from more varied sources are particularly valuable to people.

Structural Factors

The value of human capital characteristics and social networks in influencing labor market outcomes is pretty intuitive. However, we need to recognize that it is important to take into account the context in which such characteristics are employed in the labor market. For example, the value of a high school diploma is likely to vary significantly across different demographic, industrial, geographical, and political settings. In the 1960s and 1970s, when manufacturing was a staple of the US economy, workers with a high school diploma had high levels of employment and wage earnings in certain industries, such as the automobile industry. However, as the US shifted increasingly toward a service and technological industrial base, the economic situation worsened dramatically for workers with low levels of education.

The work of Peter Blau (1977) serves as a base for introducing structural influences to gain a fuller understanding of labor markets as well as intergroup relations. While Blau's macrosociological perspective has found a significant amount of support in the study of intermarriage (Blau et al. 1982), sociologists have used the theory to understand labor market outcomes including the influence that structural factors have on earnings and English fluency among immigrants (Hwang and Xi 2008; Hwang et al. 2010; Xi et al. 2010).

Group size, for instance, is a primary structural factor that has a major influence on the experiences of racial and ethnic groups in the labor market. Hubert Blalock (1967) is one of the earliest sociologists to observe the relationship between the size of a given minority group, such as African Americans, and their socioeconomic standing. Minority groups that are larger in a given area represent a threat to the existing power structure dominated by whites. As such, whites put in place practices and policies that make it difficult for minority group members to ascend the socioeconomic ladder. There is a significant amount of research that has demonstrated that Latinos tend to fare worse socioeconomically when they live in areas with a larger presence of Latinos. For example, Sáenz (1997) has shown that Chicanos (persons of Mexican origin) had higher poverty rates in places where Chicanos comprised a larger share of the overall population than in areas where they made up a smaller proportion of the population.

There are other structural characteristics that influence the labor market outcomes of minority groups. For example, residential segregation – the extent to which members of a given minority group live apart from whites – is an important factor in structuring the lives of Latinos and other minority group members. Massey and Denton (1993), in their influential book titled *American Apartheid: Segregation and the Making of the Underclass,* show the historical processes that have created high levels of residential separation between whites and blacks in many US cities. One of the important consequences of this geographic arrangement is that blacks are isolated from the opportunity structure. Thus, in the case of Latinos, people who are clustered in neighborhoods where the great majority of people are Latinos tend to have limited access to high quality schools, health care, parks, museums, libraries, and other facilities that many people in better off areas take for granted. Latinos who live in such areas also lack access to good jobs (Joassart-Marcelli 2009).

Over the last five decades, whites are increasingly found in suburban areas with Latinos and African Americans clustered in metropolitan centers. This racial living arrangement has created a spatial mismatch in jobs (Dickerson vonLockette and Johnson 2010; Massey and Denton 1993; Wilson 1987). This mismatch involves an imbalance in the location of jobs (in suburban areas) and job seekers (in metropolitan centers). This mismatch becomes even more acute when public transportation routes are not available to get people from the central cities to suburban areas, a situation that is fairly common as residents of suburban areas have tended to oppose measures to easily connect them to metropolitan centers for fear of attracting poor and minority populations. In their study of the nation's 95 largest cities, Dickerson vonLockette and Johnson (2010) found that between 1980 and 2000 Latinos tended to fare the worst in employment in cities where they were the most segregated from whites. These researchers also observed that Latinos experienced worsening employment conditions in cities where Latinos were becoming increasingly segregated.

Moreover, yet another structural attribute that is influential in labor market outcomes is the industrial diversity of a given area. Communities that have a diverse set of industrial pursuits offer their residents a wide variety of job opportunities and are better able to sustain the vicissitudes of the economy in which certain industries are affected disproportionately at a given period. In contrast, places with a narrow set of industrial options are more vulnerable to economic shifts. Immigrants and minority-group members with limited human capital resources are often routed into racial/ethnic or immigrant occupational niches where they are disproportionately located in the labor market (Douglas and Sáenz 2008; Liu 2011, 2013; Morales 2008a). Douglas and Sáenz (2008) identify 25 Mexican occupations comprising immigrant sex-specific occupational niches using 2000 census data. These occupations include job classification as agriculture laborers; meat, poultry, and seafood processing; construction; waiters/waitresses; cooks; maids and housekeeping cleaners; and janitors and building cleaners (Douglas and Sáenz 2008). Slightly more than half of Mexican immigrants worked in the 25 occupations comprising the Mexican immigrant occupational niches. Ethnic and immigrant niche jobs tend to offer workers low wages (Liu 2011, 2013) and Central American and Mexican co-ethnic jobsites are generally forms of segregated employment with limited protection from discrimination (Morales 2009).

Labor Market Patterns of Latino Groups

Data from the 2011 American Community Survey (ACS) Public-Use Microdata Sample are used to examine the labor market outcomes of Latino groups and two comparative groups (whites and blacks) along three dimensions: job attainment, job quality, and economic rewards. The results will allow us to determine how well the various Latino groups have fared in the different stages of the labor market. Because labor market outcomes vary by age, the analysis is carried out for only the "experienced labor force," that is persons 25 to 64 years of age who have the most stable labor market experiences. The analysis is also broken down by sex and for the Latino groups, place of birth. Note that among Puerto Ricans, those born on the island and mainland are part of the native-born population while those born in a different country make up the foreign-born portion of this group.

Job Attainment

We begin our analysis with the first phase of labor market outcomes – simply whether people have a job. Overall, as a whole, Latinos tend to have relatively high levels of employment with approximately 91 percent of males and 89 percent of females holding a job (table 7.1). In comparison, whites have slightly higher levels of employment while blacks have significantly lower levels of work. Nonetheless, there is a noticeable amount of variation in employment across Latino groups as well as on the basis of place of birth and gender. For example, among Latino males, foreign-born individuals are generally more likely to be working compared to native-born persons, whereas among females the opposite is the case, that is, native-born Latinas tend to be more likely to have a job than foreign-born women. High rates of employment are posted by five groups of foreign-born men (Other South American, 93.1%; Puerto Rican, 92.7%; Guatemalan, 92.3%; Mexican, 92.3%; and Other Latino, 92.0%). However, Colombian men (92.5%) and Cuban women (92.5%) lead the way in the level of employment among native-born men and women, respectively. In contrast,

Table 7.1 *Percentage of Labor Force Employed by Race/Ethnic Group, Place of Birth, and Sex among Persons 25 to 64 Years of Age, 2011*

Race/Ethnic Group	Male			Female		
	Total	Native-Born	Foreign-Born	Total	Native-Born	Foreign-Born
Mexican	91.0	88.9	92.3	89.0	90.7	87.2
Puerto Rican	88.0	87.9	92.7	87.8	87.8	88.8
Cuban	88.2	89.6	87.6	88.9	92.5	87.0
Salvadoran	91.3	91.7	91.2	90.2	91.9	90.0
Dominican	88.6	83.3	90.1	88.5	89.0	88.4
Guatemalan	92.1	90.2	92.3	84.4	87.6	83.9
Colombian	91.5	92.5	91.3	90.1	91.4	89.8
Other Central American	90.5	89.6	90.6	87.1	91.3	86.1
Other South American	92.9	91.7	93.1	91.1	88.2	91.8
Other Latino	89.4	88.7	92.0	90.0	90.4	88.6
Latino	90.6			88.9		
White	92.4			93.2		
Black	84.3			86.9		

Source: 2011 American Community Survey Public-Use File (Ruggles et al. 2010).

the groups least likely to have a job are native-born Dominican men (83.3%) and foreign-born Guatemalan women (83.9%), both of these groups having lower levels of work compared to black men and women, respectively.

One trend that is particularly noteworthy among native-born Latinos concerns the higher level of employment among Latinas compared to their male counterparts in six of the ten Latino subgroups. The gender disparity is particularly noticeable among Dominicans with native-born women having almost a 6 percentage point edge over native-born men in the rate of work. Conversely, among the foreign-born, men are more likely to hold a job compared to women across all the Latino subgroups.

A word of caution on shortcomings with the computation of the employment rate is in order. This analysis is based on persons who are part of the labor force, a group that includes persons who are currently employed as well as those who are not currently working but are seeking employment. One of the concerns with this approach is that the measure is likely to overestimate the level of employment (or underestimate the level of unemployment) simply because discouraged workers – persons who eventually give up trying to look for employment after a long period of unsuccessful attempts – are likely to exit the labor force as they no longer actively seek employment. As such, another way to deal with this problem is to simply compute the percentage of all persons (regardless of whether or not they are part of the labor force) who are employed. This measure does take into account discouraged workers, although it also includes other individuals who are not discouraged workers but are plainly not seeking a job. We illustrate the difference between the two measures using data for males aged 25–54 given that generally females, especially foreign-born Latinas, still are a bit more likely to legitimately not be part of the labor force and some people may retire before reaching retirement age, as early as when they are in their mid-50s.

We provide a general overview of the findings now (data not shown here). Overall, Latino and white men 25 to 54 years of age are quite similar, with the employment rate of all males (accounting for discouraged workers) being about 88 percent, which is as high as that of the employment rate of men in the labor force (not accounting for discouraged workers). Black men, on the other hand, are substantially more likely to include discouraged workers as only 63 percent of all black men hold a job compared to 84 percent of men in the labor force. Nonetheless, there are variations across Latino groups involving the potential impact of discouraged workers on the overestimate of employment rates. In particular, native-born Latinos tend to be more likely to be discouraged workers compared to foreign-born workers. It may be that immigrants, especially those who are unauthorized, are less selective in their job demands than their native-born counterparts. Five native-born groups of men tend to have a greater prevalence of discouraged workers (Puerto Ricans, Other Latinos, Colombians, Dominicans, and Mexicans). These findings, based on efforts to take discouraged workers into account, support the overall trends presented above showing that among Latino men, immigrants are more likely to hold a job compared to native-born individuals. As such, nuances of labor markets complicate matters involving the relationship between human capital and job attainment. Groups with high educational levels have high levels of employment, but so do immigrant groups with low levels of educational attainment. The high level of job acquisition among Latino immigrants with limited educational levels suggests that the wages offered by employers and the wages tolerated by employees may be more in line among immigrants than among native-born workers as well as the importance of social networks in assisting immigrants gain employment.

Job Quality

We now turn to the second phase of labor market outcomes, namely the quality of the job that people hold. Keep in mind that this part of the analysis involves only people 25 to 64 years of age (experienced workers) who are employed and the characteristics of the particular job that they held at the time of the survey. We use here three indicators of job quality: the median Duncan Occupational Socioeconomic Index (SEI), Latino immigrant occupational niche, and the possession of health insurance through employment. The Duncan Occupational Socioeconomic Index, commonly referred to as the SEI measure, was developed by O.D. Duncan (1961) using data from the 1950 census. The SEI is a score ranging from 0 to 100 and is based on the educational attainment level and income level associated with each occupation, with occupations having low SEI scores representing low prestigious occupations and those with high SEI scores denoting more prestigious occupations.

The Latino immigrant occupational niche is a sex-specific measure that identifies the occupations where Latinos are disproportionately concentrated on a relative and absolute basis. The approach used to identify these occupations is based on the work of Waldinger (1996; see also Douglas and Sáenz 2008; Model 1993). In particular, we first obtain two sex-specific percentages: (1) the percentage of workers in a given occupation who are Latino immigrants (p_i) and (2) the percentage of all workers (regardless of occupation) who are Latino immigrants (p_t). Subsequently, we obtain the sex-specific ratio of the percentage of workers in a given occupation who are Latino immigrants (p_i) to the percentage of all workers who are Latina/o immigrants (p_t) by the following formula:

$$\text{Ratio} = p_i/p_t$$

Finally, we use two criteria to identify sex-specific Latino immigrant jobs: (1) the ratio is 1.5 or higher and (2) there are a minimum number of workers in a given occupation (30,000 for males and 17,750 for females). The procedure identifies 25 occupations on the basis of sex in which Latino immigrants are disproportionately concentrated. A list of the occupations for men and women is found in Appendix A. Nearly half of all Latino immigrants in the country who hold a job are working in an occupation identified as a Latino immigrant job (males, 48.6%; females, 48.2%). The analysis below will examine the percentage of workers across Latino subgroups, broken down by place of birth, who are employed in the Latino immigrant occupational niche.

The third indicator of job quality is the percentage of workers who have health insurance attained through their employment.

Based on the three indicators of job quality, higher levels of job quality are associated with high levels on the SEI measure, low rates of participation in the Latino immigrant occupational niche, and high levels of health insurance coverage through one's job.

The results show clear distinctions between whites on the one hand and Latinos and blacks on the other, on the basis of job quality. For example, white workers hold much more prestigious jobs than Latino and black workers (table 7.2). However, examination of the aggregate Latino workers reveals much internal variation regarding the

Table 7.2 *Selected Characteristics Related to Job Quality by Race/Ethnic Group, Place of Birth, and Sex among Persons 25 to 64 Years of Age, 2011*

Sex and Race/Ethnic Group	Median Occupational Socioeconomic Index[a]			Percentage in Latina/o Immigrant Job[b]			Percentage with Employment Health Insurance		
	Total	Native-Born	Foreign-Born	Total	Native-Born	Foreign-Born	Total	Native-Born	Foreign-Born
Male:									
Mexican	18	33	16	41.6	22.0	54.5	38.7	51.7	29.6
Puerto Rican	32	33	18	21.2	21.0	33.2	49.3	49.4	43.6
Cuban	44	49	27	18.2	8.2	22.9	44.3	57.2	38.5
Salvadoran	18	36	16	45.0	20.5	47.9	37.2	49.5	35.7
Dominican	19	44	19	25.5	15.4	28.2	40.0	47.7	37.9
Guatemalan	16	34	15	54.9	27.0	57.5	26.3	57.5	23.3
Colombian	44	49	36	22.5	12.6	24.6	52.0	55.8	51.1
Other Central American	19	44	18	41.0	15.9	45.9	34.7	52.0	31.3
Other South American	36	49	27	26.4	10.6	29.5	47.3	60.7	44.7
Other Latino	39	41	26	21.1	18.1	31.2	51.3	53.2	44.5
Latino	19			37.2			40.6		
White	47			13.6			65.7		
Black	24			22.3			46.8		
Female:									
Mexican	40	44	18	34.7	14.4	55.8	41.1	56.5	28.4
Puerto Rican	44	44	38	15.8	15.7	27.3	50.0	50.1	43.8
Cuban	46	61	44	16.8	4.9	23.3	47.0	64.1	39.0
Salvadoran	18	44	17	52.8	16.6	57.1	36.1	54.5	34.0
Dominican	26	47	18	30.7	8.4	36.2	37.9	48.3	35.6
Guatemalan	18	44	17	54.9	13.6	60.6	28.1	54.2	25.1
Colombian	44	52	44	24.6	9.1	27.6	50.7	57.1	49.5
Other Central American	32	47	22	36.5	10.2	42.6	40.9	62.3	36.4
Other South American	44	52	44	24.4	7.3	28.1	49.5	62.8	46.8
Other Latino	46	46	44	16.9	13.2	30.5	55.0	56.7	49.1
Latina	44			31.5			42.9		
White	51			9.4			68.0		
Black	44			17.3			52.3		

[a] Based on the Duncan Occupational Socioeconomic Index (see Ruggles et al. 2010).
[b] Percent in occupations classified as "Latino immigrant jobs" (see description in text and Appendix A).

Source: 2011 American Community Survey Public-Use File (Ruggles et al. 2010).

SEI standing of the jobs that Latinos hold. In fact, native-born Cubans, Colombians, and Other South Americans, regardless of sex, work in more prestigious jobs than do whites. These are groups that have high levels of educational attainment and also tend to have lighter skin complexion compared to other Latino groups. These three groups have tended to be well integrated socioeconomically in the US. In contrast, among the native-born, Mexicans, Puerto Ricans, Salvadorans, and Guatemalans fare much less well on the basis of the socioeconomic standing of their occupations. Furthermore, as expected, foreign-born Latinos hold jobs that are located further down the socioeconomic ladder than do their native-born counterparts. Still, once again, among the foreign-born, Cubans, Colombians, and Other South Americans are at the top of the occupational socioeconomic ladder relative to other Latino foreign-born workers. Foreign-born Mexicans, Salvadorans, and Guatemalans work in jobs that are at the bottom of the occupational socioeconomic ladder. Note that overall, women work in jobs with higher socioeconomic standing compared to men. This is due to the gendered nature of occupations in which men are more likely to be employed in blue-collar jobs where educational levels are fairly low and women in administrative-support positions that tend to have moderate levels of education.

Overall, as expected, Latinos are much more likely to be working in a Latino immigrant occupational niche than blacks and particularly whites (table 7.2). Foreign-born Mexican, Salvadoran, Guatemalan, and Other Central American workers are the most likely to hold jobs in the Latino immigrant occupational niche. This is particularly the case among Guatemalan immigrants with approximately three-fifths employed in jobs where Latino immigrants are clustered. Again, Cuban, Colombian, and Other South American immigrants are the least likely to be in the Latino immigrant occupational niche. It is noteworthy that upwards of one-fifth of native-born Guatemalan, Mexican, Puerto Rican, and Salvadoran men work in jobs where Latino immigrants are concentrated. As such, US birth status does not offer native-born persons from low-ranking Latino groups a key to bypass the Latino occupational niche.

White workers fare much better than Latino and black workers when it comes to receiving health insurance through their job (table 7.2). Latino workers fare the worst in the acquisition of health insurance through their employment with only 43 percent of women and 41 percent of men enjoying this benefit. In examining the varying groups of Latinos, native-born Cubans, Colombians, and Other South Americans are the most likely to have health insurance through their employers. Mexican and Guatemalan immigrants are the least likely to receive health insurance benefits. Guatemalan immigrant men are the most disadvantaged in this regard with only 23 percent enjoying this job perk.

Thus, we have seen that Latino groups vary significantly on the basis of job quality. On the one hand, Cubans, Colombians, and Other South Americans have the better jobs, while Mexicans, Salvadorans, Guatemalans, and Other Central Americans fare much worse, especially the foreign-born members of these groups.

Economic Rewards

We now direct our attention to the third phase of labor market outcomes – economic rewards. For this segment of the analysis, we highlight three economic indicators:

median wage and salary income, median household income, and percentage of persons in poverty. This part of the analysis is based on persons 25 to 64 years of age. Note that two of the economic indicators – median household income and percentage of persons in poverty – are based on income beyond the individual's own income from employment. For example, the household income is the aggregate amount of income for all persons in the household. Similarly, poverty status is based on the aggregate income in the family and is relative to the size of the family and the presence of children. It is important also to recognize that in addition to women being at a disadvantage due to gender discrimination in the workforce, they are also at a disadvantage compared to men in the economic indicators of median household income and percent of persons in poverty given that households headed by women are less likely to consist of married couples and, thus, are more likely to include only a single income earner.

As was the case with job quality, the findings based on economic rewards clearly show that whites are situated at the higher socioeconomic levels while Latinos and blacks lag significantly behind (table 7.3). Nonetheless, in general, native-born Cubans, Colombians, Other South Americans, as well as to a certain degree Other Central Americans tend to have the highest median job incomes among Latinos. In contrast, Mexicans, Salvadorans, and Guatemalans have the lowest median wage and salary incomes among native-born Latinos. Furthermore, Mexican and Guatemalan immigrants have the lowest median wage and salary incomes, with Mexican and Guatemalan immigrant women having the lowest earnings with a median job income of $16,000. Women have significantly lower median employment earnings than men across all groups except among native-born Salvadorans in which men and women have the same median employment income ($25,000). The greatest gender disparity across racial and ethnic groups occurs among whites, with the median job income of white women being about 68 percent as high as that of white men – compared to gender-disparity levels of 80 percent among Latinos and 88 percent among blacks.

In general, in the area of median household income, the trends tend to be relatively similar to those discussed earlier (table 7.3). However, households headed by native-born Cuban, Colombian, and Other South American surpass white households in median income. Households headed by native-born Colombian men have the highest income levels with a median of $75,000 compared to the $71,000 median of white households. Despite native-born Guatemalan men having relatively low levels on other dimensions related to job quality and median job earnings, their households tend to do fairly well with a median of $64,000. However, households with native-born Mexicans, Puerto Ricans, Dominicans, and Salvadorans tend to fare less well economically among Latino households headed by native-born persons. These groups also tend to lag behind other households among households headed by foreign-born Latinos. Households headed by foreign-born Puerto Rican ($28,000) and Dominican ($28,500) women have the lowest income levels among all Latino households.

Finally, overall, Latinos and blacks are more than twice as likely as whites to have incomes below the poverty level (table 7.3). Yet, native-born Guatemalan (5.9%), Colombian (6.0%), and Other South American (6.1%) men as well as foreign-born Colombian men (8.2%) have poverty rates lower than that of white men (8.4%), while Other Latino women (9.5%) have lower rates of impoverishment than white women

Table 7.3 Selected Characteristics Related to Economic Attainment by Race/Ethnic Group, Place of Birth, and Sex among Persons 25 to 64 Years of Age, 2011

Sex and Race/Ethnic Group	Median Job Income			Median Household Income			Percentage in Poverty		
	Total	Native-Born	Foreign-Born	Total	Native-Born	Foreign-Born	Total	Native-Born	Foreign-Born
Male:									
Mexican	$25,000	$33,000	$23,000	$44,170	$57,000	$38,100	18.8	12.9	22.9
Puerto Rican	$35,000	$35,000	$32,000	$52,000	$52,000	$38,000	17.4	17.3	24.7
Cuban	$32,400	$43,000	$29,000	$53,600	$73,000	$46,000	14.6	9.3	17.0
Salvadoran	$25,000	$25,000	$25,000	$46,100	$51,000	$39,400	14.4	10.3	14.9
Dominican	$28,600	$33,000	$28,000	$45,000	$52,000	$43,000	15.4	14.5	15.7
Guatemalan	$20,000	$31,000	$20,000	$40,200	$64,000	$46,000	21.7	5.9	23.2
Colombian	$35,000	$47,000	$35,000	$57,300	$75,000	$53,000	7.8	6.0	8.2
Other Central American	$25,000	$36,000	$24,000	$47,000	$66,000	$45,000	17.7	11.8	18.9
Other South American	$34,000	$40,000	$31,500	$60,000	$73,800	$56,800	9.8	6.1	10.5
Other Latino	$35,000	$37,000	$31,000	$57,000	$56,000	$60,000	13.6	13.2	15.3
Latino	$27,000			$46,800			17.5		
White	$47,000			$71,000			8.4		
Black	$31,000			$45,400			19.3		
Female:									
Mexican	$20,000	$26,000	$16,000	$36,000	$42,800	$30,700	25.5	17.7	31.9
Puerto Rican	$28,000	$28,000	$24,000	$33,520	$33,650	$28,000	26.2	26.2	28.4
Cuban	$25,000	$32,000	$22,000	$40,000	$50,000	$35,700	17.8	11.6	20.6
Salvadoran	$18,000	$25,000	$18,000	$36,000	$37,700	$36,000	23.4	13.8	24.5
Dominican	$20,000	$28,000	$19,900	$30,000	$35,000	$28,500	27.4	24.6	28.0

Table 7.3 (*continued*)

Sex and Race/Ethnic Group	Median Job Income			Median Household Income			Percentage in Poverty		
	Total	Native-Born	Foreign-Born	Total	Native-Born	Foreign-Born	Total	Native-Born	Foreign-Born
Female									
Guatemalan	$17,000	$26,000	$16,000	$32,000	$55,000	$31,000	29.5	14.6	31.2
Colombian	$24,000	$30,000	$23,500	$47,000	$55,000	$45,000	12.1	11.0	12.3
Other South American	$25,000	$32,000	$24,000	$48,000	$54,004	$45,000	13.6	9.5	14.4
Other Latino	$26,000	$26,000	$25,000	$40,000	$40,000	$36,600	18.9	17.8	22.9
Latina	$21,600			$36,300			24.0		
White	$32,000			$56,000			10.3		
Black	$27,200			$31,220			24.7		

Source: 2011 American Community Survey Public-Use File (Ruggles et al. 2010).

(10.3%). In contrast, native-born Mexicans, Puerto Ricans, and Dominicans tend to have relatively high rates of poverty regardless of gender. Foreign-born members of these groups also have the highest prevalence of impoverishment with close to one-third of Mexican and Guatemalan women being poor. Overall, across racial and ethnic groups and place of birth, women are more likely than men to be living in poverty.

This analysis based on three phases of labor market outcomes – job attainment, job quality, and economic rewards – has provided a valuable portrait of the socioeconomic standing of Latino groups. In general, although whites tend to do better than Latinos and blacks across the variety of dimensions examined, there are certain groups that fare better, at times surpassing whites. These are consistently native-born Cubans, Colombians, and Other South Americans. Members of these groups also tend to fare well among foreign-born Latinos. In contrast, Mexicans, Salvadorans, and to a certain degree Puerto Ricans and Dominicans tend to be worse off socioeconomically, especially in the case of immigrants. Native-born Guatemalan men tended to deviate from the established pattern in the case of median household income and poverty, with their standing on these dimensions being pretty favorable relative to their position in other dimensions. It is clear that the socioeconomic fortunes are not only driven by human capital variations but also by place of birth and gender. Moreover, as noted in chapter 2, the mode of incorporation that the various groups have experienced also affects the ease or difficulty that they face in integrating socioeconomically in the US. For example, Cuban, Colombian, and Other South American immigrants have been drawn from the more prosperous and educationally advantaged segments of their country-of-origin and have received, in general, more favorable treatment and acceptance in the US, particularly in the case of Cubans.

A shortcoming associated with this analysis is that it has been fairly descriptive. We have merely provided a ranking of the diverse groups that comprise the Latino population. Nonetheless, the analysis suggests that the Latino groups vary substantially along the lines of human capital and other characteristics that are typically associated with labor market outcomes. We next seek to assess the level of wage and salary inequality after we take into account factors that are associated with earnings.

An Assessment of Earnings Inequality

As we saw in table 7.3, there are significant differences in the median wage and salary incomes of workers across race/ethnic groups, with some Latino groups being particularly at a disadvantage. Furthermore, we observed that some Latino groups actually had more favorable earnings than whites. Yet, because groups differ on a wide variety of factors related to earnings, such as on educational attainment, it is difficult to pinpoint how much of the earnings differences are due to labor market inequality, what some call the "cost of being a minority worker" (Poston et al. 1976; Sáenz and Morales 2005). Indeed, research indicates that some racial and ethnic groups pay a penalty in earnings due to their racial or ethnic group membership. In describing the research undertaken to get at this cost that persons of color pay, Sáenz and Morales (2005) point out:

These studies typically do not obtain direct measures of labor market discrimination based on race and ethnicity. However, they commonly treat differences in earnings between minority and majority workers that remain after making appropriate statistical adjustments as proxies of such discrimination. (p. 194)

Following this approach, we continue to use data from the 2011 American Community Survey Public-Use File (Ruggles et al. 2010) for persons 25 to 64 years of age who worked during the previous year (2010). We use ordinary least squares (OLS) multiple regression to conduct the analysis with our two major variables of interest being the log of the wage and salary income of workers in 2010 (the dependent variable, or the factor that we seek to explain) and race/ethnic group member (the independent variable, or the factor that we set forth as an explanation for earnings). In addition, we introduce in the model a series of control variables to account for the differences across race/ethnic groups. In particular, we use eight control variables for the analysis focusing on native-born workers: educational attainment; language spoken and English ability; self-employment status; weeks worked during the year; usual number of hours worked per week during the year; marital status; age; and region (Midwest, Northeast, South, and West) of residents. For foreign-born individuals, we use these eight control variables along with two additional control variables: years living in the US and US naturalized citizen status. The analysis seeks to determine the percentage difference in earnings that remain between each race/ethnic group and whites (the comparison group) after accounting for differences between these groups on the series of control variables. The analysis is conducted separately on the basis of place of birth and sex. Therefore, for native-born individuals, the comparison is between each native-born race/ethnic group and the native-born white group by sex; for foreign-born persons, the comparison is between each foreign-born race/ethnic group and the foreign-born white group by sex.

The results examining the relationship between race/ethnic members and earnings are presented in table 7.4 (for an examination of the results for the full model containing the relationships between earnings and all of the control variables, see Appendix B). Note that the values (coefficients) shown in table 7.4 for males and females across place-of-birth groups are in proportion format (thus they can be multiplied by 100 to obtain the percentage). Negative values indicate that the specific race/ethnic group has wages that are lower than the respective white comparison group, while positive values note that the specific race/ethnic group has wages that are higher than the comparative white group. Note also that some coefficients have asterisks. The asterisks denote statistical significance – i.e., the differences are large enough that they could not have occurred by chance – at the 0.05 level and at the 0.01 level with the latter associated with a higher level of statistical significance.

Let us take a look first at the results for native-born men. We can see that among Latino groups, even after accounting for differences in the control variables used in the analysis, five Latino groups (Mexican, Puerto Rican, Salvadoran, Other South American, and Other Latino) have wage and salary incomes that are significantly below (as indicated by negative values) those of native-born white men (table 7.4). The results show that even after differences in the control variables are accounted for, Other Latino men have wages that are 9.2 percent lower than those of white

Table 7.4 *Disparities in Wage and Salary Income Obtained from Multiple Regression Analysis for Selected Race/Ethnic Groups Relative to Whites by Place of Birth and Sex, 2011*[a]

Race/Ethnic Group	Native-Born		Foreign-Born	
	Male	Female	Male	Female
Mexican	−0.051**	−0.015**	−0.228**	−0.154**
Puerto Rican	−0.023*	0.053**	−0.300**	−0.034
Cuban	0.059**	0.080**	−0.135**	−0.028
Salvadoran	−0.068*	−0.024	−0.168**	−0.082**
Dominican	−0.044	−0.079**	−0.286**	−0.159**
Guatemalan	0.028	−0.046	−0.227**	−0.111**
Colombian	0.011	0.014	−0.195**	−0.081**
Other Central American	−0.019	0.030	−0.216**	−0.102**
Other South American	−0.070*	0.025	−0.190**	−0.093**
Other Latino	−0.092**	−0.060**	−0.125**	−0.086**
Black	−0.135**	−0.014**	−0.271**	−0.011

[a] The results from the full multiple regression model is available in Appendix B.
* Statistically significant at the 0.05 level.
**Statistically significant at the 0.01 level.

Source: 2011 American Community Survey Public-Use File (Ruggles et al. 2010).

men, with the penalty being 7.0 percent for Other South Americans, 6.8 percent for Salvadorans, 5.1 percent for Mexicans, and 2.3 percent for Puerto Ricans. On the other hand, consistent with earlier findings, native-born Cuban men actually have wages that are significantly higher (5.9%) than the wages of native-born white men. The other four native-born Latino groups (Dominican, Guatemalan, Other Central American, and Colombian) have earnings that do not differ significantly from those of native-born white men. Finally, it is important to take note that black men pay the steepest penalty for their racial membership, with this group having earnings that are close to 14 percent lower than those of whites even after differences in the control variables have been taken into account.

The results for native-born women workers are somewhat different. For example, three native-born Latina groups experience a significant earnings deficit relative to native-born white women after accounting for group differences in the control variables. In particular, Dominican women have wages that are 7.9 percent lower than white women with the gap being 6.0 percent for Other Latina women and 1.5 percent for Mexican women. On the other hand, native-born Cuban (8.0%) and Puerto Rican (5.3%) women have earnings that are significantly higher than those of native-born white women after taking differences in the control variables into account. For the remaining five groups of native-born Latina women (Salvadoran, Guatemalan, Other Central American, Colombian, and Other South American), their earnings are not significantly different from those of native-born white women. Black women, again, pay a race penalty with their wages being 1.4 percent lower than those of white women, a penalty comparable to native-born Mexican women.

The results for foreign-born workers involving the sex-specific comparisons of 11 race/ethnic groups in comparison to the foreign-born white group are stark. All of the coefficients shown in the table are negative, reflecting lower earnings among each of the race/ethnic groups in comparison to foreign-born whites and all but three are statistically significant. Overall, the groups that pay the greatest cost in the labor market include Mexicans, Dominicans, Guatemalans, and Other Central Americans, with both men and women having earnings that are particularly divergent from the earnings of their foreign-born white counterparts. In addition, foreign-born black and Puerto Rican (those not born in Puerto Rico or the US mainland) men have earnings that are steeply below those of foreign-born white men. In contrast, the three groups of foreign-born women whose earnings do not differ significantly from those of foreign-born white women are Puerto Ricans, Cubans, and blacks.

These findings examining earnings inequality provide added substance to the earlier results presented in tables 7.1–7.3. They are also instructive in another manner. Indeed, they show the divergent routes toward socioeconomic integration among the largest three Latino groups which have been in the US for the longest periods of time. Among native-born persons, Mexicans and Puerto Ricans continue to lag significantly behind whites. On the other hand, Cubans have done well socioeconomically, surpassing whites on a wide variety of socioeconomic indicators including earnings. For the other groups whose histories in the US are relatively shorter, there is quite a degree of variation as the findings here show, ranging from Colombians and Other South Americans doing fairly well and Dominicans and Salvadorans lagging behind.

Questions Related to the Future of Latino Work and Economic Life

There are several important labor market and socioeconomic trends that we need to be aware of regarding the Latino population for these are likely to play an important role in the future labor market and socioeconomic trends. These trends revolve around three groups: immigrants, teenagers, and women. These trends have major implications and questions regarding the future course of Latinos in the labor market and the economy in the coming years.

The Expanding Role of Immigrants in the Workforce

Over the last several decades, immigration has accounted for a significant proportion of the rapid growth of the Latino population. The increasing presence of immigrants has transformed the Latino workforce dramatically. The share of immigrants among Latino workers has grown from 38.5 percent in 1980 to 53.2 percent in 2010 (figure 7.1). As such, immigrants have accounted for the majority of Latino workers since 2000.

It has been nearly three decades since the US undertook major immigration reform. While immigration reform continues to be a hotly debated issue, major players in the debate have voiced their support for the passage of immigration reform including a route to citizenship among immigrants. There is also quite a bit of debate about the establishment of a guest worker program as part of immigration reform. In terms of general immigration reform, the business, labor, and religious sectors have come out in favor of reforming immigration and allowing immigrants a passage to US citizenship.

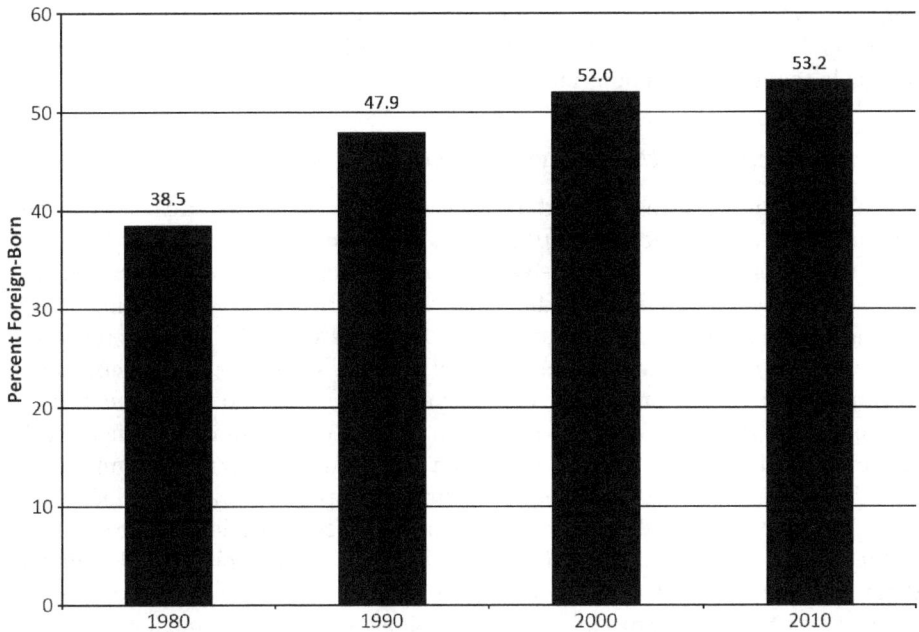

Figure 7.1 Percentage of Latino Workers Foreign-Born, 1980–2010

Source: 1980, 1990, and 2000 5% Public Use Microdata Sample (PUMS) and 2010 American Community Survey (ACS) Public-Use File (Ruggles et al. 2010).

President Obama has also pushed for immigration reform which he promised to pass when he was campaigning for election to his first presidential term. However, support for immigration reform has stalled in Congress. While the Senate passed an immigration reform bill with 67 in favor and 27 opposed in the summer of 2013, the bill emphasized border security with a plan to double the size of the Border Patrol, extend fences an additional 350 miles, and a lengthy process for citizenship attainment. Far less support exists in the Republican-dominated House, with House Republicans developing their own immigration reform proposal centered on border security and with many opposing any path to citizenship.

As the business and labor sectors realize and as figure 7.1 shows, the US is heavily dependent on immigrant labor. Immigrants are disproportionately found in many sectors of the economy, such as in construction, agriculture, hotels, restaurants, cleaning, housekeeping, childcare, and meatpacking. In fact, entrepreneurs who depend heavily on immigrant labor have expressed concern over passage of draconian anti-immigration policies in states such as Arizona and Georgia and, increasingly, as the flow of immigrants has declined in recent years (Passel et al. 2012).

Given the major obstacle that the House represents in the passage of immigration reform, the passage of immigration reform that provides a relatively expeditious path to citizenship is not likely. The failure to provide a path toward US citizenship will represent a major setback for the estimated 11 million unauthorized persons in the US, many of these Latino. Without citizenship status, Latino immigrants will continue to be relegated to low-paying, dead-end jobs with exploitative and unsafe work conditions. The lack of path to citizenship signals the scarcity of a route to more favorable economic conditions for unauthorized Latinos.

The Major Increase in Unemployment among Latino Teenagers

While the economic crisis has had a major impact on many Americans, especially Latinos (Sáenz 2008; Taylor et al. 2012b), it has been particularly devastating to youngsters. It is important that youth receive work experience, especially teenagers who are poor, for a variety of reasons including obtaining spending money, providing household assistance, and gaining responsibility. Unfortunately, today's Latino teenagers are not getting the same work experience as their older siblings or earlier generations of Latino youth. For example, the unemployment rate of Latino youth between the ages of 16 and 19 doubled from 16 percent in 1980 to 32 percent in 2010 (figure 7.2). However, youth who are in poverty have been particularly hurt by the economic crisis with their unemployment rate being approximately 44 percent in 2010 compared to a rate of 29 percent among their peers who are not poor (see also Sáenz 2014a).

These trends are particularly disturbing given the demographic trends showing that today's Latino youth will increasingly be called upon in the coming decades to serve in the US workforce to support an increasingly aging population. It is important that policymakers, educators, and community leaders view Latino youth as valuable human beings that have great potential to enhance their social, academic, and economic resources in order to be valuable contributors to their communities. Policies

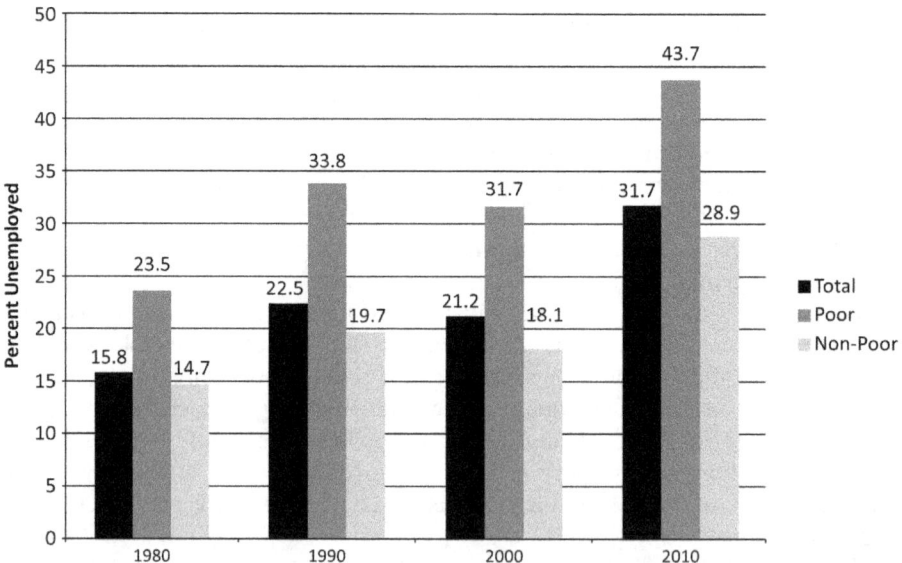

Figure 7.2 Percentage of Latino Teenagers 16 to 19 Years of Age Unemployed by Poverty Status, 1980–2010

Source: 1980, 1990, and 2000 5% Public Use Microdata Sample (PUMS) and 2010 American Community Survey (ACS) Public-Use File (Ruggles et al. 2010).

and programs designed to enhance the educational and work experience of youth, especially for those who are poor, are excellent investments in the future of these children and the communities where they will live in the future.

Former San Antonio Mayor (now US Secretary of Housing and Urban Development) Julián Castro's Pre-K 4 SA Program is a $31 million program financed by 1/8 cent sales tax to provide full-day advanced education to more than 22,000 4-year-old children over a period of eight years. Castro's program represents a model that community leaders can emulate in attempts to provide advanced educational training for youth. Indeed, President Obama has used this program as a blueprint for the development of a federal universal pre-kindergarten program (Cesar 2013).

Increasing Influence of Women in Latino Workforce and Family Finances

Over the last several decades, Latinas have increased their participation in the workforce. For example, over the course of the last four decades, the share of women among Latino workers has risen from 39 percent in 1980 to 43 percent in 2010 (figure 7.3). The relatively slow upward trend in the proportion of women in the Latino workforce is somewhat deceiving as their growth has been undercut by the faster growth of immigration laborers, disproportionately comprised of men. At the same time, however, as Latinas have gained a foothold in the workforce, their importance to family finances has surged. For instance, among in-married Latino couples (in which both spouses are Latinos), the percentage of such couples in which wives brought more money to the household than did husbands rose from 11 percent in 1980 to 20 percent in 2010.

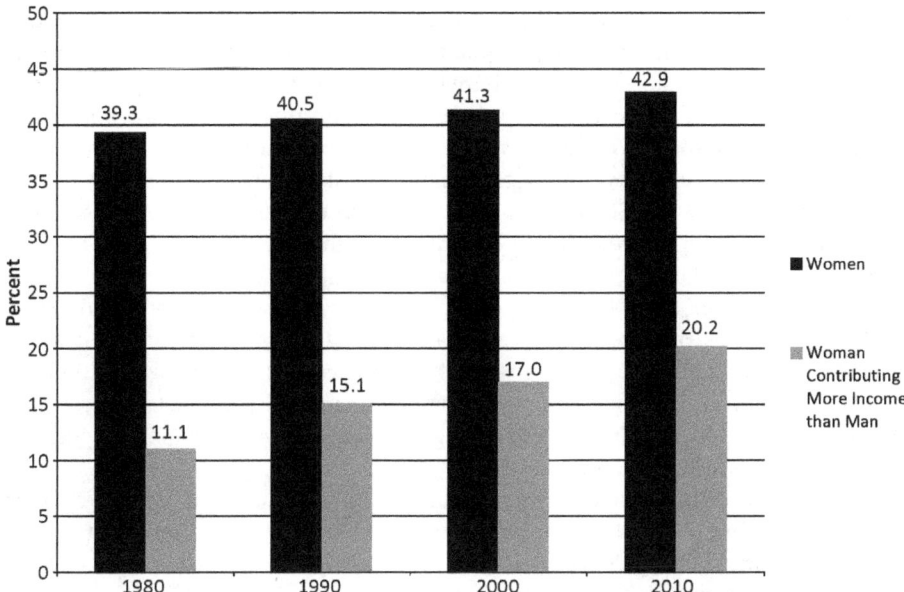

Figure 7.3 Percentage of Latino Workers who are Women and Latino Couples with Women Contributing More Income than Men, 1980–2010

Source: 1980, 1990 and 2000 5% Public-Use Microdata Sample (PUMS), and 2010 American Community Survey (ACS) Public-Use File (Ruggles et al. 2010).

The share of Latinas among the Latino workforce will certainly continue to ascend in the coming decades. There are several reasons for this expectation. First, as we saw in chapter 6, Latinas have experienced significant gains in educational attainment and they now surpass Latino men on level of education. As women attain higher levels of education, their rate of labor force participation increases. Second, as we saw above, foreign-born Latinas continue to have relatively low levels of employment activity. As such, as more of these women enter the labor force this will contribute to the increasing share of women among the group's workers. Finally, as we will observe in chapter 8, the share of families that are headed by Latinas has increased substantially over the last several decades. Under such circumstances, women will increasingly join the workforce in efforts to increase economic resources for their families.

The increasing presence of Latinas in the workforce has important implications and calls for the establishment of policies and programs to allow them to be able to support family and work life. The lack of affordable childcare continues to be a major obstacle for women workers, particularly for those with limited resources. As it stands, it is not logical for poor women to work for low wages when most of their earnings go to pay for the care of their children. In addition, programs that allow young girls to gain information on a variety of careers are important for providing them options for continuing their education after high school.

Summary

This chapter has provided an overview of the work and economic patterns of the Latino population. We overviewed a variety of theoretical perspectives that sociologists and other social scientists have used to understand the different stages of labor market outcomes: job attainment, job quality, and economic rewards. The examination of contemporary data shows that there is a great degree of variability in the work and economic experiences of the diverse groups that comprise the Latino population. In particular, while some groups fare well socioeconomically (Cubans, Colombians, and Other South Americans), other groups are not as fortunate (Mexicans, Puerto Ricans, Dominicans, and Salvadorans). In addition, analysis seeking to assess the extent to which Latino workers pay a penalty for their race/ethnic membership demonstrates that Latino immigrants along with native-born Mexicans, Puerto Ricans, Dominicans, Salvadorans, and to a certain extent Colombians and Other South Americans earn significantly less than their white counterparts, even when group differences in control variables are taken into account. Finally, we highlighted three important trends in the Latino workforce involving immigrants, teenagers, and women and outlined some policies and programs that can be developed to enhance human resources and economic returns.

The work and economic activities of Latinos is important for all phases of their lives such as in the sphere of education, contribution to the larger society, and toward greater economic stability in their golden years. One area that is intimately related to the work and economic activities of Latinos is the family. Indeed, family life affects one's work and economic conditions which subsequently are important in supporting and sustaining families. We now turn to an examination of the family life of Latinos.

8 Families

Being family oriented is one of the most distinguishable characteristics associated with Latinos. Indeed, the family unit has been a central aspect of the racialization of groups of color in the US, including Latinos. For instance, in the political realm the low social and economic standing of Latinos has been blamed on the family, which is ironic given that the marginalized social standing of blacks has been attributed to perceptions of family disintegration.

Academically, perceptions of dysfunctional Latino families arguably gained momentum after the work of anthropologists Oscar Lewis who is best known for the "culture of poverty" framework. Recall that although the concept of the "culture of poverty" has been misapplied, it has come to be used to portray poor people of color as having a dysfunctional culture without ambition. Oscar Lewis published two books on Latino families and the culture of poverty – *Five Families: Mexican Case Studies in the Culture of Poverty* (1959) and *La Vida: A Puerto Rican Family in the Culture of Poverty – San Jose and New York* (1965) that focused on a single Puerto Rican family in the "culture of poverty." Lewis's work unintentionally contributed to stereotypes of Mexican-origin and Puerto Rican families as culturally deficient and as a social problem for American society (Zambrana 2011). Today, most scholarly discourse does not attribute commitment to the family as a factor explaining Latino inequality (Zambrana 2011).

Perceptions of Latino family dysfunctionality can also occur through comparative analysis. Intentionally or unintentionally, studies contrasting whites and Latinos at times assume the former is the standard by which all other racial/ethnic groups are judged (Zambrana 2011). While not all comparative work depicts Latino families as dysfunctional, we need to be cautious of scholarship that supports the unequal treatment of ethnic families based on a superior-versus-inferior binary (Bonilla-Silva 2013).

In this chapter, we begin with an overview of theoretical perspectives that have been used to understand Latino families. In particular, we present a discussion of culture versus structural perspectives used to examine Latino families. Second, we use data from the American Community Survey (ACS) (2011) to examine various trends related to family composition for various race/ethnic groups by sex and place of birth. Third, we highlight some of the issues affecting the future of Latino families such as mixed-status families and households, family separations due to transnationalism and deportations, and same-sex couples.

Culture versus Structural Perspectives

Central to the early frameworks in family sociology is the embracement of European cultural norms that have served as a guide to theorize about racial/ethnic groups, including Latinos, in the US (Thornton 2005; Zambrana 2011). As such, Zambrana (2011, p. 39) argued that it is essential to "interrogate the epistemological roots of the intellectual traditions (family theory and assimilation/acculturation theory) that have been used to capture the lived experiences of Latino subgroups in the United States." Thus, fundamental to theoretical perspectives applied to Latino families are debates of culture versus structure. Below we elaborate on some of the ways in which the culture vs. structure debate surfaces in studies on Latino families.

Families, Sex Roles, and Latino Culture

A central question in studies of Latino families is whether family patterns originate from culture or structure. Although cultural explanations are used to account for stability of behaviors over time occurring in the context of large-scale social and economic changes (Swidler 1986), they remain controversial. Some cultural explanations can be controversial for two reasons: (1) they blame the victim or stress that groups are responsible for their own marginalized positions in society and/or (2) they ignore the social structure in which actors are embedded (Landale and Oropesa 2007). This is not to say that cultural frameworks should not be considered, rather that it is important to determine whether behavior is culturally-specific (rooted in socio-cultural-historical processes) or situation-specific (reactions to the existing socio-environment).

Two cultural perspectives rooted in the Latino family that can be controversial are *marianismo* and *machismo*. The concept of *marianismo* is based on the Catholic ideal of the Virgin Mary, used to highlight women's role as the self-sacrificing mother who suffers for her children (Ramirez 1990). In Latin America mothers are expected to self-sacrifice for the sake of the family (Chant with Craske 2003), while fathers are associated with authority, protection, and guidance of the family through participation in public spheres (Arriagada 2002). Numerous studies have questioned the applicability of *marianismo* to Latina mothers. For instance, motherhood is actually defined more broadly in Latin America. As such, mothers are not expected to be confined to the private sphere but to be proactive in public spheres such as employment outside of the home, political participation, and/or migration (Abrego 2009; Schirmer 1993). Even in the US a comparative study of Latina and white females in a public university found no differences in gender ideologies and behavior (Franco et al. 2004). Similarly, a study based on Mexican American students enrolled in a southwestern university found that attitudes toward the female role in the workplace and parental responsibility for child care reflected more Euro-American orientations (Gowan and Treviño 1998).

In contrast to *marianismo*, *machismo* emphasizes the role as head of household versus fatherhood (Cauce and Domenech-Rodríguez 2002). Early feminist perspectives describe *machismo* as "an exaggerated masculinity, physical prowess, and male chauvinism" (Baca Zinn 1994, p. 74). *Machismo* has had a wide range of conceptualizations. The most controversial are those that depict Latino males as tyrannical or hyper-masculine. This is ironic given that nine out of an estimated 29 women who have been elected presidents of their countries since the 1970s have been from Latin America and the Caribbean (Romero 2013). Yet, characterizations of *machismo* continue to largely depict Latino men as dominant fathers and husbands (Cauce and Domenech-Rodríguez 2002).

Others have painted *machismo* more positively or have questioned the applicability of the concept by highlighting Latino men's roles as providers, protectors, and representatives of their families (Mirande 1997), or have highlighted the structural factors that sustain and benefit from *machismo* (Saucedo and Morales 2010). Despite Latino male characterizations as *"machistas"* (male chauvinists), scholarship has documented the value of *familismo* (the importance of the family over the individual) which extends to fathers' household participation and childcare activities (McLoyd et al. 2000). For example, compared to white fathers, Latino fathers are more parentally engaged with their children (Leavell et al. 2012; Tamis-LeMonda et al. 2009). Moreover, in cases where Latino fathers are less engaged in caregiving than whites and African Americans, it is attributed to their low educational levels that relegate them to working more hours at low-paying jobs which pulls them away from caregiving activities (Leavell et al. 2012). The scholarship on the household division of labor also raises questions about the applicability of *machismo* to Latino males. Among Latino families both genders roughly agree on perceptions that men should do housework, that it is alright for the wife to be the primary earner, and that women have the right to use and decide the methods of birth control (Hurtado et al. 1992).

Structural Explanations of Latino Family Circumstances

One of the most important advancements in family studies in the 1990s is the emphasizing of social-structural characteristics (McLoyd et al. 2000). While referring to immigrant families, Foner (1997) elegantly stated "the family is seen as a place where there is a dynamic interplay between structure, culture, and agency – where creative culture-building takes place in the context of external social and economic forces as well as immigrants' pre-migration cultural frameworks" (p. 961). Some of the most important structural factors to consider are those that are associated with poverty which influence divorce, non-marital childbearing, and female-headed households (Landale and Oropesa 2007). It is crucial for studies on Latino families to account for structural inequality at the neighborhood, community, and educational institutional levels and its influence on family processes, family relationships, and gender-role expectations (Zambrana 2011). Indeed, in a comparative study of Mexican, Puerto Rican, and white families, structure is more important than culture given that higher social class is associated with living further away from family members and a reduction in the likelihood of living with family (Sarkisian et al. 2006). Consequently, family practices and culture should be differentiated in order to avoid attributing differences simply to culture (Sarkisian et al. 2006).

Familismo

Familisimo, or familism, is perhaps the concept that has received the most attention in the study of Latino families. Two of the most prevalent components associated with *familismo* are prioritizing the family over individual needs and conceptualizing family beyond the nuclear to the extended. First, the concept of *familismo* has been a central element describing Latinos living in the US and in Latin America for over 40 years (Fussell and Palloni 2004; Hurtado 1995; Landale and Oropesa 2007; Moore with Cuéllar 1970; Rodriguez 2000; Smith-Morris et al. 2012). One of the earliest usages of familism/*familismo* is seen in Moore with Cuéllar (1970), who described it as the most significant part of life for Mexican Americans in South Texas as it is a main source of obligations and emotional and economical support. Second, *familismo* also emphasizes the importance of contributing to the well-being of both the nuclear and the extended family (Cauce and Domenech-Rodríguez 2002; Keefe 1984; Smith-Morris et al. 2012; Tienda and Angel 1982). These attributes anchor the Latino culture as one that values the collective over the individual (Ramirez 1990). In sum, the literature suggests that Latinos' commitment to family is qualitatively and quantitatively different than that of non-Latino whites (Vega 1995).

Scholars have identified various dimensions of *familismo* including structural/demographic (e.g., family size, marriage, and family structure), attitudinal/normative (e.g., values placed on the family), and behavioral (e.g., activities that fulfill family roles and degree of interaction between families and kin networks) (Baca Zinn 1994; Valenzuela and Dornbusch 1994). Below we address the literature that directly examines each of these dimensions of *familismo*.

Demographic and structural *familismo*
Demographic and structural *familismo* refers to characteristics associated with family structure including family size and marriage. It is important to consider family structure given its influence on several factors in the life course as well as family and child well-being (Zambrana 2011). The family structure of Latino families has been distinguishable from white families over the last several decades. For example, Latina females are less likely to be married, more likely to be heads of household, and are more likely to have children at younger ages outside of marriage than white females (Cauce and Domenech-Rodríguez 2002). We will address this particular dimension of familism in the next section, where we examine trends in marriage, family, and household arrangements among Latinos.

Attitudinal/normative and behavioral *familismo*
Attitudinal or normative *familismo* refers to values that are placed on the family while behavioral *familismo* alludes to activities involving the fulfillment of family roles and interactions among family members. While both of these forms of *familismo* are distinct, they both have been applied to similar topics including family closeness, perceptions of or the role of the extended family, and living in geographical proximity to family (nuclear and extended), as well as to an array of social processes such as education, immigrant settlement, health, criminal activity and delinquency, among others. Below we thematically organize our discussion of attitudinal/normative and behavioral *familismo*.

As discussed previously, one of the distinguishing features of *familismo* is the importance of the family. Among Latinos, family is central for survival (Massey et al. 1995). Puerto Rican mothers, for instance, place much more emphasis on family closeness and respect for authority than on independence and assertiveness (Gonzales Ramos et al. 1998). In times of trouble Mexican immigrants are more likely to speak to a relative compared to a friend than whites are (Cauce and Domenech-Rodríguez 2002). Moreover, among whites proximity is the major determinant when deciding who to ask for help, whereas Latinos prefer family support (Cauce and Domenech-Rodríguez 2002).

Also, as briefly mentioned above, embedded in the concept of *familismo* is the importance of not only the nuclear but the extended family. Latinos hold a strong sense of family unity that includes extended family networks (Hidalgo 1998; Hurtado 1995; Trueba 1999; Zambrana 2011). Comeau (2012), for instance, found that Latinos and blacks maintained more frequent contact with both nuclear and extended family members than whites. This pattern suggests that whites establish more refined distinctions between nuclear and extended family members.

Another indicator of *familismo* is living in geographical proximity. Latinos place higher value on geographical closeness to family and kin (Hurtado 1995). Indeed, Keefe (1984) found Mexican Americans are less geographically mobile even when controlling for socioeconomic status. In a comparative study in Los Angeles, Mexican immigrants were more likely to have kin in town, to be related to people in the household, and to have visited more households weekly than whites (Keefe 1984).

Debates on *familismo*

Despite the wide support for the concept of *familismo*, there are several points of contestation. First, utilizing the anthropological lens, Smith-Morris et al. (2012) found through nostalgic recollections of Mexican migrants that community is equally or more important than family. Second, others disagree about whether *familismo* is restricted to Latino culture given that other racial/ethnic groups are also family-centered (Vega 1995; Zambrana 2011). For instance, *familismo* has also been found among blacks (Comeau 2012). Finally, there is disagreement on the impact of *familismo* on social processes. For instance, in contrast to the positive depictions of *familismo* described above, this concept has also been connected to downward mobility for Mexican Americans (Harris 1980) and as a source of surveillance and pressure on reproductive decisions (Maternowska et al. 2010).

Trends in Marriage, Family, and Households among Latinos

Data from the 2011 American Community Survey (ACS) Public-Use Micro-data Sample are used to examine trends in family composition of Latino groups and two comparative groups (whites and blacks) along five dimensions: (1) marriage and divorce, (2) intermarriages, (3) heterosexual and same-sex cohabitations, (4) female headed households with no husband present, and (5) living with extended family members and residing alone. Because sex is such an important factor in family studies, all analyses are conducted separately for females and males. Furthermore, other central determinants that impact Latino family structure are included, in particular, Latino subgroup and place of birth. Note that the analysis presented below is based on individuals 25 to 44 years of age. This age band is used to control for age differences across racial and ethnic groups. For example, if we considered all individuals 15 years or older, it is likely that some groups, such as Mexicans, would have very low rates of marriage, due principally to the youthfulness of the population.

Marriage and Divorce

We begin our analysis by examining the prevalence of marriage (table 8.1). Overall, there are some general patterns. First, Latinos and whites are fairly similar with their

Table 8.1 *Marriage and Divorce Characteristics among Persons 25 to 44 Years of Age by Race/Ethnic Group, Sex, and Place of Birth, 2011*

Race/Ethnic Group	Percentage of Persons 25–44 Years of Age Currently Married								Divorce Rate[a]						
	Male			Female					Male			Female		
	Total	Native-Born	Foreign-Born	Total	Native-Born	Foreign-Born			Total	Native-Born	Foreign-Born	Total	Native-Born	Foreign-Born
Mexican	53.1	44.0	59.6	56.6	48.2	63.7			17.2	30.4	10.0	19.8	29.3	13.6
Puerto Rican	40.8	40.9	—	38.3	38.2	—			30.1	30.5	—	37.9	37.6	—
Cuban	47.9	42.2	52.4	51.1	46.9	54.4			21.1	34.3	12.5	33.1	39.4	28.8
Salvadoran	47.0	29.7	49.8	49.7	38.0	51.5			9.9	24.6	8.5	21.8	3.9	23.7
Dominican	43.6	29.0	50.3	43.0	35.4	46.0			21.3	31.3	18.6	33.1	45.1	29.7
Guatemalan	43.8	31.5	45.2	52.6	47.4	53.4			10.7	35.6	8.8	9.5	18.9	8.3
Colombian	51.1	46.3	53.0	58.6	42.9	63.3			28.5	14.0	33.4	55.4	30.2	60.4
Other Central American	41.5	36.2	42.8	44.9	37.0	47.1			17.1	9.1	18.7	25.1	34.5	23.0
Other South American	52.4	42.9	55.0	56.2	42.7	59.9			26.4	27.7	26.2	27.6	27.2	27.7
Other Latino	42.8	39.5	53.9	46.2	43.1	56.5			28.7	33.1	17.8	45.7	49.6	35.0
Latino	50.2	42.4	56.3	53.1	45.1	60.1			18.7	30.2	12.0	24.1	32.3	18.5
White	53.3			58.9					28.5			30.3		
Black	33.1			29.0					39.2			39.4		

[a]Number of persons divorced in the past year per 1,000 married persons (including married and separated individuals as well as persons who were divorced or widowed in the past year).

Source: 2011 American Community Survey Public-Use File (Ruggles et al. 2010).

rates of marriage (above 50%); in contrast, less than one-third of blacks are married. Second, foreign-born Latinos are more likely to be married compared to native-born Latinos. Third, overall among Latinos, women are more likely than men to be married.

There are significant variations across Latino groups on their prevalence of marriage. Among the foreign-born, three-fifths or more of Mexican (63.7%), Colombian (63.3%), and Other South American (59.9%) women and Mexican men (59.6%) are married. In contrast, the lowest rates of marriage among the foreign-born occur among Central American (Salvadoran, Guatemalan, and Other Central American, 42.8%) and Dominican men and women. Among native-born Latinos, the highest levels of marriage (45% or higher) occur among Colombian (46.3%) and Mexican (44.0%) men and Mexican (48.2%), Guatemalan (47.4%), and Cuban (46.9%) women. On the other hand, less than one-third of native-born Dominican (29.0%), Salvadoran (29.7%), and Guatemalan (31.5%) men are married, with native-born Dominican women (35.4%) also having low rates of marriage.

We now examine the prevalence of divorce among the different racial and ethnic groups. We compute the divorce rate as the number of persons divorced in the past year per 1,000 married persons. Again, there are certain overall patterns. First, Latinos, as a whole, have lower divorce rates than whites and blacks. Blacks, in particular, have the highest level of divorce among both sexes. Second, in general, among Latinos, women have a higher divorce rate than men. Third, native-born Latinos have substantially higher divorce rates than foreign-born individuals.

There is also wide variation in the prevalence of divorce across Latino groups. For example, among foreign-born Latinos, the lowest divorce rates take place among Guatemalan women (8.3%) along with Salvadoran (8.5%), Guatemalan (8.8%), and Mexican (10.0%) men. In contrast, foreign-born Colombians (men, 33.4%; women, 60.4%) have the highest levels of divorce as is the case with foreign-born Other Latina women (35.0%). Among native-born Latinos, four groups have low levels of marital dissolution (Salvadoran women, 3.9%; Other Central American men, 9.1%; Colombian men, 14.0%; and Guatemalan women, 18.9%). On the other hand, several groups of native-born Latinos, particularly women, have divorce rates above 35%: Other Latina women, 49.6%; Dominican women, 45.1%; Cuban women, 39.4%; Puerto Rican women, 37.6%; and Guatemalan men, 35.6%.

In-marriages and Out-marriages

Next we examine another demographic family characteristic – the degree of racial and ethnic in-marriage (endogamy or marriage inside the race/ethnic group) and out-marriage (exogamy or marriage outside of one's group). Historically, scholars interested in racial/ethnic boundaries have viewed marriages as the litmus test of the salience between racial/ethnic boundaries (Landale and Oropesa 2007). We illustrate trends in endogamy and exogamy across race/ethnic groups.

We begin our discussion by examining the percentage of Latino husbands that married within their ethnic group. Overall, compared to whites and blacks, Latinos have the lowest percentage of in-group marriages, reflecting, in part, the rigid black–white color line in the US (table 8.2). Specifically, among husbands 95 percent of whites married within their racial/ethnic group, followed by 86 percent of blacks,

Table 8.2 *In-marriages and Out-marriages among Married Individuals by Race/Ethnic Group, Sex, and Place of Birth, 2011*

Place of Birth and Race/Ethnic Group	Race/Ethnic Identity of Wives or Husbands					Race/Ethnic Identity of Husbands or Wives				
	In-group[a]	Other Latino	White	Black	Other	In-group[a]	Other Latino	White	Black	Other
Total:										
Mexican	81.5	3.5	13.0	0.4	2.0	80.2	3.7	13.9	1.0	2.2
Puerto Rican	50.3	16.3	26.4	3.8	7.0	52.4	13.7	25.7	5.7	8.2
Cuban	64.0	16.5	17.1	0.9	2.4	68.6	10.9	18.4	1.1	2.1
Salvadoran	67.5	25.7	5.0	0.5	1.8	66.2	25.4	6.5	0.6	1.9
Dominican	75.4	14.5	6.9	1.6	3.2	64.0	20.6	10.0	3.8	5.4
Guatemalan	57.6	33.5	7.0	0.3	1.9	59.0	29.2	9.8	1.4	2.0
Colombian	62.5	16.1	19.4	0.3	2.0	46.6	22.9	27.1	1.6	3.4
Other Central American	50.5	29.1	15.4	2.7	5.0	43.4	28.7	21.3	4.5	6.6
Other South American	58.0	19.5	20.3	0.2	2.2	53.9	15.1	28.0	1.2	3.0
Other Latino	45.1	12.2	37.1	0.9	5.6	44.5	12.6	36.8	2.1	6.1
Latino	81.9	—	15.4	0.8	1.9	79.9	—	17.0	1.6	1.5
White	94.6	2.6	—	0.3	2.5	95.5	2.3	—	0.7	1.5
Black	86.3	2.8	7.9	—	3.0	93.8	1.5	3.6	—	1.1
Native-Born										
Mexican	65.0	3.7	27.3	0.8	3.2	60.0	3.3	32.4	2.2	2.1
Puerto Rican	50.2	16.2	26.5	3.8	3.3	58.9	5.3	27.8	6.0	2.0
Cuban	33.9	16.7	44.6	2.1	2.7	27.0	17.0	50.7	3.0	2.3
Salvadoran	39.1	34.5	18.8	2.5	5.1	17.9	39.0	37.4	3.6	2.1
Dominican	43.7	20.7	21.4	7.6	6.6	17.9	42.6	28.0	8.6	2.9
Guatemalan	20.5	49.1	26.8	1.4	2.2	9.5	32.7	50.2	6.9	0.7

Colombian	28.4	14.9	51.1	0.5	5.1	8.4	24.7	61.6	3.0	2.3
Other Central American	21.2	26.2	40.9	7.1	4.6	7.3	23.9	53.9	10.8	4.1
Other South American	22.1	25.6	47.0	0.3	5.0	7.8	17.4	69.5	2.9	2.4
Other Latino	40.9	10.5	42.4	1.1	5.1	40.0	8.7	44.6	2.4	4.3
Latino	65.5	—	29.4	1.6	3.5	58.4	—	36.1	3.2	2.3
Foreign-Born:										
Mexican	91.7	3.5	4.1	0.1	0.6	94.3	3.9	1.1	0.1	0.6
Cuban	73.5	16.4	8.5	0.5	1.1	88.5	7.9	2.9	0.3	0.4
Salvadoran	69.6	25.1	3.9	0.3	1.1	75.3	22.8	0.7	0.0	1.2
Dominican	80.5	13.5	4.5	0.6	0.9	83.5	11.3	2.3	1.7	1.2
Guatemalan	60.5	32.4	5.4	0.2	1.5	69.6	28.4	1.2	0.2	0.6
Colombian	68.4	16.2	14.0	0.2	1.2	70.2	21.7	5.9	0.8	1.4
Other Central American	55.7	29.6	10.9	1.9	1.9	63.7	31.3	3.1	0.9	1.0
Other South American	63.3	31.4	16.3	0.2	-11.2	79.0	13.8	5.5	0.3	1.4
Other Latino	58.9	17.4	20.0	0.5	3.2	59.7	25.6	10.5	1.0	3.2
Latino	92.8	—	6.1	0.2	0.9	96.8	—	2.0	0.3	0.9

[a] Ingroup marriages are those in which the husband and wife are members of the same specific race/ethnic group.

Source: 2011 American Community Survey Public-Use File (Ruggles et al. 2010).

and 82 percent of Latinos. Of the Latino husbands that married outside of their own group, the majority married whites (15.4%).

Latina wives have slightly lower percentages of in-group marriages (79.9%) than Latino husbands (81.9%), but otherwise patterns of in-group marriages are similar. In particular, white wives have the highest percentage of in-group marriages (95.5%), followed by blacks (93.8%), and Latinas have the lowest (79.9%). Also, similar to Latino husbands, among those who married outside of their racial/ethnic group, the majority are married to whites (17.0%).

There are some general patterns within the Latino population. For example, while the majority of Latino married individuals are wedded to a co-ethnic, foreign-born Latinos are much more likely to be in such a marriage compared to native-born Latinos. Indeed, among foreign-born Latinos, 97 percent of women and 93 percent of men have a spouse from their own ethnic group. In comparison, among native-born Latinos about two-thirds of men and nearly three-fifths of women are married within their own ethnic group – when they marry out, they are most likely to marry whites (women, 36.1%; men, 29.4%).

Furthermore, there are significant variations in types of marriage across Latino groups by place of birth and sex. Among native-born Latinos, Mexicans are the most likely to have a spouse who is also Mexican (men, 65.0%; women, 60.0%), followed by Puerto Ricans (men, 50.2%; women, 58.9%). In contrast, Guatemalans (men, 20.5%; women, 9.5%), Colombians (men, 28.4%; women, 8.4%), Other Central Americans (men, 21.2%; women, 7.3%), and Other South Americans (men, 22.1%; women, 7.8%) have the lowest in-marriage rates, particularly in the case of women. Yet, when Guatemalans marry out, they are more likely than these other groups to marry a person from another Latino subgroup, while Colombians, Other Central Americans, and Other South Americans are most likely to marry whites. For instance, 62 percent of Colombian women have a white husband. The high prevalence of intermarriage with whites among Colombians, Other Central Americans, and Other South Americans not only reflects high socioeconomic standing of these groups, but also their relatively small group size. Blau's (1977) research on intermarriage shows that racial/ethnic groups that are relatively small tend to have contact mostly with people who are not from their own racial/ethnic group, thus promoting the establishment of relationships with people outside of one's group.

Heterosexual and Same-Sex Cohabitation Rates

In this section we provide data trends in cohabitation among heterosexual and same-sex couples. It is important to consider this issue given that marriage patterns in the US cannot be considered in isolation from cohabitation as there is an inverse relationship between the two (Brown et al. 2008; Landale and Oropesa 2007; Smock 2000). This portion of the analysis is based on rates which are measured for each sex group as the number of persons of different sex in a relationship involving a householder and an unmarried partner of a different sex per 1,000 married persons in a given sex group.

Beginning with heterosexual couples, the highest cohabitation rates are found among native-born females (table 8.3). In particular, black females have a cohabitation rate of 243.7 followed by native-born Latina females (214.2). For all racial-place

Table 8.3 *Heterosexual and Same-Sex Cohabitation Rates by Race/Ethnic Group, Sex, and Place of Birth, 2011*

Race/Ethnic Group	Heterosexual Cohabitation Rate[a]							Same-Sex Cohabitation Rate[b]						
	Male			Female				Male			Female			
	Total	Native-Born	Foreign-Born	Total	Native-Born	Foreign-Born	Total	Native-Born	Foreign-Born	Total	Native-Born	Foreign-Born			
Mexican	156.7	180.7	141.7	165.7	212.5	132.9	7.7	13.8	3.9	7.6	14.3	3.0			
Puerto Rican	195.9	191.1	—	271.4	296.5	—	20.0	19.3	—	17.9	19.6	—			
Cuban	133.2	199.6	112.3	131.5	184.1	106.4	14.4	29.7	9.6	10.7	16.9	7.7			
Salvadoran	242.2	391.6	230.6	206.4	287.4	191.2	8.9	39.3	6.5	1.7	9.4	0.3			
Dominican	193.6	365.4	165.6	205.2	243.5	188.9	4.4	23.5	1.3	7.0	15.7	3.3			
Guatemalan	299.2	352.0	295.0	203.7	130.5	219.3	13.2	39.8	11.1	9.9	26.4	6.4			
Colombian	125.5	269.5	100.7	81.9	97.6	72.3	13.9	44.3	8.7	7.9	8.9	7.3			
Other Central American	225.6	262.6	219.0	243.2	215.4	258.7	12.7	65.8	3.2	5.2	6.0	4.8			
Other South American	130.6	264.6	110.5	96.2	93.6	97.7	13.5	73.4	4.5	5.8	6.0	5.7			
Other Latino	142.8	151.9	113.4	146.4	162.6	91.7	17.7	19.4	12.3	18.4	18.8	17.1			
Latino	164.8	187.1	150.0	171.2	214.2	137.6	10.1	17.9	4.9	8.7	15.0	3.9			
White	87.3			92.4			10.3			11.5					
Black	137.0			243.7			8.2			15.5					

[a] For each specific sex group, the number of persons of different sex in a relationship involving a householder and an unmarried partner of a different sex per 1,000 married persons in the given sex group.

[b] For each specific sex group, the number of persons of the same sex in a relationship involving a householder and an unmarried partner of the same sex per 1,000 married persons in a given sex group.

Source: 2011 American Community Survey Public-Use File (Ruggles et al. 2010).

of birth-sex groupings, females have higher cohabitation rates than their male counterparts – the exception being foreign-born Latina females and Latino males. The lowest cohabitation rate exists among white males with 87.3. Native-born Latinos have cohabitation rates twice as high as the rates of white males (187.1 vs. 87.3).

Another interesting characteristic displaying the heterogeneity of Latinos in heterosexual cohabitation rates is illustrated in variations by subgroups/national-origin/ancestry. To begin with, the native-born are more likely to cohabitate than the foreign-born across all Latino subgroups and sexes. Some native-born Latino groups, all of which are males, have rates that are over 350 (Salvadoran, Dominican, and Guatemalan). Furthermore, among the native-born, three subgroups have rates over 250 but less than 300 among males (Colombian, Other Central American, and Other South American) and two subgroups among females (Puerto Rican and Salvadoran). The lowest heterosexual cohabitation rates are found among Colombian and Other South American females. Indeed, five subgroups have rates less than 100 all of which are found among females (native-born and foreign-born Colombian, native-born and foreign-born Other South American, and foreign-born Other Latinas).

We now turn to same-sex cohabitation rates. These rates are calculated as the number of persons of the same sex in a relationship involving a householder and an unmarried partner of the same sex per 1,000 married persons in a given sex group. Overall, the native-born population has higher same-sex cohabitation rates. Specifically, native-born Latino males have the highest same-sex cohabitation rate with 18, followed by native-born Latinas and black females with rates of approximately 15. The lowest same-sex cohabitation rates are found among foreign-born Latinos (males, 4.9% and females, 3.9%).

There are some interesting variations among same-sex cohabitation rates within Latino subgroups. For instance, the highest rates are found among Latino native-born males: Other South Americans (73.4), Other Central Americans (65.8), and Colombians (44.3). The lowest same-sex cohabitation rates exist among foreign-born Mexicans, Salvadorans, Dominicans, Other Central Americans, and Other South Americans.

One caveat is in order for the same-sex cohabitation rates. It is very difficult to obtain information about couples in a homosexual relationship. We cannot verify that the data presented here for same-sex cohabitating couples are actually in a homosexual relationship. As such, readers should interpret the data presented above with some caution.

Children Living in Family Households with Female Householders

Next we examine the percentages of children living in family households with female householders and no husband present by race/ethnicity and place of birth. Overall, blacks are more likely than other groups to have households headed by females without a husband present and with children present. As such, nearly three-fifths of black children live in female-headed households with no husband present (57.5%), followed by nearly one-third of native-born Latino children, one-fifth of foreign-born Latino children, and more than one-sixth of white children (table 8.4).

When considering Latino subgroup differences and place of birth, there are important variations regarding the proportions of children living in female-headed

Table 8.4 *Percentage of Children in Family Households with Female Householders and No Husband Present by Race/Ethnic Group and Place of Birth, 2011*

Race/Ethnic Group	Total	Native-Born	Foreign-Born
Mexican	27.2	27.8	19.1
Puerto Rican	47.8	47.8	—
Cuban	26.5	27.2	22.1
Salvadoran	28.5	28.9	24.2
Dominican	50.6	52.5	39.3
Guatemalan	25.4	26.8	17.7
Colombian	24.6	26.5	15.4
Other Central American	35.9	36.0	34.6
Other South American	21.3	21.8	19.2
Other Latino	30.7	31.3	13.7
Latino	29.8	30.5	20.7
White	17.5		
Black	57.5		

Source: 2011 American Community Survey Public-Use File (Ruggles et al. 2010).

households with no husband present. Specifically, almost half of Puerto Rican (47.8%) and half of native-born Dominican (50.6%) children are living in female-headed households with no husbands present. On the other hand, five subgroups, all foreign-born, have less than one-fifth of children in this household type, resembling the percentages seen among whites – Mexicans (19.19%) Guatemalans (17.7%), Colombians (15.4%), Other South Americans (19.2%), and Other Latinos (13.7%).

Households with Extended Families and Living Alone

The last feature of family structure that we consider is adults living with extended family members and those living alone. The results show that native-born Latinos have higher percentages of adults living with extended family members compared to foreign-born individuals. Indeed, over 30 percent of native-born Latino males and females are living in households with extended family arrangements (table 8.5). Yet, blacks approximate these levels with 27.8 percent of males and 23.4 percent of females living with extended family. Similar to the patterns of blacks, foreign-born Latino males and Latina females both have 24 percent of individuals living with extended family.

While differences between males and females are not too pronounced, place of birth seems to be an important characteristic in identifying patterns of Latino adults living in households with extended family members. The highest prevalence of this type of living arrangement – over 55 percent – are found among native-born males and females in three groups – Salvadorans, Dominicans, and Guatemalans. On the other hand, several Latino subgroups have a quarter or fewer adults living with extended family members all of which are foreign-born Latino males (Mexicans,

Table 8.5 Selected Household Arrangement Characteristics by Race/Ethnic Group, Sex and Place of Birth, 2011

Race/Ethnic Group	Percentage of Adults Living as Extended Family Members						Percentage of Adults Living Alone					
	Male			Female			Male			Female		
	Total	Native-Born	Foreign-Born	Total	Native-Born	Foreign-Born	Total	Native-Born	Foreign-Born	Total	Native-Born	Foreign-Born
Mexican	30.5	38.1	23.5	28.3	33.0	23.3	5.6	7.3	4.2	5.1	6.9	3.2
Puerto Rican	26.8	27.0	—	23.2	23.2	—	11.1	11.1	—	11.7	11.6	—
Cuban	27.4	34.6	24.1	29.4	32.0	28.2	10.4	9.9	10.6	11.0	8.2	12.2
Salvadoran	32.6	61.0	25.9	30.8	55.0	25.4	3.9	3.6	3.9	3.9	3.7	3.9
Dominican	39.5	59.4	30.8	30.2	47.2	24.7	6.0	5.8	6.1	6.8	5.7	7.1
Guatemalan	30.9	58.4	26.4	29.6	55.3	24.3	3.8	5.0	3.6	3.2	3.6	3.1
Colombian	27.2	45.6	21.4	26.7	36.2	24.4	8.7	7.9	8.9	6.9	7.6	6.7
Other Central American	28.9	47.4	23.3	27.1	37.8	24.0	6.3	7.9	5.8	7.2	11.2	6.1
Other South American	27.2	43.8	23.0	26.3	37.6	23.5	7.7	7.7	7.7	7.4	7.1	7.5
Other Latino	25.7	27.9	16.5	23.0	23.7	20.4	12.1	12.9	9.0	13.6	14.6	9.9
Latino	29.9	36.3	23.9	27.6	31.2	23.9	6.7	8.4	5.1	6.6	8.4	4.8
White	14.9			12.8			13.4			16.4		
Black	27.8			23.4			14.8			16.8		

Source: 2011 American Community Survey Public-Use File (Ruggles et al. 2010).

Cubans, Colombians, Other Central Americans, Other South Americans, and Other Latinos) and females (all groups except for Cubans). This pattern questions research that finds that immigrants are more likely to live in households with extended family given their newcomer status where they need time to find a job and learn a new language (Zambrana 2011), though this may be due to the lack of kin living nearby.

In contrast to living with family members are those that live alone. Overall, non-Latino adults are almost twice as likely as native-born Lations to live alone. In particular, the largest percentages of adults living alone are among white and black females, both of which have approximately 16 percent of adults living alone. Their male counterparts have slightly lower percentages with 13.4 percent among whites and 14.8 percent among blacks. The lowest percentages of adults living alone are found among foreign-born Latinos. Indeed, foreign-born Latinos and foreign-born Latinas each have about 5 percent of adults living alone. In terms of subgroup variations, the largest percentages are between 11 and 15 percent among native-born males (Puerto Ricans and Other Latinos), native-born females (Puerto Ricans, Other Central Americans, and Other Latinas), and foreign-born Cuban females.

Questions Related to the Future of Latino Families

Transnationalism, Family Separation, and Parenting

Smith-Morris et al. (2012) eloquently describe the complexity of family among migrants as being "simultaneously a reason to go, a reason to stay, and the reason to return; family is the destination and that which was left 'at home'" (p. 51). In the sociology of Latino families an emerging field is the study of the effects of globalization on families, particularly those who are separated by migratory processes or transnational families. Dreby (2006) defines transnational families as consisting of "members of the nuclear unit (mother, father, and children) [living] in two different countries" (p. 33). This family structure arose as a strategy for economic survival where one or more of the core family members migrate internationally while some or all of the dependents stay in the home country (Abrego 2009; Schmalzbauer 2005). While this pattern of family separation in migration streams to the US has been recently conceptualized as "transnationalism," it is not a new trend (Foner 1997; Glenn 2002; Massey et al. 1987; Robles and Watkins 1993).Yet, it is increasingly important to consider given the prevalence of transnationalism among Latin American migrants (Suárez-Orozco et al. 2002) and the prolonged time it takes to reunite with family members (Dreby 2010).

There are many burdens associated with the separation of immigrant families. For instance, transnational families have the added burden of dealing with geographical distances that hamper the maintenance of family ties and inequalities that block their economic stability (Abrego 2009). Suárez-Orozco et al. (2002) note that the stress of family separation has negative consequences for the mental health and educational outcomes of children. Studies of transnational families consisting of migrant parents and non-migrant children have examined parenting practices (Abrego 2009; Dreby 2006; Menjivar and Abrego 2009) and the emotional costs to transnational families (Hondagneu-Sotelo and Avila 1997; Suárez-Orozco et al. 2002), especially among families where the mother is away (Abrego 2009).

There are some interesting variations in transnational parenting along gender lines. Dreby (2010), for instance, highlights the gendered inequalities in transnational parenting and the emotional hardships it adds to families. While mothers and fathers parent in similar ways (i.e., phone calls, gifts, and economic remittances), the expectation that mothers be the emotional caregiver remains, which creates conflict when mothers try to re-establish connections with their children (Nazario 2007).

Examining how gender differences in transnational parenting influence economic remittances, Abrego (2009) argued that even though migrant fathers earn more than migrant mothers, families where the father had migrated did not thrive more than those in which the mother migrated. Indeed, some of the father-away families were barely surviving economically compared to mother-away families. Abrego (2009) attributed this to a couple of causes. First, mother-away families tend to receive more consistent remittances in comparison to father-away families due to the social construction of motherhood as a selfless and morally superior family member where the needs of the children are prioritized ahead of their own (Abrego 2009). Second, migrant mothers stay committed to their children even when their relationship status changes, whereas fathers associate fathering as a material responsibility. Therefore, if the partnership ends, fathers also diminish their ties with their children in contrast to the mother (Abrego 2009).

Deportations

In contrast to political rhetoric about the importance of family unity, federal administrative policies have separated families through deportations. Indeed, the Illegal Immigration Reform and Immigrant Responsibility Act (IIRIRA) of 1996 broadened the types of crimes in the US (including misdemeanors) for which a legal resident can be detained and deported. Yet, in 1996 deportations was not as pressing an issue as it is today. The administration of President Obama has deported more immigrants than the George W. Bush administration (Lopez and Gonzalez-Barrera 2013b). For comparative purposes we calculated the average deportations of *non-criminal* migrants based on data from the Department of Homeland Security (DHS). We found that President Obama removed 1,266,803 non-criminal and 1,066,954 criminal migrants between 2009 and 2014 (US Department of Homeland Security 2013; US Immigration and Customs Enforcement 2014). Indeed, President Obama's average annual removal of non-criminal migrants for 2009–14 is 211,133 in comparison to 161,416 for President George W. Bush's two-term period (2001–8) (US Department of Homeland Security 2011, 2012). For instance, in 2011, 392,000 migrants were removed from the US of which only 48 percent were for breaking US laws, including drug trafficking, driving under the influence, and entering the country illegally (Lopez and Gonzalez-Barrera 2013b). While these trends are a concern for all migrants, they are especially disconcerting for Mexicans. In 2009, for example, more than 70 percent of deportees were Mexican according to Department of Homeland Security data (Passel and Cohn 2012).

Deportations not only impact the individual migrant but the entire family. Deportations produce a range of "unintended consequences" including "fracturing families and placing women in many harmful situations, specifically leaving mothers in emotional pain and severe danger of lasting physical and mental harm" (Gomes and Ross-Sheriff 2011, p. 122). In cases where one or both parents are deported, the children remain in the US in the care of other family members or friends.

To date most scholarly attention has focused on parent–child separations due to migration, while less attention has been given to families separated by detentions and deportations. An exception is Beckles Flores (2011) who describes how attachment bonds are uniquely impacted by parent–child separation due to deportation. Indeed, deportations cause immediate and long-term effects on the self, the parent(s), and the family. Unmitigated by sufficient coping skills, the intense stress caused by deportation leaves children at risk for feeling isolated, abandoned, hopeless, angry, and scared.

Mixed-Status Households

Another issue impacting Latino families is households with members of mixed-citizenship statuses. According to the National Council of La Raza (2009), about 62 percent of Latino households are mixed-status households, meaning that one or more people living in the household are undocumented immigrant(s). As such, some family members may be US citizens, others could be documented (various types of visas), and still others may be unauthorized. This situation translates to inequality among household members.

To date, most of the research on mixed-status households concerns the utilization of social services. Latino undocumented parent(s) may be apprehensive to seek services for their US-born children given fears of deportation or detention. Yet, Xu and Brabeck (2012) found that Latino families headed by undocumented parents access services for their children at equivalent rates to those of documented parents. In particular, fears of deportation are counteracted by undocumented parents' utilization of their social networks to help them navigate the system.

On the other hand, in cases of Latino children who are in the welfare system and in need of alternative housing, mixed-status households present a challenge. While the number of Latino children in need of alternative family placements has doubled in the last 15 years, kinship placements are a challenge in mixed-status households (Ayón et al. 2013). Before being placed in a home, all the residents of the household must pass background checks which create fears of deportation for undocumented members.

Latino Same-Sex Couples

Another issue that has received minimal attention relates to how the current political climate is affecting same-sex Latino couples. An exception is the work of Cahill (2009) who argued that anti-gay family policies have a disproportionate impact on Latino and black same-sex couples. In particular, anti-gay policies have a stronger adversarial impact on Latino same-sex couples than on white same-sex couples because they are more likely to be raising children, earn less, and are less likely to own their home. For instance, according to the National Gay and Lesbian Task Force Policy Institute, among couples where both partners are Latino, 58 percent of male same-sex couples are raising children compared to 19 percent of white male same-sex couples. In regards to females, couples where both partners are Latinas are over twice as likely to be raising children compared to white same-sex couples (66% vs. 32%, respectively) (Cahill 2009).

Furthermore, Latinos in same-sex partnerships are disproportionately impacted by immigration policies given that the US Citizenship and Immigration Services does not recognize same-sex couple families. In particular, Latino gay men with Latino partners are 17 times more likely than white men in same-sex couples and six times more likely than Latino men in Latino inter-ethnic same-sex couples to report they are not US citizens. In regards to females in same-sex partnerships, couples where both partners are of Latin origin are significantly more likely to be non-citizens than white men and white women in same-sex partnerships (Cahill 2009). Cahill (2009) concluded that despite anti-gay movements that seek to divide communities of color from gay communities, Latino LGBT (lesbian, gay, bisexual, and transgender) families would benefit significantly from non-discrimination policies and from protection offered by family recognition given their social demographic characteristics.

Summary

This chapter provided an overview of the theoretical debates in studies about Latino families. Given that early scholarship on Latino families utilized the culture of poverty framework, culture versus structure theoretical discussions are central to examining Latino families. Yet, individual approaches to culture lead to remedies that are also individualistic rather than focusing on the structural context that reproduce social and economic inequalities among Latino families.

In addition, we presented data that demonstrated the manner in which Latinos generally depart from whites and blacks in terms of family/household structural patterns. In particular, the findings show wide variations in the family and household arrangements as well as marriage patterns across Latino groups, particularly along the lines of place of birth.

Moreover, we raised some important issues that are currently affecting the status of Latino families that we suspect will continue to impact them in the future if precautions are not taken. Most of the issues highlighted concern the status of immigrants who are a significant segment of Latino families. The socioeconomic and political dynamics surrounding migration and citizenship in the US hamper the incorporation of unauthorized migrants (and legal permanent residents to some extent) and create challenges for Latino families.

The family has long represented a source of social support for Latinos. For many Latinos, religion has played an important role in the provision of social support as well as spiritual guidance. We now turn our attention in the next chapter to examine the religious life of Latinos.

9 Religion

Religion has sustained Latinos and their families throughout their lives in their countries-of-origin and in the US. The Catholic roots of Latinos extend deeply to their Latin American provenance and the colonial period in which Latin Americans were transformed in so many ways, including their religion (Matovina 2012; Palmer-Boyes 2010; Treviño 2006). As Mexicans and other Latin Americans have made their way to the US, they have brought with them their religion which continues to be predominantly Catholic.

Despite some declines over the last few decades, Catholicism continues to represent the religion of choice for more than two-thirds (68%) of Latinos in the US (Pew Research Center's Hispanic Trends Project 2007a). Latinos continue to be distinct from mainstream Catholics in numerous ways (Palmer-Boyes 2010; Pew Research Center's Hispanic Trends Project 2007a). For example, Palmer-Boyes (2010) observes that Latinos are distinct from other Catholics in two ways: (1) based on cultural norms and (2) based on the immigrant status of congregants. In addition, Latino Catholics deviate from the more traditional and official practices that epitomize being Catholic – "Mass attendance, communion, and involvement in parish life" (Palmer-Boyes 2010). Latinos are more likely to engage in broader practices and activities beyond the confines of the more traditional and official practices. As such, many Latinos are seen as "popular Catholics" with common practices "more loosely related to institutional involvement, characterized instead by cultural rituals and devotions rooted in indigenous heritage and often fused with civic and social celebrations" (Palmer-Boyes 2010, p. 305). Such celebrations include baptisms, weddings, funerals, *las Posadas* (annual nine-day celebration reenacting Joseph and Mary's trek from Nazareth to Bethlehem), and the Feast of the Virgin of Guadalupe (Palmer-Boyes 2010). Moreover, Latino Catholics are significantly more likely than other Catholics to incorporate charismatic activities into their worship. Charismatic conventions include speaking in tongues, raising of hands, clapping, shouting, and jumping (Palmer-Boyes 2010). Latinos are five times more likely than non-Latino Catholics to worship in a charismatic fashion (Pew Research Center's Hispanic Trends Project 2007a). Furthermore, Latino parishes are more likely than non-Latino parishes to have social services and programs that cater to the needs of immigrants, providing such services as English-language courses, citizenship training courses, job training, and assistance with immigration-related matters (Martini 2012; Matovina 2012; Odem 2004; Palmer-Boyes 2010; Stevens-Arroyo 2010; Sullivan 2000). Finally, Latino Catholics are more likely than other Catholics to pray to saints and to Our Lady of Guadalupe rather than directly to God (Krause and Bastida 2011). It is felt that because of the purity of the saints and the belief that they inhabit heaven with God, they are in a much better position to intercede on their behalf than are people themselves (Krause and Bastida 2011; Oktavec 1995).

Over the last several decades, we have seen growing numbers of Catholics convert to Protestant and evangelical religions (Ellison et al. 2005; Hunt 1999; Matovina 2012). Latinos who leave the Catholic faith in favor of a different religion report that their reason for doing so was that they were searching for a smaller and more intimate group as well as more active engagement (Matovina 2012). Furthermore, these individuals tend to be drawn to a more "direct and personal experience of God" in the Protestant religion (Matovina 2012, p. 106). Nonetheless, as suggested by the religious marketplace perspective, some Latinos maintain attachments with multiple religions. Despite the growing numbers of Latinos breaking away from the Catholic faith, however, Putnam and Campbell (2010) note that the defection of Latinos from Catholicism is not an anomaly – rather, their defection rate is lower than that of whites.

This transformation is due to the influences of the major Latino demographic force stemming from immigration and a youthful population (Palmer-Boyes 2010; Pew Research Center's Hispanic Trends Project 2007a; Poyo 2010). From 1970 to 2000, the Latino Catholic population increased by 18 million, accounting for nearly 90 percent of the overall national Catholic growth during this period (Poyo 2010). Today Latinos account for approximately one-third of US Catholics (Matovina 2012; Pew Research Center's Hispanic Trends Project 2007a). Furthermore, Latinos will fuel the projected growth of the US Catholic population over the next several decades, which will result in Catholics outnumbering Protestants in the younger ages for the first time ever by 2043 and in overall population by the mid-twenty-first century (Skirbekk et al. 2010). Putnam and Campbell (2010) observe that the US Catholic Church will become an institution with a majority Latino population in the near future.

The impact of Latinos on American religion extends beyond the Catholic Church. Over the last several decades the share of Latinos who belong to non-Catholic denominations has expanded (Barton 2010; Sánchez Walsh 2010). While still more than two-thirds (68 percent) of Latinos are Catholic, 15 percent are evangelical Protestant, 5 percent are mainline Protestants, and 3 percent belong to other Christian denominations (Pew Research Center's Hispanic Trends Project 2007a). The proselytizing and recruitment of Latinos on the part of non-Catholic denominations promises to be more intense as their memberships decline due to an aging white population. Furthermore, due to the movement of Latinos to new-destination areas, the influence of Latinos on American religion extends to locations beyond the regions where Latinos have historically been concentrated (López-Sanders 2012; Matovina 2012).

This chapter provides an overview of the religious life of Latinos. We begin with an examination of the deep historical roots of Catholicism extending back to the colonial period and the unique form of the religion that emerged in Mexico involving the blending of traditional Catholic and indigenous influences. Subsequently, we highlight theoretical perspectives that are useful in understanding the role that religion plays in the lives of Latinos. Moreover, we discuss contemporary trends related to religion among Latinos, including demographic and socioeconomic variations across people who belong to different religions. Finally, we draw attention to major questions and issues that are likely to have an impact on the religious life of Latinos in the near future.

Historical Ties of Latinos to Catholicism and Our Lady of Guadalupe

The roots of the Latino experience in the Americas extend back to the conquest of the indigenous population at the hands of Spanish colonizers. While indigenous people had been in the Americas for centuries, the Italian navigator, Christopher Columbus, exploring on behalf of the Spanish crown, made four round-trip voyages to the Americas between 1492 and 1503. The Catholic religion of Latinos represents yet another strong legacy stemming from the Spanish conquest. The Spanish colonizers, armed with their superior weaponry including cannons, demolished indigenous religions. For example, Hernan Cortez reached the Aztec empire located in Tenochtitlan, situated in present-day Mexico City, in 1519 and in a matter of a couple of years had conquered the Aztec empire (León-Portilla 1962). The conquest included the razing of Aztec temples and pyramids. As these were leveled and buried, they were replaced by crosses and eventually Catholic churches. The Spanish conquerors saw part of their mission, aside from securing the riches of the conquered, as saving the souls of the indigenous population, which they saw as heathen savages (Rodriguez 1994). Indeed, the Spanish questioned whether the indigenous people even had a soul, thus doubting that they were human (Elizondo 1980; Rodriguez 1994). Nonetheless, the indigenous population did not easily accept Catholicism and the demolition of their religions and religious beliefs. Rodriguez (1994) outlines the bitterness that the Aztec people felt after the fall of the Aztec empire:

> The people ... could not accept a religion that asked them to negate their entire metaphysics, the way they understood reality. They also could not comprehend the missionaries, who were admired and respected because of the simplicity of their lives, came from the same religion and spiritual origin as the abusive and brutal conquistadors. The Aztec insurgents of the day were fighting not merely against Spain but against Catholicism. It was evident to them that the two things were intimately connected. (p. 13)

Thus, Catholicism in Mexico, as is the case in other parts of Latin America, took on a different form. In particular, Catholicism in the Americas can best be characterized as religious syncretism which involves a blending of traditional Catholicism and indigenous influences.

The root of this melding of the two forms of religion in Mexico extends back to the apparition of the Virgin of Guadalupe to Juan Diego, an indigenous man who had recently converted to Catholicism, shortly after the fall of the Aztec empire. On December 9, 1531, Juan Diego encountered her in the hill of Tepeyac, located northwest of present-day Mexico City. Garibay (1967) describes the meeting:

> She [the Virgin] instructed him [Juan Diego] to have the Bishop Zumárraga build a church on the site. Three days later in a second appearance she told Juan Diego to pick flowers and take them to the bishop. When he presented them as instructed, roses fell out of his mantle and beneath them was the painted image of the Lady. (p. 821; see also Rodriguez 1994, p. 17)

The story describing the apparition of Our Lady of Guadalupe and the series of subsequent events is described by Elizondo (1980, pp. 75–9). Rodriguez (1994) stresses the significance of the apparition of the Virgin with her indigenous features to Juan Diego, an indigenous man, along two lines: "(1) it was the foundation of Mexican

Christianity and (2) it provided a *connection* between the indigenous and Spanish cultures" (p. 45). Thus, the apparition marked the conversion of the indigenous people and the base of Mexican Christianity (Rodriguez 1994). Indeed, the apparition represented a watershed in the conversion of the indigenous, as Rodriguez (1994) points out. Madsen (1967) notes that this form of religion is aptly called "Guadalupinist Catholicism" (p. 378; see also Rodriguez 1994, p. 45). The impact of the apparition on the conversion of indigenous people is reflected in that 9,000,000 Aztec individuals were baptized into Christianity only six years following the apparition (Elizondo 1980; Madsen 1967; Rodriguez 1994). The Virgin of Guadalupe became the symbol of Indian (Guadalupinist) Catholicism as distinct from the traditional Catholicism of the Spanish conquerors (Rodriguez 1994).

The apparition also provides a link between indigenous and Spanish cultures. This link stems from the actual name of the Virgin. The apparition involved an episode in which the Virgin paid a visit to Juan Diego's uncle who was seriously ill. The Spaniards asked the uncle if the Virgin told him her name. He responded by saying that she said her name was "Tlecuauhtlacupeuh," which in Nahuatl means *"La que viene volando de la luz como el águila de fuego* (she who comes flying from the region of light like the eagle of fire)" (Echeagaray 1981, p. 21; Rodriguez 1994, p. 46). Rodriguez (1994) notes that "The region of light was the dwelling place of the Aztec gods, and the eagle was a sign from the gods" (p. 46). The Spaniards believed that they heard the name "Guadalupe," which they immediately associated with the Guadalupe of Estremadura in Spain (Rodriguez 1994). A significant share of Spanish conquerors originated from the Spanish province of Estremadura and devotion to Our Lady of Guadalupe de Estremadura was very high at the time that the Spanish started making their way to the Americas (Rodriguez 1994). Thus, the name of Guadalupe was quickly adopted by the Spanish, although the Nahuatl language does not contain the letters "d" and "g" (Rodriguez 1994).

Nonetheless, the indigenous – through the name of Tlecuauhtlacupeuh – and the Spanish – through the name Guadalupe – were able to view the apparition in personal terms and something that could be understood and embraced from their own perspectives (Rodriguez 1994). The linkage of the apparition to the culture of each group reflected the religious syncretism that was the outcome. This syncretism involving the merging of mainstream Catholicism and indigenous religious beliefs and practices was repeated throughout Latin America to incorporate Inca and Mayan patterns (Palmer-Boyes 2010; Stanzione 2003).

Having obtained a historical context for understanding the deep historical roots of Latinos to Catholicism and to Our Lady of Guadalupe, we now turn to an overview of theoretical perspectives that are useful in understanding the contemporary religious life of Latinos.

Theoretical Perspectives

Interest in the sociology of religion has grown significantly over the last several decades. Indeed, in their review of the sociology of religion literature, Sherkat and Ellison (1999) observe that "The wealth of empirical findings about religious beliefs, commitments, and institutions and their consequences left the field open for new theoretical insights, and the trickle of theoretical perspicacity that began in the late

1970s turned into a flood by the early 1990s" (p. 378). Interest in religious matters related to Latinos has also increased tremendously. For example, our review of peer-reviewed journal articles catalogued in *Sociological Abstracts* with the combination of keywords – "religion" and "Hispanic" or "Latino" – has surged over time: 1960–9, 5 articles; 1970–9, 8; 1980–9, 19; 1990–9, 69; and 2000–9, 108. Between 2010 and 2013, in a mere three years, 67 articles had already been published, about three-fifths of the total number of 108 published during the ten years between 2000 and 2009.

Religion as Social Capital

Propelled by the Robert Putnam (2000) book titled *Bowling Alone: The Collapse and Revival of American Community*, social scientists have called significant attention to the concept of social capital over the last couple of decades. Putnam defines social capital as "connections among individuals – social networks and the norms of reciprocity and trustworthiness that arise from them" (p. 19). Religious associations represent the "producers and facilitators of social capital" (Hye-cheon et al. 2012, p. 332). Religion is at the center of many organizational and civic activities in the US. Putnam (2000) highlights the role of religion in the establishment of social capital. Accordingly, Putnam (2000) points out that "Faith communities in which people worship together are arguably the single most important repository of social capital in America" (p. 66). Bruhn (2011) adds that:

> Religion is an important source of social capital. People of like-minded faith come together to form social networks that create interest in each other's welfare and provide an ongoing resource for social support and trusting relationships. (p. 206)

As such, people with a religious orientation draw a variety of benefits from their social connections with people with whom they participate in religious services and share deep religious convictions and fellowship. In particular, such people gain a "sense of community and group solidarity" from their religious social attachments (Bruhn 2011, p. 185).

Putnam (2000) distinguishes between two types of social capital based on whether people are linked within groups or across groups. Bonding social capital involves the strengthening of social ties among people who belong to the same group or organization, such as members of a given church. In such instances, people in the social network have very close and interpersonal relations and exhibit a great amount of care for the well-being of each other. On the other hand, bridging social capital involves the linkage of people to individuals from other groups or organizations, such as across denominational groups, racial and ethnic organizations, and non-religious organizations. Typically, religious organizations tend to facilitate bonding social capital to the neglect of bridging capital (Williams and Loret de Mola 2007).

Social capital derived from religious activities is associated with a variety of favorable outcomes. We highlight here the association between social capital and the deterrence of alcohol, drugs, and crime among teenagers and health outcomes. Religion has long been observed to be a deterrent to crime and deviance. Sherkat and Ellison (1999) outline the reasons for the deterrence impact of religion on crime and deviance:

(a) the internalization of religious norms and moral messages; (b) the fear of divine punishment (the so-called "hellfire" effect); (c) the threat of social sanctions for coreligionists; (d) the desire for approval from reference groups within religious communities; and (e) the lack of exposure to (or time for) deviant pursuits due to involvement in religious activities and networks, among other possible effects. (pp. 375-6)

The context in which people participate in religious activities, replete with shared norms and expectations, social sanctions for being out of line, the pursuit of social approval from one's network, and an immersion in church-related activities that reinforces in-group associations with like-minded individuals, serve to shelter individuals from crime and deviance.

Bartkowski and Xu (2007) use a social capital of religiosity framework to understand drug use among teenagers. Drawing on the work of Putnam (2000), Bartkowski and Xu (2007) conceptualize social capital as comprised of three key components: norms, networks, and trust. In particular, Bartkowski and Xu (2007) characterize social capital as consisting of "exposure to and internalization of religious norms (gauged respectively by denominational affiliation and religious salience)"; "integration within religious networks (measured through worship service attendance as well as participation in faith-based youth groups and Scouts)"; and "expressions of religious trust (measured through trust in God)" (pp. S182-3). In their 1996 nationally representative study of high school seniors, Bartkowski and Xu (2000) found that teenagers who were more integrated into their religious networks – measured by the frequency of church attendance – had lower levels of drug use compared to their peers who were less integrated into their religious networks. Thus, youngsters connected to church life are more likely than their peers without such ties to fall for peer pressure associated with drug use. Other indicators of social capital (denominational affiliation, religious salience, religious trust, and faith-based civic participation), however, were not significantly associated with teenage drug use.

While the Bartkowski and Xu study was based on a nationally representative sample of high school seniors, it did not focus on the racial/ethnic group of respondents, aside from a variable that takes into account whether a person is black or not. Unfortunately, this is a common trend as some researchers (Hodge et al. 2011) have noted the absence of much research examining the association between religion and substance abuse and related phenomena among Latino youth. Hodge et al. (2011) use the Bartkowski and Xu social capital of religiosity to examine substance use among Mexican-origin teenagers. Based on data from a drug prevention study on fifth grade students in 39 schools located in low-income and inner-city areas and collected at four points in time, Hodge et al. (2011) also found that religious attendance – a measure of integration into religious networks – was the most important indicator of social capital deterring Mexican-origin students from substance use. Specifically, students who attended church more regularly at time 1 tended to have lower substance use at time 2 (30 days after the church attendance was measured as well as lifetime substance use at any time). Thus, there is evidence that integration and participation in religious activities provide important social bonds that allow Latino youngsters to refrain from substance use.

Similarly, research has observed the value of religion – particularly with respect to attendance in religious services – in health outcomes (Hye-cheon et al. 2012). Drawing on theoretical insights extending back to Durkheim on the integrative and regulatory functions of religion, Sherkat and Ellison (1999, p. 374) argue that people who are integrated into religious groups gain a sense of community from which they benefit emotionally and socially from feeling "loved, valued, and cared for." Furthermore, individuals who are integrated into religious communities are subject to regulatory prohibitions against the use and abuse of tobacco, drugs, and alcohol, as well as against risky and deviant behaviors, with the result being more favorable health outcomes (Bruhn 2011; Sherkat and Ellison 1999). In sum, Sherkat and Ellison (1999) argue that participation in religious activities is likely to govern personal behavior which in turn results in people having a lower likelihood of disease. In such a case, then, social capital serves as a mediator between religious attendance and health outcomes (Hye-cheon et al. 2012).

Hye-cheon et al.'s (2012) research, utilizing data from the 2006 Social Capital Community Benchmark Survey, supports the mediating role of social capital in the association between religiosity and health outcomes. In particular, Hye-cheon et al. (2012) observe that people who are more involved in religious activities tend to have greater involvement in formal groups associated with giving and volunteering – a reflection of contribution to the public good (Leonard et al. 2010), which results in more positive self-reported health. Furthermore, Strawbridge et al. (1997) found that adults in Alameda County in California, who had greater participation in their church or synagogue, tended to have lower death rates compared to those with more limited religious participation. Bruhn (2011) points out that people with more favorable risks of death tended to have better health practices, higher levels of social connections, and more stable marriages.

While these findings are based on general populations and do not focus exclusively on Latinos, there are some studies that demonstrate the value of religiosity on the health conditions of Latinos. For example, Berges et al. (2010) discovered that Mexican American elderly who had a high frequency of religious attendance (nearly once a week or more than once a week) were significantly less likely to develop disabilities associated with activities of daily living (ADL) compared to their counterparts who did not have high rates of religious attendance. This finding held even after controlling for changes in health conditions and mobility over time.

Yet, Latinos tend to deviate somewhat from other groups with respect to the recipient of their prayers. Thus, rather than praying directly to God, Catholic Latinos tend to be more likely than other groups to pray to saints and the Virgin of Guadalupe, who serve as intermediaries between the petitioner and God (Krause and Bastida 2011; Oktavec 1995; Rodriguez 1994). Based on a study of older Mexican American Catholics, Krause and Bastida (2011) found that people who attended church more frequently tended to be more likely to believe in the effectiveness of prayers to saints and the Virgin of Guadalupe. Saints play a central role for both immigrant and native-born Latinos. In the case of Latino migrant journeys, Toribio Romo, known as the "holy smuggler," is a saint known to help migrants in the desert find their way to the US (Romo 2010). Jesús Malverde, a Robin Hood-like figure who is the patron saint of drug traffickers, has been appropriated by Mexican immigrants who call on him for assistance in making the trek to the US (Murphy 2008). Among older Mexican Americans, those who pray to religious entities are more likely to believe that God is helping them control important aspects of their lives (Krause and Bastida 2011). Finally, older Mexican Americans who believe that God is assisting them in this way are more likely to be optimistic, which, in turn, is associated with more favorable health. These studies provide some evidence of the importance of religion in the lives of Latinos.

Immigration Integration

Extending back to the earliest immigrants to the US, religion has played an important role in providing adherents with an identity, support for co-religionists, and guidance in integrating into the host society. An interest in the religiosity of post-1965 immigrants has arisen since the early 1990s (Cadge and Ecklund 2007). Religious organizations have historically been helpful in the sustenance and integration of new immigrants into their new places where they settle. We highlight ways in which churches assist immigrants in the incorporation process. In particular, we provide an overview below on the dimensions related to identity maintenance, boundary expansion, civic engagement, and political participation.

Upon arrival in the US, immigrants are drawn to others like themselves. For example, at varying points in time, Irish, Italian, and Mexican immigrants have settled in ethnic enclaves, geographic settings where people from their countries were concentrated. In ethnic enclaves immigrants find others who are similar to them with respect to language, origin, culture, and socioeconomic status. Immigrants find people who can provide a variety of support adjusting to life in their new country, assistance in securing employment, and a setting where they can maintain their sense of ethnic community (Bruhn 2011; López-Sanders 2012; Warner and Wittner 1998). Religious organizations provide newcomers with a place where they can sustain their ethnic identity and culture in their new country (Cadge and Ecklund 2007).

López-Sanders (2012) conducted an ethnographic study of three churches located in the Greenville-Spartanburg-Anderson (GSA) region of South Carolina to understand how they incorporated Colombian, Mexican, and Guatemalan immigrants. López-Sanders (2012) describes the formation of three churches along racial/ethnic lines and the central role that religion plays in their members' lives. The three churches also differed in the activities that they pursue to assist Latinos incorporate into the GSA region. Of the three churches the Catholic Church of the Resurrection best illustrates the incorporation dimension associated with identity maintenance. The congregants of Resurrection are exclusively Guatemalan and the leadership consists of a white bilingual priest who presides over the sacrament along with a dozen Guatemalan lay leaders who are involved in the administrative affairs of the church. The roots of Resurrection stem from Los Angeles, the original settlement of this group of Guatemalan immigrants. The Guatemalan congregants are held together by language, the small size of the church membership, and the ethnic homogeneity of the worshippers (López-Sanders 2012). The Guatemalan immigrants are very much aware and conscious of their language and ethnic differences with other Latinos in the GSA region. In particular, they are not comfortable speaking Spanish and their Mayan language and their physical features along with their low levels of education set them apart from other Latinos in the area. López-Sanders (2012) observes that the homogeneity of the group in the church allows Guatemalans to "reproduce the social cohesion characteristics of Mayan communities in their country-of-origin" (p. 142). Moreover, the Guatemalan congregants maintain strong ties to the communities from where they originate in Guatemala as evident in the number of remittances and community projects they support in the sending community (e.g., renovation projects, funding the feasts of the patron saints of their home villages) (López-Sanders 2012). Thus, the Catholic Church of the Resurrection provides a haven for Guatemalan immigrants where they maintain their ethnicity, speak their Mayan language, and sustain ties to their home communities which help bridge their transnational existence.

A second element associated with the incorporation of immigrants concerns boundary expansion. Racial and ethnic groups exhibit social boundaries where they operate and interact with each other. Frederick Barth (1969) brought to the forefront the way in which racial/ethnic groups construct and negotiate boundaries (see Alba and Nee 2003; Frank et al. 2010).

In contrast to the experience of Guatemalans in the Catholic Church of Resurrection, López-Sanders (2012) observes that whites and Mexicans made changes in their boundaries that brought Mexicans into Harvest Church, a white non-denominational Protestant church. Harvest Church is located in a suburban area close to trailer parks and other low-income housing where Latinos live (López-Sanders 2012). The church ventured to attract Latino newcomers and to assist them integrate into the community. The church members had some contact with the local Latino workers as they either worked with them or were their employers. Some church members began to stop by the local Latino areas and encourage them to visit their church. Latinos started coming to the church and now make up 20 of the 140 families that belong to the church. The church has developed a series of activities, including bible camps and hiring a community liaison, in efforts to help integrate Latinos into the church, efforts that are somewhat difficult given language barriers across groups (López-Sanders 2012).

Yet, for the most part, it is Latinos who are being transformed rather than the white congregants themselves, as evident in their placement in the church where Latinos sit in the back with a person translating scripture from English to Spanish. Nonetheless, for the most part, Latinos have not ceded their Catholicism as well as their participation in religious-oriented rites, such as baptisms, and traditions including the celebration of the Virgin of Guadalupe (López-Sanders 2012). This is in contrast to other more traditional Protestant churches in the area that do not allow Latinos to join unless they renounce their Catholic religion. Moreover, Latinos report that they gain benefits from their attendance and participation at church, such as learning how to acculturate to white norms. For example, Mariana, a 45-year-old woman who attends the church, intimates that she learns how to think and behave by paying attention to what her "hermanos Americanos [American brothers/sisters] at church do and say" (López-Sanders 2012, p. 137). Mariana also believes that her attendance and participation in church functions shows to her employer that "she is responsible" (López-Sanders 2012), which she credits for her advancement in her job.

Again, stratified relationships in which Latinos are the beneficiaries of the so-called goodwill of whites are evident at Harvest. López-Sanders (2012) observes that Harvest's openness to Latino cultural norms and the socioeconomic benefits that come with learning Anglo-Saxon norms and developing social networks with whites comes at a price:

> This type of incorporation, however, has implications for the nature of Latino integration. In brokering this integration, the church reproduces the asymmetric position that whites and Latinos have in the social structure. For example, many white parishioners are the employers of Latino members in the church. Although the church has a participatory structure – decisions fall on members rather than on a board of directors – Latinos participate very little, if at all, in the decision-making process of the church. Latinos depend on the "charity" of white parishioners, as they are the church's major economic contributors. As such, the well-intended efforts to integrate Latinos into the community could be interpreted as patronizing or condescending. (p. 139)

Nonetheless, López-Sanders (2012) makes reference to individuals who see the relationship between whites and Latinos in Harvest Church more favorably. Joseph, the white church pastor, points out:

> We genuinely love the Hispanic community. We actually feel a connection with them. We feel that they give just as much to us as we give to them. They enrich our lives as much as we enrich theirs. So I think that they realize that we are not just there because of obligation. It is very rewarding for us to get to know them to learn about their culture, to learn about where they come from. (López-Sanders 2012, pp. 139–40)

Eulalio, a Central American immigrant, adds that "Harvest is a mix of Americans and Hispanics, but we all get along, we have good friendships, and Joseph has a gift to make everyone feel welcome" (López-Sanders 2012, p. 140).

Thus, regardless of how we view the relationship between Latinos and whites at Harvest Church, it is clear that both groups have expanded their social boundaries to relate to one another in the confines of the church and beyond.

A third manner in which religion serves to incorporate immigrants is through getting them civically engaged. Over the last couple of decades there has been growing interest in the association between religion and civic engagement (Cadge and Ecklund 2007). Cadge and Ecklund (2007) note that "Civil actions are generally voluntary, not aimed at reaping an economic profit, and are often concerned with improving some version of the common good" (p. 366). Churches and church leaders often can spur their members to become engaged in various forms of civic life to contribute to the overall common good. Latino parishes and congregations tend to be particularly active in the provision of social and community services (Martini 2012; Palmer-Boyes 2010). Such services include efforts to improve housing and schools and endeavors to reduce crime (Martini 2012). In San Antonio, Latino Catholics have a long history of civic engagement and efforts to better Latino neighborhoods through their work with San Antonio's Communities Organized for Public Service (COPS) (Matovina 2012). It has been observed that religious organizations are particularly important for Latinos in the encouragement of civic engagement as whites are more likely to engage civically through a broader set of types of organizations (Jones-Correa and Leal 2001; Verba et al. 1995).

The fourth way through which religion promotes the incorporation of immigrants and people of color is through political mobilization. Religious leaders have a significant amount of influence over their congregants, especially when they share a variety of political interests (Brown 2011; Putnam and Campbell 2010). Certainly, in the African American community religious leaders have played a prominent role in organizing and impelling their church members to vote as well as support civil rights causes (Brown 2011; Morris 1984; Williams 2003). In the Latino community, Chicano priests and nuns have been important in demanding that the Catholic Church pay more attention to issues affecting Latinos as was the case through the development of Padres Asociades para los Derechos Religiosos, Educativos, y Sociales (PADRES; Priests Associated for Religious, Educational, and Social Rights) and Las Hermanas (the Sisters), an organization for Latina women not only for nuns and not only for persons of Mexican origin. More recently, Latino parishes and congregants have been active in a variety of efforts related to the human rights of immigrants as well as in efforts to push for immigration reform (Hondagneu-Sotelo 2007; Hondagneu-Sotelo et al. 2004; Menjivar 2003).

In addition, religious leaders also stimulate their followers to support a range of conservative causes as well. These include issues involving pro-life, anti-homosexual, and related matters. Williams and Loret de Mola (2007) describe the fiery words of a Latino pastor in a Florida community:

> Pastor Rincón is politically conservative, and speaks openly in church of his fervent support for President Bush and his policies. He often employs an apocalyptic discourse and biblical literalism to denounce homosexuality and abortion, and to preach against drinking, smoking, and other pleasures "del mundo" [of the world]. (p. 244)

Research has also examined the degree to which Latinos support the role of religion in politics. Analyzing 2006 survey data from the Pew Research Center's Hispanic Trends Project and Pew Forum on Religion and Public Life, Martini (2012) discovered that Latinos with greater church participation and deeper religious beliefs are more supportive of the role of religion in the political sphere. Martini (2012) also observed that Evangelical Protestants, in particular, had the greatest degree of support for the involvement of religious organizations in politics. Using data from the 1990 Latino National Political Survey, Ellison et al. (2005) find that Latinos who are Protestants with the strongest degree of religious commitment to conservative evangelical, fundamentalist, and charismatic groups exhibit the greatest support for the most restrictive bans on abortion. In sum, Martini (2012) observes that the overall general findings related to how Latinos view the association between religion and politics "add to the mounting evidence of the role that religion can play a . . . role for Latinos in shaping public opinion" (p. 1004). The growing popularity of Protestant evangelical denominations among Latinos has implications for a turn toward more conservative political views among the population (Ellison et al. 2005).

Religious Marketplace

While Latinos have historically been Catholic, increasingly they are turning to other denominations (Hunt 1999). Given the demographic trends that we examined in chapter 4, it is certain that religious denominations will increasingly try to recruit Latinos into their fold. The religious marketplace theoretical perspective offers a context which allows us to understand the competition that takes place among religious organizations as they seek congregants (Finke and Stark 1992). The religious marketplace perspective derives from economics and more specifically the rational choice (RC) framework.

The religious marketplace perspective views religious denominations as suppliers of a religious product that is marketed to consumers in search of a religion that suits them. More specifically, Sherkat and Ellison (1999) describe the players in the religious marketplace across levels:

> Religious organizations are firms dedicated to the production of religious value. Congregations are franchises led by entrepreneurial salespeople (ministers), who create value for customers. Firms are limited in their range of product offerings, and only those lacking an organizational hierarchy (e.g., Baptists) or nourishing an institutional commitment to pluralism (e.g., Roman Catholics) can sustain much diversity. (p. 379)

Accordingly, we can think of the different religious denominations as firms such as McDonalds, Burger King, Wendy's, and so forth. The franchises (or congregations) of these firms (or religious denominations) are situated across neighborhoods, communities, and states.

Like any other product, the religious product is "produced, chosen, and consumed" (Sherkat and Ellison 1999, p. 378). Religious denominations offer a product that offers "promises of future rewards and supernatural explanations for life events and meaning" (Sherkat and Ellison 1999, p. 378). Consumers compare the varying religious products on how they deal with these big issues and they come to a determination on the selection of a particular religious product. Subsequently, people consume the selected religious product with respect to participating in the religious activities and following the religious prescriptions that adherents are expected to follow. However, in contrast to other types of products, as Sherkat and Ellison (1999) point out, the promises of the religious product cannot be truly assessed. Thus, the religious products are risky. Consumers gain reassurance more indirectly – from their social relationships derived from other congregants and religious leaders (Sherkat and Ellison 1999). Nonetheless, the uncertainty associated with the religious product leads to potential for people to eschew the product in favor of another one (religious conversion), diversify their religious portfolio (by either holding on to a primary one or connecting to other religious denominations or identifying with various denominations without a preference for any), or by exiting the religious marketplace (becoming agnostic or atheist) (Sherkat and Ellison 1999).

The religious marketplace perspective has received some criticism. It is difficult for some people to view religion as a product that is manufactured, marketed, and consumed. It is challenging for some to think about people comparing across religious denominations and assessing the costs and benefits associated with becoming a member of an array of faiths. Similar criticisms are made of the marriage market and the economic perspective of fertility. It is difficult to see love and babies as commodities, with consumers using reason to analyze costs and benefits associated with varying potential spouses and comparing whether or not to have a child or how many relative to other consumer products, respectively.

Despite these criticisms and others (see McKinnon 2011), the religious marketplace framework is a useful metaphor to make sense of how Latinos are involved in religious conversion – typically from Catholicism to other religions – and perhaps more importantly how religious denominations seek to recruit Latinos as congregants as they face membership losses due to aging white populations. With the disproportionate growth of the Latino population, we have seen how corporations and businesses market their products to Latino consumers and how political parties market their political candidates to the Latino electorate. We can also envision how religious denominations package their faiths to Latinos who are seen as potential congregants.

Religious Patterns of Latinos

We now turn to the examination of data from the 2006 Hispanic Religion Survey conducted by the Pew Research Center's Hispanic Trends Project (2007b). This data source is a nationally representative sample including 4,016 Latinos 18 years of age and older.

As noted above, Latinos continue to be Catholic with approximately two-thirds identifying with this religion (figure 9.1). Close to one-fifth of Latinos are Protestants. Among Latino Protestants, nearly half identify their specific denomination as Baptist (16.4%), Nondenominational/Independent (16.3%), and Pentecostal Church of God (14.2%). Nonetheless, roughly 8 percent – about one in 12 – of Latinos report that they do not belong to a religion or that they are secular. About two-thirds of these individuals who do not have a religion had been previously affiliated with one, with the religions they left being mostly Catholic (62.6%), Evangelical or Protestant (23.1%), and Jehovah's Witness (9.4%).

There is relative stability in religious affiliation among Latinos who have a religion. Approximately one in seven Latinos had undergone a conversion of religion (data not shown here). When they did convert, most left the Catholic religion (77.1%) and a smaller number left the Evangelical or Protestant religion (14.3%).

The 2006 Hispanic Religion Survey asked people to identify their family heritage, corresponding to their national origin group to which they belong. Overall, most of the Latino ethnic groups are Catholic, although there is a wide range (table 9.1). Catholicism is most prevalent among Mexicans (73.5%), Other South Americans

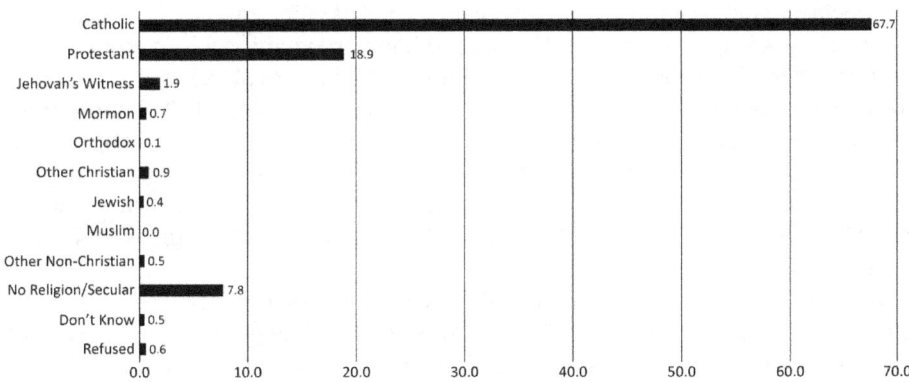

Figure 9.1 Percentage Distribution of Latinos by Religious Affiliation, 2006

Source: Compiled with data from Pew Research Center's Hispanic Trends Project (2007b).

Table 9.1 *Percentage Distribution of Latino Groups by Religious Affiliation, 2006*

Latino Group	Catholic	Protestant	Other	No Religion/Secular
Mexican	73.5	15.1	4.9	6.5
Puerto Rican	49.2	35.2	6.7	8.9
Cuban	59.9	19.3	7.0	13.8
Dominican	68.4	13.2	9.0	9.4
Salvadoran	57.2	24.8	6.5	11.5
Other Central American	60.7	22.9	4.8	11.6
Other South American	71.3	13.7	6.7	8.3
European	38.3	43.9	6.5	11.3
Other	46.3	42.9	4.4	6.4
Total	67.7	18.9	5.6	7.8

Source: Pew Research Center's Hispanic Trends Project (2007b).

(71.3%), and Dominicans (68.4%). In contrast, less than half of Puerto Ricans (49.2%), people identifying as Other (46.3%), and Europeans (38.3%) are Catholic. These three groups are the most likely to identify themselves as Protestant (European, 43.9%; Other, 42.9%; and Puerto Rican, 35.2%). Anywhere from one-fifth to a quarter of Salvadorans, Other Central Americans, and Cubans also belong to the Protestant religion. There is also some variation in the degree to which people do not hold a religion or see themselves as secular. Roughly one in eight Cubans, Salvadorans, Other Central Americans, and Europeans do not have a religious affiliation. On the other hand, few Mexicans (6.5%) and Latinos who identify themselves as Other (6.4%) do not belong to any religion.

We now develop a profile of Latinos on the basis of religion. To do this, we focus on three specific groups – Latinos who identify themselves as Catholics, those who are Protestant, and those who do not have a religion. Our analysis is limited to these three groups due to unreliable statistics for other groups because of small numbers of Latinos who belong to such religions. The profile will first examine the demographic and socioeconomic characteristics of the three groups of interest.

The three groups vary noticeably along demographic and socioeconomic lines. Protestants tend to be somewhat older with a median age of 39 compared to people without a religion being the youngest with a median age of 34 (table 9.2). Protestants are disproportionately females with 82 males per 100 females. In contrast, persons without a religion are much more likely to be male with a sex ratio of 224 males per 100 females. Moreover, Catholics are significantly more likely to be born outside of the US with two-thirds immigrating to the US. Protestants (41.7%) are the least likely to be born outside of the US.

The language and socioeconomic differences across the three groups reflect variations in the relative presence of immigrants across these groups. Thus, given the disproportionate representation of the foreign-born among Catholics, this group is the most likely to be Spanish dominant (55.0%), to have the lowest level of high school graduates (55.7%), and the lowest median household income level, with only 18 percent having an income of $50,000 or more. In contrast, Latinos who are

Table 9.2 *Demographic and Socioeconomic Profile of Latinos by Religious Affiliation, 2006*

Characteristic	Catholic	Protestant	No Religion/Secular
Median Age	36	39	34
Sex Ratio (males per 100 females)	105	82	224
Percent Foreign-Born	64.3	41.7	50.0
Language Patterns:			
English Dominant	16.1	34.6	29.9
Bilingual	28.9	30.8	32.5
Spanish Dominant	55.0	34.6	37.6
Percent High School Graduates	55.7	66.1	66.8
Pct. Household Income $50,000 or more	18.1	27.0	28.6

Source: Pew Research Center's Hispanic Trends Project (2007b).

Table 9.3 *Political Characteristics among Latinos by Religious Affiliation, 2006*

Characteristics	Catholic	Protestant	No Religion/Secular
% Registered to Vote	78.4	81.9	70.8
Political Party Affiliation:			
Republican	27.2	41.2	19.1
Democrat	59.6	49.7	62.3
Independent	8.1	6.1	12.8
Something Else	5.1	3.0	5.8
Political Views:			
Very Conservative	4.4	10.3	2.8
Conservative	32.0	37.0	28.2
Moderate	32.3	32.4	32.6
Liberal	21.9	13.8	26.8
Very Liberal	9.4	6.5	9.6

Source: Pew Research Center's Hispanic Trends Project (2007b).

Protestant and those that do not have a religion tend to be less fluent in Spanish and better off socioeconomically.

Given the important association between religion and political patterns observed in the literature, we are also interested in examining the political variations across the three groups of interest. In particular, we examine three political-related characteristics: percentage registered to vote, political party affiliation, and general political views. The two groups of Latinos who identify with a religion are more likely to be registered to vote compared to those who do not have a religion (table 9.3). In addition, while the majority of people in each of the three categories identifies with the Democratic Party, there is a significant split in the level of association with the Republican Party. More than two-fifths of Protestants (41.2%) identify with the Republican Party compared to slightly more than a quarter of Catholics (27.2%) and less than one-fifth of those without a religion (19.1%). Similarly, Protestants (47.3%) are much more likely to hold conservative views in general compared to Catholics (36.4%) and those who do not have a religion (31.0%). Overall, however, Latinos who do not have a religion tend to be more liberal than conservative (36.4% liberal vs. 31.0% conservative) compared to Catholics (36.4% conservative vs. 31.3% liberal) and especially Protestants (47.3% conservative vs. 20.3% liberal).

In sum, we see here significant variations across the three groups of interest. The immigration experience is particularly prevalent among Catholics. As we observed above, Latino Catholic congregations tend to be the most likely to focus on the provision of services and programs directed toward immigrants. We also observe the significant differences in political orientation of the three groups, with Protestants holding views that are especially conservative and Catholics being somewhat more moderate.

We now highlight some key questions related to religious patterns and trends that Latinos will confront in the near future.

Questions Related to the Future of Latino Religious Life

There are a series of important trends that impact the religious life of Latinos that we need to address and monitor. These revolve around the disproportionate growth of the Latino population and its role in the Catholic Church and as potential recruits for other religions, the secularization trend, and the impact of Pope Francis on Latinos.

The Increasing Influence of Latinos on the Catholic Church

As we saw in chapter 4, the Latino population is shaping the demography of the US and its institutions. The impact of the Latino population will expand in the coming decades due to the youthfulness of this population. The Latino population is expected to have a particularly significant sway in religious life in the US. Over the final three decades of the twentieth century, the Latino Catholic population nearly tripled and accounted for close to 90 percent of the total population growth of Catholics in the US (Poyo 2010). Today, Latinos comprise approximately one-third of US Catholics (Matovina 2012; Pew Research Center's Hispanic Trends Project 2007a). Matovina (2012) points out that in the absence of Latinos, the US Catholic Church would be experiencing severe population decline as is the case with mainline Protestant groups. The demographic influence of Latinos in the Catholic Church will expand in the near future. Indeed, already Latinos make up the majority of Catholics less than 25 years of age (Matovina 2012). Moreover, in Arizona, California, New Mexico, and Texas, Latinos represent more than three quarters of Catholics less than 18 years of age. Furthermore, the demographic influence of Latinos on the Catholic Church is also apparent in Latino new-destination areas. For example, Latino Catholics outnumber white Catholics in Georgia (Matovina 2012). Put simply, Putnam and Campbell (2010, p. 17; see also Matovina 2012, p. vii) claim that the US Catholic Church "is on its way to becoming a majority-Latino institution."

The influence of Latinos on the US Catholic Church extends beyond numbers. There are two distinct aspects of Latino Catholics that are particularly noteworthy, for they stand to potentially alter the practice of Catholicism in this country. First, Latino Catholics are much more likely than other Catholics to engage in spirit-filled religious expression as part of their worship. As noted above, while only one-eighth of non-Latino Catholics view themselves as charismatic, more than half of Latinos do (Pew Hispanic Center 2007a). Moreover, Latinos as a whole, regardless of religious faith, are more likely than non-Latinos to believe that God is an active presence in their daily lives, to pray daily, to believe in religious miracles, and to possess religious objects in their homes (Pew Research Center's Hispanic Trends Project 2007a). It is likely that with the growth of the Latino population, these beliefs and forms of worship will become a greater part of Catholicism in the US. Second, Latino Catholics tend to worship and attend churches with other Latinos. For instance, two-thirds of Latino Catholics participate in churches that have Latino clergy, where masses are in Spanish, and where the majority of attendees are Latinos, with three quarters of foreign-born and half of native-born Latinos attending such churches (Pew Research Center's Hispanic Trends Project 2007a). Hence, the disproportionate growth of Latinos in the US Catholic Church is likely to lead to more predominantly Latino churches. It will certainly be interesting to see how white Catholics will adjust to their declining numbers and potential for church closures in this changing environment.

This major demographic transformation involving the increasing influence of Latinos in the Catholic Church represents another stage in the long history between Latinos and the Catholic Church. For example, as the Mexican population grew in the early twentieth century due to people fleeing the Mexican Revolution, the Catholic Church largely neglected Mexicans with its ideological model emphasizing Americanization which stressed the abandonment of Spanish and Mexican culture in favor of English and mainstream white culture (Matovina 2012; Poyo 2010; Stevens-Arroyo 2010; Treviño 2006). There were important shifts in the relationship between Latinos and the Catholic Church beginning in the 1960s. In the midst of the Civil Rights Movement, the Second Vatican Council (1962–5) of the Catholic Church made significant changes in bringing about greater democracy, diversity, transparency, and opened the door for concerns for social justice (Stevens-Arroyo 2010). Still, however, efforts to improve the conditions of Latinos within the Catholic Church and more generally in the larger society did not originate from the mainstream Catholic structure. Rather, as the Chicano Movement emerged in the 1960s, Catholic priests, such as Ralph Ruiz, and nuns, such as Sisters Gregoria Ortega and Gloria Graciela Gallardo, played important roles in pushing for greater inclusion of Latinos and on social justice concerns affecting Latinos. Despite the more multicultural environment supporting the retention of the Spanish language and Latino cultures, Latinos continue to be disproportionately underrepresented in the hierarchy of the Catholic Church (Poyo 2010; Treviño 2006). The major question that arises is whether the increasing numbers of Latinos in the Catholic Church will translate into the actual positioning of Latinos in the higher levels of the hierarchy of the Church. Moreover, Latinos have historically been underrepresented as priests and nuns. Current trends suggest that Latino youth will forego careers as priests and nuns, which commonly has led to the importation of priests from abroad (Goodstein 2008) or even the outsourcing of prayer services to priests abroad (Rai 2004).

Secularization

Our data analysis showed that about 8 percent of Latinos do not have a religion or consider themselves to be secular. The percentage approximates the 11 percent in the general public that are secular (Goodstein 2007). However, one of the distinguishing attributes of secular Latinos is that they are more likely than those in the general public to have belonged to a particular religion in the past – two-thirds of secular Latinos with the majority former Catholics (Goodstein 2007). The secularization of Latinos has been dramatic. Indeed, data from the American Religious Identification Survey shows that the percentage of Latinos without a religion more than doubled, from 6 percent in 1990 to 13 percent in 2001 (Goodstein 2007). Some have observed that the secularization trend is not limited to higher generation Latinos, but also includes immigrants who were devout church attendees in their home country but have now abandoned church attendance and religion more generally (Goodstein 2007). To the extent that Latinos achieve greater socioeconomic mobility in the future and move away from family influences, it is likely that secularization may be an increasing reality for Latinos.

The Pope Francis Factor

Despite Latin America having the largest share of Catholics in the world (Sáenz 2005), this region has largely been overlooked in selection of popes. This changed on March 13, 2013, when Jorge Mario Bergoglio, an Argentinian, was elected the 266th pope and the first originating from Latin America. Ordained as Pope Francis, he has been an extraordinarily popular and charismatic pope who shuns luxury and comfort and who has placed a high priority on addressing the conditions of the poor and social justice concerns. Undoubtedly, Latinos feel a deep connection to Pope Francis due to his Latin American roots and his passionate attention to people on the margins. As a voice for social change in the Catholic Church, Pope Francis has the potential to bring back to the fold Catholics who have left the faith – many of these people who do not have a religion – due to dissonance between their views and those of the Catholic Church regarding a variety of issues such as contraceptive use, abortion, and the sexual abuse of children by priests that has rocked the Church. In addition, it is possible that Pope Francis will help stem the outflow of Catholics who have converted to evangelical and Pentecostal denominations. Pope Francis has shone light on issues that are important to Latinos such as immigration, human rights, poverty, and inequality. It will be interesting to see the impact he has on Latinos not only in keeping them within the religious fold, but also in how he can meet their spiritual needs.

Summary

In this chapter we provided an overview of a variety of theoretical perspectives that sociologists and political scientists have used to understand various aspects of religion related to Latinos, including the role of religion as social capital, as a vehicle to integrate immigrants, and a framework for viewing religion as a marketplace. We also examined the deep historical roots of Latinos to Catholicism as well as the unique aspects related to worship among Latinos and the strong presence of the Virgin of

Guadalupe in their lives. The examination of data from the 2006 Hispanic Religion Survey shows that while Catholicism continues to be the most popular religion among Latinos (especially among Mexicans, South Americans, and Dominicans), a significant proportion identify with the Protestant religion and another share of Latinos does not have a religion. These groups vary along demographic, socioeconomic, and political lines. In particular, Catholics are disproportionately immigrants and persons with relatively low socioeconomic status. Finally, we highlighted important trends related to the religious life of Latinos involving the increasing influence of Latinos in the Catholic Church, religious conversion, secularization, and the Pope Francis factor.

Religion has sustained many Latinos, providing a certain degree of security, predictability, and strength in dealing with all aspects of their lives that we have covered thus far. As we saw in this chapter, there is a significant association between religion and health well-being. Indeed, individuals whose lives are more intimately tied to religion tend to have more favorable health outcomes. We now turn to an examination of health and health care among Latinos.

10 Health and Health Care

Throughout the chapters we have covered thus far, we have seen that Latinos as a whole are characterized by relatively low socioeconomic levels. Latinos, particularly in the case of certain groups such as Mexicans, tend to have comparatively low levels of education, hold low-paying and physically demanding jobs with limited benefits, have high rates of poverty, and have high percentages of persons lacking health insurance. Given a well-established and long history of research observing the strong link between low socioeconomic status and high mortality (Buttenheim et al. 2010; Kitagawa and Hauser 1973; Ross and Wu 1996), it is not surprising that we would expect Latinos to die at high rates and to live relatively short lives compared to whites and other racial and ethnic groups that are better off economically. However, this is not the case. In fact, despite their many social and economic attributes that would expect us to infer that Latinos have high levels of mortality, they actually have mortality rates that are lower and life expectancies that are more favorable than whites. This pattern, referred to as the "epidemiological paradox," has been observed consistently for three decades (Arias 2012; Hummer and Chinn 2011; Markides and Coreil 1986; Markides and Eschbach 2011). There has been much research that has attempted to unravel the paradox through the examination of various explanations that have been proposed (see below).

The unanticipated favorable mortality outcomes of Latinos, however, hide other health and health care related patterns that are more disturbing. For example, Latinos lack access to health care due to their low prevalence of health care insurance, particularly among undocumented immigrants (Chavez 2012). As such, Latinos without health care insurance resort to a variety of other ways to access health care, including depending on health care at the emergency room when ailments become severe (Chavez 2012), using alternative forms of health care, and traveling to Mexico to obtain health care (Bastida et al. 2008; Horton and Cole 2011). Moreover, Latinos fare worse than whites on the prevalence of diabetes, obesity, and disability. It has thus been observed that Latinos live longer than whites, but they do so with chronic ailments.

We begin with an overview of theoretical perspectives that have been used to understand the health and mortality outcome of individuals. Subsequently, we provide a discussion of the Latino paradox and examine the different explanations that have been proposed. In addition, we examine the other side of the paradox where Latinos do not fare as well. Finally, we highlight major questions and issues that we need to recognize in order to better understand the future of Latinos in the area of health and health care.

Stratification and Cumulative Advantages/Disadvantages

One of the most enduring sociological tenets is that one's position in the social class ladder is associated with one's position in the various domains of life (Domhoff 2013; Massey 2007). Thus, people born in the upper classes are endowed with a multitude of social, economic, political, and cultural resources that allow them to get into and graduate from the most prestigious universities, earn high incomes, accumulate vast amounts of wealth, live in prestigious neighborhoods, and have strong political connections that protect their wealth and societal position (Sáenz et al. 2007a). In contrast, individuals born in the lower classes – bereft of social, economic, political, and cultural assets – are restricted to low-quality education, low levels of income, miniscule wealth, low-income neighborhoods, and do not have significant political connections (Sáenz et al. 2007a). One's social class standing also affects health and mortality outcomes.

Our sociological understanding of the link between social class and mortality extends back to a very influential research project by Evelyn Kitagawa and Phillip Hauser, two sociologists and demographers at the University of Chicago, who examined the relationship between social class and mortality among some 500,000 people who died in the US in 1960. They published their findings in a landmark book titled *Differential Mortality in the United States: A Study in Socioeconomic Epidemiology* (Kitagawa and Hauser 1973). Kitagawa and Hauser (1973) observed that white adults with the lowest education and income levels had the highest death rates and the probability of death declined with increasing educational and income levels. For example, they found that low-income women died at nearly twice the rate of high-income women.

The relationship between socioeconomic position and mortality persists today (Rogers et al. 2000). For example, among adults dying in the US in 2004, there is a strong and consistent negative association between educational level and death rate (Miniño et al. 2007). On average, US adults with less than 12 years of education had death rates that were more than three times higher than those of their counterparts with 13 or more years of schooling in 2004 (Miniño et al. 2007). Furthermore, historical data show that whites have a higher life expectancy than blacks (National Center for Health Statistics 2013). Despite the narrowing of the white–black life expectancy gap since 1990, the life expectancy of white males was still about 7 percent higher than that of black males in 2010, while white females had an advantage of 4 percent in their life expectancy compared to black females (National Center for Health Statistics 2013).

Variations in mortality and health outcomes on the basis of socioeconomic status as well as race and ethnicity reflect the advantages and disadvantages that people have due to their position in the stratification system. As people go through the life course extending from the utero stage to birth, infancy, childhood, teenage years, young adulthood, middle age, and elderly age, they have social and economic resources at their disposal to maintain their health (Geronimus et al. 2007; Ross and Wu 1996). Persons who are endowed with socioeconomic advantages – whites being disproportionately in this category – have greater access to health care, nutritious diets, living in safe and salubrious environments, and are also more likely to exercise compared to individuals with limited resources – people of color, especially African Americans,

Latinos, and Native Americans, being disproportionately in this category (Hummer 1996; Williams 1999; Williams and Jackson 2005). Over the life course, the advantages and disadvantages accumulate to produce greater disparities in health and mortality outcomes (Bowen 2009; Ross and Wu 1996). This is consistent with such adages as "success breeds further success," "failure breeds further failure," and "the rich get richer and the poor get poorer" (Ross and Wu 1996). Thus, people with greater access to quality health care have the ability to attain preventive care to minimize the risks of contracting serious health problems and can get medical care whenever illness arises. In contrast, people without health care insurance and those with limited access to quality health care may have to forego medical visits until health problems become unbearable, at which time health recovery is more difficult. Similarly, people working in physically demanding jobs, such as agricultural labor, machine operative work, meatpacking labor, construction, mining, and so forth, face the accumulation of stress on the body over time and, as such, become increasingly vulnerable to physical disabilities (Leigh and Fries 1992; Schlosser 2001), with immigrants particularly likely to work in risky and physically demanding jobs (Orrenius and Zavodny 2009).

Health disparities in old age, then, reflect the statuses that people had throughout the life course. People with more disadvantaged statuses, such as being poor, being a person of color, being an immigrant, and lacking US citizenship status, are particularly vulnerable in old age because of their cumulative disadvantages over the life course. Moreover, at the elderly stage of their lives they are likely to lack adequate socioeconomic resources to deal with the many health challenges that come at the later stages of life (Orrenius and Zavodny 2009; Schlosser 2001). Nevertheless, in the older ages demographers have often observed a mortality crossover, whereby disadvantaged groups have lower rates of mortality compared to advantaged groups. This is particularly the case when we examine the death rates of blacks and whites in the US (Eberstein et al. 2008). Accordingly, blacks have higher death rates compared to whites – regardless of sex group – at almost all age groups with the exception of the oldest age categories. Indeed, in 2010 blacks had higher death rates than whites up to the 75–79 age category, but blacks actually had lower death rates than whites in the 80–84 and 85-and-older age categories (Murphy et al. 2013). Why does this unexpected pattern arise in the older ages?

One of the most common explanations for the mortality crossover is that blacks who have made it to the older ages tend to be a hearty and hale population, whereas whites who have made it to this age have a more heterogeneous health profile. The argument is that racial and socioeconomic disparities have resulted in blacks having cumulative health problems over their lives and limited access to quality health care. In this scenario, blacks who have serious health problems die before making it to the older ages, with the result being that blacks who make it to the older ages tend to be selectively salubrious (Nam 1995). In contrast, because whites have greater access to quality health care over the life course, they are better able to postpone death, the result being that people that make it to the older ages include both hale whites as well as whites with significant health problems. As such, whites with health problems can no longer postpone death at the oldest ages and thus whites die at a higher rate than blacks at this stage of life. Nonetheless, another explanation that has been put forth to explain the mortality crossover relates to age misreporting resulting in inaccurate death rates at the older ages (Hussey and Elo 1997; Nam 1995; Preston et al. 1996).

The negative relationship between social status and mortality is strong and consistent for many groups, with the mortality distinctions between blacks and whites being particularly longlasting. This pattern in many ways is not apparent in the case of Latino mortality.

The Latino Paradox

It is now four decades since demographers first observed an unexpected pattern involving Latinos exhibiting low levels of mortality despite their low socioeconomic status and related factors that suggest that the group would have high levels of mortality. Teller and Clyburn (1974) were the first to observe this unexpected finding in their study of Latino infant mortality in Texas. A dozen years later Markides and Coreil (1986) observed the same phenomenon in their study of Latino infant mortality in the Southwest. These researchers referred to the unexpected pattern as an "epidemiological paradox." Markides and Coreil (1986; see also Hummer et al. 2007) elaborated on the paradox:

> Despite methodological limitations of much of the research, it can be concluded with some certainty that the health status of Hispanics in the Southwest is much more similar to the health status of other Whites than that of Blacks although socioeconomically, the status of Hispanics is closer to that of Blacks. This observation is supported by evidence of such key health indicators as infant mortality, life-expectancy, mortality from cardiovascular diseases, mortality from major types of cancer, and measures of functional health. On other health indicators, such as diabetes and infectious and parasitic diseases, Hispanics appear to be clearly disadvantaged relative to other Whites. (p. 253)

The favorable mortality outcome of Latinos is pretty well established over the last three decades in the areas of infant mortality, general mortality, and low birth weight (Crimmins et al. 2007; Gorman et al. 2010; Hummer et al. 2007; Markides and Eschbach 2005; Palloni and Arias 2004). The label of "epidemiological paradox" has been commonly used interchangeably with other terms such as "Hispanic paradox," "Latino paradox," and "Mexican immigrant paradox." Mexican immigrants, in particular, are associated with the paradoxical patterns involving unexpectedly favorable mortality among this group.

The Latino paradox with respect to death rates is prevalent across both sexes and age groups. Table 10.1 shows the death rates of Latinos, whites, and blacks in 2010 broken down by sex and age. Across all age and sex groups, Latinos have the lowest death rates while blacks have the highest prevalence of death. This is consistent with the Latino paradox. Moreover, the greatest advantage for Latinos over whites in terms of the level of death occurs between the ages of 25 and 49, with Latino men at these ages dying at a rate that is 30 percent lower than that of white men and Latina women dying at a level that is 40 percent lower than that of white women (figure 10.1).

Based on the favorable death rates of Latinos compared to whites and blacks, Latino babies born in 2010 are expected to outlive their white and black counterparts. Latino baby boys born in 2010 are estimated to live an average of 78.5 years (2.1 years more than white baby boys and 7.1 years more than black baby boys) and Latina baby

Table 10.1 Death Rates for Selected Race/Ethnic Groups by Age and Sex, 2010

Age	[Deaths Per 100,000 Population]					
	Male			Female		
	Latino	White	Black	Latina	White	Black
Under 1	556.8	575.9	1,281.5	462.9	480.4	1,055.7
1 to 4	25.0	27.5	45.4	20.2	21.8	34.8
5 to 9	10.0	12.5	17.9	7.6	10.2	13.9
10 to 14	12.9	16.0	23.4	10.4	11.5	17.0
15 to 19	61.2	63.9	108.0	20.4	30.1	31.9
20 to 24	97.9	123.2	200.2	32.6	46.5	60.5
25 to 29	97.4	137.6	219.0	35.5	57.8	84.7
30 to 34	104.7	150.1	243.4	42.3	76.5	114.3
35 to 39	121.7	180.8	274.7	58.2	106.9	169.2
40 to 44	173.6	253.9	366.4	94.4	156.9	248.5
45 to 49	282.6	406.9	569.2	155.6	247.9	392.0
50 to 54	439.1	607.1	918.4	240.4	365.7	607.4
55 to 59	686.1	881.6	1,462.7	357.5	508.4	853.9
60 to 64	992.8	1,233.3	2,027.9	571.4	769.4	1,181.1
65 to 69	1,450.9	1,844.8	2,802.4	874.0	1,221.1	1,730.3
70 to 74	2,229.5	2,822.4	3,947.8	1,364.2	1,945.9	2,515.2
75 to 79	3,592.4	4,518.2	5,789.4	2,349.8	3,207.2	3,760.6
80 to 84	5,795.9	7,459.8	8,566.4	4,072.2	5,420.4	5,921.1
85 and older	11,779.8	15,816.6	14,974.2	10,237.3	13,543.5	12,767.7

Source: Murphy et al. (2013).

girls born that year are expected to live an average of 83.8 years (2.7 years more than white baby girls and 6.1 years more than black baby girls) (figure 10.2). Again, these patterns are consistent with the Latino paradox.

Paradox across Latino Groups?

Limited data are available to assess whether the Latino paradox exists across certain groups that make up the overall Latino population or whether it encompasses all such groups. We use here death rates broken down across five Latino subgroups (Mexican, Puerto Rican, Cuban, Central and South American, and Other and Unknown Latino), sex groups (male and female), and 11 age groups (under 1, 1-4, 5-14, 15-24, 25-34, 35-44, 45-54, 55-64, 65-74, 75-84, and 85 and older) (Murphy et al. 2013). Note that Dominicans are included in the residual Latino subgroup titled "Other and Unknown Latino." These configurations contain 110 death rates for Latinos based on age and sex categories. More than four-fifths (91 of the 110) of the Latino death rates are lower than the respective white death rate (data not shown here). Four of the five Latino subgroups exhibit high levels of evidence supporting the Latino paradox: Cubans, 100% (all 22 Cuban death rates are lower than the respective white death rates);

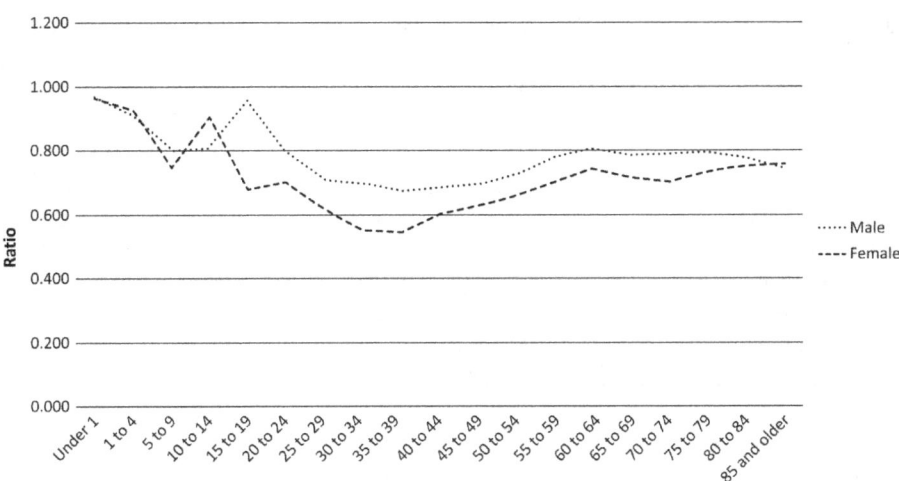

Figure 10.1 Ratio of Latino-to-White Death Rates by Age and Sex, 2010
Source: Compiled with data from Murphy et al. (2013).

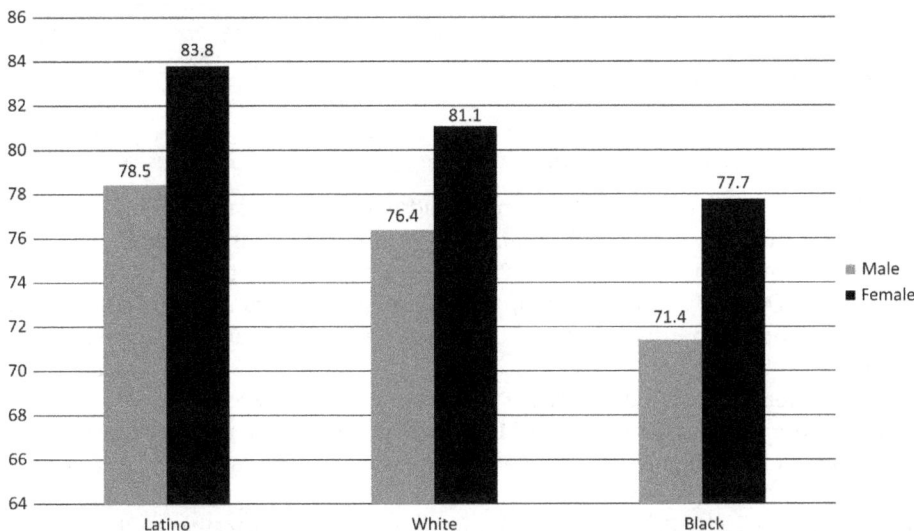

Figure 10.2 Life Expectancy at Birth for Selected Race/Ethnic Groups by Sex, 2010
Source: Compiled with data from Murphy et al. (2013).

Central and South Americans, 100%; Mexican 90.9% (the exception being death rates at age less than 1); and Puerto Rican, 81.8% (the exceptions being death rates at age less than 1 and for males aged 55–64 and 65–74). In contrast, only 40.9 percent of the death rates of the residual Other and Unknown Latino group are lower than the respective white death rates. Thus, it appears that the Latino paradox can be generalized to most of the groups that constitute the Latino population, the exception being the residual group which includes Dominicans.

Table 10.2 *Age-Adjusted Death Rates for Selected Causes of Death by Race/Ethnic Group, 2010*

Causes of Death	[Deaths Per 100,000 Population]		
	Latino	White	Black[a]
Diseases of heart	132.8	179.9	224.9
Cerebrovascular diseases	32.1	37.8	53.0
Malignant neoplasms	119.7	176.5	203.8
Chronic lower respiratory diseases	19.6	46.6	29.0
Influenza and pneumonia	13.7	14.9	16.8
Chronic liver disease and cirrhosis	13.7	9.4	6.7
Diabetes mellitus	27.1	18.2	38.7
Alzheimer's disease	18.5	26.4	20.6
Human immunodeficiency virus (HIV) disease	2.8	1.1	11.6
Unintentional injuries	25.8	42.4	31.3
Suicide	5.9	15.0	5.2
Homicide	5.3	2.5	17.7

[a] Includes Latinos who were racially identified as black.

Source: National Center for Health Statistics (2013).

Paradox across Causes of Death?

We also can assess whether the Latino paradox is valid across some of the most common causes of death. Table 10.2 shows the age-adjusted death rates for Latinos, whites, and blacks across 12 of the most common causes of death. For two-thirds of the 12 causes of death, whites have higher age-adjusted death rates than do Latinos. In particular, whites have higher levels of deaths in the three most common causes of death (diseases of the heart, cerebrovascular diseases, and malignant neoplasms) – 53 percent of white deaths in 2010 were due to these three diseases compared to 47 percent of Latino deaths (Murphy et al. 2013). In contrast, Latinos have higher age-adjusted death rates than whites in one-third of the 12 causes of death (chronic liver disease and cirrhosis, diabetes mellitus, human immunodeficiency [HIV] disease, and homicide). Overall, blacks have the highest age-adjusted death rates compared to Latinos and whites for seven of the 12 causes of death. In general, there is some support for the generalizability of the Latino paradox for causes of death, especially with respect to the most common causes of death.

Explanations for the Latino Paradox

What accounts for the Latino paradox? There have been several explanations proposed to resolve the paradox. First, it has been suggested that the paradox is due, at least in part, to the selectivity of immigrants. For long it has been established that immigrants are distinct in the countries from which they originate in a variety of ways, one of these being health. Immigrants who come to the US tend to be healthier than people who do not migrate from the country-of-origin (Jasso et al. 2004; Landale et al. 1999; Markides and Eschbach 2005; Palloni and Arias 2004; Palloni and Morenoff 2001). As such, given that Latino immigrants are a healthy lot, it is reasonable that they will have favorable health and mortality outcomes in the US. The migration selectivity explanation extends to Latina immigrant women who tend to have healthier infants than other women (Hummer et al. 2007).

Second, it is proposed that the elements of the culture of Latino immigrants protect them in a variety of ways. Cultural dimensions that produce favorable outcomes include a high degree of importance for the family (familism); participation in supportive social networks; diets which are rich in vegetables, grains, and legumes; and relatively low levels of the use of alcohol, tobacco, and drugs (Abraído-Lanza et al. 2005; Pérez et al. 2001; Reichman et al. 2008; Zambrana et al. 1997). The importance of culture in favorable health outcomes is evidenced by worsening health and mortality as Latino immigrants live longer in the US and acculturate (Horevitz and Organista 2013; Kaestner et al. 2009; Kimbro et al. 2012). The association between culture and health is also evident among Latina immigrant mothers (de la Rosa 2002; Sussner et al. 2008). Furthermore, there is a growing body of literature showing that Latinos who live in Latino areas with higher shares of immigrants tend to be healthier than those living in areas with fewer Latino immigrants (Aranda et al. 2011; Eschbach et al. 2005; McFarland and Smith 2011; Osypuk et al. 2010; Patel et al. 2003).

Third, it has also been posited that the Latino paradox represents a statistical artifact rather than reality or at least is not as strong as it appears. The underlying problem, according to this argument, is that there is inconsistency between the numerator and denominator used to generate death rates due to problems associated with age misreporting, inconsistencies in reporting of race and ethnicity, and return migration (Lariscy 2011; Liao et al. 1998). For example, it has been suggested that there tends to be the misreporting of age with the result being more people in the older ages (the denominator in the computation of death rates), resulting in artificially lower death rates. In addition, death records may have inaccurate information regarding the race and ethnicity of deceased individuals, especially if persons other than family members fill out this information on death certificates (e.g., funeral directors, physicians, etc.), leading to the populations comprising the numerator and denominator in the calculation of death rates being different. Furthermore, return migration is problematic when immigrants living in the US become ill and return to their country-of-origin – if such persons die in the home country, their death is recorded there rather than in the US, resulting in an artificially lower death rate in the US. The phenomenon associated with the return of ill individuals to the home country to die is referred to as the salmon bias, a term coined by Pablos-Mendez (1994). In general, there is a growing volume of research suggesting that the Mexican paradox is authentic rather than due to a statistical artifact (Elo et al. 2004; Hummer et al. 2007).

While the Latino paradox suggests that Latinos tend to die at lower rates and live longer lives than whites and other groups, there is also a significant amount of information indicating that Latinos suffer significantly from an array of health problems and from the lack of adequate health care.

Table 10.3 *Causes of Death for which Latinos Have Higher Age-Adjusted Death Rates Compared to Whites, 2010*[a]

Causes of Death	Latino	White	Latino/White Ratio
Viral hepatitis	3.3	1.9	1.74
Human immunodeficiency (HIV) diseases	2.8	1.1	2.55
Malignant neoplasms of stomach	5.8	2.7	2.15
Malignant neoplasms of liver and intrahepatic bile ducts	8.8	5.2	1.69
Malignant neoplasm of cervix uteri	1.4	1.0	1.40
Diabetes mellitus	27.1	18.2	1.49
Essential hypertension and hypertensive renal disease	7.8	6.9	1.13
Alcoholic liver disease	6.8	4.7	1.45
Other chronic liver disease and cirrhosis	6.9	4.7	1.47
Cholelithiasis and other disorders of gallbladder	1.1	1.0	1.10
Renal failure	12.5	12.1	1.03
Assault (homicide) by discharge of firearms	3.4	1.4	2.43
Assault (homicide) by other & unspecified means & their sequelae	1.9	1.1	1.73
Alcohol-induced deaths	9.1	7.8	1.17

[a] The causes of death for Latinos included here are those where the Latino age-adjusted death rate is 1.0 or higher and the causes are specific causes rather than general causes of death.

Source: Murphy et al. (2013).

The Other Side of the Latino Paradox

Evidence from the Latino paradox suggests that Latinos are overachievers in the area of mortality. Latinos tend to fare much better than expected with respect to avoiding death and actually living long lives. However, Latinos are not as fortunate in other areas such as elevated risks of dying from particular diseases, disability, risky behavior and lifestyles, and the lack of adequate health care. We will now examine each of these areas.

Prominent Causes of Death for Latinos

As noted earlier, Latinos fare better than whites on many causes of death, including some diseases that take a heavy toll on people – heart disease, cancer, and cerebrovascular disease. There are only a handful of diseases in which Latinos fare comparatively worse than whites. Table 10.3 shows 14 causes of death for which Latinos have age-adjusted death rates of 1.0 or higher (to ensure that causes of death with very small number of deaths are not included in the analysis) and for which Latinos have higher age-adjusted death rates than whites. The seven causes of death with the highest death rates among Latinos include diabetes mellitus (27.1 deaths per 100,000 people), renal failure (12.5), alcohol-induced deaths (9.1), malignant neoplasms of liver and intrahepatic bile ducts (8.8), essential hypertension and hypertensive renal disease (7.8), other chronic liver disease and cirrhosis (6.9), and alcoholic liver disease (6.8). The seven causes of death with the greatest relative risk of dying (measured by the ratio of the Latino-to-white death rates) for Latinos compared to whites are human immunodeficiency (HIV) diseases (ratio of 2.55 based on the Latino death rate divided by the white death rate), assault (homicide) by discharge of firearms (2.43), malignant neoplasms of stomach (2.15), viral hepatitis (1.74), assault (homicide) by other and unspecified means and their sequelae (1.73), malignant neoplasms of liver and intrahepatic bile ducts (1.69), and diabetes mellitus (1.49).

There are certain commonalities associated with the 14 causes of death. The causes of death are largely associated with lifestyle and risky behavior. For example, three causes are directly related to liver problems, which are commonly associated with heavy alcohol use. Other causes of death are associated with alcohol use (alcohol-induced deaths), smoking (stomach cancer), unprotected sex, multiple sexual partners (viral hepatitis, HIV diseases, and cervical cancer), and violence (both causes of death associated with homicide). Still other causes of death – primarily hypertension-related disease, gallbladder problems, and type-2 diabetes – are associated with the lack of healthy diets featuring fruits and vegetables, obesity, and lack of exercise. As such, it appears that a change in lifestyle behaviors and modifications in risky behavior could result in healthier Latinos and even lower death rates.

Risky Behavior among Adolescents

Children are at risk for engaging in an array of behaviors that are risky to their health and well-being. The degree to which they are exposed to such possibilities varies greatly and is influenced by many factors including the schools they attend, the neighborhoods where they live, the peers with whom they associate, as well as the level of guidance from their parents. Table 10.4 presents information on the percentage of students in grades 9 to 12 who engage in a series of health risk behaviors.

Of the nine behaviors, Latino youth are most likely to have engaged in sexual intercourse (boys, 53.0%; girls, 43.9%), having sex without the use of a condom (36.6%; 47.0%), being in a physical fight (44.4%; 28.7%), and riding in a vehicle with someone who has been drinking alcohol (30.7% among both boys and girls). In addition, approximately one-fourth of Latino boys have carried a weapon in the last 30 days, while slightly more than one-fifth of Latina girls have seriously considered suicide. Compared to white and black youngsters, Latino youth are the most likely to have thought about suicide, ridden or driven a vehicle with drinking involved, and had sex without using a condom. Note in particular the gender differences in not using a condom during sex and physically forced to have sex, situations in which girls – regardless of race and ethnicity – are much more at risk compared to boys. Obviously, the risky behaviors examined here are associated with a litany of serious consequences

Table 10.4 *Percentage of Students in Grades 9 to 12 Engaging in a Series of Health Risk Behaviors by Race/Ethnic Group and Sex, 2011*

Health Risk Behaviors	Male			Female		
	Latino	White	Black	Latina	White	Black
Seriously considered suicide (last 12 months)	12.6	12.8	9.0	21.0	18.4	17.4
In a fight (last 30 days)	44.4	37.7	45.8	28.7	20.4	32.3
Carried a weapon (last 30 days)	24.5	27.2	21.0	7.5	6.2	7.5
Rarely or never wore a seatbelt	10.1	7.3	12.6	8.4	5.1	8.0
Rode with a driver who had been drinking alcohol (last 30 days)	30.7	20.5	22.5	30.7	23.8	23.2
Drove while drinking alcohol (last 30 days)	11.5	8.9	7.8	7.8	7.0	4.0
Ever had sexual intercourse	53.0	44.0	66.9	43.9	44.5	53.6
Did not use a condom at last sex (among those having sex in last three months)	36.6	33.7	24.6	47.0	46.6	46.2
Physically forced to have sex	5.4	3.2	6.1	11.2	12.0	11.0

Source: National Center for Health Statistics (2013).

including injury, arrest, pregnancy, the contracting of a sexually transmitted disease, and death, all situations that can severely alter the life course of teenagers.

Obesity

Many of the health problems that Americans face are associated with the increasing prevalence of obesity (Monteverde et al. 2010). Obesity is associated with unhealthy diets lacking fruits and vegetables, lack of exercise, and sedentary lifestyles. The poor often have ready access to inexpensive processed unhealthy food and lack access to nutritious foods. The rise of obesity has been especially apparent among Latinos, especially children. The National Hispanic Caucus of State Legislators (2010) has called the obesity of Latinos a "national crisis," and asserts that "For Latino communities, the obesity epidemic has reached crisis, with many states and communities reporting Latino obesity at staggering proportions, with Latino children becoming obese earlier in their lives" (p. 8). It goes on to warn that "Increasing rates of obesity in Latino children suggest that, unless policy-makers take action, the subsequent generation will be less healthy as it ages, affecting among other things, health care costs" (p. 9).

A significant share of the Latino population is considered obese as defined by a body mass index (BMI) of 30 or higher. Data are available for Mexicans, whites, and blacks to assess the prevalence of obesity among males and females in different age groups for the 2007–10 period. Overall, Latino boys have the highest obesity levels compared to white and black youngsters with nearly one-fifth of Mexican boys 2–5 years of age being obese, close to a quarter of Mexican boys 6–11 years of age, and

Table 10.5 *Percentage of Persons Obese by Race/Ethnic Group, Age, and Sex, 2007–2010*

Age Group	Male			Female		
	Mexican	White	Black	Mexican	White	Black
2 to 5 years	19.1	8.8	15.7	9.9	9.2	14.2
6 to 11 years	24.3	18.6	23.3	22.4	14.0	24.5
12 to 19 years	27.9	17.1	21.2	18.0	14.6	27.1
20 years and older[a]	35.6	33.2	38.1	44.2	33.2	54.2

[a] Age-adjusted percentages.

Source: National Center for Health Statistics (2013).

more than a quarter of Mexican boys 12–19 years of age (table 10.5). Mexican girls are less likely to be obese with their obesity rates being generally lower than those of black girls and higher than white girls. However, among adults, Mexican women (44.2%) are more likely than Mexican men (35.6%) to be obese. Black adults are somewhat more likely to be obese compared to Mexican adults, with white adults posting the lowest levels of obesity. The obesity rates of Mexican adult men and women have increased steadily over time, while the prevalence of obesity has also climbed among Mexican boys 2–5 years of age and among Mexican girls 6–11 and 12–19 years of age. These trends are disturbing and put at risk the mortality advantages that we observed above.

Disability

While Latinos have an advantage over whites and blacks in the area of mortality, the advantage is somewhat different in the area of disability. We present data here for the percentage of persons across age and sex groups who have any disability for Latinos, whites, and blacks. The list of possible disabilities includes cognitive difficulty, ambulatory difficulty, independent living difficulty, self-care difficulty, vision difficulty, and hearing difficulty. Overall, blacks have the highest levels of disability throughout the age spectrum (figure 10.3). There are noticeable differences between Latinos and whites, however. In particular, Latinos have relatively lower levels of disabilities than whites up to the 45–49 age category among females and the 50–54 age category among males. Thereafter whites have lower rates of disability. As such, there is a disability crossover between Latinos and whites.

The disability crossover is likely driven by the selectivity of Latino immigrants. As we learned earlier, Latino immigrants tend to be positively selected from the countries from where they originate, with people with disabilities being less likely to immigrate to the US. However, the situation is a bit more complicated because in order to get the more complete panorama of the disability crossover, we need to examine whites, foreign-born Latinos, and native-born Latinos. For both males and females, the selectivity of Latino immigrants is clear, as they have lower disability rates compared to both whites (up to the 60–64 age category) and native-born Latinos (up to the 65–69 age category) (figure 10.4). Why would Latino immigrants suddenly

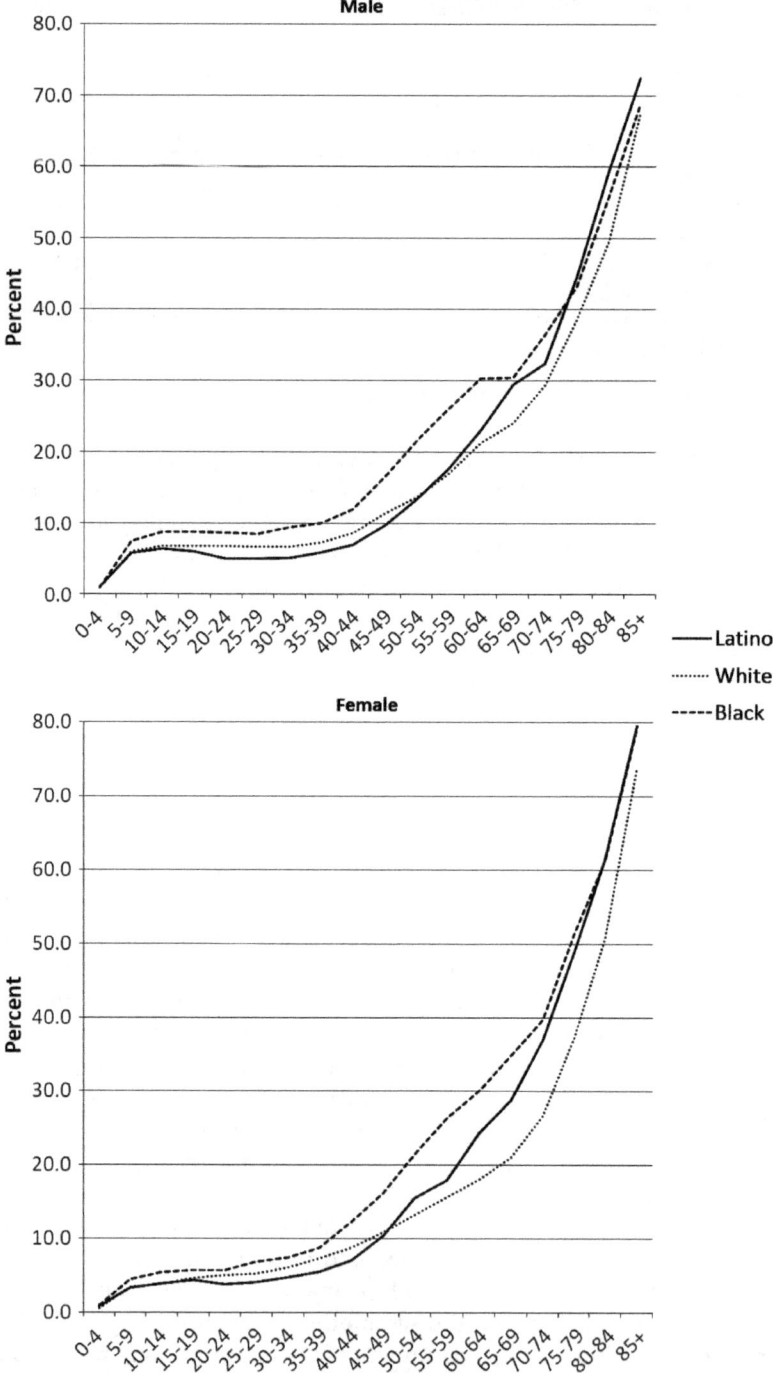

Figure 10.3 Percentage of Persons with a Disability by Race/Ethnic Group, Age, and Sex, 2011

Source: 2011 American Community Survey (ACS) Public-Use File (Ruggles et al. 2010).

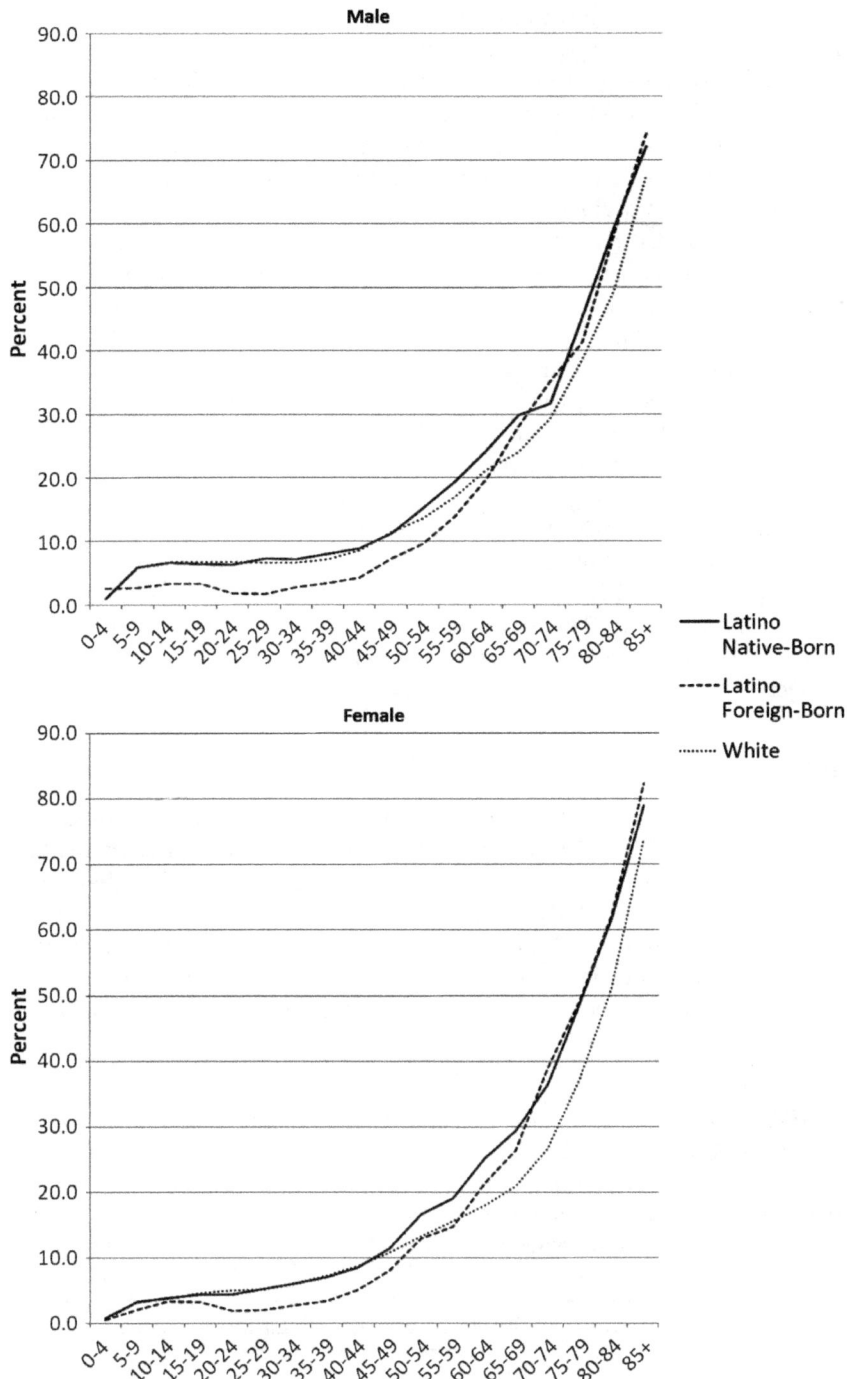

Figure 10.4 Percentage of Persons with a Disability among Native-Born Latinos, Foreign-Born Latinos, and Whites by Age and Sex, 2011

Source: 2011 American Community Survey (ACS) Public-Use File (Ruggles et al. 2010).

have higher rates of disability as they reach the elderly ages? Latino immigrants are more likely than other groups to work in physically demanding jobs which take a toll on the body (see chapter 7). Thus, it is likely that by the time Latino immigrants reach the older ages, the wear-and-tear impact on the body becomes more debilitating. Because whites, in particular, tend to be employed in more prestigious occupations, their body is not subjected to physical demands on the job as much as Latinos.

However, the story is a bit different when we compare the prevalence of disability among native-born Latinos and whites. Not subject to health selectivity, native-born Latinos have fairly comparable rates of disability relative to whites (figure 10.4). Nonetheless, the occurrence of disability diverges, with whites having lower levels of disability and Latinos having escalating rates in the late 20s for males and late 40s for females. This trend provides further evidence that Latinos are not a monolithic group and that their health status varies significantly by place of birth.

It is clear, then, that while Latinos live longer than whites and blacks, they do so with a greater prevalence of disability, especially relative to whites. Given the high incidence of diabetes among Latinos (and blacks as well), Latinos are at risk of worsening health conditions with the onset of a configuration of diabetes, obesity, and disability. People who are obese are at greater risks of diabetes and people who have diabetes are at risk of becoming physically disabled with increasing probabilities of loss of sight and limbs. Due to the limited resources of Latinos and the undocumented status of a noticeable share of the population, they tend to have health care challenges.

Health Care Needs

Latinos have significant health care needs compared to other race/ethnic groups. For example, one-third of Latino adults do not have a usual source of health care, a rate that is twice as high as that of whites and about 1.5 times higher than that of blacks (table 10.6). Similarly, Latino children 6–17 years of age are almost three times as likely as white children of those ages and nearly twice as likely as black children to not have a usual source of health care. In fact, Latino children are more likely to have gone the last year without a health care visit compared to white and black children.

Table 10.6 *Percentage of Persons Without a Usual Source of Health Care by Race/Ethnic Group and Age, 2010–2011*

Age Group	Percentage Without Usual Source of Health Care			Percentage of Children Without a Health Care Visit in Last Year		
	Latino	White	Black	Latino	White	Black
Under 6 years	2.6	2.0	4.5	6.7	3.5	5.9
6 to 17 years	10.2	3.6	5.8	16.4	9.0	11.1
18 to 64 years	33.3	15.8	22.1	—	—	—

Source: National Center for Health Statistics (2013).

The high prevalence of health care needs of Latinos reflects the high rate of lack of health care insurance, the undocumented status of a significant share of Latinos, as well as the types of jobs that many Latinos hold, which are low-paying and without significant benefits (see chapter 7).

Lack of Health Care Insurance: A Major Impediment to Meeting Health Care Needs

Latinos stand out among racial and ethnic groups with respect to the lack of health care insurance coverage (Sáenz 2010), which makes their low mortality particularly surprising. Overall, 30 percent of Latinos lack health insurance compared to 11 percent of whites and 19 percent of blacks. Across age groups, Latinos are much more likely than whites and blacks to not have insurance in 2011 (figure 10.5). Approximately one in eight Latino children, more than two in five Latino adults 18–64 years of age, and one in 20 Latino elderly lack insurance coverage. Latino children are 2.4 times more likely than white children to need insurance, with Latino adults 18–64 years of age being almost three times as likely as white adults of these ages to not have insurance. While health insurance coverage is pretty much universal for white and black elderly, this not the case for Latino elderly.

The absence of health care insurance coverage among Latinos, however, varies by place of birth and citizenship status. The lack of insurance is lowest among Latinos born in the US followed by Latino immigrants who are naturalized citizens with Latino immigrants who are not naturalized citizens being the most likely to not have insurance (see figure 10.5). Across the three age groups, a high percentage of Latinos

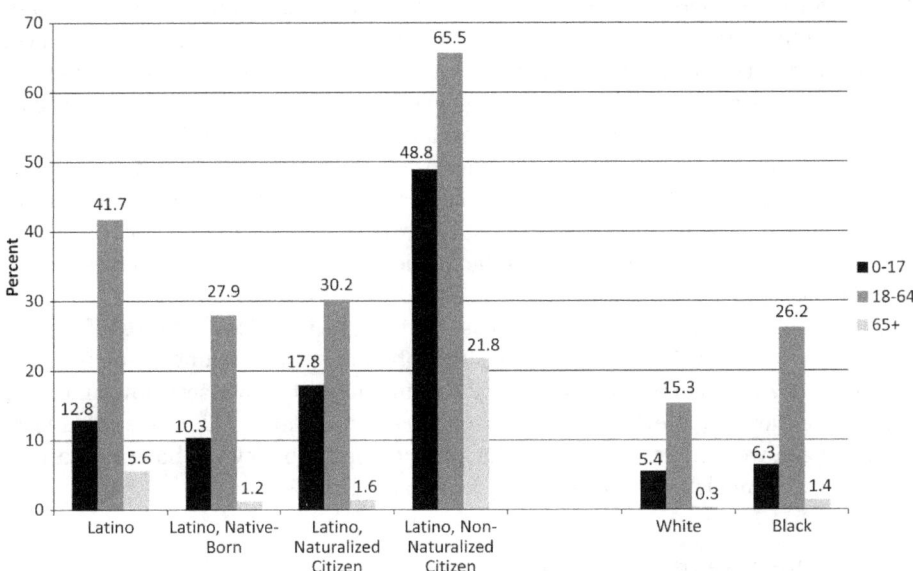

Figure 10.5 Percentage of Persons without Health Care Insurance by Race/Ethnic Group, Age, and Place of Birth/Citizenship Status, 2011

Source: 2011 American Community Survey (ACS) Public-Use File (Ruggles et al. 2010).

who are not US citizens do not have insurance coverage: nearly half of children, two-thirds of adults 18–64 years of age, and more than one-fifth of elderly. Nonetheless, even US-born Latinos are nearly twice as likely as whites to lack health care coverage, though their levels are more similar to those of blacks.

As we have seen in earlier chapters, there are noticeable variations in the socioeconomic standing of the different groups that constitute the overall Latino population. Table 10.7 shows the percentage of people in Latino subgroups that lack health insurance broken down by age group and place of birth. Overall, the level of health insurance deprivation ranges from groups with low rates consisting of Puerto Ricans (14.8% lack insurance), Other Latinos (19.2%), and Dominicans (21.1%) to groups with high rates including Guatemalans (46.0%), Salvadorans (38.6%), and Mexicans (32.5%). Indeed, across age groups and place of birth, Guatemalans, Salvadorans, and Mexicans stand out with the highest levels lacking insurance, even among the native-born.

It has been suggested that the lack of health care insurance and the high costs of health care in the US prompt Latinos, especially Mexicans, to travel to Mexico for affordable health care involving visits to doctors, dentists, as well as to obtain medicine (Bastida et al. 2008; Horton and Cole 2011). Research has shown that such travel is not restricted to people living along the US–Mexico border but also among those living further away from the border (Wallace et al. 2009). Moreover, it has been observed that even Latinos with health insurance travel to Mexico for health care (Seid et al. 2003; Wallace et al. 2009), while still others even forego attaining insurance in the US in favor of the less expensive and more flexible health care system in Mexico (Brown 2008).

Given the broad segment of the Latino population that depends on travel to Mexico for health services, there are elements beyond costs and the lack of health insurance that motivate Latinos to opt for the attainment of health care in Mexico. Horton and Cole (2011) observe a list of reasons that Latinos give more often for their preference for travel to Mexico in search of health services. These include the low cost of health care, speed at which they are attended, the potency of medication in Mexico rather than the concern for extended diagnosis, costlier treatment, and impersonal form of health care delivery in the US (Horton and Cole 2011). Yet, it is important to understand that many Latinos may find it costly to travel into Mexico and, of course, the surging violence, especially along the Mexican side of the border, makes it difficult for people to make the trip.

The Affordable Care Act, also known as Obamacare, promises to make affordable health care insurance widely available, although people who are undocumented are not eligible. While, at the time of writing, we will not be able to assess how much the Affordable Care Act alleviates the insurance needs of Latinos and others for at least another year, we can get a glimpse of the impact that this policy will have by examining one state that already has a similar program in place.

Health Care Insurance and the Case of Massachusetts

The state of Massachusetts, under the administration of Governor Mitt Romney, passed a policy that provided its residents access to affordable health care insurance. Today, Massachusetts leads all states with the lowest percentage of persons who

Table 10.7 Percentage of Persons Without Health Care Insurance by Race/Ethnic Group, Age, and Place of Birth, 2011

Race/Ethnic Group	Total				Native-Born				Foreign-Born			
	Total	0–17	18–64	65+		0–17	18–64	65+		0–17	18–64	65+
Mexican	32.5	14.3	45.7	6.3		11.5	30.8	1.3		51.9	60.3	11.4
Puerto Rican	14.8	5.4	21.5	1.0		5.3	21.3	1.0		30.3	33.5	3.0
Cuban	25.0	9.7	36.1	2.7		7.7	22.3	1.2		23.2	44.3	2.8
Salvadoran	38.6	15.4	50.3	13.3		12.3	34.5	8.1		43.9	54.1	13.5
Dominican	21.1	8.0	28.4	6.2		5.9	23.7	1.9		20.1	30.3	6.5
Guatemalan	46.0	13.7	61.3	15.5		11.1	32.4	3.8		27.3	66.7	15.6
Colombian	26.6	10.3	34.2	10.7		7.2	26.9	0.0		24.8	36.4	11.1
Other Central American	36.6	12.0	48.3	4.7		8.3	26.5	1.3		46.1	55.1	5.0
Other South American	27.9	11.3	35.8	11.2		6.7	21.7	5.3		33.1	39.7	11.4
Other Latino	19.2	9.4	26.9	2.2		8.3	23.7	0.5		40.0	40.0	8.1
Latino	29.9	12.8	41.7	5.6		10.3	27.9	1.2		44.9	55.3	9.3
White	10.8	5.4	15.3	0.3								
Black	18.6	6.3	26.2	1.4								

Source: 2011 American Community Survey Public-Use File (Ruggles et al. 2010).

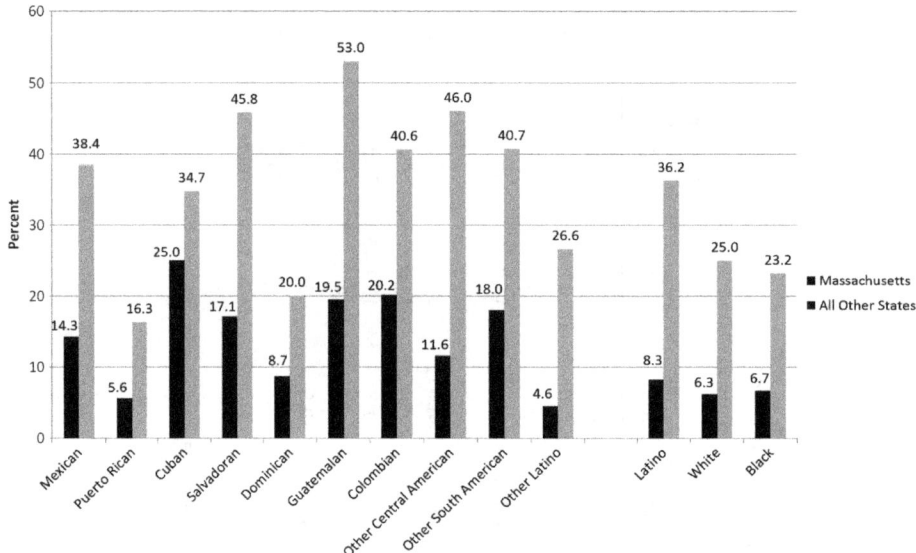

Figure 10.6 Percentage of Persons in Poverty without Health Care Insurance by Race/Ethnic Group and State of Residence, 2011

Source: 2011 American Community Survey (ACS) Public-Use File (Ruggles et al. 2010).

lack insurance with only 3.6 percent of its population not having insurance in 2011. We want to assess the percentage of Latinos who lack insurance in Massachusetts compared to those living in all other states. One of the problems in making this comparison is that Latinos who live in Massachusetts may be selective on a variety of characteristics compared to Latinos who live in all other states. To deal with this problem, we focus the analysis only on individuals who are defined as being in poverty. As such, these individuals are much more likely to be comparable on an array of attributes, such as socioeconomic status, regardless of whether they live in Massachusetts or elsewhere.

The comparison of the percentage of the poor who lack health care insurance coverage between Massachusetts residents and those from all other states reveals some interesting trends. Across race/ethnic groups, the poor living in Massachusetts are much more likely to enjoy health care coverage compared to the poor residing in all other states (including the District of Columbia). Overall, the Latino poor outside of Massachusetts are four times more likely to not have insurance coverage compared to Latino poor living in Massachusetts (figure 10.6). Dominicans and Puerto Ricans, the two groups with the largest presence in Massachusetts, can be highlighted to observe the different insurance outcomes between people in Massachusetts and those living elsewhere. Dominican poor in Massachusetts (8.7%) are much less likely to lack insurance compared to Dominican poor elsewhere (20.0%); the same patterns exist among the Puerto Rican poor (Massachusetts residents, 5.6%; people in other states, 16.3%). Obviously, the Affordable Care Act has the potential to meet the large needs for health care insurance coverage among many Latinos.

Questions Related to the Future of Latino Health and Health Care

There are several important trends regarding Latino health and health care that we need to recognize due to their significance in shaping the future patterns of health well-being among Latinos in the near future. We highlight here trends regarding immigration and *narco* violence; changing marriage and family life and aging; and obesity. These trends have important implications for how Latinos will fare in terms of their health in the future.

Immigration and Narco Violence

As we have seen in this chapter, the favorable aspects of Latino health and health care are associated in one form or another with immigration and transnational forms of health care. For example, favorable death rates, life expectancy, and disability levels reflect the selectivity of Latino immigrants on the basis of health status. In addition, Latinos have relied on travel to Mexico to address their health care needs. However, over the last several years we have seen major reductions in the flow of Latino immigrants, especially those originating from Mexico, to the US. In fact, the latest estimates indicate that the net balance between international movement between Mexico and the US is practically zero or even a slightly higher volume of people leaving the US to Mexico than vice versa (Passel et al. 2012). If the reduction of Mexican immigration persists over time, there will be fewer immigrants who come with their salubrious conditions, diets, and lifestyles. As such, the reduced number of Mexican immigrants would represent a declining share of the overall Latino population with the result being worsening death rates, longevity, and disability levels in the overall Latino population.

Moreover, if the *narco* violence that has plagued Mexico endures, travel to Mexican border areas will continue to be prohibitive. Thus, under such conditions, Latinos will be increasingly cut off from the health care safety valve that Mexican border communities have represented. Undocumented immigrants, in particular, face dire possibilities in meeting their health care needs. Indeed, these individuals are not eligible to access affordable health care insurance under the Affordable Care Act and the high level of militarization and security of the US–Mexico border makes it extremely difficult to travel to Mexico in search of health services. For undocumented immigrants who tend to toil in low-paying jobs, emergency rooms will increasingly represent the last-resort health care source.

Changing Marriage and Family Patterns

Latino marriage and family life has been restructured in a variety of ways which ultimately impact the family support system of Latinos. The increasing levels of apprehensions and deportations of Latino immigrants during the Obama administration have spurred the splitting of families across countries. Furthermore, heightened border security and the militarization of the US–Mexico border have trapped Latino undocumented immigrants in the US, separating them for long periods of time from aging parents as well as spouses and their children in

Mexico. In addition, an increasing prevalence of marriage instability alongside declining birth rates among Latinos in the US as well as in Latin America stands to weaken the family support system. Such changes in marriage and family life have significant implications for the health care needs of Latinos, particularly in the coming years, as we will see a significant aging of the Latino population in the US as well as in Latin America. Increasingly health care is a binational reality for Latino families whose members are living in different countries (Montes de Oca et al. 2012).

The continued failure to pass immigration reform policies in the US does not bode well for the future of the family in meeting the health care needs of a future aging population. Certainly we have also seen a reversal of family-friendly immigration policies in the US. Furthermore, immigration proposals that Congress has drafted have primarily prioritized the further security of the border with much less emphasis on the establishment of a path to US citizenship for undocumented immigrants.

Obesity

The escalating levels of obesity among Latinos have the potential to have devastating impacts on the future health and economic well-being of Latinos. Obesity is associated with a variety of chronic diseases including diabetes, hypertension, heart disease, and particular types of cancer (Monteverde et al. 2010; World Health Organization 2000). Moreover, the onset of chronic diseases is also likely to limit the mobility of individuals, thus promoting a more sedentary lifestyle that does not include exercise. As we learned above, the causes of death that disproportionately affect Latinos are related to obesity, lifestyle choices, and diet. Programs and policies need to increasingly promote healthy choices among Latinos.

Nonetheless, we need to understand that the choices that people make involving diet, exercise, and other lifestyle choices do not occur in a vacuum. Rather they take place in a larger cultural, physical, and economic environment which sets limitations. For example, many popular foods that Latinos enjoy are unhealthy. These include such foods as *bañuelos, barbacoa, chile rellenos, chimichangas, empanadas, enchiladas,* flour tortillas, *gorditas, menudo, mofongo, nachos, pan dulce, quesadillas,* refried beans, and tamales. Often these foods can be modified with healthier ingredients to make them less harmful. Yet, there needs to be some modification of attitudes toward such alterations. In addition, poor Latinos tend to be located in segregated areas where they have few options for the acquisition of healthy foods, including fresh fruits and vegetables, and for engaging in exercise due to the lack of parks. For many Latinos who live in "food deserts" in many US cities, local stores are disproportionately convenience stores, fast-food outlets, and liquor stores. Furthermore, eating a healthy diet tends to be more expensive than unhealthy food, which is cheap and convenient. Thus, the environments where Latinos with limited resources live tend to promote unhealthy diets and lifestyle choices. Policymakers need to invest in improving the availability of parks and recreational facilities in poor Latino communities and to develop incentives for the establishment of supermarkets and farmers markets that provide broad availability of fruits, vegetables, and other healthy foods in these communities.

These are certainly major challenges that policymakers and other community leaders must tackle in establishing policies and programs that provide healthier environments to allow people with limited resources to make healthier choices in their diets and lifestyles. In addition, there needs to be the implementation of immigration policies that help support and sustain families to enhance rather than weaken the family support system that is crucial in meeting the health care needs of family members. Finally, there needs to be options for undocumented persons and others who cannot afford health insurance under Obamacare to ensure that they have access to preventive health care that can ward off medical catastrophes at early stages.

Summary

This chapter has provided an overview of the health and health care patterns of Latinos. We provided an overview of the theoretical perspectives that for long have shown that people with limited socioeconomic resources tend to fare worse in mortality and health compared to individuals who are well off socioeconomically. We presented data that demonstrated that Latinos depart from this general pattern and represent an epidemiological paradox. Accordingly, despite their low socioeconomic profile along with a variety of related factors, Latinos actually have lower death rates and live longer than do whites. We provided an overview of several explanations that have been put forth to explain the Latino paradox. We also demonstrated the other side of the paradox which reveals a variety of areas where Latinos do not fare as well as whites and other groups. Finally, we highlighted several major trends that have major implications for the future course of Latino health and health care.

We observed in this chapter that the other side of the paradox included disproportionate causes of death and practices related to violence and at-risk behavior. We now turn to an overview of crime and victimization among Latinos.

11 Crime and Victimization

There are several illustrations of disparate treatment of blacks and Latinos in the criminal justice system. To begin, racial profiling, the use of race alone as a criteria for deciding to stop or detain someone, continues today and is justified by police, arguably because crime rates are higher in black and Latino communities. Yet, according to some research, while three quarters of motorist and traffic violations were perpetrated by whites, four-fifths of the searches were on people of color (Cannon 1999). The American Civil Liberties Union (2008) even proclaimed that racial profiling has reached epidemic proportions due to the "war on drugs," where police disproportionately target young black and Latino men perceived to be drug couriers.

Moreover, when compared to whites, blacks and Latinos are assessed higher bail, are less successful with plea bargains, are more likely to be found guilty, and are given longer sentences (Anderson and Taylor 2011). Indeed, young black and Latino men are sentenced more harshly than any other group and are less likely to be released on probation (Bales and Piquero 2012). Additionally, in homicide cases, if the victim is white, blacks and Latinos receive longer sentences (Curry 2010). Furthermore, black and Latino communities are policed more heavily than white neighborhoods. This is a concern given that Latinos perceive the police as a threatening rather than as a protective force (Menjivar and Bejarano 2004; Weitzer and Tuch 2005). These are just some of the illustrations of racial inequality against people of color in comparison to whites in the criminal justice system.

Most of the literature on race and crime has focused on black–white disparities, but the scholarship on the criminalization, victimization, and criminal patterns of Latinos has been growing. Indeed, Martinez (2008) argues that while data on Latinos are rare, the information that exists confirms the need for data on Latinos to adequately address racial/ethnic crime disparities. Similarly, a study on property crime on the predominately Latino Texas counties along the US–Mexico border concludes that incorporating information for both native- and foreign-born Latinos is important for expanding our knowledge on how economic and social conditions relate to crime (Allen and Cancino 2012).

Thus far, scholarship on Latinos and crime has largely focused on males, immigrants, and on violent crimes. In particular, despite the structural disadvantages of Latino immigrants (e.g., high poverty, low levels of education, lack of adequate housing, etc.), they have lower rates of crime than blacks, whites, and native-born Latinos (Hagan and Palloni 1999; Kubrin and Ishizawa 2012; Martinez 2008, 2013; Martinez and Lee 2000; Martinez and Stowell 2012; Martinez and Valenzuela 2006; Ousey and Kubrin 2009; Sampson 2008; Sampson and Bean 2006; Stowell et al. 2009; Thomas 2011). This pattern is known as the "Latino immigrant crime paradox," similar to the Latino epidemiological paradox examined in the previous chapter. The crime paradox has received an increasing amount of research attention. Moreover, most of the literature on Latinos and crime has focused on violent crime in contrast to property and other minor crimes (Martinez 2008). This is mostly due to reliable data on violent crimes being more accessible than data on other forms of crime. Lastly, most of the Latino scholarship on crime has focused on males and the poor. This is largely attributed to what Rios (2011) calls the "youth control complex," where young boys coming of age are subjected to the social control of various institutions and treated like criminals for being poor, young, black or Latino, and male.

This chapter presents an overview of patterns of criminalization, victimization, and criminal behavior among Latinos. We begin by illustrating some historical and contemporary examples of how Latinos are criminalized in US society. We then focus on criminological theories that have been used to examine Latino victimization and criminal activity. Next, we present some of the trends in criminalization and victimization utilizing data from the Pew Research Center's Hispanic Trends Project's 2008 National Survey of Latinos and the National Longitudinal Study of Adolescent Health (Add Health) (2008). Finally, we conclude by posing major questions that are important for the future study of Latinos and crime as well as policy considerations.

Latinos and Social Constructions as Criminals

Institutional perspectives examine racism from a societal/structural perspective rather than on a biological or cultural basis. According to institutional perspectives, racism is a result of decisions and policies concerning race that are overtly or covertly subordinating groups of color, such as Latinos, in an effort to maintain social control over them and sustain the status quo. Scholars have described such patterns as institutional racism. Below we describe the criminalization of Latinos in US society by examining how the historical image of the Mexican *bandido* (bandit) to the present-day shapes immigrant policies and laws that endorse the criminalization of Latino immigrants and Latino communities (both native-born and foreign-born).

To describe the criminalization of Chicanos (persons of Mexican origin born in the US) in American society, Mirande's (1987) *Gringo Justice* provides an outline of historical examples of racism. First, the criminalization of Chicanos resulted not from being more prone to crime, but by varying from mainstream society in terms of culture, worldviews, economic, political, and justice systems. Second, in the aftermath of the Mexican-American War, Chicanos were rendered landless and were displaced politically and economically, becoming a vital source of cheap labor for the development of the US capitalist system. Third, Chicanos were labeled as *bandidos* due to their active resistance against white encroachment while not having the power to repel the images of criminality placed upon them. Thus the image of the *bandido* served to legitimize their economic, political, and legal exploitation. Fourth, as Chicanos became displaced economically and politically, they became concentrated in ethnically and residentially homogeneous neighborhoods or *barrios* (neighborhoods with predominantly Latino populations). This *barrioization* made it possible to maintain a constant supply of cheap labor without "contaminating" white society. Fifth, conflict with law enforcement grew during the twentieth century. Indeed, the image of the violent *bandido* from the 1900s continues to be the most prevalent image of Mexicans in popular culture (Martinez 2013).

A notable example of the criminalization of Latinos and the breakdown in law enforcement in the twentieth century is the zoot suit riots. Escobar (2008) describes the tension between Mexican American young men and boys wearing a distinctive style of dress called a zoot suit and the white servicemen and police officers in Los Angeles between June 3 and June 10, 1943. The riots began when servicemen attacked zoot suiters, beating them, tearing off their clothes, and leaving them bleeding and naked in the streets. The Los Angeles Police Department (LAPD) allowed this violence against the Mexican American community to occur by only stepping in after the violence had occurred. Moreover, while they only arrested a handful of servicemen, they incarcerated over 600 Mexican Americans for disturbing the peace. The rioting then escalated to attacks on all Mexican Americans, which highlights the violation of Mexican American rights. This is just one of the incidents displaying anti-Mexican racism during this period.

Today's criminalization of Latinos is largely attributed to administrative policies and laws aimed at controlling immigration and border communities that disproportionately target all Latinos regardless of their citizenship status. Latinos, particularly Mexicans, have been involved in what Massey et al. (2002) call "circular patterns of migration," wherein target earners have historically migrated to the US for a temporary period of time and then return to their sending countries. This migratory pattern declined with the Immigration Reform and Control Act (1986) and border operations – such as Operation Hold the Line in El Paso (1993), Operation Gatekeeper in San Diego (1994), and the Border Safety Initiative (1998) (Massey et al. 2002) – and other initiatives involving a concentration of agents and technology in the US–Mexico border to provide a "show of force" to potential "illegal" border crossers (Customs and Border Protection 2010). These border control measures are part of what nongovernmental organizations (NGOs) and others refer to as the "militarization of the border," given the use of war-like discourse, military technology, and military personnel.

This is the context in which Bejarano et al. (2012) argue that violence surfaces, exposing migrants and subjugated border regions to militarized measures used by nation-states to stop migration flows, drug trafficking, and terrorism. Indeed, border enforcement measures have increased in the wake of the terrorist attacks on September 11, 2001. Although the perpetrators of 9/11 entered the US legally with student visas and not through the US–Mexican border, border security became a national priority, leading to the establishment of the Department of Homeland Security (DHS) on March 1, 2003. To date, such legal and administrative measures that focus on national security measures and militarization of the US–Mexico border contribute to shaping an image of Latinos as criminals.

It is only in recent history that clandestinely crossing the border without proper documentation became a crime, as it used to be only an administrative violation. DHS's Operation Streamline, initiated in 2005, required federal criminal prosecution and imprisonment of unlawful border crossers, thus largely targeting migrants with no criminal history (Lydgate 2010). Therefore, Latinos migrating to the US are now criminalized for migratory patterns that are largely responses to economic development in Latin America and labor demands in the US. In a comprehensive study of Operation Streamline, Lydgate (2010) observes that the program redirects crucial resources needed to fight violent crime along the border, fails to reduce undocumented immigration, and violates the US Constitution. Moreover, due to the targeted structural criminalization, such as the administrative policies described above, Latinos are interacting more than ever with police, courts, and prisons. This is a concern given that Latino confidence in the US criminal justice system is closer to mirroring the views of blacks who have been historically discriminated against by it (Lopez and Livingston 2009).

The legal restrictions against undocumented Latino immigrants do not stop at the border. While laws aimed to regulate immigration and border control are the responsibility of the federal government, individual states have developed immigration policies as a response to the perceived inability of the federal government to control migration flows from the southern border. State-level policies aimed to control immigration not only criminalize undocumented Latinos, but also their families and consequently the entire Latino community. One of the most notable efforts by states to implement immigration law is Arizona's SB 1070, signed in April 2010 (Sáenz et al. 2011), and amended as HB 2162, that legalized the *intensified* surveillance of Latinos, leading to more criminal arrests and detentions of Latinos by state and local police (Heyman 2010). This law in essence legalizes the racial profiling of Latinos by giving local and state law enforcement the authority to arrest Latinos on "reasonable suspicion" of being undocumented. Critics have claimed that SB 1070 violates the civil rights of Latinos by subjecting them to racial profiling (Golash-Boza 2012). This law then extends border control measures to local communities at the border and beyond by encouraging the criminalization of Latinos. In June 2012 the US Supreme Court ruled in *Arizona v. United States* upholding the Arizona law that requires police to check the legal status of any person they already stopped or arrested, although other parts of this law were ruled unconstitutional.

While SB 1070 targets all undocumented migrants, it is disproportionately aimed at Latinos as they represent the majority of migrants in states that have adopted such policies. Indeed, Sáenz et al. (2011) identify a racial threat phenomenon where demographic changes in Arizona are linked to the implementation of SB 1070. Specifically, from 1980 to 2008 Arizona experienced a growth in the foreign-born population from 18 percent to 33 percent. During this timeframe, the state's Latino population doubled while white representation decreased. Other regions adopting such administrative and legal forms of social control are new migrant destination areas that are experiencing similar demographic shifts as Arizona for the first time (e.g., Alabama, Georgia, and Pennsylvania). Hazelton, Pennsylvania, for instance, passed the Illegal Immigration Relief Act (IIRA) in 2006, which Longazel (2013) conceives as a racial degradation ceremony performed after an allegation of a Latino-on-white homicide which occurred in the background of demographic shifts and a weakening economy. Longazel (2013) contends that in the passage of IIRA, officials heavily relied on racialized rhetoric of the war on crime which socially constructs Latinos as "illegal" and "unlawful" and consequently leads to the marginalization of immigrant communities and the sustaining of the racial order of white hegemony.

Aligned with the increasing power given to local policing of immigration is the Secure Communities initiative. Secure Communities is an administrative policy forming a partnership between US Immigration and Customs Enforcement (ICE) and local- and state-level law enforcement aimed at removing criminal "aliens." It is based on a federal information-sharing partnership between ICE and the Federal Bureau of Investigation (FBI) that helps identify criminal aliens (US Immigration and Customs Enforcement 2015). Under Secure Communities, the FBI automatically sends fingerprints to the DHS to check against its immigration databases. If these checks reveal that an individual is unlawfully present in the US, ICE takes enforcement action, prioritizing the removal of individuals who present the most significant threats to public safety, including those with repeated immigration law violations.

The Border Network for Human Rights (BNHR) (2015), an advocacy organization along the US–Mexico border, argues that while initiatives such as Secure Communities and border militarization are implemented under the guise of national security, they are in violation of community security. Specifically, the discourse and practice of "national security" is not in line with that of "community security" given that it contributes to the marginalization of the border region and its large Latino communities by increasing surveillance and the criminalization of this population. Moreover, accenting the racialization of deportation practices, it is Afro-Caribbean small-time drug peddlers and Latino undocumented workers that DHS targets for removal rather than the "worst of the worst" (Golash-Boza 2012).

Policies, such as the ones discussed above and others, contribute to what some scholars call the *immigration industrial complex* (Diaz 2012; Douglas and Sáenz 2013; Fernandez 2007; Golash-Boza 2012). Fernandez (2007), for instance, claims that attempts to criminalize immigrants in addition to creating parallels between migrants and terrorists in the post 9/11 era have fueled policies that created the profit-making immigration industrial complex focused on detention and deportation of migrants. Detention centers resemble prisons and are intended to house individuals and entire families, including children, who are awaiting hearings, deportation, or to be bonded out. The immigration industrial complex for Latinos is comparable to the experiences of blacks in the post-civil rights era, where the prison industrial complex served in the disappearance of people of color from society (Diaz 2012). According to Douglas and Sáenz (2013), the rise of the immigration industrial complex is due to an association between the criminalization of immigrants and a corresponding growth in detention facilities. According to data from the US DHS, the immigrant detainee population has expanded from 9,011 in 1996, to 20,429 in 2001, 19,409 in 2006, and to 33,330 in 2011 (Douglas and Sáenz 2013; Siskin 2007, 2012). The growth in the demand for detention facilities has led to the privatization of migration centers. These policies have made corporations such as the Corrections Corporation of America (CCA) increase their stock market value nine-fold (Douglas and Sáenz 2013), thus making it possible to become rich from incarcerating people (Diaz 2012; Hallinan 2001). Not surprisingly CCA has made significant political contributions of an estimated $3.1 million from 2003 to 2012 (Douglas and Sáenz 2013). Supporting such views, Golash-Boza (2012) argues that powerful interests capitalizing from the detention and deportation of immigrants make immigration reform extremely difficult.

Criminological Theoretical Frameworks

As previously mentioned, most of the literature on race and crime has focused on black–white disparities (Martinez 2013). However, Latinos are gaining more scholarly attention due to the Latino immigrant crime paradox that discredits societal assumptions about immigrants having high levels of criminal behavior and societal perceptions that examine all Latinos, regardless of citizenship, through the immigrant lens. The following discussion highlights some of the most prevalent theoretical frameworks used to examine the criminalization of Latinos and their criminal behavior and victimization.

The labeling theory provides a useful framework to study the criminalization of Latinos. Labeling theory stresses that society creates deviance by creating rules and laws in which the violation of these rules/laws constitutes deviance for individuals who do not have enough power to avoid such labels (Eitzen et al. 2013). Even though deviant behavior cuts across social class and race, it is the undereducated, poor, and ethno-racial minorities that are disproportionately labeled as deviant in the criminal justice system. Therefore, labeling theory emphasizes the role of society in defining what is illegal and assigning a deviant status to certain individuals who break those rules (Eitzen et al. 2013). Eventually people who are imputed the deviant label can internalize it to the extent that it dominates their identities and behaviors.

In the case of Latinos, labels such as "bandido," "illegal," "foreigner," and "criminal," have been placed on them and their communities systematically (Mirande 1987; Rios 2011). Such labeling is the basic premise behind racial profiling, where police stop black and Latino drivers for routine traffic violations to search for evidence of criminal activity such as drugs or guns (Eitzen et al. 2013), and in the case of Latinos, unauthorized citizenship status. Moreover, in describing the stigmatized labels imposed on young Latino and black males, Rios (2011) calls this process the "labeling hype," where agents of social control (i.e., schools, police, probation officers) systematically target these youths as a criminal risk, thus creating a cycle of criminalization.

Other perspectives used to examine Latino criminality are aligned with the *culture of poverty* thesis. Simply stated, the culture of poverty perspective argues that criminality results from low-income individuals' adaptation to their deprived structural conditions. In this view the poor embody different values than the rest of society and these cultural differences not only explain their poverty but their crime and deviancy. Arguably expanding upon this framework the *subculture of violence* thesis posits that violence becomes normalized and it is an expected means for dispute resolution in structurally disadvantaged areas (i.e., poor neighborhoods). For instance, black (Dance 2005) and Latino male youths (Rios 2011) display "tough front" subcultures that develop in the streets – not a result of being cruel, hyper-masculine, and/or resistant, but as a resilience based on trying to succeed in a system that has systematically excluded them. At the macro level, however, there is less support for subculture of violence perspectives (Sampson 1985), suggesting that structure is more important than culture.

Attention has turned from cultural perspectives to examining the association between structural disadvantages and crime. For example, an early framework studying the structural component is Cloward and Ohlin's (1960) *opportunity structure* that builds on Robert Merton's theory of delinquency (Merton 1949). According to this thesis, the opportunity structure represents access to societal institutions (e.g., employment and schooling) as a means for supporting oneself and achieving goals. Merton argues that there is some consensus over major values but when society does not provide equal access to legitimate means for achieving those goals, it will result in deviance/delinquency. As such, being relegated to disadvantaged neighborhoods may encourage individuals to turn to crime as a means to overcome blocked opportunities (Martinez 2013).

Expanding upon the association between structural disadvantages and crime, Sampson and associates (Sampson and Bean 2006; Sampson and Wilson 1995) devised the *racial invariance thesis* to explain black-white racial disparities in crime and which has been found to be applicable to Latinos as well (Martinez 2008). The racial invariance thesis accentuates the role of concentrated disadvantage and racial segregation. Concentrated disadvantage has two dimensions: (1) the convergence of an assortment of negative economic and social conditions (e.g., joblessness, welfare dependency, poverty, family disruption, and residential instability) and (2) the concentration of these conditions in specific geographic areas (Martin et al. 2011; Wilson 1987). Consequently, due to structural racism Latinos and blacks have been relegated to neighborhoods with concentrated disadvantages and racial segregation, both of which are associated with crime rates, in particular violent crime (Martin et al. 2011). Ulmer et al. (2012), for instance, examined racial disparities and structural sources of those disparities and found that family structure and poverty are important in driving racial disparities and crime.

Another theoretical perspective based on the neighborhood level that has been used to examine Latinos and crime is the *social disorganization* framework that posits that crime is spatially concentrated in certain neighborhoods and structural conditions exert disparate influences on various types of crime across communities (Shaw and McKay 1942). A key feature of this social disorganization perspective is that structural economic conditions do not directly influence crime but that crime is a result of the breakdown of informal social control that is associated with deteriorating structural conditions (Allen and Cancino 2012). In particular, according to the social disorganization thesis, in disorganized areas community institutions are not able to work together to protect the values of residents and to control their behavior to conform to common goals and values, thus creating a space for crime to prosper (Bursik 1988).

In the case of Latinos, an assumption behind the *social disorganization* theory is that social change, such as demographic changes that come along with new settlements of Latinos, is associated with the breakdown of social institutions which weakens social control and allows for crime to flourish. Yet, the applicability of the social disorganization framework is questionable in the case of Latinos, particularly Latino immigrants. Even though Bankston (1998) argued that immigrants may undermine established institutions and hinder the establishment of common values, current research does not support this. Indeed, the argument that immigration reduces crime is substantially supported in the literature (Kubrin and Ishizawa 2012; Martinez and Lee 2000; Martinez and Stowell 2012; Martinez et al. 2010; Ousey and Kubrin 2009; Stowell et al. 2009; Thomas 2011). Sampson (2008) even argues that immigration is partially responsible for the dramatic drop in crime in the US since the 1990s. Moreover, in a study of social disorganization along the predominately Latino Texas border, the percentage of foreign-born (mostly Latino) is negatively related to juvenile property crime in urban areas (Allen and Cancino 2012). Furthermore, as ethnic heterogeneity increases in border counties, signifying a decrease in Latino concentration, property crime rates among juveniles in rural areas rise (Allen and Cancino 2012).

In spite of the racial profiling and the criminalization of Latinos, crime statistics illustrate the Latino immigrant crime paradox (Sampson and Bean 2006).

The homicide rates for Latinos are lower than those of other impoverished racial/ethnic groups (Martinez 2013). Thus, in contrast to common public opinion, Latino immigrants have lower levels of homicide than expected given their economic deprivation (Martinez 2008). Moreover, Latino immigrants are less involved in crime than the native-born despite being more vulnerable to disparate treatment in the criminal justice system, especially at the pre-trial stage (Hagan and Palloni 1999).

The Latino immigrant crime paradox has also been found at the macro level. For instance, crime is considerably lower in immigrant neighborhoods despite high rates of poverty and other structural disadvantages in these areas (Kubrin and Ishizawa 2012; Stowell 2007). Furthermore, this relationship appears to be robust, emerging among immigrant groups from different national origins, including those from Central America and Mexico and across different cities and time periods (Martinez and Stowell 2012; Martinez et al. 2010).

To explain the association between low crime rates and immigration, Martinez (2013) and Martinez and Valenzuela (2006) developed the *immigrant revitalization theory* to describe how immigration revitalizes impoverished urban neighborhoods with hard-working families and new businesses, therefore lowering crime. Indeed, Martinez (2013) claims that the low prevalence of homicide among Latino immigrants is due to the strong social support found in Latino neighborhoods which aids in reducing criminal behavior. This argument is in contrast to the social disorganization perspective. Moreover, if there were an association between immigration and violent crime, Latinos and Latino communities would have experienced the bulk of that crime given the heavy representation of migrants from Latin America in the US (Martinez 2008).

Trends on Victimization and Perceptions of Crime

National crime data reveal some important trends concerning Latino victimization and criminal activity. For example, Latinos are more likely to be victims of robbery than non-Latinos, at a rate comparable to that of blacks (Martinez 2008). Moreover, according to findings from the National Longitudinal Study of Adolescent Health (Add Health) (2008), Chicanos report a higher proportion of violent victimization and criminal activity compared to other Latino groups (Martinez 2008). For instance, one of the largest disparities involves Chicanos being at least twice as likely to report being jumped or assaulted than Mexicans, Puerto Ricans, Other Latinos, and Central Americans and three times more likely than Cubans (Martinez 2008). Furthermore, Latinos are three times more likely than whites to be victims of homicide but are three times less likely to be killed when compared to blacks (Martinez 2008). Below we utilize the Pew Research Center's Hispanic Trends Project's 2008 National Survey of Latinos and the National Longitudinal Study on Adolescent Health (2008) to present additional data trends on perceptions of the local policing of immigration enforcement, percentage of Latinos that have been stopped by police and asked about their citizenship status, deportation concerns, exposure to violence, and views on neighborhood safety.

Figure 11.1 illustrates Latino perceptions on whether immigration enforcement should be the responsibility of the federal government or local police departments.

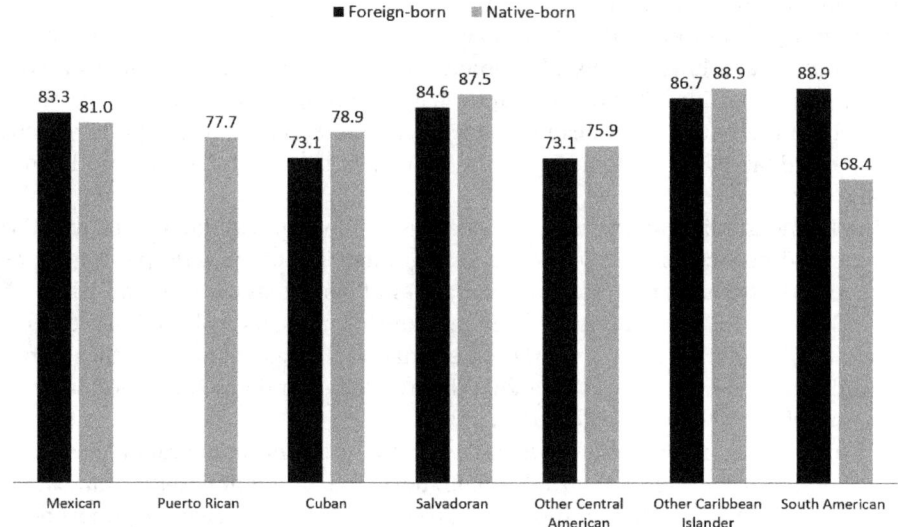

Figure 11.1 Percentage of Latinos who Perceive that Immigration Enforcement Should be the Responsibility of the Federal Government and Not Local Police

Source: Compiled with data from the 2008 National Survey of Latinos (Pew Research Center's Hispanic Trends Project 2008).

Based on the Pew Research Center's Hispanic Trends Project's 2008 National Survey of Latinos, it is evident that Latinos generally disapprove of local police handling immigration enforcement that is normally the responsibility of the federal government. Specifically, over 80 percent of Mexicans (foreign-born and native-born), Salvadorans (foreign-born and native-born), Other Caribbean Islanders (foreign-born and native-born), and foreign-born South Americans believe that immigration enforcement should be the responsibility of the federal government and not local police. In terms of the range, native-born Other Caribbean Islanders and foreign-born South Americans have the highest percentage (88.9%) of individuals believing that immigration enforcement should be dealt with by the federal government rather than local police, with native-born South Americans having the lowest level of agreement with this view (68.4%).

These data show that the local policing of immigration is not just a concern for the foreign-born but for Latinos in general. Indeed, there are not vast differences between foreign-born and native-born groups on perceptions regarding the local policing of immigration enforcement. Moreover, only among Mexicans and South Americans are foreign-born individuals more inclined to perceive that immigration enforcement is the responsibility of the federal government and not local police.

Figure 11.2 presents the percentage of Latinos that were stopped by police and asked about their citizenship status. According to data from the National Survey of Latinos (2008), close to 10 percent of both foreign-born and native-born Mexicans have been stopped by the police and asked about their immigration status. It is also necessary to recognize that these data are under-reported considering that at the time of the data collection, summer of 2008, such policies were controversial and

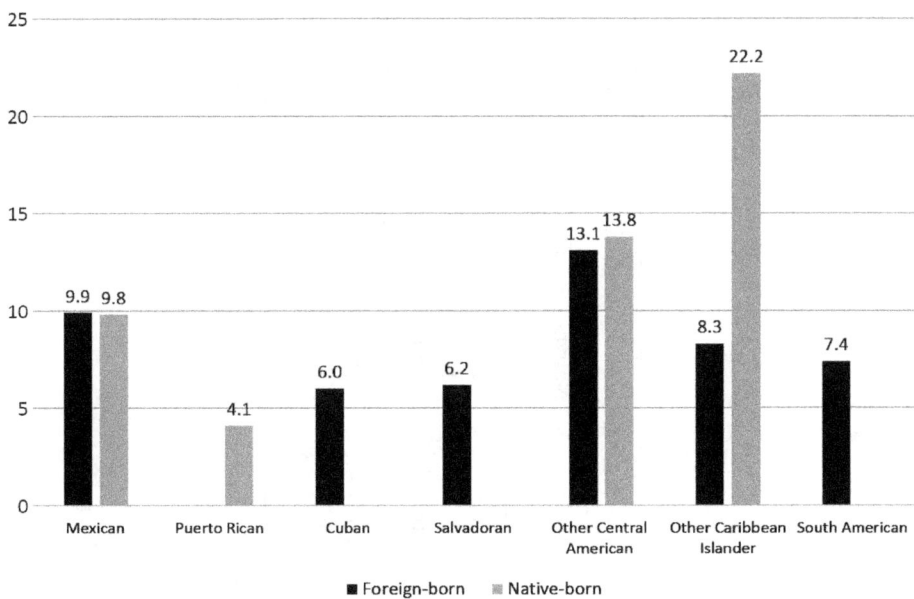

Figure 11.2 Percentage of Latinos Stopped by Police and Asked About Immigration Status, by Latino Group

Source: Compiled with data from 2008 National Survey of Latinos (Pew Research Center's Hispanic Trends Project 2008).

sparsely implemented. Currently, the number of such programs has increased. For example, while Secure Communities was a pilot program in 2008, it has grown each consecutive year, and became fully implemented nationwide in 2013 (US Immigration and Customs Enforcement 2015) (see below). What is important to point out is that, according to these data, the local policing of immigration status not only affects foreign-born individuals but also US-born Latinos. Furthermore, the policing of immigration status also affects Mexican-origin individuals more so than most other Latinos. The disproportionate impact of this practice on the Mexican-origin population could be attributed to the local policing of immigration not being equally implemented across the nation but more so in regions that are experiencing growth in Mexican immigration.

Table 11.1 presents the percentages of Latinos who, regardless of their citizenship status, are concerned about themselves, relatives, or friends being deported. Based on the 2008 National Survey of Latinos, it is evident that deportations of self, relatives or friends are a serious concern for immigrant Latinos, more so than native-born Latinos. In part due to administrative policies, such as Secure Communities and the local policing of immigration enforcement discussed above, the Obama administration has featured record-breaking levels of deportations. Not surprisingly, table 11.1 demonstrates that Latinos with the highest concern regarding deportations are the foreign-born. Specifically, the Latino group most worried about deportations is Mexican immigrants, with 77.0 percent having at least some worry about deportations, followed by 69.5 percent of Other Central American immigrants, 68.8 percent of Salvadoran immigrants, 66.5 percent of South

Table 11.1 Degree of Concern Regarding Deportations of Self, Relatives, or Friends by Place of Birth (%)

	A lot		Some		Not Much		Not at All	
	Foreign-born	Native-born	Foreign-born	Native-born	Foreign-born	Native-born	Foreign-born	Native-born
Mexican	57.0	19.3	20.0	19.9	8.8	11.6	14.1	48.8
Puerto Rican		24.7		11.5		12.3		51.4
Cuban	31.3	5.6	18.0	11.1	10.4	27.8	40.3	55.6
Salvadoran	54.7	62.5	14.1	0.0	10.9	0.0	20.3	37.5
Other Central American	53.3	17.2	16.2	13.8	6.7	17.2	23.8	51.7
Other Caribbean Islander	44.8	22.2	13.8	0.0	22.4	33.3	19.0	44.4
South American	49.3	10.5	17.2	15.8	7.4	5.3	25.9	68.4

Source: 2008 National Survey of Latinos (Pew Research Center's Hispanic Trends Project 2008).

American immigrants, and 58.6 percent of foreign-born Other Caribbean Islanders. It is highly probable that this worry is affecting the mental health and the stability of Latino communities (Sáenz et al. 2011), although more research is needed in this area.

Furthermore, while Latino immigrants are more heavily impacted by concern for deportations, this issue also affects native-born Latinos. In particular, 62.5 percent of native-born Salvadorans worry a lot about deportations, followed by 39.2 percent of Mexican Americans and 31 percent of native-born Other Central Americans who are at least somewhat concerned, and 36.2 percent of Puerto Ricans who have at least some worry. The group that is the least impacted by worries about deportations is native-born Cubans, with only one-sixth reporting at least some worry.

Based on data from the National Longitudinal Study on Adolescent Health (2008), figure 11.3 presents the percentage of Latinos that had a weapon pulled on them at least once in the past year by race, ethnicity, and place of birth. White youth are less likely to be subjected to violence in comparison to Latinos and blacks. Specifically, native-born Latinos (20.5%) are twice as likely as whites (10.1%) to have been threatened with a weapon at least once in the last year. Particularly alarming is that native-born Puerto Rican and Mexican American youth are approximately three times more likely than whites to experience such threat.

For all Latino subgroups, except for Cubans, the native-born are more likely to be subjected to violence than the foreign-born. Specifically, the native/foreign-born gap in exposure to violence is evident in statistics of being threatened with a weapon. For example, the exposure to violence gap ranges from native-born Latino Others being over four times as likely to be threatened with a weapon in contrast to their foreign-born counterparts (4.3% vs. 17.6%) to the native-born being almost twice as likely to be threatened with a weapon than their foreign-born co-ethnics

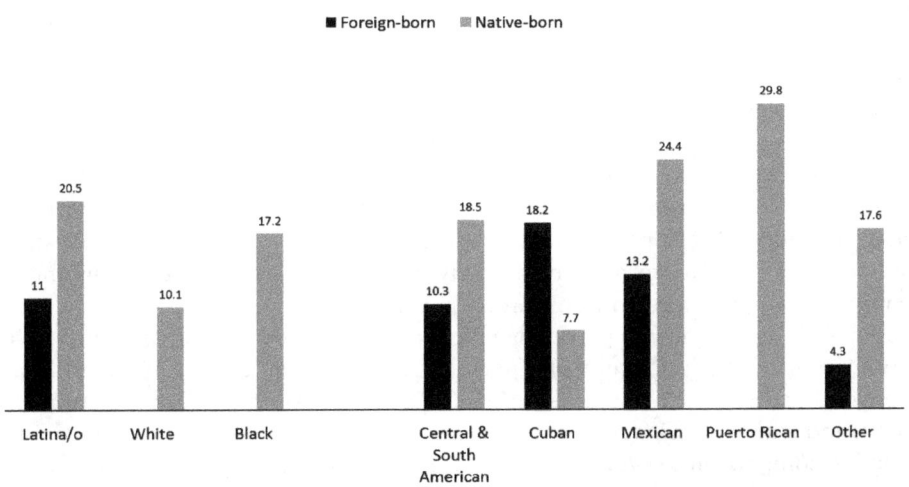

Figure 11.3 Percentage of Youth who Have Had a Knife/Gun Pulled on Them in the Past Year, by Race/Ethnic Group and Place of Birth

Source: Compiled with data from National Longitudinal Study on Adolescent Health (Add Health) (2008).

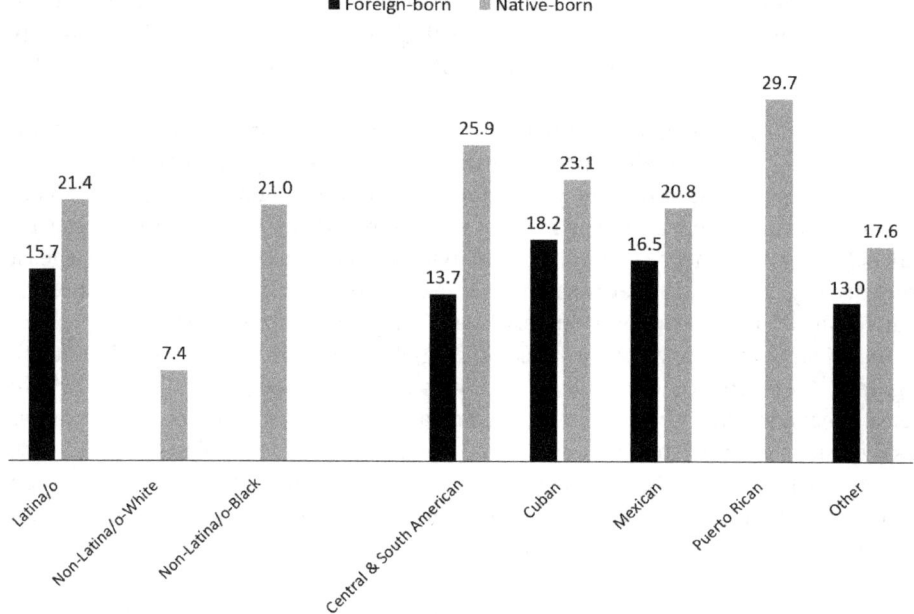

Figure 11.4 Percentage of Youth who Saw a Shooting or Stabbing at Least Once in the Past Year, by Race/Ethnic Group and Place of Birth

Source: Compiled with data from National Longitudinal Study on Adolescent Health (Add Health) (2008).

in the case of Mexicans (13.2% vs. 24.4%) and Central and South Americans (10.3% vs. 18.5%).

Figure 11.4 shows the percentage of youth who saw a shooting or stabbing at least once in the past year by race/ethnic group and place of birth. In comparison to whites, foreign-born Latinos are twice as likely and native-born Latinos are three times more prone to have witnessed a violent act in the last year. Particularly disconcerting is that Puerto Rican youth are four times more likely to have seen a shooting or stabbing at least once in comparison to whites. Moreover, comparable to the percentage of black youth, native-born Mexicans, Cubans, and Central and South Americans are about three times more likely than whites to have seen a stabbing or shooting in the past 12 months. In terms of place of birth, among all Latino subgroups the native-born are more likely to have seen a shooting or stabbing in comparison to their foreign-born counterparts.

Figure 11.5 presents the percentage of youth who do not feel safe in their neighborhood by race/ethnic group and place of birth based on data from the National Longitudinal Study on Adolescent Health (2008). Foreign-born Latinos are three times and native-born Latinos are over twice as likely to feel unsafe in their neighborhood in comparison to whites. About 27 percent of both foreign-born Mexican and Cuban youth reported being unsafe in their neighborhoods, which is close to four times higher than whites. In terms of place of birth, Latino immigrants feel less secure in their neighborhoods in comparison to their native-born counterparts across all Latino subgroups.

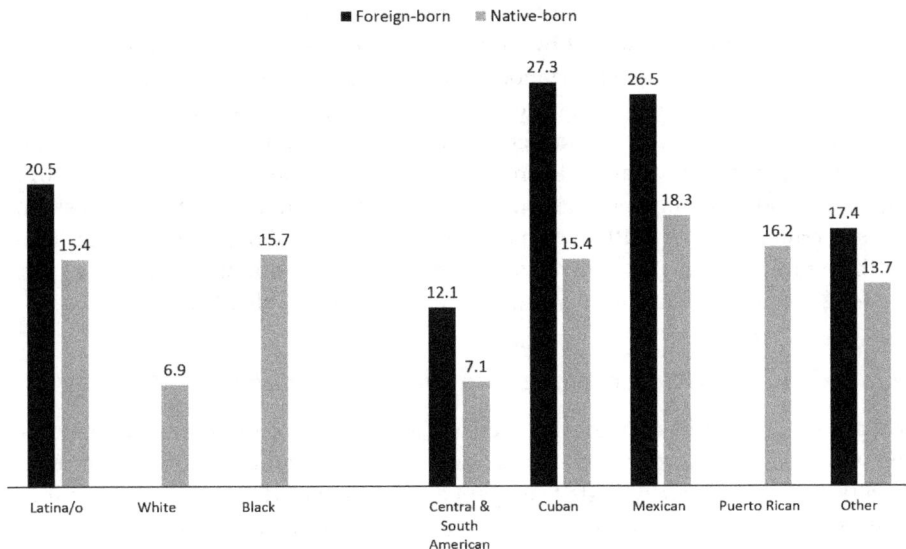

Figure 11.5 Percentage of Youth who Do Not Feel Safe in Their Neighborhood, by Race/Ethnic Group and Place of Birth

Source: Compiled with data from National Longitudinal Study on Adolescent Health (Add Health) (2008).

Questions Related to the Future of Latino Crime and Victimization

In this section we highlight some of the major issues concerning Latino criminal behavior and victimization that are likely to affect the future stability of this group. Below we discuss the structural violence and resiliency that are associated with crime and victimization, laws and policies aimed to militarize the border, and the hyper-criminalization and victimization of Latino youth. These topics are relevant not only for future academic research but also for public policy.

Structural Violence and Resiliency

How should violence be conceptualized in the crime literature? For the most part the criminal justice and criminology literature concentrates on physical violence. In a separate literature on social inequality, violence is conceptualized as not only physical but as emotional, psychological, and even economic. A theoretical framework that helps to understand various forms of victimization is structural violence. A basic premise of structural violence as a theoretical approach examines how violence is a consequence of a society's macro-level inequalities that occur when a group of people suffers from avoidable conditions while others do not (Chasin 2004; Farmer 2004). Thus, violence can take on different forms and is a direct result of structural inequalities.

Another question is how to acknowledge and study "victims" and "victimization" without painting a picture of passive individuals? Expanding upon the structural violence perspective, Morales and Bejarano (2008, 2009) and Bejarano et al. (2012) developed the *border sexual conquest* thesis. One of the premises behind border sexual conquest is that conquest (i.e., victimization) and attempts to conquer are ongoing and continue to be met by strong opposition (Morales and Bejarano 2009). As such, when discussing victimization, it is important to also acknowledge the resiliency and resistance against that violence. Although in this chapter we have discussed how Latinos are criminalized and victimized, there are several examples of how they are active agents of resistance. Even in the case of criminal behavior, Rios (2011) argues that "some of their non-serious offenses were committed as acts of resistance to being criminalized" (p. 103) when referring to Latino and black male youth. Thus, youth committed crime not only in search of respect and honor but also as a revolt against a system of exclusion and punitive control that they clearly understand.

Border Control and the Criminalization and Victimization of Latinos

What is the impact of military-like tactics used to control the flow of people and goods through the border on migrants and the Latino concentrated border communities? Border security costs taxpayers an estimated $18 billion per year which is more than the combined budgets of the Federal Bureau of Investigation (FBI), Bureau of Alcohol, Tobacco, Firearms and Explosives (ATF), US Marshals, Drug Enforcement Administration (DEA), and Secret Service (Border Network for Human Rights 2015). Even more importantly are the costs associated with human lives. Border-control policing initiatives have expanded from the apprehension and prevention-of-entry of migrants clandestinely crossing the border to also include drug enforcement and anti-terrorism policing (Bejarano et al. 2012; Dunn 1996). This surge in border enforcement has increased the number of deaths at the border (Bejarano et al. 2012; Cornelius 2001; Dunn 1996). The Border Network for Human Rights (2015) notes that an estimated 500 migrants die each year trying to avoid border militarization by crossing into dangerous natural terrain. The militarization not only affects the migrants but residents on both sides of the border. Two telling cases are the youths that were shot and killed by border enforcement agents along the US–Mexico border. First, Ezequiel Hernandez, Jr., a teenager, was shot dead in 1997 by a Marine on reconnaissance for the Border Patrol in Redford, Texas. Second, more recently, in 2010, a Mexican 14-year-old boy was shot and killed by a Border Patrol agent while still on the Mexican side of the border after throwing rocks along the international port of entry. As of May 2013, the Border Network for Human Rights (2015) observes that the current immigration reform proposal (S.744) recommends still further expansion of border control operations with the following militaristic measures:

- Adding 20,000 Border Patrol agents to the current 21,000
- At least 700 miles of border fencing as triple walls must be completed
- Deployment of the National Guard
- 85 fixed watch towers
- 488 fixed remote video surveillance systems
- 232 mobile surveillance systems
- 4,425 ground sensors
- 820 thermal and night vision goggles
- 6 VADER radar systems

- 17 UH-1N helicopters
- 8 AS-350 light enforcement helicopters
- 15 Blackhawk Helicopters
- 30 marine vessels
- 18 drones (unmanned aerial vehicles)

Nowhere else in the country are residents subjected to these war-like conditions that exist for Latino communities along the US–Mexico border. As such, the civil rights of the 7,000,000 border residents from San Diego, California to Brownsville, Texas are in question (Border Network for Human Rights 2015).

Native-born Latino Youth and Social Death

A critical issue to consider that will deeply impact the stability of Latinos in the US is the various institutional mechanisms of social control that result in the criminalization of native-born Latino youth. Drawing on Orlando Patterson's (1982) concept of "social death," where individuals are systematically denied their humanity, Rios (2011) describes the experiences of Latino youth as "social incapacities," or the process by which punitive social control becomes a tool to marginalize and keep them from thriving. Moreover, there is gender inequity where females are less likely to be sentenced to prison than males for property and drug offenses and to receive shorter sentences for violent offenses (Rodriguez et al. 2006). In a study based on Texas felony drug offenders during the height of the "war on drugs," Curry and Corral-Camacho (2008) found that Latino males are more likely to go to prison, concluding that they pay an additional penalty due to their gender and ethnicity. In conjunction with hyper-criminalization is the exposure to violence confronted by native-born Latino youth. What are the social and psychological costs associated with navigating such violence? From a structural violence perspective, why are young males of color subjected to violent social environments in contrast to white youth?

Summary

This chapter has provided an overview of the study and trends on Latino criminalization, criminal behavior, and victimization. We began by highlighting some historical and contemporary examples of how the law and the criminal justice system disproportionately aim to criminalize Latinos and Latino communities, from images of the Mexican "*bandido*" rooted in the aftermath of the Mexican-American War, to the zoot suit riots of the 1940s, and today's immigration enforcement policies. We then presented an overview of the criminological theoretical frameworks that are used to examine Latino criminalization, criminal behavior, and the Latino immigrant crime paradox in which Latino immigrants exhibit low criminal behavior despite the structural disadvantages they face.

In addition, we provided an overview of patterns of criminal behavior and victimization among Latinos. The results show some consistencies across Latino groups with respect to their attitudes regarding the use of local policing of immigration and worries about deportation, as well as in the experiences with being stopped by local police and questioned about their immigration status. Moreover, Latino youth, especially the native-born, report a significant level of personal victimization and the witnessing of violent crimes, although Latino foreign-born youth do not feel safe in their neighborhoods. Finally, we provided a discussion on issues that need to be considered in current and future discussions on Latino criminal behavior and victimization.

As we discussed in this chapter, the image of Latinos as criminals and thugs has been around since Mexicans were incorporated into the US. The mass media has been one vehicle that has created and promoted this image of Latinos. In the next chapter, we provide an overview of the mass media and its portrayal of Latinos.

12 Mass Media

The mass media has historically played an important role in fostering and presenting a portrait of Latinos locally, nationally, and internationally. As the Latino population has become more diverse along a variety of dimensions – generational status, national origin, language use, and socioeconomic status – it has become increasingly difficult to determine this image. Nonetheless, because many Americans know relatively little about Latinos and the diversity that characterizes the group, many people rely on the mass media's depiction of Latinos. Historically, Latinos have been presented in stereotypical fashion. Moreover, despite the major importance of Latinos in the demographic patterns of the US, Latinos continue to be disproportionately absent from the big screen, television, and other forms of mass media.

The absence of representation of Latinos in the mass media results in the continuation of stereotypical images in the portrayal of Latinos. Thus, the mainstream media tends to present Latinos and frame issues involving them in a certain fashion. For example, the mainstream media tends to stress immigration-related matters, resulting in the continuation of an image of Latinos as immigrants. In contrast, the Spanish-language media also engages in the construction of counternarratives that give voice to people who have been marginalized in mainstream society.

Yet, traditional forms of mass media, including television and newspapers, do not have a monopoly in the creation and dissemination of images and framing of matters related to Latinos. This is particularly the case with the technological advancements – such as email, Facebook, Twitter, blogs, and other forms of communication – which provide voice to a large swath of the population with mercurial speed in which images and stories can be dispersed. Such technology has made it possible to spread positive and negative images of Latinos and the major issues that affect the community.

In this chapter, we began with a discussion of theoretical perspectives that help us understand the framing of Latinos in the mass media. Subsequently, we provide a discussion of the important role that the Spanish-language media has played in providing a more complete portrait of Latinos compared to that of the mainstream media. Furthermore, we illustrate the distinct ways in which Latinos are framed in the mainstream and Spanish-language mass media. Moreover, we assess the relative presence of Latinos in a variety of dimensions of the mass media. Finally, we highlight some of the major issues involving Latinos and the mass media in the near future.

Theoretical Overview

The mass media plays an important role in shaping public opinion on particular issues as well as groups such as Latinos (Markert 2010; McConnell 2011). In the case of groups of color, the mass media is particularly important in shaping opinions that members of the dominant group hold given the lack of knowledge about the group and limited interaction with minority-group members. For example, Markert (2010) reports on a study that he undertook involving 136 white and black college students concerning their interaction with and opinions about Latinos. He found that both sets of students had a minimal number of friends and acquaintances that are Latino. Furthermore, Markert (2010) observed that students who had the greatest levels of animosity toward Latinos were more likely than other students to have been exposed to stories, shows, or news reports that presented Latinos in a negative fashion compared to students who had lower levels of antagonism toward Latinos.

The mass media essentially packages issues, individuals, and groups of people through frames which are presented to the general public. McConnell (2011) describes the role that framing plays in establishing an image about certain groups as well as attributes that are associated with them:

> Scholars invoking the framing perspective explore media professionals' use of media texts as organizing devices that structure information and help shape the social world . . . Through framing, members of the media create particular interpretations through the selection, emphasis and juxtaposition of material . . . Consequently, media organizations help produce discourses that do not simply reflect an objective reality. (p. 181)

As Hall (1997) argues, such discourse packages what is significant, pertinent, and true for people of color (see also McConnell 2011). Without the nuances of the diversity that exists within groups of color, the group is packaged efficiently for the audience to consume and form opinions. The framing of groups of color – especially Latinos and African Americans – tends to provide images as the "other," people who are not like "us." Thus, Latinos and African Americans tend to be portrayed as law breakers, criminals, hypersexual, aggressive, and so forth (McConnell 2011; Van Dijk 1991). Leo Chavez (2008) has documented in great detail the Latino Threat Narrative which portrays Latinos as criminals who are a threat to American ideals and institutions and who are not worthy of social services and education (see also Flores-Yeffal et al. 2011; Santa Ana 2002). This is a portrait that certainly does not engender empathy toward the plight of Latino unauthorized immigrants and, by extension, Latinos in general.

There are three theoretical perspectives that we highlight here to help us understand how Latinos are framed and the issues and attributes that are associated with them. These include the racial formation, power threat, and critical race theory perspectives.

Racial Formation Perspective

The racial formation perspective, developed by Michael Omi and Howard Winant (1994), describes how race is socially constructed through social, economic, and political forces and how it operates at the micro level (personal interactions) and at the macro level (institutions, laws, mass media, etc.). The racial formation perspective is especially useful in making sense of the role of the mass media in crafting frames and narratives to relay the storyline about groups of color and their societal standing (McConnell 2011). As McConnell (2011) asserts, "extensive research documents that members of the media actively construct ideologies and metaphors about racial and ethnic minorities in the US, select which information is relevant to readers, shape their depictions in texts and associated photographs and limit the variety of those depictions" (p. 181).

As noted above, Latinos and African Americans tend to be depicted negatively as violent individuals who are prone to crime and who are outside of the mainstream. When the specter of Latinos as criminals and as threats to US ideals is raised, it is easy to see how people in the mainstream increase their level of hostility and distaste for "those" people (Chavez 2008; Santa Ana 2002). In addition, when Trayvon Martin was portrayed as a black man up to no good in a gated white community – the common frame that the mainstream "knows" – it was with ease that many in the mainstream no longer saw Martin as a scared teenager but as an aggressive man who did not belong where he was when he was murdered (Sáenz 2014b). In contrast, when the mass media holds whites as the "norm," as a group without race, it supports white hegemony and white privilege, thus placing whites at the top of the racial hierarchy (Feagin 2013; Jensen 1998; McConnell 2011; Omi and Winant 1994). Accordingly, the mass media, as do other societal institutions, support and sustain the existing racial hierarchy.

Power Threat Perspective

The power threat perspective (or group size perspective), developed by Hubert Blalock (1967), overviewed in chapter 6, provides some insights to understand the role of the mass media in framing Latinos, particularly with recent modifications to the original theory (Markert 2010; Weimann 2000). In its original formulation, Blalock (1967) argued that as a minority group increases in size, it becomes an economic and political threat to the dominant group, at which time – in order to protect its position of power – the dominant group establishes barriers in the form of policies and practices to limit the economic and political power of the minority group. Over the nearly 50 years since the development of the power threat perspective, a lot has changed. In particular, while the perspective focuses primarily on African Americans, Latinos now form the largest minority groups. In addition, while the perspective placed emphasis on competition over economic resources and political power, due to the more limited influence of the mass media half a century earlier, the perspective did not take into account the role of the mass media in enhancing competition and in limiting opportunities for the minority group (Markert 2010).

Since the development of the power threat perspective, the mass media has played an increasingly powerful role in the development of frames, narratives, and images that can instantly define situations involving minority-majority relations and stir collective action to correct threats that the minority group poses to the dominant group (Markert 2010). Moreover, technological innovations, such as email, Facebook, and Twitter, can distribute mass media products instantaneously and widely. It has been suggested that the intensity of the competition rises when the minority group is quite distinct from the dominant group (Markert 2010). Markert (2010) asserts that, accordingly, Latinos stand out from whites along the lines of their undocumented status and the perceived resistance toward learning English. Markert (2010) points out that over the last several decades there has been a shift from a greater predominance of news stories involving legal immigration over undocumented immigration to the opposite pattern. For example, Lee's (1998) research based on newspaper articles related to immigration published in *The New York Times* between 1965 and 1995 showed that reporting turned predominantly to undocumented immigration beginning in 1975 with a 6:1 ratio in stories on undocumented immigration to legal immigration. Markert's (2010) replication revealed that the ratio had climbed to 30:1 during the period from 1996 to 2005 and the large majority of stories on undocumented immigration focused on Latinos. In reality, as we observed back in chapter 4, the majority of Latinos – approximately three-fifths – were born in the US and, thus, are not immigrants, much less undocumented immigrants.

Similarly, as the Latino population has grown, there has been opposition to bilingual education programs as well as an increase in the number of states around the country that have adopted English as the official language (Markert 2010). Opposition to bilingual education has been magnified further by the inaccurate belief among many opponents that bilingual education involves the instruction of students only in Spanish (Huddy and Sears 1990; Markert 2010). Rising attacks on bilingual education in California led to the passage of Proposition 227 which mandated that instruction in public schools be only in English (Markert 2010). Relatedly, 31 states have made English their official language (Pro English 2014); this list includes six of the ten states with the most Latinos: Arizona, California, Colorado, Florida, Georgia, and Illinois. Again, in actuality, upwards of 70 percent of Latinos 5 years of age and older speak English, with 50 percent being bilingual (speaking Spanish at home and speaking English well or very well) and an additional 21 percent speaking English at home (Sáenz 2010).

In sum, Markert (2010) seeks to extend Blalock's (1967) power threat perspective as a mediating variable that "affects the intensity of the public's hostility toward Hispanics, regardless of their population size, because media attention may make the group seem larger than it actually is, and thus more threatening" (p. 321). Inaccurate perceptions suggesting that the Latino population is larger than reality is fueled by news stories which tend to describe the growth to the Latino population in superlative terms often imbued with natural disaster prose, e.g., wave, surge, flood, etc. (Markert 2010; McConnell 2011).

Critical Race Theory

Critical race theory (CRT), developed by legal scholars such as Derrick Bell and Richard Delgado, originated as a critical response to critical legal studies and civil rights research in the 1970s when gains from civil rights legislation waned (Delgado and Stefancic 2001; Milner and Howard 2013). In addition, CRT was critical of critical legal studies and civil rights scholarship for sidestepping the profound links between the legal system and racism. López (2006) points out that laws create racial categories and support the subordination of groups of color. One of the elements of CRT that is particularly relevant to our understanding of the role that the mass media plays in framing Latinos is the counterstory or counternarrative that provides voice to marginalized people. As Waterman (2013) notes:

> Counterstory-telling is an important element of CRT ... Counterstories reveal the lived experiences of non-dominant groups that are typically not acknowledged by the dominant society. The popular notion that *the victor writes the history* is the

common person's understanding . . . that not all stories are told. CRT insists that those stories be told. (p. 340)

Thus, as the mainstream mass media presents images, depictions, frames, narratives, and stories about groups of color, minority media sources provide counterimages, counterdepictions, counterframes, counternarratives, and counterstories that originate from the group and which serve to correct or provide greater nuance to tales put forth by the mainstream media.

Having provided an overview of three theoretical perspectives that allow us to gain an understanding of the framing of Latinos, we now turn to a historical overview of the Spanish-language media and how it differs in many respects from the mainstream in its coverage of the Latino population. As we will see below, the Spanish-language mass media continues to be valuable in offering a counternarrative to the shallow and often stereotypical narrative that the mainstream media constructs.

Historical Overview of Spanish-Language Mass Media

There is a common tendency to focus exclusively on the mainstream mass media in its treatment of Latinos. Nonetheless, the Spanish-language media has a long history in the US. The first Spanish-language newspaper, New Orleans' *El Misisipí*, was published in 1808 (Gutiérrez 2013). In 1938, at the time that San Antonio's *La Prensa* celebrated its 25th anniversary, it published an inventory of 451 Spanish-language periodicals published in the US (Gutiérrez 2013).

The mainstream English-language and Spanish-language mass media differ significantly in their coverage of Latinos. Gutiérrez (2013) notes the differences between the two. He provides an overview of the mainstream media method of appealing to an audience and in its views regarding people of color:

> They [mainstream media] seek to attract viewers, readers, and listeners by offering news, programs, or movies with broad appeal to people from different races, ages, sexes, income, and demographic categories. Although they reach multicultural, multiracial audiences, Anglo media have tended to view people of diverse cultures through eyes that see Anglo Americans as the norm and others as apart from the norm. This "us and others" media view has offered less accurate images, reporting, and coverage of people of color and the communities in which they live. This is especially apparent in the Anglo media's portrayal and coverage of Latinos. (p. 100)

Gutiérrez (2013) describes the contrasting way in which the Spanish-language and mainstream media view and portray Latinos:

> Latino media are produced by, for, and about Latinos and their communities. Their success in drawing audiences and ultimately advertisers is built on having a close connection with the wide range of activities and issues of interest to Latinos in the US. They are more closely linked to their audiences and play important roles in explaining the US to their readers, listeners, and viewers, while also covering news in Latin America. (p. 100)

Further, David Hayes-Bautista, Professor of Medicine and Director of the Center for the Study of Latino Health and Culture at the University of California, Los Angeles, illustrates the difference between the two media in its coverage of Latinos:

> In the mainstream media, almost the only time you see a minority is a crime or welfare story, something negative. In the Spanish-language media, you also get the human interest, the arts and sport stories . . . Latinos are reduced to only one slice in the Anglo media, while in the Spanish media, a whole community is presented. (quoted in Gutiérrez 2013, p. 100; see also Garza 1997, p. 134)

The mainstream historically has had little knowledge of Latinos. For example, Gutiérrez (1977) conducted an analysis of magazine articles published between 1890 and 1970. He observed that relatively few stories reported on Latinos and the few that were written tended to depict Latinos as a problem or crisis. Gutiérrez (2013) notes that:

> When Latinos were covered in Anglo news media during much of the 20th century, the editors, news directors, and reporters often used shorthand word symbols to trigger stereotypes of the Latinos seen as posing a threat, such as "Zoot Suiters" in the 1940s, "Wetbacks" [sic] in the 1950s, "Chicano Militants" in the 1960s, and "Illegal Aliens" in the 1970s and 1980s. (p. 102)

The lack of knowledge concerning Latinos on the part of the mainstream media is illustrated in a 1967 magazine article in *The Atlantic* titled "A Minority Nobody Knows" (Rowan 1967; see also Gutiérrez 2013). Gutiérrez (2013) suggests that when the mass media did start paying attention to this minority nobody knows, "their stories sometimes revealed more of their own lack of knowledge or their Anglo preconceptions than the realities of the people they tried to cover" (p. 103). For example, the gulf separating white reporters and the Latino community is evident in a 1967 *Time* magazine article on East Los Angeles, a predominantly Mexican area in Los Angeles, which is described as "tawdry taco joints and rollicking cantinas . . . the reek of cheap wine . . . the fumes of frying tortillas . . . the machine gun patter of slang Spanish" (quoted in Gutiérrez 2013, p. 103; see also *Time* 1967). Rubén Salazar, a reporter for the *Los Angeles Times*, asserted at a conference held in San Antonio in 1969 that "It's as if the media, having finally discovered Mexican Americans, is not amused that under the serape and sombrero is a complex Chicano instead of a potential Gringo" (quoted in Gutiérrez 2013, p. 103; see also Salazar 1969). The following year Salazar was killed by a Los Angeles County sheriff's deputy during the National Chicano Moratorium.

Aside from providing the more profound counternarrative to the shallow narrative of the mainstream media, the Spanish-language media serve a variety of other functions related to the Latino community. Luis Leal, a scholar of Mexican, Chicano, and Latin American literature, lists these functions:

> political and social activism; promotion of civic duties; the defense of the population against the abuse of the authorities and other organized groups; the sponsoring of national and religious holidays; the provision of an outlet for the public to express their ideas in the form of letters or to express their activity in the form of poems, short stories, essays, and an occasional serialized novels [sic] . . . Not less important has been the publication of community social news (cited in Gutiérrez 2013, p. 105; original in Leal 1989, p. 159).

Gutiérrez (2013) summarizes the uniqueness of the Spanish-language press and its coverage of Latinos in contrast to the mainstream media:

> One common theme across all Latino media is coverage of an active, engaged, and ambitious people looking to make a better life for themselves and others in the US,

first in print and later other media. Recognizing the fullness of Latino experiences in the US, these media show Latinos as participants, not bystanders, in events that shaped the nation and their communities. Such representation and documentation is important in countering prevailing images of Latinos as passive, unambitious, and uncultured additions to the nation. By documenting the literate tradition of Latinos and their use of new media technologies as they were developed, a more complete history of the nation and its communities can be told to a wider public. (p. 106)

The Spanish-language media, then, portray Latinos as real people with agency who make important contributions to their communities and country. Latinos are seen as people who have a long history in the US, who are vested in this country, and who belong here.

We can gain an understanding of the importance of the Spanish-language media in its role in calling attention to Latinos and key issues that affect them. The spring of 2006 saw major waves of marches throughout the country bringing together undocumented immigrants along with family, friends, and supporters protesting the draconian HR 4437 – the Sensenbrenner Bill – which among a variety of provisions sought to enhance criminal penalties against undocumented immigrants and to make helping and abetting undocumented immigrants a felony act. These marches, known as the Immigrant Rights Marches, also called for immigration reform with particular emphasis on the development of a path to US citizenship for undocumented immigrants. The marches caught the mainstream media off guard (Gutiérrez 2013). The mainstream media quickly placed the events within its handy, tried-and-true "sleeping giant" narrative. Accordingly, the marches represented the Latino sleeping giant being rousted from its slumber (Gutiérrez 2013). The mainstream media itself had, in fact, been in a stupor as the planning of the massive marches were underway for some time earlier, illustrating its lack of connection to the Latino community and its grassroots organizations.

In fact, the Spanish-language media played a major role in the organizing of Latinos. Radio personalities, most prominently Eduardo Sotelo (known as *El Piolín*), played an important part in "spreading advance word of the marches, where they would happen, and who should participate" (Gutiérrez 2013, p. 99). Yet, as Gutiérrez (2013) points out, other forms of Spanish-language mass media such as television networks (Univision and Telemundo) and newspapers played an important role as well. The morning of the 500,000-person march in Los Angeles started with the thunderous headline titled "*A Las Calles!*" ("To the Streets!") on the front page of *La Opinión*, one of the leading Spanish-language newspapers in the country, housed in Los Angeles (Gutiérrez 2013).

In addition, as the traditional mass media sought answers to its query about whether the marches represented an awakening of Latinos on the national political scene, it began to learn more about the history of Latino protest (Gutiérrez 2013). For example, on *The NewsHour with Jim Lehrer*, Félix Gutiérrez asserted that this was nothing new – *El Clamor Público* (The Public Clamor), a Los Angeles Spanish-language newspaper, back in 1855 was a forceful voice of protest calling attention to equal rights violations of Mexicans following the Treaty of Guadalupe Hidalgo (PBS NewsHour 2006). Gutiérrez also told of Pedro J. González, a radio personality, who opposed the repatriation of Mexicans during the Great Depression in the 1930s, *La Opinión*'s critical coverage of Operation Wetback in the 1950s, among other important protests on the part of the Spanish-language mass media (PBS NewsHour 2006). In sum, the Spanish-language media provided a valuable counternarrative to the sleeping-giant narrative that the mainstream media erected.

We have presented an overview of the uniqueness of the Spanish-language media and its important role in presenting a counternarrative to the often superficial and stereotypical narrative that the mainstream promotes. We now turn to a discussion in which we draw attention to how the mainstream and Spanish-language media differ in their framing of Latinos in the print media.

The Framing of Latinos in the Print Media

The newspaper is an important mass media source that is quite effective in shaping opinions on political issues and on certain groups, such as groups of color and immigrants. The newspaper is a valuable source for researchers today as newspaper articles are digitalized which allow them to be compiled, culled, and sorted. Thus, scholars can analyze text and images to assess how issues or groups are framed and how the framing varies across media sources, such as mainstream versus ethnic media. We illustrate below how Latinos are portrayed in a variety of contexts.

Framing Latino Population Growth in Georgia

As shown in chapter 4, the Latino population in the US has increased more rapidly than other racial and ethnic groups. Newspapers around the country readily run headline stories about the growth of the Latino population following the release of population figures by the US Census Bureau. McConnell (2011) analyzed 70 newspaper articles appearing in the *Atlanta Journal-Constitution* between 2000 and 2003 to see how they reported the growth of different racial and ethnic groups in Gwinnett County, a suburban area that is part of the Atlanta Metropolitan Statistical Area (MSA), between 1990 and 2000.

McConnell's (2011) results indicate that while the four major racial and ethnic groups (whites, blacks, Latinos, and Asians) in Gwinnett County increased between 1990 and 2000, newspaper articles overwhelmingly focused on growth in the Asian and, especially, Latino populations. Only one-fifth of articles actually reported the growth across all four racial and ethnic groups. In contrast, 71 percent of the articles concentrated primarily on the increase of the Latino population, with 59 percent reporting principally on the growth of the Asian population. In fact, none of the articles focused exclusively on gains in the white or black populations, although the absolute growth of each of these groups was larger than that of Latinos and Asians.

Furthermore, even though whites make up the largest segment of the population of Gwinnett County and they accounted for the largest share of the county's growth between 1990 and 2000, their role in Gwinnett County's population change was minimized. Rather, the focus was especially on Latino growth through the use of superlative words as illustrated by the following description:

> Gwinnett's population, with a whopping 657 per cent increase in Hispanics in the past decade, now claims the greatest number of Latinos in the Atlanta region. More are coming, too, furthering Gwinnett's explosive growth. (Chapman 2001; see also McConnell 2011, p. 187)

Again, minimizing the role of whites in Gwinnett County's population growth, another article focuses on the growth of gangs alongside the increase of non-white groups:

> Their names are colorful, sometimes menacing: La Gran Familia, Latin Lords, Asian Piru Bloods, Insane Blood Gangstas. There are many reasons gangs have flourished in Gwinnett, experts say, including an explosion of immigrants seeking better economic circumstances ... According to the 2000 Census, Gwinnett's Hispanic population grew from fewer than 9,000 in 1990 to 64,000 in 2000 – more than a sevenfold increase. More than 50 of the 175 gangs identified by Gwinnett police have Latino roots. The Asian community's numbers swelled even more spectacularly, from fewer than 1,000 residents in 1990 to 42,768 just a decade later. Police have identified 28 gangs with Asian ties. The black population quadrupled from 1990 to 2000, rising to 78,224. Officials estimate 20 to 30 predominantly black gangs in Gwinnett. Police have also identified a handful of white gangs and many white youths who are members of gangs with Asian, African-American or Latino roots. (Mungin and Davis 2003; see also McConnell 2011, p. 189)

The framing of non-white growth is simple – the massive growth of non-whites has brought an influx of gangs. This particular newspaper article illustrates the methodological caution that must be exercised in reporting percentage changes which McConnell (2011) points out, namely that an elevated percentage change is oft due to a very small population base at the earlier point in time in the comparison (e.g., 1990). Certainly, such reporting leads to the impression that the Latino population is larger than actuality. In many Latino new-destination areas, such as Georgia, extraordinary high levels of growth were due largely to very small population sizes at the beginning of the comparative period.

The Framing of Latinos in Virginia

Virginia represents another new-destination area for Latinos. Stewart et al. (2011) conducted an analysis of the discourse on undocumented immigration in articles appearing in *The Virginian-Pilot*, which serves the Hampton Roads region of Virginia – including Virginia Beach, the state's largest city – between 1994 and 2006. These researchers undertook two studies – the first based on articles, editorials, and letters to the editor appearing in the newspaper between 1994 and 2006 to examine the salience of the term "illegal immigrants" in these texts, and the second based on an examination of two local events (an undocumented immigrant drunk driver who killed two teenage girls in a crash and undocumented workers employed for a Verizon contractor) associated with undocumented workers that occurred in 2007.

The findings of Stewart et al. (2011) suggest newspaper reports constructed "illegal immigrants" as a metonym – a word or phrase used as a substitute for something else – for Latino immigrants. Thus, just as "Washington" is used to represent the federal government, "illegal immigrant" is used to signify Latino immigrants. The analysis reveals discourse showing the threat that Latinos represent: "Local policy let this illegal immigrant [Alfredo Ramos, the drunk driver] flout the law" (Stewart et al. 2011, p. 20); Ramos described in court as having a "zombie like demeanor" and unable to "muster any visible remorse" (Stewart et al. 2011, p. 21); "While we have heard repeated apologies from Hispanic leaders, most recently in announcing an alliance of sorts with MADD to combat drunk driving, I've yet to hear an apology from the people in the Hispanic community" (Stewart et al. 2011, p. 21).

Stewart et al. (2011) report a few incidences in which whites took action in response to their suspicions that some Latinos were in the country illegally. In addition, Stewart et al.'s (2011) interviews with local Latinos demonstrated that Latinos feared a backlash. Stewart et al. (2011) describe the feelings of local Latinos:

> These Latino community members clearly sensed that they were perceived as a threat by the majority and worked to counter stereotypes that were developing within the local news media. These out-group responses to this news discourse show how its rhetorical force is created through widespread public participation in the construction and definition of the illegal immigrant ... This rhetorical force is strongly tied to the marker of race; despite being longtime residents and established business owners in the community they perceived that their identities as Latinos are still constrained by dominant media constructions of (illegal) immigrants. (p. 23)

This research project shows how the construction of the "illegal immigrant" term came to represent all Latinos in the Hampton Roads region of Virginia. Latinos clearly became marked as the "other," individuals that do not belong in the community.

Framing a Wise Latina

Thus far, we have examined how the mainstream media has framed, constructed, and represented Latinos, as a group, in two new-destination areas. We now shift to how a particular individual Latina woman was framed differently by the mainstream media and the Spanish-language media. On May 26, 2009 President Barack Obama nominated Sonia Sotomayor to the Supreme Court. As the nomination process went into effect, pundits, journalists, legislators, and the general public began looking into her background, experience, politics, and legal decisions (Nielsen 2013). Nielsen (2013) conducted an analysis of 124 news articles related to Sotomayor that appeared in *The New York Times* (76 articles) and *El Diario-La Prensa* (48 articles) – a Spanish-language newspaper located in New York City – between the date of her nomination (May 26, 2009) and one week after she was sworn (August 15, 2009). Nielsen's (2013) analysis was based on the use of critical race theory and the intersectionality perspective, which takes into account the intersection between race, class, and gender.

The results of Nielsen's (2013) analysis clearly show that the two newspapers framed Sotomayor distinctly. In particular, the two outlets differed significantly in how they framed the issue of diversity. The articles in *The New York Times* focused primarily on the *burden of diversity* with the discourse centered on concerns that Sotomayor has in-group biases and favoritism toward Latinos. In contrast, *El Diario* articles emphasized the benefit of diversity, highlighting the favorable attributes that she brings to the job such as opening doors of opportunities for others.

The newspapers also diverged in the way that they defined the catchphrase "wise Latina" which was culled from a 3,932-word speech that Sotomayor had delivered at the University of California, Berkeley School of Law in 2002 (Nielsen 2013). In the speech she states "I would hope that a wise Latina woman with the richness of her experiences would more often than not reach a better conclusion than a white male who hasn't lived that life" (Nielsen 2013, p. 127). The articles in *The New York Times* containing the catchphrase were either based on her opponents who found it to be racist or characterized as reverse racism, or based on her supporters who offered apologies for Sotomayor (Nielsen 2013). In contrast, *El Diario* "reclaimed the phrase as an expression of pride" (Nielsen 2013, p. 127). *El Diario* saw the value in what a wise Latina brings to legal discourse. Nielsen (2013) points out that the reclamation of the catchphrase reached the marketplace: "The reclamation of 'wise Latina' created a marketing boom, with everything from mouse pads to baby bibs bearing phrases such as 'I love Wise Latinas' or 'Future Wise Latina'" (p. 127).

Moreover, the two newspapers varied also in the way that they covered and analyzed Sotomayor. Nielsen (2013) finds that the articles in *The New York Times* tended to highlight her ethnicity over other salient personal attributes. In contrast, *El Diario* articles presented a fuller panorama of Sotomayor, drawing on her ethnicity, class, and gender.

In sum, consistent with critical race theory, while *The New York Times* framed and developed a narrative on Sotomayor, *El Diario* represented the counternarrative. As Nielsen summarizes:

> *El Diario* provided a counternarrative to the *Times* in all aspects of this study from frames to news packages to exemplars, metaphors, and catchphrases . . . by challenging mainstream media messages about racism, by including the stories of people who have experienced oppression, and by avoiding an Anglo-as-norm standpoint. (p. 129)

Having now provided some illustrations on how the print media frames and develops narratives on Latinos and the role that the ethnic media plays in presenting counterframes and counternarratives, we now provide a discussion of how Latinos are marketed.

Latino Spin: The Marketing of Latinos

We have seen above how the mainstream mass media has defined and portrayed Latinos. There is a long history of Latinos being portrayed on the big screen as well as the small screen as criminals, thugs, bandits, shiftless, people who are in this country illegally, and who do work that no one else wants to do (Rodríguez 2008). The phrase "illegal immigrant" has come to signify "Latino immigrant" and to a certain extent "Latino" (Stewart et al. 2011). Samuel Huntington (2004) a decade ago targeted Latinos as a threat to national ideals, democracy, and institutions. Clearly, there are a lot of negative images in place that vilify Latinos.

There are counterimages that have developed over the last couple of decades that attempt to counter these images. However, in contrast to the counternarrative from the critical race theory that calls attention to racism and the legal systems and institutions that create and support the subordination of people of color, these counterimages tend to be colorblind and attempt to make Latinos palatable to mainstream society (Dávila 2008; del Rio 2012; Guillem and Briziarelli 2012). Arlene Dávila (2008) refers to these counterimages as the "Latino spin." We discuss here how the Latino spin packages Latinos as a cultural product and as an economic product.

Subsequently, we highlight two major projects that have sought to correct stereotypical images associated with Latinos and how these can be classified as part of the Latino spin genre.

In response to portrayals of Latinos in negative fashion associated with criminality, dishonesty, laziness, and other forms of moral turpitude, advocates of Latinos have constructed descriptions of Latinos that emphasize their hard-work ethic, strong family values, and conservative ideals (Dávila 2008). Dávila (2008) recalls interviewing Raul Yzaguirre, former president of the National Council of La Raza, in 2006, when he reflected about the biggest challenge being to correct the stereotypes that had been perpetuated against Latinos. Yzaguirre states:

> We have to understand and internalize that Hispanics are the hardest working of Americans, the most patriotic of Americans, the most family oriented and entrepreneurial of Americans. Everything that is supposed to be uniquely American we embody. We originated these arguments a long time ago and I'm happy that they are being picked up but they are not picked up enough. The average American does not hear these arguments. When I make them to an Anglo audience they say, wow! They are surprised to learn that Hispanics have higher participation in the labor force, that they work more hours per week. These are surprising facts. (Dávila 2008, p. 33)

In addition, Jorge Ramos (2004; see also Dávila 2008), Univision anchor, argues that Latino conservative values, encompassed by opposition to abortion, homosexuality, and divorce, are the cherished values that Americans hold dearly. He further asserts that through their strong moral and family values, Latinos make important contributions to the American moral fabric. Moreover, Lionel Sosa, highly successful advertising agent commonly contracted by Republican candidates, is fond of saying that the first time he met Ronald Reagan (prior to him becoming president), Reagan told him "Hispanics are Republicans, they just don't know it" (Dávila 2008, p. 59). These messages tend to draw Latinos as a homogeneous group of people that are just like regular white Americans. Latinos are not subverting and invading the US; they are strengthening its morals.

In contrast to the image of Latinos as poor people dependent on public assistance, the Latino-spin counterimage emphasizes the hard-work ethic of Latinos, upward mobility, entrepreneurial spirit and the expanding purchasing power of Latinos. There is often pride that American employers prefer to hire Latino immigrants over African American, native-born Latino, and even white workers, with the notion that Latino immigrants outperform other workers (see Wilson 1997). Of course, one of the reasons why US employers prefer Latino immigrants, especially those without documents, is that they can pay them lower wages and they are less likely to complain due to their lack of US citizenship. Furthermore, there is increasing attention to the growing Latino middle class and to the expanding Latino purchasing power. Indeed, according to the University of Georgia's Selig Center for Economic Growth (2012), the $1.2 trillion buying power of Latinos in 2012 is larger than the market of all but 13 countries around the world. While the Spanish-language Univision television station is a major promoter of the large and growing Latino market, it goes way beyond the Spanish-language media (Dávila 2008). For example, Dávila (2008) calls attention to an email that an Hispanic marketing agency owner sent to his clients: "Recognize that in just seven years, the 43 million plus Hispanics in the US today will have spending power equivalent to 60 percent of all 1.3 billion Chinese" (p. 71). The message is clear – Latinos represent major dollars for the business community.

The cultural and economic packaging of Latinos shows the importance of Latinos to the US and its economy. The message is completely colorblind, as the issue of race is completely invisible from these narratives. There is no reference to the many Latino children who are poor, the many Latinos who are working but still poor, and the many Latinos who do not have health care insurance. There is no mention of the exploitation that many Latinos encounter in their jobs. In fact, it has been suggested that there are some Latino political and economic leaders who make sure that statistics that make Latinos look bad do not see the light of day. One analyst indicates that a report that he produced for the Puerto Rican Legal Defense Education Fund (PRLDEF) in 2004, which showed that Puerto Ricans were three times more likely to be poor than the national average, received much negative reaction from community leaders who wanted this fact buried because it would make Puerto Ricans look bad (Dávila 2008). Certainly when the emphasis is on presenting an image of Latinos as successful and content, the important concerns of people on the margins are hidden away.

We now turn to two major undertakings that sought to deal either with stereotypical or incomplete representations of Latinos in a Latino-spin fashion. These two venues are the multimedia project *Americanos: Latino Life in the US/La Vida Latina en los Estados Unidos* which started in 1999 (del Rio 2012; see also Olmos et al. 1999) and the CNN two-part documentary *Latino in America* which aired in 2009 (Guillem and Briziarelli 2012; see also O'Brien 2009).

Esteban del Rio (2012) conducted a study analyzing the *Americanos* project. We highlight his work here. The project began in the late 1990s and involved collaboration between actor Edward James Olmos, sociologist Lea Ybarra, and photojournalist Manuel Monterrey, in partnership with the Smithsonian Institution and Time Warner (del Rio 2012). Olmos points out that the project had two aims: "1) to present the diversity of Latinidad as a cultural signifier; and 2) . . . to build a coherent cultural unity for Latina/os" (del Rio 2012, p. 191; see also Sanches 1999). del Rio (2012) offers a critique of the exhibit. He argues that the exhibit kept a white audience in mind and points out that the work is couched within the multicultural and universalism frameworks, where despite our differences that we celebrate, in reality we are all the same as shown by the daily rituals in which Latinos engage. One photographer claims in the exhibit's brochure:

> By revealing our commonality through the daily rituals of home, family, and community, others can see that Latinos are a vital part of America and that we are more than the stereotypes portrayed in most of today's media. I hope that this exhibition can show America that we are all the same. (Goldson 1999; see also del Rio 2012, p. 186)

One segment of the exhibit hails the American Dream and what Latinos can achieve through hard work. One part of the American Dream section features the story and photographs of US Representative from California Xavier Becerra's family. Becerra reflects on the life of his parents and what they have accomplished:

> Maria Teresa and Manuel married in Mexico and moved to California. Manuel helped build our nation from the ground up, laying pipe and concrete. While raising four children, Maria Teresa worked and attended night school to learn English . . . They were able to buy their first home. Now in retirement, Manuel and Maria Teresa

> own many homes. They are an American success story and they are my parents. (del Rio 2012, p. 194)

As del Rio (2012) points out, however, the exhibit is devoid of the discussion of political struggle as well as structural inequality, thus creating a sanitized colorblind portrait that makes mainstream America comfortable (del Rio 2012). del Rio notes that few photographs feature the many activists that have struggled to bring justice to Latinos over their long history in this country. Yet, the few photographs that show such individuals present them in a passive manner, e.g., a small group of union employees protesting against an unfair labor contract with the University of Southern California; a poet, artist, and activist sitting at his desk; and Luis Valdez, Teatro Campesino founder, shown sitting off to the side of a stage (del Rio 2012).

Obviously in exhibits such as this one that involve partnerships with governmental institutes (Smithsonian Institution) and corporations (Time Warner), the messaging is affected by what such sponsors require and the limitations that they have. As such, while *Americanos* confronted the many stereotypical images of Latinos, it did so in a multicultural, universalistic, colorblind, and ahistorical fashion – a way which is palatable and not offensive to the mainstream (del Rio 2012).

The second work that we will examine is CNN's two-part documentary *Latino in America*, hosted by Soledad O'Brien, which was aired in 2009. We highlight here the research of Guillem and Briziarelli (2012) in which they analyzed *Latinos in America* along with Latino audience reaction. The producers of the documentary aimed to examine "how Latinos are reshaping our communities and culture and forcing a nation of immigrants to rediscover what it means to be an American" (O'Brien 2009; see also Guillem and Briziarelli 2012). Soledad O'Brien, CNN anchor and someone who is both Latina and Irish, served as the host of the documentary.

Guillem and Briziarelli's (2012) findings offer a number of critiques of the documentary. Overall, these researchers suggest the documentary reflects a two-way street involving assimilation – on the one hand, the show highlights the obstacles that Latinos encounter when they retain their Latino ethnicity, and on the other, the fact that Latinos are redefining the mainstream. Guillem and Briziarelli (2012) observe three paths that the documentary describes in which Latinos try to improve their socioeconomic situation: (1) the loss of ethnic identity and the achievement of socioeconomic success; (2) the retention of Latino ethnicity and the barrier that it represents in attaining socioeconomic success; and (3) the maintenance of Latino ethnicity alongside socioeconomic success. Of the stories featured in the documentary that fit exclusively into one of these paths, four related to the first path, seven to the second, and eight to the third. Guillem and Briziarelli (2012) call attention to problems in the two most popular paths. First, the latter path, the one in which people reconcile their ethnicity and socioeconomic attainment, the individuals who are featured are not typical of the Latino cross section, but are persons who are either celebrities or people in the entertainment industry, such as Eva Longoria and Chef Lorena Garcia (Guillem and Briziarelli 2012). Even in the case of Chef Lorena who immigrated to the US, she is not the typical Latina immigrant, as initially she was going to attend law school and ended up pursuing a career as a chef (Guillem and Briziarelli 2012). Second, in the second path, the one in which people maintain their Latino ethnicity and encounter problems with socioeconomic achievement, a representative story is a Puerto Rican young man whose dream is to be a police officer, but his lack of English skills and thick accent prevent him from passing a requisite exam. He fails yet another attempt, but insists that he will keep trying. As Guillem and Briziarelli (2012) point out, the stories involving such failures end on an optimistic note as O'Brien lauds their insistence that they will keep on trying and she does not critically examine the systemic inequities that keep people from achieving their dream.

Guillem and Briziarelli (2012) additionally analyze more than 500 commentaries from Latino viewers regarding the documentary. One of the main criticisms that the audience leveled against the documentary was that the primary emphasis was on failure rather than success. In particular, many audience commentators indicated that they viewed the path involving the maintenance of Latino ethnicity and the obstacle that it represented in attaining socioeconomic success as a failure rather than as a success as depicted by O'Brien. In addition, viewers were critical about the over-representativeness of celebrities as the people who have kept their ethnicity and achieved socioeconomic success. Viewers suggested that there are many successful Latinos in the community from other walks of life who could have been featured.

In the end, while the documentary did feature the diversity that characterizes the Latino population, there were limitations in presenting an accurate representation of Latinos as well as the structural inequities that block opportunities for Latinos. Like *Americanos, Latino in America* comes across as a feel-good overview of Latinos, with the documentary not addressing underlying inequities that produce and maintain racial subordination.

Mass Media Patterns Concerning Latinos

As in the other chapters, we have examined the current standing of Latinos on the subject matter being covered in the particular chapter – in this case, mass media. In contrast to the other chapters, there are limited sources of data available to undertake a systematic analysis of the state of Latinos in the mass media. As such, in this section we provide information on general patterns that we have observed in the literature and in related sources.

The Representation of Latinos in Movies and Television

Over the history of Hollywood movies there has been an increase in the number of Latino actors, although Latinos continue to be portrayed in stereotypical manners (Rodríguez 2008). Yet, despite these gains, Latinos continue to be disproportionately underrepresented and to play supporting rather than leading roles (Rodríguez 2008). For example, a recent study by researchers at the University of Southern California's Annenberg School for Communication and Journalism analyzed 500 top-grossing movies and 20,000 speaking characters appearing between 2007 and 2012 (Keegan 2013). The study found that while Latinos account for approximately 26 percent of all movie ticket sales, they account for only 4 percent of all speaking parts in the movies analyzed over the period (Keegan 2013). In contrast, while whites constituted 56 percent of all moviegoers, they comprise 76 percent of all speaking parts (Keegan 2013). Moreover, true to the stereotypical image of sexual objects, Latina women are the most likely racial/ethnic-gender group to be shown nude or donning sexy clothing (Keegan 2013). In addition, Latinos did not appear or fare much better on television. For example, a study of prime-time television shows in March 2007 appearing on ABC, CBS, FOX, and NBC revealed that Latinos accounted for only 5 percent of characters in these shows (Monk-Tanner et al. 2010) with an even smaller percentage (3 percent) a decade earlier (Mastro and Greenberg 2000).

Moreover, Latinos continue to be absent from movies and television in yet another way. In particular, Latinos are noticeably removed from movies and television series that are based in particular locales where Latinos are well represented. For example, Rodríguez (2008) observes that in the movie *Ghost*, which came out in 1990 and took place in New York, where Latinos at the time comprised a quarter of the city's population, Latinos were completely absent, save for "the repellent villain and a confused spiritualist seeker" (p. 192). In addition, the hit series *Seinfeld* which aired from 1989 to 1998, which also took place in New York, featured almost exclusively white people. Latinos were absent from this series with a few exceptions including the Puerto Rican parade episode in which one of the regular characters, Kramer, accidentally sets a Puerto Rican flag on fire and proceeds to stomp on it, which drew the rage of Puerto Rican bystanders. The episode received much complaint from the Latino community for showing the Puerto Rican flag being burned and stomped and the portrayal of Puerto Ricans as aggressive. Similarly, the HBO-aired series *Curb Your Enthusiasm*, which featured Larry David – the creator of *Seinfeld* – as the star, was based in Los Angeles but hardly included any Latino characters except for an occasional maid. Rodríguez (2008) further notes that Latinos are also virtually absent – aside from isolated parts as criminals or people performing cleaning jobs – in other major Hollywood movies including *Beverly Hills Cop, Beverly Hills Cop II, Down and Out in Beverly Hills, Forrest Gump, Pretty Woman, Terminator 2,* and *Rambo First Blood Part 2* (Rodríguez 2008).

The Representation of Latinos on News Shows

While the Latino population is driving the US demography, is an increasingly important segment of the voting population, and is likely to account for the large majority of the nation's population growth over the coming decades, they are virtually invisible among political commentators discussing current political events and the future of the US. This represents yet another paradox, where the rising demographic and political strength of the Latino population does not translate to a representative voice in the mass media discussing important political issues. Jamie Reno (2012) in an article titled "Why Don't We Have More Hispanic Talking Heads?" commenting a few days after the November 2, 2012 election describes this situation:

> There's been a lot of talk on all the English-language television networks since the election about the increasing power of the Latino vote – but virtually all of the television pundits pontificating about this subject this past week have been non-Hispanic. On MSNBC's *Morning Joe* on Friday morning, for example, all four white males over 50 sat around and talked about the election, including the Latino vote.

In fact, of the 23 MSNBC anchors and hosts listed on the network's website, apparently only one is Hispanic.

And while CNN has CNN en Español, on the main network only two of the 21 anchors and hosts are Hispanic: Soledad O'Brien and Zoraida Sambolin.

Furthermore, in his book titled *Juan in a Hundred: The Representation of Latinos on Network News*, Otto Santa Ana (2013) observes that less than 1 percent of all news covered on the evening news programs of ABC, CBS, CNN, and NBC focus on Latinos, with the miniscule number of such stories slanted in a negative direction.

The Representation of Latinos in Newspaper Articles

Latinos do not fare much better in printed media. To examine the prevalence of articles in *The New York Times*, we searched for the keywords "Hispanic" or "Latino" using LexisNexis Academic and selected the "On-High similarity" option in the Duplicate option. In addition, articles defined as "unclassified documents" were excluded. There are two caveats to take into account with the analysis overviewed below. First, the identified articles merely contain the word "Latino" or "Hispanic" and thus the gist of the content may not be related specifically to Latinos. Second, beginning in 2007 *The New York Times* started using blogs which have become quite popular since 2011 and these are not taken into account in figure 12.1; the number of blogs containing the words "Latino" or "Hispanic" since 2007 are the following: 4 in 2007, 4 in 2008, 4 in 2009, 10 in 2010, 302 in 2011, 732 in 2012, and 413 in 2013. For these time periods, we present data excluding and including blogs when differences are significant.

Over the period between 1980 and 2013, we found a total of 40,857 articles excluding blogs and 42,326 when blogs are taken into account in *The New York Times* – translating to an average of roughly 1,202 and 1,245 articles per year, respectively. Figure 12.1 presents the average annual articles containing the word "Latino" or "Hispanic" for four time periods: 1980–9, 1990–9, 2000–9, and 2010–13, with the latter period subdivided into the average annual number excluding blogs and including blogs. There is a general increase in the number of articles related to Latinos over the periods covered. However, if we do not account for blogs in the last time period (2010–13a), there was a decline of about 18 percent in articles between the 2000–9 and 2010–13 periods. However, if blogs are taken into account (2010–13b) there was a small increase of close to 7 percent during this time frame. Despite the general upward trend in the number of articles in *The New York Times* containing the word "Latino" or "Hispanic," it has not kept up with the much greater growth of the Latino population during the last several decades. For example, as noted in chapter 4, the Latino population more than tripled between 1980 and 2010, while the average annual number of articles making reference to this population in the major US newspaper rose much slower between 1980–9 and 2010–13 – rising 23 percent when blogs are not included and 61 percent when they are.

Furthermore, supplementary analysis shows that the articles related to Latinos are increasingly tied to immigration. We conducted this part of the analysis by computing the percentage of articles containing the word "Latino" or "Hispanic" that also contain the word "immigration" or "immigrant." Figure 12.2 shows the percentage of articles making reference to immigration over the four time periods; note that we only use the figures for the 2010–13 period based on the exclusion of blogs given that there was not much of a difference in the percentage regardless of whether or not blogs were included. There is a rising share of articles related to Latinos that are also

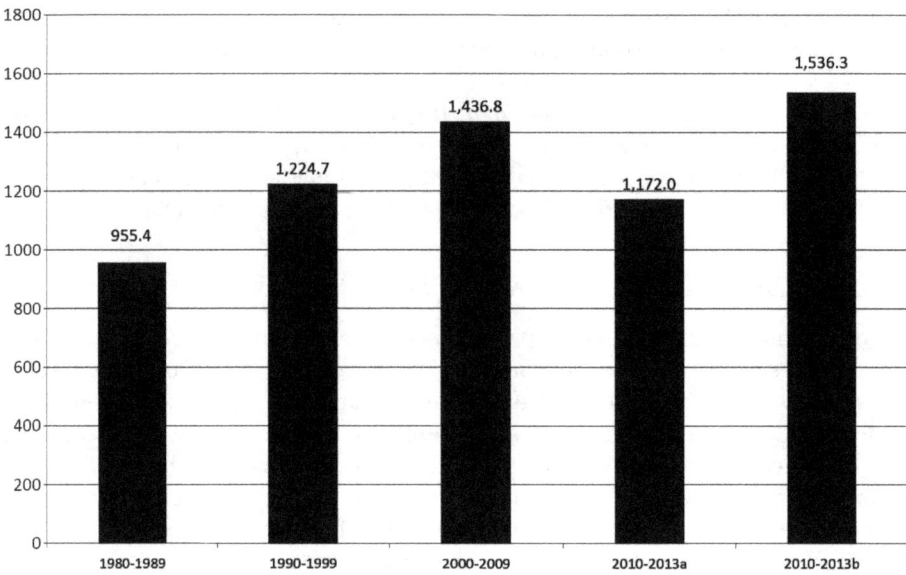

Figure 12.1 Average Annual Number of Articles in *The New York Times* Containing "Latino" or "Hispanic", 1980–2013

Note: 2010–13a excludes blogs while 2010–13b includes blogs.

Source: Compiled with data from LexisNexis Academic search.

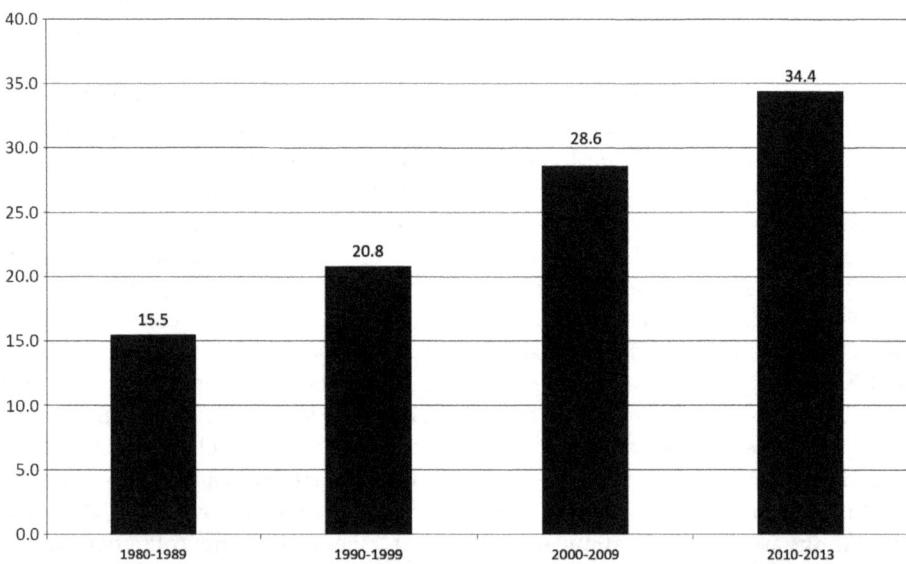

Figure 12.2 Percentage of Articles in *The New York Times* Containing "Latino" or "Hispanic" that Also Contain "Immigration" or "Immigrant", 1980–2013

Source: Compiled with data from LexisNexis Academic search.

connected to immigration, with the percentage rising steadily from roughly one-sixth in the 1980–9 period to one-third in the 2010–13 period.

The overall trends related to the relative absence of Latinos in the mass media in general and in positions of political commentary on television are consistent with the assertion that Marco Portales (2000) makes that Latinos are "crowded out" in the mass media and, by extension, in the public consciousness. As Portales (2000) suggests,

> African Americans have spokespeople ... who continue to speak out against the distortions and misrepresentations. With two or possibly three not very widely known exceptions, Latinos have not had the benefit of being defended or promoted by known voices or champions. Cesar Chavez spoke out for the California field migrant workers in the 1960s, but the leaders envisioned by enlightened intellectuals like Carey McWilliams and other less known Chicano activists in the late 1960s simply have not materialized during the last thirty years. (p. 57)

The absence of such individuals in the Latino community today is apparent in that the Immigrant Rights marches of 2006 took place without a clearly recognized leader. Furthermore, when Taylor and Lopez (2010) at the Pew Research Center's Hispanic Trends Project queried a sample of Latinos in 2010 about whom they consider to be the most important Latino leader in the nation, nearly two-thirds responded that they did not know with an additional one-tenth indicating that there is no one who fits the bill. Supreme Court Justice Sonia Sotomayor was identified as the most recognized Latino leader in the country by only 7 percent of the sample, followed by Illinois Congressman Luis Gutiérrez with 5 percent, then-mayor of Los Angeles Antonio Villaraigosa with 3 percent, Univision anchorman Jorge Ramos with 2 percent, and an open "other" category receiving 8 percent of the response. Taylor and Lopez (2010) jest that the job of national Latino leader is open.

The absence of a clearly recognized national Latino leader in part reflects the disproportionate absence of Latinos in the mass media and stage of public dialogue. In some ways, the absence of Latinos in a variety of media sources and public dialogue reflects the view of Latinos as newcomers – as a people who are immigrants – a view that ignores the fact that the majority of Latinos were born in the US and a certain segment of the population has been here for many generations.

Questions Related to the Future of Latinos and the Mass Media

There are a number of questions that we need to keep an eye on in the coming decades related to the imaging of Latinos in the mass media in light of their disproportionate influence on the demography of the country. We examine two areas below – the framing of Latinos in the context of expanding numbers and the future of the Spanish-language media.

The Framing of Latinos in the Context of Expanding Numbers

As we saw in chapter 4, the Latino population is projected to drive the demography of the US in the coming decades. The relative size of the Latino population is expected to rise and these shifts are no longer limited to a few regions of the country where Latinos have been historically concentrated, as Latinos have increasingly moved to new-destination areas. Earlier in this chapter, we examined Blalock's theoretical insights on how the growing presence of minority groups represents a threat to the dominant group which then erects barriers and policies to limit the political and economic power of the minority group. In recent reformulations of Blalock's theory, the mass media has been introduced as an increasingly important resource that the dominant group uses to control the "threat" of the growing minority group through the framing of the group and salient political issues.

The growing numbers of Latinos will certainly lead to the mounting of efforts on the part of segments within the white community to portray Latino immigrants – and by extension, Latinos in general – as people who do not belong in the country, who are here illegally, and who negatively impact the communities where they live. It remains to be seen whether the growing numbers of Latinos and their increasing purchasing power will lead to more objective or sympathetic framing of Latinos on the part of the traditional mass media. Undoubtedly, the mainstream mass media will need to enhance the recruitment of Latinos as journalists, news analysts, correspondents, and commentators in order to gain a fuller understanding of Latinos and to include them in the ongoing dialogue concerning issues that affect Latinos. Currently, data from the 2010 American Community Survey Public-Use File suggests that Latinos account for approximately 8 percent of news analysts, reporters, and correspondents in the country. Other sources provide alternate statistics. For example, the American Society of News Editors reported that in 2012 Latinos represented only 4.1 percent of journalists working in daily newspapers; the Radio Television Digital News Association announced that Latinos made up 7.3 percent of local television news employees and 2.6 percent of radio news workers (Gutiérrez 2013). Nonetheless, as illustrated above, these individuals are severely underrepresented among commentators – the talking heads – addressing critical issues affecting the country and world on popular news programs.

The Future of the Spanish-Language Media

The Spanish-language media is a strong presence in the lives of Latinos and in closely reporting on Latinos and the issues that affect them. As we have seen above, the Spanish-language media play an important role in providing a counternarrative to what the mainstream offers concerning Latinos. The large-scale growth of the Latino population bodes well for the popularity of Spanish-language media in the future. For the first time ever, in June 2013 the Univision television network attracted more viewers among the coveted 18–34 and 18–49 age groupings than did English-language networks (ABC, CBS, FOX, and NBC) (Lopez 2013). The success of Univison has been concentrated in entertainment shows, such as *telenovelas* (Spanish-language soap operas) as well as local news shows, particularly in large cities (Lopez 2013).

However, there are some trends that do not bode as well for the future growth of Spanish-language media. First, there are significant signals over the last several years that point to the decline of immigration stemming from Latin America, especially from Mexico. For example, the level of immigration from Mexico has dropped significantly with a net outflow from the US to Mexico recently (Passel et al. 2012). In addition, due to rapidly falling fertility rates, Mexico will have fewer people in the age groups (e.g., 15–34) that have fueled the immigration of its workforce toward the US. Second, over the last several years there has been a tendency for Latinos to get their news (from television, print, radio, and the internet) in English (Lopez and Gonzalez-Barrera 2013a). For instance, a growing percentage of Latinos – 82 percent in 2012 compared to 78 percent in 2006 – report obtaining at least part of their news in English (Lopez and Gonzalez-Barrera 2013a). During the same period, there has been a fall in the share of Latinos who get at least some of their news in Spanish or in both Spanish and English (Lopez and Gonzalez-Barrera 2013a). If the volume of immigrants coming to the US from Latin America continues to decline, a greater share of Latinos will be born in the US, a group that is increasingly proficient in English. Thus, both of these trends – declining immigration alongside a rising share of Latinos being English-speakers (31 million Latinos are now proficient in English, the highest number ever) (Lopez 2013) – have the potential to negatively impact the expansion of Spanish-language media. Nonetheless, Latinos place a high premium on being bilingual and a large segment of native-born Latinos have immigrant parents, who provide a link to the Spanish language (Lopez 2013).

In sum, overall there are mixed patterns involving the future of Spanish-language media. We envision that this media will continue to grow, though the growth is likely to be somewhat tempered in the future given current trends in immigration and English proficiency. As such, we see the Spanish-language media continuing to play an important role in telling the story of Latinos and engaging the community on salient political issues.

Summary

In this chapter we introduced several theoretical perspectives that are useful in understanding the treatment of Latinos in the mass media. In addition, we provided an overview of the long history of the Spanish-language media in more fully reporting on the Latino population and the variety of functions it plays in the lives of Latino communities compared to the mainstream media. Moreover, we illustrated the way that the mainstream and Spanish-language media differ in their portrayal of Latinos. We also provided a discussion of how Latinos are packaged through what is referred to as the "Latino spin." Additionally, we assessed the representation of Latinos in the mass media which revealed the continued underrepresentation of Latinos, particularly as political commentators contributing to debates on current and future policy issues. Finally, we spotlighted some important questions that have major implications for the future concerning the treatment of Latinos in the mass media.

We now turn to the concluding chapter in which we highlight some of the major patterns from all the chapters covered in the book thus far. The chapter will address how Latinos are changing our understanding of race relations in this country as well as discuss the impact that Latinos will have on the various societal institutions.

13 Conclusions

Despite being viewed as an immigrant group with only a brief history in the US, Latinos have a long historical presence in the US as evident in the land, architecture, and culture of the Southwest. Latinos continue to make important contributions to the fabric of the US. Moreover, due largely to its youthfulness, the Latino population will increasingly be the driver of the US demography and will disproportionately affect all of the nation's institutions in the near future. The ascending importance of Latinos will be felt in schools and universities, the workforce, the consumer market, the voting booth, the patient rolls, the pews of houses of worship, the content of the mass media, and beyond. Yet, despite their growing significance to the future of the US, Latinos continue to be absent in discussions related to understanding current issues and policies and in planning for the future of the country.

This, at least in part, reflects the challenges that Latinos pose to a country that has had a relatively static framework for understanding race relations. Indeed, the US continues to feature a black–white framework, extending back to the institution of slavery, for making sense of racial matters in this country. The many groups that have immigrated to the US have been forced into this dichotomy. In fact, many groups such as the Irish and Italians were initially seen as black while over time they came to be accepted as white. Today, because of the growing presence of Latinos, the question about where Latinos fit in the racial framework of this country is not trivial.

Latinos also challenge sociological theories that have been used to understand the integration of racial and ethnic groups into American society. For long the assimilation perspective was used to understand the progress of white immigrant groups with the general view that in approximately three generations, white ethnic groups became integrated into the US mainstream. Yet, the two groups of Latinos that have the longest presence in the US – Mexicans and Puerto Ricans – continue to lag significantly behind not only whites but numerous other Latino groups that have been in the US for a shorter period of time. Certainly the assimilation perspective does not hold much weight for understanding the experiences of Mexicans, Puerto Ricans, and other non-white groups in the US.

This chapter considers some of the challenges that Latinos are making to the understanding of racial and integration matters in the US. We provide a discussion of an emerging theoretical framework that describes how the US is changing with respect to how it sees race and how groups in the country are positioned along the hierarchy of the stratification system. We subsequently address structural and systemic obstacles that need to be confronted and challenged in order for Latinos to be integrated into the US and to facilitate their thriving in US society. We also highlight three crucial areas that need to be addressed through the development of policies and programs to improve the lives of Latinos. Finally, we highlight the many ways in which Latinos will increasingly impact US institutions in the coming decades.

The Shift from a Bi-Racial to a Tri-Racial Framework

Eduardo Bonilla-Silva (2001, 2004, 2013) has made major contributions to the development of theoretical frameworks to understand the workings of white supremacy – how it was established, the means at its disposal that it uses to maintain its dominant position, and the adjustments that it makes to deal with challenges that allow it to persist. Just as we see how the capitalist system has been able to maintain its dominant position, Bonilla-Silva helps us see how white supremacy has persisted through countless centuries. Throughout its existence, the bi-racial framework has been part of the system that has maintained white supremacy in the US. As whites established themselves as the dominant group in the US, the standing of racial and ethnic groups depended on whether they were seen as white or black (the "other").

As we suggested earlier, some immigrant groups, most prominently Irish and Italians, coming to the US were originally seen as very different from the US white mainstream and, as such, were viewed as black. Over time, these groups distanced themselves from blacks and in some instances were involved in violence against blacks, as was the case with Irish attacking blacks in the Cincinnati race riots of 1829 (Taylor 2005), New York City draft riots in 1863 (Harris 2003), and Chicago race riots of 1919 (Tuttle 1996). Eventually Irish, Italians, and other similar groups became accepted as white (Ignatiev 2008; Roediger 2005).

A number of significant demographic, social, and political changes in the US over the last several decades, however, are increasingly challenging the bi-racial framework that has been in place in this country for centuries. In particular, the US population is undergoing major shifts in its racial and ethnic composition. The share of the dominant white population is waning and will continue to do so in the coming decades. In contrast, the proportion of the population that is non-white is expanding and will continue to do so throughout the twenty-first century, driven largely by the growth of the Latino population as well as the Asian population. Further, the passage of Civil Rights legislation brought about changes in racial discourse in the US, shifting from overt racism to a softer, covert, and colorblind form of racism and the way people in the US think about race (Bonilla-Silva 2001, 2004, 2013). In essence, the storyline that has emerged in the US mainstream is that we are now beyond race, particularly in light of the US electing its first black president. Accordingly, people who continue talking about the continued existence of racism in the US are accused of trying to inflame racial divisions. Finally, over the last several decades, there have been certain Asian and Latino groups that have been able to ascend the socioeconomic scale while others continue to lag behind, as we have seen above in the case of Latinos.

In light of such changes and how the white supremacy system makes adjustments to maintain its dominance, Bonilla-Silva (2004) argues that the US is moving from a bi-racial toward a tri-racial framework – one similar to that found in Latin America and the Caribbean (Bonilla-Silva 2004; Wade 1997). Historically, Latin American and Caribbean societies have undertaken ways to whiten the population in light of disproportionate growth of darker skinned people in these countries (e.g., indigenous, black, and mestizo populations). For example, light-skinned elites in these countries have sought to whiten the population through selective immigration from Europe and the redefinition of racial categories to allow certain non-whites to join the ranks of the white elite (Bonilla-Silva 2004; Helg 1990; Loveman and Muñiz 2007; Rodríguez 2000; Telles 2006). Bonilla-Silva suggests that the transformation toward a tri-racial framework in the US will occur through highly assimilated and light-skinned persons being allowed to become white as well as the creation of "honorary whites," a group of people that will be almost white receiving certain white privileges but still subject to some inequality – not being exclusive members of the select white group. In particular, Bonilla-Silva (2004) proposes that the tri-racial categories in the US will consist of: (1) Whites consisting of "whites, new whites (Russians, Albanians, etc.), assimilated white Latinos, some Multiracials, assimilated (urban) Native Americans, and a few Asian origin people"; (2) Honorary Whites composed of "light-skinned Latinos, Japanese Americans, Korean Americans, Asian Americans, Chinese Americans, Middle Eastern Americans, most Multiracials, and Filipino Americans"; and (3) Collective Black comprised of "Vietnamese Americans, Hmong Americans, Laotian Americans, dark-skinned Latinos, blacks, new West Indian and African immigrants, and reservation-bound Native Americans" (p. 933). The original white–black racial framework exists at the poles of the tri-racial framework with honorary whites serving as an intermediary group.

Thus, although there continues to be a lack of data to assess the skin color of Latinos and the overall population in general, following Bonilla-Silva's tri-racial framework, the diverse set of Latinos in the US will span across the three categories that Bonilla-Silva outlines. First, completely assimilated light-skinned Latinos are likely to be part of the white category. Second, light-skinned Latinos who are well off economically are likely to be part of the honorary white group. Third, dark-skinned Latinos are likely to be part of the collective black category.

While this categorization is useful in understanding the role that skin color and socioeconomic standing plays in the positioning of Latino individuals across the emerging tri-racial framework in the US, it does not directly address the socioeconomic ranking and level of integration of Latino groups in the US.

The Stratification of Latino Groups

In this book, we have provided an overview of the diverse histories of Latino groups and the varying ways in which they were initially incorporated into the US. We also provided analyses showing variations across Latino groups on the basis of their social and economic characteristics. Overall, three groups – Cubans, Colombians, and Other South Americans – rank consistently high on the set of social and economic attributes that we examined. These groups tend to share certain commonalities – they tend to be of lighter skin color and members of these groups immigrated to the US with favorable socioeconomic resources. In a relatively short period of time, these groups have made impressive gains socially and economically in the US. In fact, in some instances, these groups surpass whites on certain social and economic indicators. Furthermore, foreign-born members of these groups consistently have more favorable social and economic standing compared to native-born members of other Latino groups that have been in this country for a long time, namely Mexicans and

Puerto Ricans. Moreover, these three groups, especially among native-born individuals, have high rates of intermarriage with whites.

In contrast, certain other groups – Mexicans, Puerto Ricans, Dominicans, Salvadorans, Guatemalans, and Other Central Americans – tend to consistently fall at the lower levels of social and economic rankings among Latino groups. These groups tend to have certain commonalities including a greater prevalence of people with darker skin as well as indigenous features compared to other Latino groups as well as immigrants coming to the US with limited socioeconomic resources. Particularly problematic is that Latino groups that were originally incorporated into the US – ranging from approximately 50 years ago in the case of Dominicans, to more than 110 years ago in the case of Puerto Ricans, and to more than 160 years ago in the case of Mexicans – continue to be positioned at the lowest tiers of the social and economic hierarchy among Latinos. While some scholars (Perlman 2005) suggest that Mexicans today are following the path of Italians a century ago, our analysis suggests that Mexicans, as a whole, continue to lag behind socioeconomically compared to other Latino groups that have been in this country less time. Of course, the long history of African Americans in the US and their continual positioning at the bottom of the US stratification system illustrates the structural aspects of this problem.

The Structural Aspects of Racial and Ethnic Stratification

The sociological roots of the study of race and ethnicity in the US are in the tradition of the assimilation perspective developed by Robert Park (1950) and later modified by Milton Gordon (1964). This particular theoretical approach worked fairly well in explaining the experiences of white ethnic groups immigrating to the US. For the most part, the process toward integration of these groups involved initial settlement in ethnic enclaves living alongside co-ethnics, experiences of hostility in the form of discrimination and prejudice against the group, followed by increasing levels of educational attainment, loss of the native language, and movement to suburban areas among subsequent generations. As mentioned above, in general, it took roughly three generations for white ethnic groups to fully integrate into US society. The commonality of these groups is that they were white, an attribute that was necessary to gain US citizenship over a long period of US history. Even though some of these groups, such as the Irish and Italians, were originally viewed as black or non-white, eventually they attained white membership alongside access to white privilege.

Ira Katznelson (2005), in his book titled *When Affirmative Action Was White: An Untold History of Racial Inequality in Twentieth-Century America*, offers a historical overview of the privileges and advantages that whites have enjoyed due to their white race. The narrative associated with the assimilation perspective, in line with the country's Horatio Alger individual-oriented myth, is that success or failure is due simply to the individual person. Given the upward mobility that white ethnics experienced in the US, the belief continues to be that if one works hard, plays by the rules, and becomes American through abandoning one's culture and language, then people eventually can get ahead and succeed. Accordingly, if people are unwilling to dedicate themselves in this way, they only have themselves to blame for their failure.

Such individualistic thinking blinds people from recognizing the structural factors that create and sustain racial stratification. Structural explanations of racial stratification argue that racism and racial inequality are systemic – etched in the foundations of the nation's institutions, laws, practices, policies, and general attitudes (Bonilla-Silva 2001, 2013; Feagin 2006, 2013). The contemporary low positioning of many Latinos – especially Mexicans, Puerto Ricans, Dominicans, and Central Americans – reflects historical structural patterns that have defined Latinos as not belonging in the US – as the other – as people who could be easily deported and who had no interest in bettering themselves educationally. For much of the twentieth century Mexicans in Texas and elsewhere in the Southwest were allowed to attend only segregated Mexican-only schools even after the *Brown v. Board of Education* (1954) ruling. Mexican schools were deplorably unequal compared to white schools. In these schools, Mexican students were commonly punished for speaking Spanish, experienced humiliation due to their culture, and were deloused. In such a setting, not surprisingly, few Mexican students made it to high school and even fewer graduated from high school.

In the mid-1950s the US Supreme Court outlawed "separate but equal" schools in its 1954 *Brown v. Board of Education* decision. From the outset, white political officials protested the ruling and delayed complying with laws calling for the end of separate schools. When school desegregation was finally instituted, whites took steps to ensure that the desegregation ruling would be subverted. Whites used all means at their disposal alongside assistance from state and local officials and the court system to subvert school desegregation. In particular, whites sent their children to private schools and moved to white suburban areas (Clotfelter 2004). Moreover, the *Milliken v. Bradley* ruling of 1974, indicating that students could not be moved across school districts to achieve school desegregation, marked what Clotfelter (2004) refers to as "the beginning of a retreat from the proactive pursuit of racial balance as a judicial objective" (p. 31). Today, public schools are more segregated than they were toward the end of the 1960s (Orfield and Lee 2007). Orfield and Lee (2007) observe that:

> On a national scale, the segregation of Latino students has grown the most since the civil rights era. Since the early 1970s, the period in which the Supreme Court recognized Latinos' right to desegregation there has been an uninterrupted national trend toward increased isolation. Latino students have become, by some measures, the most segregated group by both race and poverty and there are increasing patterns of triple segregation – ethnicity, poverty and linguistic isolation. (p. 31)

While many Americans continue to believe that education is the great equalizer – that everyone starts from the same position in the public education system – that is not the case (Sáenz et al. 2007a). From the start, Latino children are less likely to be enrolled in pre-kindergarten schooling than children from other racial and ethnic groups, which places them behind the starting line when they enter kindergarten. Moreover, many Latino students attend poorly funded and highly segregated schools that provide them a low quality education (Kozol 1991, 2005; Orfield and Eaton 1996). As such, it is not surprising that the education system tends to reproduce existing school inequality along racial and socioeconomic lines (Sáenz and Siordia 2012; Sáenz et al. 2007a).

More generally, in response to the disproportionate growth of non-whites, especially Latinos, whites have used a variety of means at their disposal to stem the social, economic, and political standing of these groups (Sáenz 2012a). For example, in

Texas, at a time when Latino children became the majority group of students in the state's public schools, the state legislature in 2011 gutted $5.4 billion from the state's educational budget to public schools (Sáenz 2012a). Similarly, gerrymandering practices and voter identification policies disproportionately impact certain groups such as Latinos, blacks, and the poor (Sáenz 2012a). Furthermore, the rising incarceration of Latinos and blacks leads to their disenfranchisement at least, in some cases, for a certain period of time (Sáenz 2012a; Sáenz et al. 2007a). Nonetheless, despite these policies and practices affecting Latinos and African Americans disproportionately, consistent with the post-Civil Rights era discourse, they are colorblind – not specifically targeting these groups. It is certain that in the coming years, as the share of the Latino population increases further and that of the white population declines progressively, whites will forge similar actions to limit the political power of Latinos and to restrict their socioeconomic possibilities.

Thus, efforts to deal with structural impediments blocking Latinos from upward mobility must come through combatting these forces by strengthening political power among Latinos. At present, the demographic numbers of Latinos do not translate to actual political power. As we have seen, the Latino population is quite young with one-third of Latinos today being less than 18 years of age and thus ineligible to vote. One sign of optimism is the consistently large numbers of Latino children, beginning in 2012, who will be reaching 18 years of age over the next 18 years (2012-30). The nearly 17.6 million children in 2012 translates to approximately 976,000 Latino 18 year olds every year during this period – a strong cadre of potential voters, though some of these are not US citizens and a small number would also be subject to emigration or death. In addition, one-third of Latinos 18 years of age or older are not US citizens and thus not eligible to vote. Furthermore, only 58.7 percent of Latinos who are eligible to vote are actually registered to vote – this compares to a rate of 71.9 percent among whites and 73.1 among blacks (File 2013). Finally, in the last presidential election only 48 percent of Latino registered voters actually voted – compared to 62.2 percent of whites and 66.2 percent of blacks (File 2013). Obviously, there needs to be greater effort to register Latinos and to make sure that they actually turn out to vote. The Southwest Voter Registration and Education Project (SVREP), founded by the late Willie Velasquez, is the major Latino organization with this function. SVREP has also organized the Latina/o Academy which provides training to local Latino candidates and elected officials. As the presidential election of 2012 showed, Latinos are already becoming a major force in national politics. However, the significance of the Latino vote and its potential power will grow stronger in the coming years as Latino youth turn 18 years of age and unauthorized Latinos become US citizens, translating to a larger Latino populace. Ultimately, political power among Latinos will allow for dealing with major structural obstacles that continue to block Latinos from greater political participation and upward mobility.

Yet, the growing diversity of the Latino population stands to divide the political strength of the population. As we have seen, there is a certain segment of the Latino population – Cubans, Colombians, and Other South Americans – that has become integrated into the US and another segment that has not fared as well, particularly in the case of Mexicans, Puerto Ricans, and Dominicans, groups that have been in this country for a lengthy period of time. Certainly, there are rifts between Latino groups positioned at an elevated level and at a low level socioeconomically. In addition, even within Latino groups, people who are better off economically and those who are not doing well are likely to differ in the issues that they consider important as well as the political party that they are most likely to support. While the Democratic Party has counted on the growing Latino population being Democrat, upward mobility and, as we observed earlier, association with evangelical denominations are likely to move some Latinos toward the Republican Party.

In efforts to maximize political power to tackle structural impediments, Latino political leaders will need to forge alliances across racial and ethnic groups. For example, Bonilla-Silva (2004) suggests that in the emerging tri-racial society, the collective-Black and the honorary-White groups will need to recognize their common interests and forge ties. Similarly, Latinos will need to develop stronger ties with blacks, Asians, Native Americans, and progressive whites to maximize their political strengths. The US racial stratification system was built with the establishment of the country and has been fortified over the last five centuries. It will not crumble easily. Even in a country that is undergoing massive demographic shifts that will lead shortly to a population in which whites will be outnumbered by nonwhites, whites will continue to be the dominant group possessing economic, political, and social power. Corporate boardrooms, the halls of Congress, and the bench of the Supreme Court will still be filled disproportionately by whites. Nonetheless, the establishment of intergroup political linkages across groups of color will begin to make dents in America's racial-stratification house.

Three Crucial Areas for Improving the Lives of Latinos

The political institution represents the key for Latinos to exert influence to better their social, economic, and political position in the US – the route through which the growing Latino numbers translate to political substance. The political institution and the political power that Latinos attain will be important in pressing for fundamental changes in immigration, education, and work. These three areas are significant for they represent crucial areas through which other institutions such as the family and health are supported and sustained. We will discuss below the significance of the areas of immigration, education, and work.

Immigration

There is a long history of immigration from Latin America to the US that extends throughout the twentieth century and into the twenty-first century. The latest estimates of the undocumented immigration population stands at approximately 11.7 million, with Mexicans accounting for 52 percent of this total (Passel et al. 2013). The last major immigration policy that involved the question of citizenship status occurred nearly three decades ago in 1986 when the Immigration Reform and Control Act was passed. Immigration has been a hotly debated topic since the passage of this law. Over the course of the twenty-first century, thus far it appeared that immigration reform policy would be enacted at two points in time. In 2001 it appeared that President George W. Bush had support for the passage of immigration reform policy, only to see this possibility evaporate as 9/11 changed the playing field. In 2007, at the time of the massive Immigrant Rights marches, it appeared that immigration reform policy would be developed, only to fall through in Congress. Over the last year (2013–14) there have been signs of possible passage of immigration reform policy with the House stalling this idea. Nonetheless, even the current Senate Bill focuses primarily on border security with the establishment of a path toward citizenship occupying a secondary position and involving a lengthy process.

Despite the major contention in Congress, particularly in the House, over immigration reform, there is much consensus outside of Capitol Hill. Indeed, there is much support for immigration reform among a wide variety of sectors including the religious, business, labor, law enforcement, and human rights sectors. The litany of strange bedfellows is best characterized by Ali Noorani, executive director of the National Immigration Forum, who points out that immigration reform has wide support spanning the three B's – bibles, badges, and business (Noorani 2014). Immigration reform within the Latino community has taken heightened importance in light of the nearly 2,000,000 people that have been deported during the Obama administration, leading to the moniker of "Deporter-in-Chief" for President Obama (Gamboa 2014). Unfortunately, the congressional process on immigration reform and President Obama have continued to postpone taking any executive action to enact some form of immigration reform.

The lives of millions of Latinos who hold unauthorized status in the US are on the line. The current situation has increased the splitting of families across countries. In addition, unauthorized immigrants continue to experience exploitation of their labor and human rights without much defense. As we observed earlier, Latino immigrants – particularly Mexicans, Dominicans, Guatemalans, and Salvadorans – have particularly dire socioeconomic standing and many lack health care insurance. The passage of immigration reform that includes a path toward citizenship is important in getting Latino undocumented immigrants out of the shadows. The granting of legal status and, ultimately, citizenship status would significantly enhance the possibility of upward mobility among this segment of the Latino community.

Of course, forces that are attempting to limit the political power of Latinos oppose extending citizenship status to undocumented immigrants. The narrative of the US being a white country that is being invaded by hordes of non-whites is alive and well in many circles as characterized nearly a decade ago by Samuel Huntington (2004). Furthermore, powerful sectors that are benefiting from the undocumented status of immigrants, such as the private-sector detention center industry, oppose immigration reform involving a path toward citizenship.

Education

While there have been modest gains in the educational area among Latinos over the last few years, Latinos continue to lag behind other racial and ethnic groups in educational attainment. As noted above, from the outset, Latino children start at a disadvantage given their high levels of poverty alongside low levels of pre-school enrollment. Therefore, when Latino children enter kindergarten they are already significantly behind many of their peers from other racial and ethnic groups. Recent efforts to provide pre-school education to children in San Antonio, New York City, as well as in the states of Oklahoma and New York are steps in the right direction. Indeed, the early years are extremely important in the cognitive development of children. Moreover, Latino students are disproportionately attending segregated schools that are severely underfunded and which offer relatively low quality education. This is a long and contentious issue related to how public schools are funded in the US. Policymakers need to ensure that students with so many strikes against them are not further jeopardized by being in schools that are inadequately funded and equipped to prepare them for educational success. As we see a further divide in age along racial and ethnic lines – with an increasingly older white population and a younger increasingly Latino population – there will certainly be opposition from whites on educational funding. There needs to be a recognition of the importance of Latino children as an asset rather than a liability, especially given the significant role that they will play in the labor force and economic institution in the coming decades. This will involve an ultimate acknowledgement from the larger society, that Latinos represent "our" children rather than "their" children, something that involves the deracialization of Latinos.

In addition, the favorable signs that we have seen recently related to the greater percentage of Latinos that are going on to college represent welcome news. Yet, the majority of Latinos in higher education are in two-year community colleges. While this is a step in the right direction after decades of the disproportionate absence of Latinos on college campuses, there needs to be the development of effective bridge programs that allow Latino community college students to make the transition to four-year universities where they can further thrive and develop their academic abilities.

These recommendations for the improvement of educational attainment among Latinos have major implications for the improvement of the lives of Latinos. For example, higher levels of educational attainment result in more favorable odds of obtaining employment, a high quality job, and higher wages. In addition, jobs with greater socioeconomic prestige are associated with greater job benefits including health insurance, opportunities for upward mobility, and so forth. Furthermore, educational attainment is associated with the development of critical thinking which allows people to enhance their lives and their human possibilities. Moreover, educational attainment is associated with greater civic engagement and political participation. Hence, educational attainment provides a bundle of possibilities that open economic, political, and social opportunities for Latinos. Given the demographic trends that we observed earlier, the future labor force and economy of the US will depend heavily on today's Latino youth who will increasingly be the nation's workforce, consumers, and entrepreneurs. As the economy shifts progressively toward a greater emphasis on globalization and technology, an educated workforce is essential for national success.

Again, oppositional forces favoring the continued existence of white supremacy are against investments to improve the educational environment of Latinos. For these opposing forces, the perpetuation of educational inequality ensures that Latinos remain on the margins of society where they continue to exert limited political power and civic engagement. It is in these circles that we often hear the phrase that "college is not for everyone."

Work

Latinos exhibit one of the highest rates of employment across racial and ethnic groups in the country, particularly in the case of immigrants. Nevertheless, it is clear that Latinos, as a whole, continue to have elevated poverty rates. As such, many Latinos are working-poor. While Latinos are employed, they happen to be working in jobs that pay low wages and that do not lift them out of poverty. This is particularly the case for persons – immigrants but also some groups of native-born Latinos – who are employed in immigrant niches where immigrant labor is concentrated. There has been some discussion over the last year about the need to increase the minimum hourly wage. The current federal minimum wage for exempt workers is $7.25 per hour (US Department of Labor 2014a). A person earning a minimum wage of $7.25 working 40 hours per week over 52 weeks in the year has an annual salary of $15,080 – a very low salary that does not elevate people out of poverty. As of January 1, 2014, five states in the South (Alabama, Louisiana, Mississippi, South Carolina, and Tennessee) do not have a minimum wage law while four others (Arkansas, minimum wage of $6.25; Georgia, $5.15; Minnesota, $6.15; and Wyoming, $5.15) have minimum wage rates below the federal rate of $7.25 (US Department of Labor 2014b). Thus, a worker employed full-time year-round in Georgia or Wyoming would earn a mere $10,712. On the other hand, the states of Washington ($9.32) and Oregon ($9.10) have the highest minimum hourly wages. In order to improve the lives of the working-poor, it is important that policymakers raise the minimum wage hourly rate. This will provide the poor with at least some degree of relief concerning escalating costs that they face.

In addition, Latino teenagers, especially those who are poor, have been hit hard by the economic recession. Overall, the unemployment rate of Latino teenagers stood at 45 percent in 2011 and at 56 percent among Latino teenagers who are classified as poor (Sáenz 2014a). In contrast, overall white teenagers are much less likely to be unemployed with a rate of 27 percent. While historically teens of color were more likely to be employed compared to white teens, there has been a reversal today. It appears that for whites – especially those who are well off – having a job is part of establishing an extracurricular profile to be competitive in gaining entry to certain universities, with youth of color being disadvantaged in yet another manner. Policymakers, educators, and businesspeople can work collaboratively to establish work opportunities for Latino youth to allow them to gain some economic resources, to gain responsibility and experience, as well as become aware of career opportunities.

Moreover, poor women face major challenges in balancing work and childcare needs due to their low income levels. This is particularly difficult for unmarried or unpartnered poor women who cannot rely on a spouse or partner to assist with childcare responsibilities. Poor women who have limited social support cannot afford childcare expenses on the small paychecks that they earn. Policymakers need to seek ways to create policies and programs that provide affordable childcare for parents with limited resources who are working.

Again, as we have pointed out above, forces that oppose improving the lives of Latinos as well as the poor in general are against the policy recommendations that we offer here. People taking such positions argue that the government should not be involved in the lives of people when it comes to raising the minimum wage laws, creating employment opportunities for youth, and establishing affordable childcare.

The policy recommendations that we have made here in three areas that are particularly important for improving the lives of Latinos as well as their socioeconomic standing in the US are ambitious and will require resources and wide political support. These recommendations fall in the category referred to as "social programs," which in the current political environment raise red flags and the ire of many Republicans and, in particular, its Tea Party segment. Certainly in the current political environment the passage of such policies is difficult. The development of political coalitions among people of color and progressive whites that we have described earlier is particularly important in gaining some political traction to improve the lives of Latinos and others that have been long on the margins of society. It will also require a shift in the thinking of policymakers from short-term thinking to long-term planning in order to make important and strategic investments today to reap valuable benefits in the coming decades. Fortunately, despite the continued barriers that we have outlined, the growing numbers of Latinos that demographers project throughout the twenty-first century will make them a more significant part of American society and potentially will improve their political strength.

The Implications of the Growing Latino Population on Societal Institutions

We have asserted in this book that Latinos are the engine of the US population. Indeed, the Latino population is driving the demography of the US. The future of the US will depend greatly on the fortunes of the Latino population. The last time that the US experienced such a dramatic impact on all of its societal institutions was the tremendous growth of its population that was born between 1946 and 1964, a group that was dubbed the "baby boomers." The baby boom cohort has had a tremendous impact on all societal institutions as it has gone through its life cycle. For example, at infancy baby boomers had an impact on baby necessities and products; at the childhood stage they had an impact on the building of schools and the number of teachers that were needed; at the young adulthood phase they had an impact on the number of faculty positions to educate them in colleges and universities, they affected the number of jobs that were needed to accommodate them in the labor force, and they also impacted attitudes regarding war, sex, race, gender, environment, and music; at the middle age stage they have impacted the marketing of products, travel, and leisure; and now as they reach retirement age, baby boomers will impact the health care industry, the demand for assisted-care facilities, and so forth. Given the youthfulness of the Latino population and its significance in the changing demography of the US over the coming decades, Latinos will have an important impact on all US institutions.

Education Institution

Given the youthfulness of the Latino population, Latino youth will represent a growing share of our nation's students at the K-12 level. The changing racial and ethnic profile of US schools can be illustrated by recent changes in the US child population. Between 2000 and 2011, the number of white children declined by 4.9 million, while the number of Latino children rose by 5.1 million; thus, the massive decline of white children was more than offset by the growth of Latino children (Sáenz 2014a). During this 11-year period, blacks and American Indians and Alaska Natives also experienced drops in their number of children.

These recent trends fuel further racial and ethnic changes in the country's child population that are on the horizon. Indeed, demographers project that the white share of the US child population will progressively drop from 52.7 percent in 2012 to 32.9 percent in 2060, while the Latino proportion of this population will climb from 23.9 percent in 2012 to 38.0 in 2060 (Sáenz 2014a). Thus, some time by 2020, non-whites will represent the majority of the US child population, with Latinos becoming the largest group some time between 2050 and 2060. In fact, these patterns are already reality in five southwestern states that have child populations in which Latinos represent the largest racial/ethnic group: New Mexico, California, Texas, Arizona, and Nevada. It is very clear then that Latinos represent the engine of the US population. It is also essential that policymakers make investments in providing Latino children the educational skills that they will need to succeed educationally. Certainly they are expected to become an even larger share of students on college campuses.

Economic Institution

Latinos will have an important impact on the economic institution. For example, already Latinos are projected to account for three quarters of the new entrants into the US labor force between 2010 and 2020 (Kochhar 2012b). The share of Latinos among new labor force entrants will only increase over the coming decades. This is why it is so important that investments be made today to ensure that today's Latino youth succeed in the educational system in order to enhance their chances for economic success in the future. Some industries that will be largely affected by the aging of baby boomers, such as the health care and eldercare industries, will depend heavily on Latinos to fill these new jobs. Moreover, the US consumer base will be increasingly Latino with the purchasing power of Latinos expected to increase significantly alongside its projected population growth (Selig Center for Economic Growth 2012). The latest $1.2 trillion buying power of Latinos in 2012 is larger than the market of all but 13 countries around the world. Businesses in the US will depend heavily on Latino consumers to buy their products. Furthermore, Latinos stand to disproportionately represent the growth of entrepreneurs and self-employed workers in the coming decades. Latinos are already experiencing significant growth in such business ventures (Valdez 2011). As such, again, it is important that investments be made in the educational preparation of Latino youth today to ensure that they reach their maximum social and economic potential in the future.

Political Institution

Over the last half century, Latinos have shifted from a relatively small regional minority concentrated in certain parts of the country to the nation's largest minority group which increasingly has the strength to sway national, state, and local elections. As suggested above, the Latino populace will grow significantly over the coming decades as Latino youth reach voting age alongside foreign-born individuals who become US naturalized citizens. Indeed, it is estimated that the Latino electorate will double by 2030 (Taylor et al. 2012a). In addition, as Latinos gain political strength, political slates will progressively include Latino candidates.

On a national scale, presidential and related elections will shift dramatically when projected demographic changes turn Texas into a blue state. Texas currently has a major age split along the lines of race and ethnicity, which has major implications for changing the political landscape in the state. In particular, whites represented the majority group numerically at ages above 35 in 2010, while Latinos represented the plurality at ages less than 35 with slightly more than half (50.6) of children 0–4 years of age being Latino. Furthermore, population projections for Texas indicate that by 2020 Latinos will outnumber whites with the share of Latinos rising from 41.7 percent in 2020 to 53.9 percent in 2050, while the proportion of whites falls noticeably from 40.6 percent in 2020 to 27.5 percent in 2050. This demographic shift representing the growth of Latinos and the decline of whites has reverberating effects from the local to the national levels. The political influence of Latinos will be prominent once Texas turns Democratic, which is only a matter of time.

Health Institution

We have seen that Latinos pose a paradox in our understanding of mortality. Despite being a population that possesses a bundle of attributes – such as high poverty, low education, and low health insurance coverage – that suggest that Latinos have high rates of mortality and truncated longevity, Latinos actually have lower mortality rates and higher life expectancies compared to whites. Yet, as we saw in chapter 10, there is another side of the paradox that is less favorable. In general, Latinos are likely to live longer than whites, but they do so with a greater prevalence of disability, diabetes, and obesity. Moreover, Latinos are much less likely than other racial and ethnic groups to have health insurance coverage and to receive adequate health care. Thus, particularly as Latinos age, they will place an increasing stress on the health care system. As such, it is crucial that Latinos have access to preventive health care that will allow for identifying health problems at an early stage when they can be treated, rather than at late stages when it is more difficult and costly to cure.

Moreover, as we suggested above, as baby boomers reach retirement age between 2011 and 2029, there will be greater demand for health care providers. Given the rising presence of Latinos in the labor force, today's Latinos will be part of the workforce that provides health care for an increasingly aging US population, largely made up of whites. It is essential that Latinos receive educational training opportunities to fill medical professional occupations.

Religious Institution

The projected growth of the Latino population will impact the religious institution dramatically. As observed in chapter 9, Latinos are the driving force behind the changing demography of the US Catholic population. They accounted for 90 percent of the entire growth of the Catholic Church in the country between 1970 and 2000 (Poyo 2010). Latinos now account for one-third of US Catholics (Matovina 2012; Pew Research Center's Hispanic Trends Project 2007a), with their numbers expected to grow significantly in the coming decades. Putnam and Campbell (2010) point out that Latinos will become the majority in the US Catholic Church in the near future. In fact, Latinos already constitute the majority of Catholics less than 25 years of age

(Matovina 2012). In addition, observers also suggest that Latinos will transform the Church through their unique aspects of worship such as engaging in spirit-filled religious expression and related practices (Pew Research Center's Hispanic Trends Project 2007a).

Furthermore, as other religious denominations experience dwindling memberships due to aging white populations, these will increasingly seek to recruit Latinos into their fold. We have already seen over the last few decades a rising percentage of Latinos who are converting to Evangelical and Pentecostal religions.

Military Institution

Given the increasing Latino population throughout the twenty-first century, Latinos will also have an impact on the military institution. Latinos will increasingly be part of US forces protecting the country and participating in future wars. For many Latinos throughout their presence in the US, the military has represented a career option. Latinos have fought valiantly on the battlefield and have been decorated with medals of honor for these deeds (Buffalo Soldier 2014; Voces Oral History 2014).

Summary

This chapter has provided an overview of the highlights and implications that we have covered in the previous chapters. In particular, we called attention to how the growing Latino population has challenged the longstanding US racial framework and sociological perspectives for understanding race relations in this country. We drew attention to the usefulness of Bonilla-Silva's (2004) theorizing, which argues that the US is shifting from a bi-racial to a tri-racial framework and the role that Latinos play in this shift. We also discussed the stratification that we have observed in our analysis presented earlier in the book, which shows that some groups, marked by lighter skin and socioeconomic advantages at the time of immigration, have fared well in the US, while others have continued to lag significantly behind, particularly disturbing in the case of groups (Mexicans, Puerto Ricans, and Dominicans) that have been in this country for a long period of time. We also discussed the structural and systemic elements of white supremacy that need to be confronted and challenged in order for Latinos and other groups of color to make inroads in social, economic, and political arenas. Finally, we called attention to the multitude of ways in which Latinos will impact the nation's institutions in the coming decades.

The Latino population has a long history in the US extending back to the original incorporation of Mexicans through the signing of the Treaty of Guadalupe Hidalgo at the conclusion of the US–Mexico War in 1848. This treaty created the Mexican American people. Over the span of the ensuing nearly 170 years, the Latino population has been transformed in so many ways including changes in the name of the group, the large numbers of groups that constitute the Latino population, the diverse histories that link them to the US which promoted immigration to this country, and the divergent paths toward integration that they have experienced. It is clear that Latinos have left a significant mark on the history of the US. The aging of the white population alongside the youthfulness of the Latino population will result in a significant expansion of the Latino population throughout the twenty-first century. As such,

Latinos are the driving force behind the US population – its engine of population change. The growing Latino population will continue to make important contributions to the US throughout the century. Latinos will play an increasingly important role in each of the country's institutions. Thus, it is essential that Americans gain a closer understanding and appreciation of the Latino population and that policies and programs be established to improve the lives of the Latino population to ensure that they reach their full human potential and to shift from the margins of society to its core.

Appendices

A. List of Occupations Comprising "Latino Immigrant Jobs" by Sex

Code[a]	Occupation
Men:	
4020	Cooks
4030	Food preparation workers
4110	Waiters and waitresses
4130	Miscellaneous food preparation and serving related workers
4140	Dishwashers
4210	First-line supervisors of landscaping, lawn service, and groundkeeping workers
4220	Janitors and building cleaners
4230	Maids and housekeeping cleaners
4250	Grounds maintenance workers
6050	Miscellaneous agricultural workers including animal breeders
6220	Brickmasons, blockmasons, and stonemasons
6230	Carpenters
6240	Carpet, floor, and tile installers and finishers
6260	Construction laborers
6330	Drywall installers, ceiling tile installers, and tapers
6420	Painters, construction and maintenance
6515	Roofers
7810	Butchers and other meat, poultry, and fish processing workers
8140	Welding, soldering, and brazing workers
8220	Miscellaneous metal workers and plastic workers
8800	Packing and filling machine operators and tenders
8965	Other product workers including semiconductor processors and cooling and freezing equipment operators
9600	Industrial truck and tractor operators
9610	Cleaners of vehicles and equipment
9640	Hand packers and packaging
Women:	
2860	Miscellaneous media and communication workers
4020	Cooks
4030	Food preparation workers
4130	Miscellaneous food preparation and serving related workers
4140	Dishwashers

4220	Janitors and building cleaners
4230	Maids and housekeeping cleaners
4600	Childcare workers
4610	Personal care aides
5610	Shipping, receiving, and traffic clerks
6040	Agricultural products graders and sorters
6050	Miscellaneous agricultural workers including animal breeders
7700	First-line supervisors of production and operating workers
7750	Miscellaneous assemblers and fabricators
7800	Bakers
7810	Butchers and other meat, poultry, and fish processing workers
8220	Miscellaneous metal workers and plastic workers
8300	Laundry and dry-cleaning workers
8310	Pressers, textile, garment, and related materials
8320	Sewing machine operators
8740	Inspectors, testers, sorters, samplers, and weighers
8800	Packing and filling machine operators and tenders
8965	Other product workers including semiconductor processors and cooling and freezing equipment operators
9620	Hand laborers and freight, stock, and material movers
9640	Hand packers and packaging

[a] American Community Survey (ACS) Occupation Code.

Source: 2011 American Community Survey Public-Use File (Ruggles et al. 2010).

B. Results of Multiple Regression Analysis Examining the Relationships between Selected Predictors and the Logged Wage and Salary Income by Place of Birth and Sex, 2011[a]

Race/Ethnic Group	Native-Born		Foreign-Born	
	Male	Female	Male	Female
Intercept	6.32**	5.96**	7.011**	6.38**
Mexican	−0.051**	−0.015**	−0.228**	−0.154**
Puerto Rican	−0.023*	0.053**	−0.300**	−0.034
Cuban	0.059**	0.080**	−0.135**	−0.028
Salvadoran	−0.068*	−0.024	−0.168**	−0.082**
Dominican	−0.044	−0.079**	−0.286**	−0.159**
Guatemalan	0.028	−0.046	−0.227**	−0.111**
Other Central American	−0.019	0.030	−0.216**	−0.102**
Colombian	0.011	0.014	−0.195**	−0.081**
Other South American	−0.070*	0.025	−0.190**	−0.093**
Other Latino	−0.092**	−0.060**	−0.125**	−0.086**
Black	−0.135**	−0.014**	−0.271**	−0.011
Some High School	0.003	−0.004	0.027**	0.021
High School Graduate	0.222**	0.193**	0.073**	0.099**

Some College	0.336**	0.341**	0.160**	0.222**
College Graduate	0.796**	0.759**	0.620**	0.625**
Bilingual	−0.030**	−0.017**	−0.110**	−0.056**
Monolingual Spanish	−0.121**	−0.073**	−0.224**	−0.176**
Self-employed	−0.115**	−0.205**	−0.099**	−0.080**
Worked 14–26 weeks	0.962**	0.952**	0.988**	1.012**
Worked 27–39 weeks	1.464**	1.460**	1.446**	1.433**
Worked 40–47 weeks	1.828**	1.814**	1.779**	1.754**
Worked 48–49 weeks	2.007**	1.934**	1.916**	1.839**
Worked 50–52 weeks	2.193**	2.135**	2.039**	2.019**
Usual hours worked per week	0.031**	0.042**	0.025**	0.035**
Married	0.315**	0.136**	0.182**	0.077**
Age 35–44	0.342**	0.264**	0.217**	0.148**
Age 45–54	0.418**	0.314**	0.226**	0.136**
Age 55–64	0.385**	0.337**	0.161**	0.132**
Midwest	−0.139**	−0.145**	−0.099**	−0.116**
South	−0.099**	−0.125**	−0.094**	−0.130**
West	−0.010**	−0.013**	−0.044**	−0.033**
In US 5–9 years	—	—	0.088**	0.106**
In US 10–14 years	—	—	0.126**	0.150**
In US 15–19 years	—	—	0.140**	0.169**
In US 20–24 years	—	—	0.186**	0.207**
In US 25 or more years	—	—	0.257**	0.285**
Naturalized citizen	—	—	0.095**	0.087**
Adjusted R^2	0.691	0.713	0.586	0.651
N	611,584	595,782	79,051	59,330

Source: 2011 American Community Survey Public-Use File (Ruggles et al. 2010).

Note: The comparison groups for dummy variables are: Whites; 0–8 years of education; persons who speak English at home; people who are not self-employed; persons who worked 1–13 hours; persons who are not currently married; persons 25–34 years of age; persons living in the Northeast; and for foreign-born persons: persons who have lived in the US less than 5 years and persons who are not naturalized citizens.

[a]The results are used to generate the coefficients appearing in table 7.4.
*Statistically significant at the 0.05 level.
**Statistically significant at the 0.01 level.

References

Abraído-Lanza, Ana F., Maria T. Chao, and Karen R. Flórez. 2005. "Do Healthy Behaviors Decline with Greater Acculturation?: Implications for the Latino Mortality Paradox." *Social Science & Medicine* 61: 1243–55.

Abrego, Leisy. 2009. "Economic Well-Being in Salvadoran Transnational Families: How Gender Affects Remittance Practices." *Journal of Marriage and Family* 71(4): 1070–85.

Acuña, Rodolfo. 1972. *Occupied America: The Chicano Struggle for Liberation*. New York: Harper and Row.

Acuña, Rodolfo. 2014. *Occupied America: A History of Chicanos*, 8th edn. New York: Pearson Education.

Aguirre, B.E., Rogelio Sáenz, and Brian Sinclair. 1997. "Marielitos Ten Years Later: The Scarface Legacy." *Social Science Quarterly* 78(2): 487–507.

Alarcón, Amado, Josiah Heyman, and María Cristina Morales. 2014a. "The Occupational Placement of Spanish–English Bilinguals in the New Information Economy: The Health and Criminal Justice Sectors in the US Borderlands with Mexico," in R.M. Callahan and P.C. Gándara (eds.), *The Bilingual Advantage: Language, Literacy, and the Labor Market*. Clevedon, Bristol: Multilingual Matters.

Alarcón, Amado, Antonio Di Paolo, Josiah Heyman, and María Cristina Morales. 2014b. "Returns to Spanish–English Bilingualism in the New Information Economy: The Health and Criminal Justice Sectors in the Texas Border and Dallas-Tarrant Counties," in R.M. Callahan and P.C. Gándara (eds.), *The Bilingual Advantage: Language, Literacy, and the Labor Market*. Clevedon, Bristol: Multilingual Matters.

Alba, Richard and Victor Nee. 2003. *Remaking the American Mainstream: Assimilation and Contemporary Immigration*. Cambridge, MA: Harvard University Press.

Allen, Jonathan and Jeffrey Cancino. 2012. "Social Disorganization, Latinos, and Juvenile Justice in the Texas Borderlands." *Journal of Criminal Justice* 40(2): 152–63.

Alvarez, R. Michael and Lisa Garcia Bedolla. 2003. "The Foundations of Latino Voter Partisanship: Evidence from the 2000 Election." *Journal of Politics* 65: 31–49.

Alvarez, Rodolfo. 1973. "The Psycho-Historical and Socioeconomic Development of the Chicano Community in the United States." *Social Science Quarterly* 53(4): 920–42.

American Civil Liberties Union. 2008. "About the Campaign Against Racial Profiling." March 20. Accessed at https://www.aclu.org/racial-justice/about-campaign-against-racial-profiling on October 30, 2014.

American Civil Liberties Union. 2014. "Shelby County vs. Holder." Accessed at https://www.aclu.org/voting-rights/shelby-county-v-holder on March 24, 2014.

Amuedo-Dorantes, Catalina and Cynthia Bansak. 2011. "The Impact of Amnesty on Labor Market Outcomes: A Panel Study Using the Legalized Population Survey." *Industrial Relations* 50(3): 443–71.

Anderson, Margaret L. and Howard F. Taylor. 2011. *Sociology: The Essentials*. Belmont, CA: Wadsworth Cengage Learning.

Aranda, Elizabeth M. 2007. *Emotional Bridges to Puerto Rico: Migration, Return Migration, and the Struggles of Incorporation*. Lanham, MD: Rowman & Littlefield.

Aranda, María, Laura A. Ray, Soham Al Snih, Kenneth J. Ottenbacher, and Kyriakos S. Markides. 2011. "The Protective Effect of Neighborhood Composition on Increasing Frailty among Older Mexican Americans: A Barrio Advantage?" *Journal of Aging and Health* 23(7): 1189–217.

Archibold, Randal C. 2010. "In Wake of Immigration Law, Calls for an Economic Boycott of Arizona." *New York Times*, April 26. Accessed at http://www.nytimes.com/2010/04/27/us/27arizona.html?_r=0 on March 7, 2014.

Argote-Freyre, Frank. 2006. *Fulgencio Batista: From Revolutionary to Strongman*. New Brunswick, NJ: Rutgers University Press.

Arias, Elizabeth. 2012. "United States Life Tables, 2008." *National Vital Statistics Reports* 61(3). Hyattsville, MD: National Center for Health Statistics.

Arriagada, Irma. 2002. "Cambios y Desigualdad en Las Familias Latinoamericanas." *Revista de CEPA* 77: 143–61.

Ayala, Maria I. 2012. "The State of Research in Latino Academic Attainment." *Sociological Forum* 27(4): 1037–45.

Ayón, Cecilia, Eugene Aisenberg, and Andrea Cimino. 2013. "Latino Families in the Nexus of Child Welfare, Welfare Reform, and Immigration Policies: Is Kinship Care a Lost Opportunity?" *Social Work* 58(1): 91–4.

Baca Zinn, Maxine. 1994. "Adaptation and Continuity in Mexican-Origin Families," in R.L. Taylor (ed.), *Minority Families in the United States: A Multicultural Perspective*. Englewood Cliffs, NJ: Prentice Hall.

Bacon, David. 2011. "The Rebirth of Solidarity on the Border." *Truthout*, June 7. Accessed at http://truth-out.org/index.php?option=com_k2&view=item&id=1508:the-rebirth-of-solidarity-on-the-border on May 17, 2013.

Balderrama, Francisco E. and Raymond Rodríguez. 2006. *Decade of Betrayal: Mexican Repatriation in the 1930s*, rev. edn. Albuquerque, NM: University of New Mexico Press.

Bales, William D. and Alex R. Piquero. 2012. "Racial/Ethnic Differentials in Sentencing to Incarceration." *Justice Quarterly* 29(5): 742–73.

Bankston, Carl L. III. 1998. "Youth Gangs and the New Second Generation: A Review Essay." *Aggression and Violent Behavior* 3: 35–45.

Barrera, Mario. 1979. *Race and Class in the Southwest*. Notre Dame, IN: University of Notre Dame Press.

Barth, Frederik (ed.). 1969. *Ethnic Groups and Boundaries: The Social Organization of Culture Difference*. London: Allen and Unwin.

Bartkowski, John P. and Xiaohe Xu. 2007. "Religiosity and Teen Drug Use Reconsidered: A Social Capital Perspective." *American Journal of Preventive Medicine* 32(6S): S182–94.

Barton, Paul. 2010. "Latino American Religion: Mainline Protestants," in C.H. Lippy and P.W. Williams (eds.), *Encyclopedia of Religion in America*. Washington, DC: CQ Press.

Bastida, Elena, H. Shelton Brown, and José A. Pagán. 2008. "Persistent Disparities in the Use of Health Care along the US–Mexico Border: An Ecological Perspective." *American Journal of Public Health* 98(11): 1987–95.

Batalova, Jeanne and Aaron Terrazas. 2010. "Frequently Requested Statistics on Immigrants and Immigration to the United States." *Migration Information Source*, December 9. Accessed at http://www.migrationinformation.org/USFocus/display.cfm?ID=818 on June 15, 2013.

Bean, Frank D. and Marta Tienda. 1988. *The Hispanic Population of the United States*. Newbury Park, CA: Russell Sage Foundation.

Becker, Gary S. 1975. *Human Capital: A Theoretical and Empirical Analysis, with Special Reference to Education*, 2nd edn. New York: Columbia University Press.

Beckles Flores, Erika. 2011. "Waiting for Your Return: A Phenomenological Study on Parental Deportation and the Impact of the Family and the Parent-Child Attachment Bond." Ph.D. Dissertation, Syracuse University.

Bejarano, Cynthia, Maria Cristina Morales, and Said Saddiki. 2012. "A Comparative Analysis of the Mexico-US and Moroccan–Spanish Regions: Understanding Conquest through a Border Lens," pp. 27–41 in J.M. Loyd (ed.), *Beyond Walls and Cages*. Tucson, AZ: University of Arizona Press.

Benjamin-Alvarado, Jonathan, Louis DeSipio, and Celeste Montoya. 2009. "Latino Mobilization in New Immigrant Destinations: The Anti-HR 4437 Protest in Nebraska's Cities." *Urban Affairs Review* 44(5): 718–35.

Berges, Ivonne-Marie, Yong-Fang Kuo, M. Kristen Peek, and Kyriakos S. Markides. 2010. "Religious Involvement and Physical Functioning among Older Mexican Americans." *Journal of Aging* 12(1): 1-10.

Bidwell, Charles E. and Noah E. Friedkin. 1988. "The Sociology of Education," pp. 449-71 in N.J. Smelser (ed.), *Handbook of Sociology*. Newbury Park, CA: Sage Publications.

Bishin, Benjamin G., Karen M. Kaufmann, and Daniel Stevens. 2012. "Turf Wars Local Context and Latino Political Development." *Urban Affairs Review* 48(1): 111-37.

Blalock, Hubert M. 1967. *Toward a Theory of Minority-Group Relations*. New York: John Wiley & Sons.

Blau, Peter M. 1977. *Inequality and Heterogeneity*. New York: Free Press.

Blau, Peter M., Terry C. Blum, and Joseph E. Schwartz. 1982. "Heterogeneity and Intermarriage." *American Sociological Review* 47(1): 45-62.

Blauner, Robert. 1972. *Racial Oppression in America*. New York: Harper and Row.

Bonilla-Silva, Eduardo. 1997. "Rethinking Racism: Toward a Structural Interpretation." *American Sociological Review* 62: 465-80.

Bonilla-Silva, Eduardo. 2001. *White Supremacy and Racism in the Post-Civil Rights Era*. Boulder, CO: Lynne Rienner.

Bonilla-Silva, Eduardo. 2004. "From Bi-Racial to Tri-Racial: Towards a New System of Racial Stratification in the USA." *Ethnic and Racial Studies* 27(6): 931-50.

Bonilla-Silva, Eduardo. 2013. *Racism without Racists: Colorblind Racism and the Persistence of Racial Inequality in America*, 4th edn. Lanham, MD: Rowman & Littlefield.

Border Network for Human Rights. 2015. Border Network for Human Rights. El Paso, TX: BNHR. Accessed at www.bnhr.org on January 12, 2015.

Bourdieu, Pierre. 1974. "The School as a Conservative Force: Scholastic and Cultural Inequalities," in J. Eggleston (ed.), *Contemporary Research in the Sociology of Education*. New York: Harper & Row.

Bourdieu, Pierre. 1977. "Cultural Reproduction and Social Reproduction," in J. Karabel and A.H. Halsey (eds.), *Power and Education Ideology*. New York: Oxford University Press.

Bowen, Mary Elizabeth. 2009. "Childhood Socioeconomic Status and Racial Differences in Disability: Evidence from the Health and Retirement Study (1998-2006)." *Social Science & Medicine* 69(3): 433-41.

Bowler, Shaun, Stephen P. Nicholson, and Gary M. Segura. 2006. "Earthquakes and Aftershocks: Race, Direct Democracy, and Partisan Change." *American Journal of Political Science* 50(1): 146-59.

Brown, Henry Shelton. 2008. "Do Mexican Immigrants Substitute Health Care in Mexico for Insurance in the United States? The Role of Distance." *Social Science & Medicine* 67: 2036-42.

Brown, R. Khari. 2011. "Religion, Political Discourse, and Activism among Varying Racial/Ethnic Groups in America." *Review of Religious Research* 53: 301-22.

Brown, Susan, Jennifer Van Hook, and Jennifer Glick. 2008. "Generational Differences in Cohabitation and Marriage in the US." *Population Research and Policy Review* 27(5): 531-50.

Bruhn, John G. 2011. *The Sociology of Community Connections*. New York: Springer.

Buffalo Soldier. 2014. *Hispanic–American Medal of Honor Recipients*. Accessed at http://www.buffalosoldier.net/Hispanic-AmericanMedalofHonorRecipients.htm on April 12, 2014.

Bursik, Robert J. 1988. "Social Disorganization and Theories of Crime and Delinquency: Problems and Prospects." *Criminology* 26(4): 519-52.

Bustamante, Jorge. 1972. "The 'Wetback' as Deviant: An Application of Labeling Theory." *American Journal of Sociology* 77(4): 706-18.

Buttenheim, Alison, Noreen Goldman, Anne R. Pebley, Rebecca Wong, and Chang Chung. 2010. "Do Mexican Immigrants 'Import' Social Gradients in Health to the US?" *Social Science & Medicine* 71(7): 1268-76.

Cadge, Wendy and Elaine Howard Ecklund. 2007. "Immigration and Religion." *Annual Review of Sociology* 33: 359-79.

Cahill, Sean. 2009. "The Disproportionate Impact of Antigay Family Policies on Black and Latino Same-Sex Couple Households." *Journal of African American Studies* 13(3): 219-50.

Cannon, Angie. 1999. "DWB: Driving While Black." *US News & World Report*, March 15: 72.

Card, David. 1990. "The Impact of the Mariel Boatlift on the Miami Labor Market." *Industrial and Labor Relations Review* 43(2): 245-57.

Cauce, Ana Mari and Melanie Domenech-Rodríguez. 2002. "Latino Families: Myths and Realities," pp. 3-26 in Josefina M. Contreras, Kathryn A. Kerns, and Angela M. Neal-Barnett (eds.) *Latino Children and Families in the United States: Current Research and Future Directions*. Westport, CT: Praeger.

Cave, Damen. 2013. "In Mexican Villages, Few Are Left to Dream of U.S." *New York Times*, April 3. Accessed at http://www.nytimes.com/2013/04/03/world/americas/new-wave-of-mexican-immigrants-seems-unlikely.html?hp on April 3, 2013.

Cavendish, Richard. 1998. "The Sinking of the Maine." *History Today* 48 (2): 33.

Center for Disease Control and Prevention. 2013a. *CDC Wonder: Compressed Mortality 1999-2010 Request*. Data extraction file. Atlanta: Center for Disease Control and Prevention. Accessed at http://wonder.cdc.gov/controller/datarequest/D91;jsessionid=4292298407529A2D031E6851BE812CA5 on March 20, 2013.

Center for Disease Control and Prevention. 2013b. *CDC Wonder: Natality, 2003-2006 Request*. Data extraction file. Atlanta: Center for Disease Control and Prevention. Accessed at http://wonder.cdc.gov/controller/datarequest/D27 on March 20, 2013.

Center for Disease Control and Prevention. 2013c. *CDC Wonder: Natality, 2007-2010 Request*. Data extraction file. Atlanta: Center for Disease Control and Prevention. Accessed at http://wonder.cdc.gov/controller/datarequest/D66;jsessionid=A308078E9F86A38DE67223BCF87E62F4 on March 20, 2013.

Center for Immigration Studies. 1995. "Three Decades of Mass Immigration: The Legacy of the 1965 Immigration Act." Washington, DC: Center for Immigration Studies.

Cesar, Maria Luisa. 2013. "Obama Official Lauds Pre-K 4 SA, Touts President's Universal Pre-K Plan." *San Antonio Express-News*, April 24. Accessed at http://www.mysanantonio.com/news/education/article/Obama-official-lauds-Pre-K-4-SA-touts-4461031.php on September 2, 2013.

Chant, Sylvia with Nikki Craske. 2003. *Gender in Latin America*. New Brunswick, NJ: Rutgers University Press.

Chapman, Dan. 2001. "Gwinnett No. 1? Steady Growth May Put County in Top Spot by 2008." *Atlanta Journal-Constitution*, March 24: 1B.

Chasin, Barbara H. 2004. *Inequality and Violence in the United States: Casualties of Capitalism*. New York: Humanity Books.

Chavez, Leo R. 2008. *The Latino Threat Narrative: Constructing Immigrants, Citizens, and the Nation*. Stanford, CA: Stanford University Press.

Chavez, Leo R. 2012. "Undocumented Immigrants and Their Use of Medical Services in Orange County, California." *Social Science & Medicine* 74(6): 887-93.

Chetty, Raj, Nathaniel Handren, Patrick Kline, and Emmanuel Saez. 2013. *The Equality of Opportunity Project*. Cambridge, MA: The Equality of Opportunity Project, Harvard University.

Clotfelter, Charles T. 2004. *After Brown: The Rise and Retreat of School Segregation*. Princeton, NJ: Princeton University Press.

Cloward, Richard A. and Lloyd E. Ohlin. 1960. *Delinquency and Opportunity: A Theory of Delinquent Gangs*. Glencoe, IL: Free Press.

Cohen, Laurie. 1998. "Free Ride: With Help from INS, U.S. Meatpacker Taps Mexican Work Force." *Wall Street Journal*, October 15: A1.

Comeau, Joseph A. 2012. "Race/Ethnicity and Family Contact Toward a Behavioral Measure of Familialism." *Hispanic Journal of Behavioral Sciences* 34(2): 251-68.

Cornelius, Wayne. 2001. Death at the Border: Efficiency and "Unintended" Consequences of US Immigration and Control Policy 1993-2000. Working Paper 27, Center for Comparative Immigration Studies. University of California San Diego. Accessed at http://www.ccis-ucsd.org/PUBLICATIONS/wrkg27.PDF on October 2, 2009.

Crandall, Russell. 2006. *Gunboat Democracy: U.S. Interventions in the Dominican Republic, Grenada, and Panama*. Lanham, MD: Rowman & Littlefield.

Crimmins, Eileen M., Jung Ki Kim, Dawn E. Alley, Arun Karlamangla, and Teresa Seeman.

2007. "Hispanic Paradox in Biological Risk Profiles." *American Journal of Public Health* 97: 1305-10.

Curry, Theodore R. 2010. "The Conditional Effects of Victim and Offender Ethnicity and Victim Gender on Sentences for Non-Capital Cases." *Punishment & Society* 12(4): 438-62.

Curry, Theodore R. and Guadalupe Corral-Camacho. 2008. "Sentencing Young Minority Males for Drug Offenses: Testing for Conditional Effects between Race/Ethnicity, Gender and Age during the US War on Drugs." *Punishment & Society* 10(3): 253-76.

Dance, Jannelle. 2005. *Tough Fronts: The Impact of Street Crime on Schooling*. New York: Routledge.

Dávila, Arlene. 2001. *Latino Inc.: The Marketing and Making of a People*. Berkeley, CA: University of California Press.

Dávila, Arlene. 2008. *Latino Spin: Public Image and the Whitewashing of Race*. New York: New York University Press.

Dawson, Michael. 1994. *Behind the Mule: Race and Class in African-American Politics*. Princeton, NJ: Princeton University Press.

de la Garza, Rodolfo O. and Jeronimo Cortina. 2007. "Are Latinos Republican But Just Don't Know It? The Latino Vote in the 2000 and 2004 Presidential Elections." *American Politics Research* 35: 202-23.

de la Rosa, Ivan A. 2002. "Perinatal Outcomes among Mexican Americans: A Review of an Epidemiological Paradox." *Ethnicity & Disease* 12: 480-7.

del Rio, Esteban. 2012. "Accentuate the Positive: *Americanos* and the Articulation of Latina/o Life in the United States." *Journal of Communication Inquiry* 36(3): 179-201.

Delgado, Richard and Jean Stefancic. 2001. *Critical Race Theory: An Introduction*. New York: New York University Press.

DeVitt, Rachel. 2011. "Cheat Sheet: Latino Crossovers." *Rhapsody.com*, October 5. Accessed at http://blog.rhapsody.com/2011/10/crossovers.html on February 2, 2013.

Diaz, Jesse, Jr. 2012. "Prison and Immigration Industrial Complexes: The Ethnodistillation of People of Color and Immigrants as Economic, Political, and Demographic Threats to the US Hegemony." *International Journal of Criminology and Sociology* 1: 265-84.

Dickerson vonLockette, Niki T. and Jacqueline Johnson. 2010. "Latino Employment and Residential Segregation in Metropolitan Labor Markets." *DuBois Review* 7(1): 151-84.

Dinan, Stephen. 2012. "Obama Administration Sets Deportation Record." *Washington Post*, December 21. Accessed at http://www.washingtontimes.com/news/2012/dec/21/obama-administration-sets-deportation-record/ on June 22, 2013.

Domhoff, G. William. 2013. *Who Rules America?: The Triumph of the Corporate Rich*, 7th edn. New York: McGraw-Hill.

Donato, Katharine M. and Blake Sisk. 2012. "Shifts in the Employment Outcomes among Mexican Migrants to the United States, 1976-2009." *Research in Social Stratification and Mobility* 30(1): 63-77.

Douglas, Karen Manges and Rogelio Sáenz. 2008. "No Phone, No Vehicle, No English, and No Citizenship: The Vulnerability of Mexican Immigrants in the United States," pp. 161-80 in A. Hattery, D.G. Embrick, and E. Smith (eds.), *Race, Human Rights and Inequality*. Lanham, MD: Rowman and Littlefield.

Douglas, Karen Manges and Rogelio Sáenz. 2013. "The Criminalization of Immigrants and the Immigration-Industrial Complex." *Daedalus, the Journal of the American Academy of Arts & Sciences* 142(3): 199-227.

Dreby, Joanna. 2006. "Honor and Virtue: Mexican Parenting in the Transnational Context." *Gender and Society* 20: 32-59.

Dreby, Joanna. 2010. *Divided by Borders: Mexican Migrants and Their Children*. Berkeley, CA: University of California Press.

Duncan, Otis Dudley. 1961. "A Socioeconomic Index for All Occupations," pp. 109-38 in A. Reiss, Jr., *Occupations and Social Status*. Glencoe, IL: Free Press.

Dunn, Timothy. 1996. *The Militarization of the US–Mexico Border 1978-1992: Low-Intensity Conflict Doctrine Comes Home*. Austin, TX: Center for Mexican American Studies Books.

Dunn, Timothy. 2009. *Blockading the Border and Human Rights: The El Paso Operation that Remade Immigration Enforcement.* Austin, TX: University of Texas Press.

Durand, Jorge and Douglas S. Massey. 2003. "The Costs of Contradiction: US Border Policy 1986–2000." *Latino Studies* 1(2): 233–52.

Eberstein, Isaac W., Charles B. Nam, and Kathleen M. Heyman. 2008. "Causes of Death and Mortality Crossovers by Race." *Biodemography and Social Biology* 54(2): 214–28.

Echeagaray, José Ignacio (ed.). 1981. *Album Conmemorativo del 450 Aniversario de la Apariciones de Nuestra Señora de Guadalupe.* Mexico City: Ediciones Buena Nueva.

Eitzen, Stanley D. and Maxine Baca Zinn. 2007. *In Conflict and Order: Understanding Society.* Upper Saddle, NJ: Pearson.

Eitzen, Stanley D., Maxine Baca Zinn, and Kelly Eitzen Smith. 2013. *In Conflict and Order: Understanding Society.* Upper Saddle, NJ: Pearson.

Elizondo, Virgilio P. 1980. *La Morenita: Evangelizer of the Americas.* San Antonio, TX: Mexican American Cultural Center.

Ellison, Christopher G., Samuel Echevarria, and Brad Smith. 2005. "Religion and Abortion Attitudes among US Hispanics: Findings from the 1990 Latino National Political Survey." *Social Science Quarterly* 86: 192–208.

Elo, Irma T., Cassio M. Turra, Bert Kestenbaum, and B. Reneé Ferguson. 2004. "Mortality among Elderly Hispanics in the United States: Past Evidence and New Results." *Demography* 41(1): 109–28.

English, T.J. 2009. *Havana Nocturne: How the Mob Owned Cuba and Lost It To the Revolution.* New York: HarperCollins.

Eschbach, Karl, Jacqueline Hagan, Nestor Rodriguez, Rubén Hernández-León, and Stanley Bailey. 1999. "Death at the Border." *International Migration Review* 33(2): 430–54.

Eschbach, Karl, Jonathan D. Mahnken, and James S. Goodwin. 2005. "Neighborhood Composition and Incidence of Cancer among Hispanics in the United States." *Cancer* 103(5): 1036–44.

Escobar, Edward. 2008. "Race and Criminal Justice," pp. 291–300 in Abby Ferber, Christina M. Jimenez, Andrea O'Reilly Herrera, and Dena R. Samuels (eds.), *The Matrix Reader: Examining the Dynamics of Oppression and Privilege.* New York: McGraw-Hill.

Esparza, Adrian X. and Angela J. Donelson. 2008. *Colonias in Arizona and New Mexico: Border Poverty and Community Development Solutions.* Tucson, AZ: University of Arizona Press.

Evans, Diana, Ana Franco, J.L. Polinard, James P. Wenzel, and Robert D. Wrinkle. 2012. "Ethnic Concerns and Latino Party Identification." *The Social Science Journal* 49(2): 150–4.

Farmer, Paul. 2004. "An Anthropology of Structural Violence." *Current Anthropology* 45: 305–25.

Feagin, Joe R. 2006. *Systemic Racism: A Theory of Oppression.* New York: Routledge.

Feagin, Joe R. 2010. *Racist America: Roots, Current Realities and Future Reparations,* 2nd edn. New York: Routledge.

Feagin, Joe R. 2013. *The White Racial Frame: Centuries of Racial Framing and Counter-Framing,* 2nd edn. New York: Routledge.

Feagin, Joe and Danielle Dirks. 2005. "Who Is White? College Students' Assessments of Key US Racial and Ethnic Groups." Paper presented at the annual meeting of the Southern Sociological Society.

Fernandez, Deepa. 2007. *Targeted: Homeland Security and the Business of Immigration.* New York: Seven Stories Press.

File, Thom. 2013. *The Diversifying Electorate – Voting Rates by Race and Hispanic Origin in 2012 (and Other Recent Elections).* Current Population Survey P20-568. Washington, DC: US Census Bureau.

Finke, Roger and Rodney Stark. 1992. *The Churching of America: Winners and Losers in Our Religious Economy.* New Brunswick, NJ: Rutgers University Press.

Flores-Yeffal, Nadia Yamel, Guadalupe Vidales, and April Plemons. 2011. "The Latino Cyber-Moral Panic Process in the United States." *Information, Communication & Society* 14(4): 568–89.

Foner, Nancy. 1997. "The Immigrant Family: Cultural Legacies and Cultural Changes." *International Migration Review* 31(4): 961–74.

Franco, Jamie L., Laura Sabattini, and Faye J. Crosby. 2004. "Anticipating Work and Family: Exploring the Associations among Gender-Related Ideologies, Values, and Behaviors in Latino and White Families in the United States." *Journal of Social Issues* 60(4): 755–66.

Frank, Reanne and Patrick Heuveline. 2005. "A Crossover in Mexican and Mexican-American Fertility Rates: Evidence and Explanations for an Emerging Paradox." *Demographic Research* 12(4): 77-104.

Frank, Reanne, Ilana Redstone, and Bo Lu. 2010. "Latino Immigrants and the US Racial Order." *American Sociological Review* 75(3): 378-401.

Fry, Richard. 2006. "The Changing Landscape of American Public Education." Washington, DC: Pew Research Center's Hispanic Trends Project.

Full-Service Restaurants. 2012. "With Ethnic Food on the Rise, Diners Seek Authenticity." *FSR Breaking News*, March 1. Accessed at http://www.fsrmagazine.com/content/ethnic-food-rise-diners-seek-authenticity on February 2, 2013.

Furman, Nelly, David Goldberg, and Natalia Lusin. 2010. *Enrollments in Languages Other Than English in United States Institutions of Higher Education, Fall 2009*. New York: Modern Language Association.

Fussell, Elizabeth and Alberto Palloni. 2004. "Persistent Marriage Regimes in Changing Times." *Journal of Marriage and Family* 66(5): 1201-13.

Gamboa, Erasmo. 2000. *Mexican Labor & World War II*. Seattle, WA: University of Washington Press.

Gamboa, Suzanne. 2014. "Deporter-in-Chief Label Ups the Pressure for Action from Obama." *NBC News*, March 6. Accessed at http://www.nbcnews.com/news/latino/deporter-chief-label-ups-pressure-action-obama-n45346 on April 11, 2014.

Garcia, Eugene. 2001. *Hispanic Education in the United States*. Lanham, MD: Rowman and Littlefield.

García, Ofelia. 2009. "Racializing the Language Practices of US Latinos: Impact in Their Education," pp. 101-15 in Jose A. Cobas, Jorge Duany, and Joe R. Feagin (eds.), *How the United States Racializes Latinos: White Hegemony & Its Consequences*. Boulder, CO: Paradigm Publishers.

Garibay, Angel. 1967. "Our Lady of Guadalupe," pp. 821-22 in *New Catholic Encyclopedia, Vol. VIII*. New York: McGraw-Hill.

Garza, Melita Marie. 1997. "Hola America! Newsstand 2000," pp. 129-36 in E.E. Dennis and E.C. Pease (eds.), *The Media in Black and White*. New Brunswick, NJ: Transaction Press.

Gearing, Jes. 2010. "The Most Popular Foreign Languages: Foreign Language Enrollment in US Schools." *Beyond Words Language Blog*, April 5. Accessed at http://www.altalang.com/beyond-words/2010/04/05/the-most-popular-foreign-languages-foreign-language-enrollment-in-u-s-schools/ on April 24, 2014.

Geronimus, Arline, John Bound, Danya Keene, and Margaret Hicken. 2007. "Black-White Differences in Age Trajectories of Hypertension Prevalence among Adult Women and Men, 1999-2002." *Ethnicity and Disease* 17(1): 40-8.

Glazer, Nathan. 1987. "The Emergence of an American Pattern," pp. 11-23 in R. Takaki (ed.), *From Different Shores: Perspectives on Race and Ethnicity in America*, 2nd edn. New York: Oxford University Press.

Glenn, Evelyn Nakano. 2002. *Unequal Freedom: How Race and Gender Shaped American Citizenship and Labor*. Cambridge, MA: Harvard University Press.

Golash-Boza, Tanya. 2009. "A Confluence of Interests in Immigration Enforcement: How Politicians, the Media, and Corporations Profit from Immigration Policies Destined to Fail." *Sociology Compass* 3(2): 283-94.

Golash-Boza, Tanya. 2012. *Immigration Nation: Raids, Detentions, and Deportations in Post-9/11 America*. Boulder, CO: Paradigm Publishers.

Goldsmith, Pat Antonio. 2004. "Schools' Racial Mix, Students' Optimism, and the Black-White and Latino-White Achievement Gaps." *Sociology of Education* 77: 121-47.

Goldson, E. 1999. *Americanos: Latino Life in the United States/La Vida de los Latinos en los Estados Unidos*. Washington, DC: Smithsonian Institution.

Gomes, Maria, and Fariyal Ross-Sheriff. 2011. "The Impact of Unintended Consequences of the 1996 US Immigration Reform Act on Women." *Affilia: Journal of Women and Social Work* 26(2): 117-24.

Gómez, Christina. 2000. "The Continual Significance of Skin Color: An Exploratory Study of Latinos in the Northeast." *Hispanic Journal of Behavioral Sciences* 22: 94-103.

González, Juan. 2000. *Harvest of Empire: The History of Latinos in America*. New York: Penguin Books.

González, Juan. 2012. "Preface," pp. xi–xii in O. Santa Ana and C. González de Bustamante (eds.), *Arizona Firestorm: Global Immigration Realities, National Media, and Provincial Politics*. Lanham, MD: Rowman & Littlefield.

Gonzalez-Ramos, Gladys, Luis H. Zayas, and Elaine V. Cohen. 1998. "Child-Rearing Values of Low-Income, Urban Puerto Rican Mothers of Preschool Children." *Professional Psychology: Research and Practice* 29(4): 377–82.

Goodstein, Laurie. 2007. "For Some Hispanics, Coming to America Also Means Abandoning Religion." *New York Times*, April 15. Accessed at http://www.nytimes.com/2007/04/15/us/15hispanic.html?pagewanted=all on February 11, 2014.

Goodstein, Laurie. 2008. "Serving US Parishes, Fathers Without Borders." *New York Times*, December 28. Accessed at http://www.nytimes.com/2008/12/28/us/28priest.html?pagewanted=all on February 11, 2014.

Gordon, Milton M. 1964. *Assimilation in American Life: The Role of Race, Religion, and National Origins*. New York: Oxford University Press.

Gorman, Bridget K., Elaine Howard Ecklund, and Holly E. Heard. 2010. "Nativity Differences in Physical Health: The Roles of Emotional Support, Family, and Social Integration." *Sociological Spectrum* 30: 671–94.

Gouveia, Lourdes and Rogelio Sáenz. 2000. "Global Forces and Latino Population Growth in the Midwest: A Regional and Subregional Analysis." *Great Plains Research* 10: 305–28.

Gowan, Mary and Melanie Treviño. 1998. "An Examination of Gender Differences in Mexican-American Attitudes toward Family and Career Roles." *Sex Roles* 38(11–12): 1079–93.

Granovetter, Mark S. 1973. "The Strength of Weak Ties." *American Journal of Sociology* 78(6): 1360–80.

Grasmuck, Sherri and Ramón Grosfoguel. 1997. "Geopolitics, Economic Niches, and Gendered Social Capital among Recent Caribbean Immigrants in New York City." *Sociological Perspectives* 40(3): 339–63.

Greenwood, Michael J. 1985. "Human Migration: Theory, Models, Empirical Studies." *Journal of Regional Science* 25(4): 521–44.

Guillem, Susana Martínez and Marco Briziarelli. 2012. "We Want Your Success! Hegemony, Materiality, and *Latino in America*." *Critical Studies in Media Communication* 29(4): 292–312.

Gutiérrez, David. 1995. *Walls and Mirrors: Mexican Americans, Mexican Immigrants, and the Politics of Ethnicity*. Berkeley, CA: University of California Press.

Gutiérrez, Félix F. 1977. "Chicanos and the Media," in M.C. Emery and T.C. Smythe (eds.), *Readings in Mass Communication: Concepts and Issues in the Mass Media*, 3rd edn. Dubuque, IA: William C. Brown.

Gutiérrez, Félix F. 2013. "More Than 200 Years of Latino Media in the United States," in National Park System Advisory Board (ed.), *American Latinos and the Making of the United States: A Theme Study*. Washington, DC: National Park System.

Hagan, John and Alberto Palloni. 1999. "Immigration and Crime in the United States," pp. 367–87 in J.P. Smith and B. Edmonston (eds.), *The Immigration Debate*. Washington, DC: National Academy Press.

Hajnal, Zoltan and Taeku Lee. 2011. *Race, Immigration and (Non) Partisanship in America*. Princeton, NJ: Princeton University Press.

Hall, Stuart. 1997. "The Work of Representation," pp. 13–74 in S. Hall (ed.), *Representation: Cultural Representations and Signifying Practices*. London: Sage.

Hallinan, Joseph T. 2001. *Going up the River: Travels in a Prison Nation*. New York: Random House.

Hamilton, Darrick, Arthur H. Goldsmith, and William Darity. 2008. "Measuring the Wage Costs of Limited English: Issues with Using Interviewer Versus Self-Reports in Determining Latino Wages." *Hispanic Journal of Behavioral Sciences* 30(3): 257–79.

Harris, Craig, Alicia Beard Rau, and Glen Creno. 2010. "Arizona Governor Signs Immigration Law; Foes Promise Fight." *The Arizona Republic*, April 24. Accessed at http://www.azcentral.com/news/articles/2010/04/23/20100423arizona-immigration-law-passed.html on March 7, 2014.

Harris, Leslie M. 2003. *In the Shadow of Slavery: African Americans in New York City, 1626–1863*. Chicago, IL: University of Chicago Press.

Harris, Richard J. 1980. "An Examination of the Effects of Ethnicity, Socioeconomic Status and Generation on Familism and Sex Role Orientations." *Journal of Comparative Family Studies* 11: 173–93.

Hauser, Robert M., Solon J. Simmons, and Devah I. Pager. 2000. *High School Dropout, Race-Ethnicity, and Social Background from the 1970s to the 1990s*. New York: Russell Sage Foundation.

Helg, Aline. 1990. "Race in Argentina and Cuba, 1880–1930: Theory, Policies, and Popular Reaction," pp. 37–69 in R. Graham (ed.), *The Idea of Race in Latin America, 1870–1940*. Austin, TX: University of Texas Press.

Hempel, Lynn M., Julie A. Dowling, Jason D. Boardman, and Christopher G. Ellison. 2013. "Racial Threat and White Opposition to Bilingual Education in Texas." *Hispanic Journal of Behavioral Sciences* 35(1): 85–102.

Hernández, Kelly Lytle. 2006. "The Crimes and Consequences of Illegal Immigration: A Cross-Border Examination of Operation Wetback, 1943 to 1954." *Western Historical Quarterly* 37: 421–44.

Hernández, Ramona. 2002. *The Mobility of Workers under Advanced Capitalism: Dominican Migration to the United States*. New York: Columbia University Press.

Hernández, Ramona. 2004. "On the Age Against the Poor: Dominican Migration to the United States." *Journal of Immigrant and Refugee Services* 2(1–2): 87–107.

Hernández-León, Rubén and Víctor Zúñiga. 2000. "'Making Carpet by the Mile': The Emergence of a Mexican Immigrant Community in an Industrial Region of the US Historic South." *Social Science Quarterly* 81(1): 49–66.

Hero, Rodney, F. Chris Garcia, John Garcia, and Harry Pachon. 2000. "Latino Participation, Partisanship, and Office Holding." *Political Science and Politics* 33(3): 529–34.

Heyman, Josiah. 2010. "Arizona's Immigration Law – S.B.1070." *News: A Publication of the Society for Applied Anthropology* 21(3): 23–26.

Hidalgo, Nitza. 1998. "Toward a Definition of a Latino Family Research Paradigm." *Qualitative Studies in Education* 11(1): 103–20.

Hines, Barbara. 2006. "An Overview of US Immigration Law and Policy Since 9/11." *Texas Hispanic Journal of Law and Policy* 12(9): 9–28.

Hobbs, Frank and Nicole Stoops. 2002. *Demographic Trends in the 20th Century*. Census 2000 Special Reports, Series CENSR-4. Washington, DC: US Government Printing Office. Accessed at http://www.census.gov/prod/2002pubs/censr-4.pdf on March 14, 2013.

Hodge, David R., Flavio F. Marsiglia, and Tanya Nieri. 2011. "Religion and Substance Use among Youths of Mexican Heritage: A Social Capital Perspective." *Social Work Research* 35(3): 137–46.

Hoffman, Abraham. 1974. *Unwanted Mexican Americans in the Great Depression: Repatriation Pressures 1929–1939*. Tucson, AZ: University of Arizona Press.

Hondagneu-Sotelo, Pierrette (ed.). 2007. *Religion and Social Justice for Immigrants*. New Brunswick, NJ: Rutgers University Press.

Hondagneu-Sotelo, Pierrette and Ernestine Avila. 1997. "'I'm Here, but I'm There': The Meanings of Latina Transnational Motherhood." *Gender and Society* 11(5): 548–71.

Hondagneu-Sotelo, Pierrette, Genelle Gaudinez, Hector Lara, and Billie C. Ortiz. 2004. "There's a Spirit that Transcends the Border: Faith, Ritual, and Postnational Protest in the US–Mexico Border." *Sociological Perspectives* 47: 133–59.

Horevitz, Elizabeth and Kurt C. Organista. 2013. "The Mexican Health Paradox: Expanding the Explanatory Power of the Acculturation Construct." *Hispanic Journal of Behavioral Sciences* 35(1): 3–34.

Horton, Sarah and Stephanie Cole. 2011. "Medical Returns: Seeking Health Care in Mexico." *Social Science & Medicine* 72: 1846–52.

Huddy, Leonie and David O. Sears. 1990. "Qualified Public Support for Bilingual Education: Some Policy Implications." *Annals of the American Academy of Political and Social Science* 508(1): 119–25.

Hummer, Robert A. 1996. "Black-White Differences in Health and Mortality: A Review and Conceptual Model." *The Sociological Quarterly* 37(1): 105–25.

Hummer, Robert A. and Juanita J. Chinn. 2011. "Race/Ethnicity and US Adult Mortality: Progress, Prospects, and New Analyses." *Du Bois Review* 8(1): 5–24.

Hummer, Robert A., Daniel A. Powers, Starling G. Pullum, Ginger L. Gossman, and W. Parker Frisbie. 2007. "Paradox Found (Again): Infant Mortality among the Mexican-Origin Population in the United States." *Demography* 44(3): 441–57.

Hunt, John. 1964. "The Psychological Basis for Using Pre-School Environment as an Antidote for Cultural Deprivation." *Merrill-Palmer Quarterly* 10: 209–48.

Hunt, Larry L. 1999. "Hispanic Protestantism in the United States: Trends by Decade and Generation." *Social Forces* 77: 1601–23.

Huntington, Samuel P. 2004. *Who Are We? The Challenges to America's National Identity*. New York: Simon & Schuster.

Hurn, Christopher J. 1993. *The Limits and Possibilities of Schooling: An Introduction to the Sociology of Education*, 3rd edn. Needham Heights, MA: Allyn and Bacon.

Hurtado, Aida. 1995. "Creations, Combinations, and Evolutions: Latino Families in the United States," pp. 18–38 in R.E. Zambrana (ed.), *Understanding Latino Families, Scholarship, Policy, and Practice*. Thousand Oaks, CA: Sage.

Hurtado, Aida, David E. Hayes-Bautista, R. Burciaga Valdez, and Anthony C.R. Hernandez. 1992. *Redefining California: Latino Social Engagement in a Multicultural Society*. Los Angeles, CA: UCLA Chicano Studies Research Center.

Hussey, Jon M. and Irma T. Elo. 1997. "Cause-Specific Mortality among Older African Americans: Correlates and Consequences of Age Misreporting." *Social Biology* 44(3–4): 227–46.

Hwang, Sean-Shong and Juan Xi. 2008. "Structural and Individual Covariates of English Language Proficiency." *Social Forces* 86: 1079–104.

Hwang, Sean-Shong, Juan Xi, and Yue Cao. 2010. "The Conditional Relationship between English Language Proficiency and Earnings among US Immigrants." *Social Forces* 33(9): 1620–47.

Hye-cheon, Karen, Kim Yeary, Songthip Ounpraseuth, Page Moore, Zoran Bursac, and Paul Greene. 2012. "Religion, Social Capital, and Health." *Review of Religious Research* 54: 331–47.

Ignatiev, Noel. 2008. *How the Irish Became White*. New York: Routledge.

Jasso, Guillermina, Douglas S. Massey, Mark R. Rosenzweig, and James P. Smith. 2004. "Immigrant Health: Selectivity and Acculturation," pp. 227–66 in N.B. Anderson, R.A. Bulatao, and B. Cohen (eds.), *Critical Perspectives on Racial and Ethnic Differences in Health in Later Life*. Washington, DC: National Academies Press.

Jensen, Robert. 1998. "White Privilege Shapes the U.S." *Baltimore Sun*, July 19: 1C, 4C.

Joassart-Marcelli, Pascale. 2009. "The Spatial Determinants of Wage Inequality: Evidence from Recent Latina Immigrants in Southern California." *Feminist Economics* 15: 33–72.

Johnson, Lyndon B. 1965. "Remarks at the Signing of the Immigration Bill, Liberty Island, New York, October 3, 1965." Selected Speeches and Messages of LBJ. Austin, TX: LBJ Presidential Library. Accessed at http://www.lbjlib.utexas.edu/johnson/archives.hom/speeches.hom/651003.asp on May 18, 2013.

Jones-Correa, Michael A. and David Leal. 1996. "Becoming 'Hispanic': Secondary Pan-ethnic Identification among Latin-American-Origin Populations in the United States." *Hispanic Journal of Behavioral Sciences* 18: 214–54.

Jones-Correa, Michael A. and David L. Leal. 2001. "Political Participation: Does Religion Matter?" *Political Research Quarterly* 54: 751–70.

Kaestner, Robert, Jay A. Peterson, Danya Keene, and Arline T. Geronimus. 2009. "Stress, Allostatic Load, and Health of Mexican Immigrants." *Social Science Quarterly* 90(5): 1089–111.

Kandel, William and Emilio Parrado. 2005. "Restructuring of the US Meat Processing Industry and New Hispanic Destinations." *Population and Development Review* 31(3): 447–71.

Katznelson, Ira. 2005. *When Affirmative Action Was White: An Untold History of Racial Inequality in Twentieth-Century America*. New York: W.W. Norton & Company.

Kaufmann, Karen M. 2003. "Cracks in the Rainbow: Group Commonality as a Basis for Latino and African-American Political Coalitions." *Political Research Quarterly* 56(2): 199-210.

Keefe, Susan E. 1984. "Real and Ideal Familism among Mexican Americans and Anglo Americans: On the Meaning of 'Close' Family Ties." *Human Organization* 43(1): 65-70.

Keegan, Rebecca. 2013. "USC Study: Minorities Still Under-Represented in Popular Films." *Los Angeles Times*, October 30.

Kimbro, Rachel Tolbert, Bridget K. Gorman, and Ariela Schachter. 2012. "Acculturation and Self-Rated Health among Latino and Asian Immigrants to the United States." *Social Problems* 59(3): 341-63.

Kitagawa, Evelyn M. and Philip M. Hauser. 1973. *Differential Mortality in the United States: A Study in Socioeconomic Epidemiology.* Cambridge, MA: Harvard University Press.

Kochanek, Kenneth D., Jiaquan Xu, Sherry L. Murphy, Arialdi M. Miniño, and Hsiang-Ching Kung. 2011. "Deaths: Final Data for 2009." *National Vital Statistics Reports* 60(3). Hyattsville, MD: National Center for Health Statistics.

Kochhar, Rakesh. 2012a. *The Demographics of the Job Recovery.* Washington, DC: Pew Research Center's Hispanic Trends Project.

Kochhar, Rakesh. 2012b. *Labor Force Growth Slows, Hispanic Share Grows.* Washington, DC: Pew Research Center's Hispanic Trends Project.

Koestler, Fred L. 2013. "Operation Wetback." *Handbook of Texas Online.* Denton, TX: Texas State Historical Association. Accessed at http://www.tshaonline.org/handbook/online/articles/pqo01 on May 10, 2013.

Kozol, Jonathan. 1991. *Savage Inequalities.* New York: Crown.

Kozol, Jonathan. 2005. *The Shame of the Nation: The Restoration of Apartheid Schooling in America.* New York: Crown Publishers.

Krause, Neal and Elena Bastida. 2011. "Prayer to the Saints or the Virgin and Health among Older Mexican Americans." *Hispanic Journal of Behavioral Sciences* 33: 71-87.

Kubrin, Charis and Hiromi Ishizawa. 2012. "Why Some Immigrant Neighborhoods Are Safer than Others: Divergent Findings from Los Angeles and Chicago." *The Annals of the American Academy of Political and Social Science* 641(1): 148-73.

Lacey, Marc. 2011. "Rift in Arizona as Latino Class is Found Illegal." *New York Times*, January 7. Accessed at http://www.nytimes.com/2011/01/08/us/08ethnic.html?pagewanted=all&_r=0 on April 14, 2014.

LaFeber, Walter. 1984. *Inevitable Revolutions: The United States in Central America.* New York: Norton.

Lakshmanan, Indira A.R. 2008. "US Election Highlights Puerto Rico's 'Unequal' Status." *New York Times*, May 20. Accessed at http://www.nytimes.com/2008/05/20/world/americas/20iht-letter.1.13044789.html on March 31, 2014.

Landale, Nancy S. and R.S. Oropesa. 2007. "Hispanic Families: Stability and Change." *Annual Review of Sociology* 33: 381-405.

Landale, Nancy, R.S. Oropesa, and Bridget K. Gorman. 1999. "Immigration and Infant Health: Birth Outcomes of Immigrant and Native Women," pp. 244-86 in D.J. Hernandez (ed.), *Children of Immigrants: Health, Adjustment, and Public Assistance.* Washington, DC: National Academy Press.

Lariscy, Joseph T. 2011. "Differential Record Linkage by Hispanic Ethnicity and Age in Linked Mortality Studies: Implications for the Epidemiological Paradox." *Journal of Aging and Health* 23(8): 1263-84.

Leadership Conference, The. 2014. "Voting Rights Act." Accessed at http://www.civilrights.org/voting-rights/vra/ on March 27, 2014.

Leal, Luis. 1989. "The Spanish-Language Press Function and Use." *The Americas Review* 17(3-4): 157-62.

Leavell, Ashley Smith, Catherine S. Tamis-LeMonda, Diane N. Ruble, Kristina M. Zosuls, and Natasha J. Cabrera. 2012. "African American, White and Latino Fathers' Activities with Their Sons and Daughters in Early Childhood." *Sex Roles* 66(1-2): 53-65.

Leavitt, Parker and Nathan Gonzalez. 2010a. "At Phx. rally, 2,800 vow to thwart immigrant law." *The Arizona Republic*, April 26. Accessed at http://azstarnet.com/news/local/govt-and-politics/article_335334a2-913b-596b-80e0-a060a64b5148.html on March 7, 2014.

Leavitt, Parker and Nathan Gonzalez. 2010b. "Immigration Law Protested by More than 2,500 at State Capitol: Diverse Groups Join Forces for March, Demonstration." *The Arizona Republic*, April 25. Accessed at http://www.azcentral.com/community/mesa/articles/2010/04/25/20100425immigration-law-protest-arizona.html on April 24, 2014.

Lee, Everett S. 1966. "A Theory of Migration." *Demography* 3(1): 47–57.

Lee, Kenneth K. 1998. *Huddled Masses, Muddled Laws*. Westport, CT: Praeger.

Leigh, J. Paul and James F. Fries. 1992. "Disability in Occupations in a National Sample." *American Journal of Public Health* 82 (11): 1517–24.

León-Portilla, Miguel. 1962. *The Broken Spears: The Aztec Account of the Conquest of Mexico*. Boston, MA: Beacon Press.

Leonard, Tammy, Rachel T.A. Croson, and Angela C.M. de Oliveira. 2010. "Social Capital and Public Goods." *The Journal of Socioeconomics* 39: 474–81.

Lewis, Amanda. 2003. *Race in the Schoolyard: Negotiating the Color Line in Classrooms and Communities*. New Brunswick, NJ: Rutgers University Press.

Lewis, Oscar. 1959. *Five Families: Mexican Case Studies in the Culture of Poverty*. New York: Basic Books.

Lewis, Oscar. 1965. *La Vida: A Puerto Rican Family in the Culture of Poverty – San Jose and New York*. New York: Random House.

Lewis, Oscar. 1966. "The Culture of Poverty." *Scientific American* 215: 19–25.

Leyva, Yolanda Chávez. 2002. "The Revisioning of History Es Una Gran Limpa: Teaching and Historical Trauma in Chicana/o History." *La Voz de Esperanza* 15(7): 10–12.

Liao, Youlian, Richard S. Cooper, Guichan Cao, Ramon Durazo-Arvizu, Jay S. Kaufman, Amy Luke, and Daniel L. McGee. 1998. "Mortality Patterns among Adult Hispanics." *American Journal of Public Health* 88: 227–32.

Liu, John M., Paul M. Ong, and Carolyn Rosenstein. 1991. "Dual Chain Migration: Post-1965 Filipino Immigration to the United States." *International Migration Review* 25(3): 487–513.

Liu, Kathy Yang. 2011. "Employment Concentration and Job Quality for Low-Skilled Latino Immigrants." *Journal of Urban Affairs* 33(2): 117–42.

Liu, Kathy Yang. 2013. "Latino Immigration and the Low-Skill Urban Labor Market: The Case of Atlanta." *Social Science Quarterly* 94(1): 131–57.

Livingston, Gretchen and D'Vera Cohn. 2012. *US Birth Rate Falls to a Record Low; Decline is Greatest among Immigrants*. Washington, DC: Pew Research Center's Hispanic Trends Project.

LoBreglio, Kiera. 2004. "The Border Security and Immigration Improvement Act: A Modern Solution to a Historic Problem?" *St. John's Law Review* 78(3): 933–64.

Longazel, Jamie G. 2013. "Moral Panic as Racial Degradation Ceremony: Racial Stratification and the Local-Level Backlash against Latino/a Immigrants." *Punishment & Society* 15(1): 96–119.

López, Ian Haney. 2006. *White by Law: The Legal Construction of Race*. New York: New York University Press.

Lopez, Mark Hugo. 2013. "What Univision's Milestone Says about US Demographics." Washington, DC: Pew Research Center's Hispanic Trends Project.

Lopez, Mark Hugo and Ana Gonzalez-Barrera. 2013a. "A Growing Share of Latinos Get Their News in English." Washington, DC: Pew Research Center's Hispanic Trends Project.

Lopez, Mark Hugo and Ana Gonzalez-Barrera. 2013b. "High Rates of Deportations Continue Under Obama Despite Latino Disapproval." Washington, DC: Pew Research Center's Hispanic Trends Project.

Lopez, Mark Hugo and Ana Gonzalez-Barrera. 2013c. "Inside the 2012 Latino Electorate." Washington, DC: Pew Research Center's Hispanic Trends Project.

Lopez, Mark Hugo and Gretchen Livingston. 2009. "Hispanics and the Criminal Justice System: Low Confidence, High Exposure." Washington, DC: Pew Research Center's Hispanic Trends Project.

López-Sanders, Laura. 2012. "Bible Belt Immigrants: Latino Religion Incorporation in New Immigrant Destinations." *Latino Studies* 10(1-2): 128-54.

Loveman, Mara and Jeronimo O. Muñiz. 2007. "How Puerto Rico Became White: Boundary Dynamics and Inter-Census Racial Reclassification." *American Sociological Review* 72(6): 915-39.

Luibheid, Eithne. 1997. "The 1965 Immigration and Nationality Act: An 'End' to Exclusion." *Positions* 5(2): 501-22.

Lundholm, Nicholas B. 2011. "Cutting Class: Why Arizona's Ethnic Studies Ban won't Ban Ethnic Studies." *Arizona Law Review* 53(3): 1041-88.

Lydgate, Joanna. 2010. "Assembly-Line Justice: A Review of Operation Streamline." The Chief Justice Earl Warren Institute on Race, Ethnicity & Diversity. University of California, Berkeley Law School.

MacCormack, John. 2012. "Immigrant Deaths Soar in South Texas." *San Antonio Express-News*, December 30. Accessed at http://www.mysanantonio.com/news/local_news/article/Border-woes-no-longer-just-on-the-border-4155003.php on April 1, 2014.

Madsen, William. 1967. "Religious Syncretism," pp. 369-91 in M. Nash (ed.), *Social Anthropology*. Vol. 6. *Handbook of Middle American Indians*. Austin, TX: University of Texas Press.

Markert, John. 2010. "The Changing Face of Racial Discrimination: Hispanics as the Dominant Minority in the USA – A New Application of Power-Threat Theory." *Critical Sociology* 36(2): 307-27.

Markides, Kyriakos S. and Jeannine Coreil. 1986. "The Health of Hispanics in the Southwestern United States: An Epidemiological Paradox." *Public Health Reports* 101: 253-65.

Markides, Kyriakos S. and Karl Eschbach. 2005. "Aging, Migration, and Mortality: Current Status of Research on the Hispanic Paradox." *Journals of Gerontology, Series B: Psychological Sciences* 60B: 68-75.

Markides, Kyriakos S. and Karl Eschbach. 2011. "Hispanic Paradox in Adult Mortality in the United States," pp. 227-240 in R.G. Rogers and E.M. Crimmins (eds.), *International Handbook of Adult Mortality*. New York: Springer.

Martin, Joyce A., Brady E. Hamilton, Stephanie J. Ventura, Michelle J.K. Osterman, Elizabeth C. Wilson, and T.J. Matthews. 2012. "Births: Final Data for 2010." *National Vital Statistics Reports* 61(1). Hyattsville, MD: National Center for Health Statistics.

Martin, Monica J., Bill McCarthy, Rand D. Conger, Frederick X. Gibbons, Ronald L. Simons, Carolyn E. Cutrona, and Gene H. Brody. 2011. "The Enduring Significance of Racism: Discrimination and Delinquency among Black American Youth." *Journal of Research on Adolescence* 21(3): 662-76.

Martinez, George A. 1997. "The Legal Construction of Race: Mexican-Americans and Whiteness." *Harvard Latino Law Review* 2: 321.

Martinez, Ramiro, Jr. 2008. "Latino Crime and Delinquency in the United States," pp. 114-26 in H. Rodríguez, R. Sáenz, and C. Menjívar (eds.), *Latinas/os in the United States: Changing the Face of América*. New York: Springer.

Martinez, Ramiro, Jr. 2013. *Latino Homicide: Immigration, Violence, and Community*, 2nd edn. New York: Routledge.

Martinez, Ramiro, Jr. and Matthew T. Lee. 2000. "Comparing the Context of Immigrant Homicides in Miami: Haitians, Jamaicans and Mariels." *International Migration Review* 34(3): 794-812.

Martinez, Ramiro, Jr. and Jacob I. Stowell. 2012. "Extending Immigration and Crime Studies: National Implications and Local Settings." *Annals of the American Academy of Political & Social Science* 641(1): 174-91.

Martínez, Ramiro, Jr. and Abel Valenzuela (eds.). 2006. *Immigration and Crime: Race, Ethnicity, and Violence*. New York: New York University Press.

Martínez, Ramiro, Jr., Jacob I. Stowell, and Matthew T. Lee. 2010. "Immigration and Crime in an Era of Transformation: A Longitudinal Analysis of Homicides in San Diego Neighborhood, 1980-2000." *Criminology* 48(3): 797-829.

Martini, Nicholas F. 2012. "'La Iglesia' in Politics? Religion and Latino Public Opinion." *Social Science Quarterly* 93(4): 988-1006.

Massey, Douglas S. 2007. *Categorically Unequal: The American Stratification System*. New York: Russell Sage Foundation.

Massey, Douglas S. and Nancy Denton. 1993. *American Apartheid: Segregation and the Making of the Underclass*. Cambridge, MA: Harvard University Press.

Massey, Douglas S. and Kristin E. Espinosa. 1997. "What's Driving Mexico–US Migration? A Theoretical, Empirical, and Policy Analysis." *American Journal of Sociology* 102(4): 939–99.

Massey, Douglas S. and Emilio Parrado. 1994. "Migradollars: The Remittances and Savings of Mexican Migrants to the USA." *Population Research and Policy Review* 13: 3–30.

Massey, Douglas, Rafael Alarcon, Jorge Durand, and Humberto Gonzalez. 1987. *Return to Aztlan: The Social Process of International Migration from Western Mexico*. Berkeley, CA: University of California Press.

Massey, Douglas S., Joaquín Arango, Graeme Hugo, Ali Kouaouci, Adela Pellegrino, and J. Edward Taylor. 1993. "Theories of International Migration: A Review and Appraisal." *Population and Development Review* 19(3): 431–66.

Massey, Douglas S., Ruth E. Zambrana, and Sally Alonzo Bell. 1995. "Contemporary Issues in Latino Families: Future Directions for Research, Policy, and Practice," pp. 190–3 in Ruth E. Zambrana (ed.), *Understanding Latino Families*. Thousand Oaks, CA: Sage.

Massey, Douglas S., Jorge Durand, and Nolan J. Malone. 2002. *Beyond Smoke and Mirrors: Mexican Immigration in an Era of Economic Integration*. New York: Russell Sage Foundation.

Massey, Douglas S., Joaquín Arango, Graeme Hugo, Ali Kouaouci, Adela Pellegrino, and J. Edward Taylor. 2005. *Worlds in Motion: Understanding World Migration at the End of the Millennium*. New York: Oxford University Press.

Mastro, Dana E. and Bradley S. Greenberg. 2000. "The Portrayal of Racial Minorities on Prime Time Television." *Journal of Broadcasting and Electronic Media* 44: 690–703.

Maternowska, Catherine, Fátima Estrada, Lourdes Campero, Cristina Herrera, Claire D. Brindis, and Meredith Miller Vostrejs. 2010. "Gender, Culture and Reproductive Decision-Making among Recent Mexican Migrants in California." *Culture, Health & Sexuality* 12(1): 29–43.

Matovina, Timothy. 2012. *Latino Catholicism: Transformation in America's Largest Church*. Princeton, NJ: Princeton University Press.

McConnell, Eileen Diaz. 2011. "An 'Incredible Number of Latinos and Asians': Media Representations of Racial and Ethnic Population Change in Atlanta, Georgia." *Latino Studies* 9(2/3): 177–97.

McDonald, Steve, Nan Lin, and Dan Ao. 2009. "Networks of Opportunity: Gender, Race, and Job Leads." *Social Problems* 56(3): 385–402.

McFarland, Michael and Cheryl A. Smith. 2011. "Segregation, Race, and Infant Well-Being." *Population Research and Policy Review* 30: 467–93.

McKinnon, Andrew M. 2011. "Ideology and the Market Metaphor in Rational Choice Theory of Religion: A Rhetorical Critique of 'Religious Economies.'" *Critical Sociology* 39(4): 529–43.

McLoyd, Vonnie C., Ana Mari Cauce, David Takeuchi, and Leon Wilson. 2000. "Marital Processes and Parental Socialization in Families of Color: A Decade Review of Research." *Journal of Marriage and Family* 62: 1070–93.

Menjívar, Cecilia. 2000. *Fragmented Ties: Salvadoran Immigrant Networks in America*. Berkeley, CA: University of California Press.

Menjívar, Cecilia. 2003. "Religion and Immigration in Comparative Perspective: Catholic and Evangelical Salvadorans in San Francisco, Washington, D.C., and Phoenix." *Sociology of Religion* 64(1): 21–45.

Menjívar, Cecilia and Leisy Abrego. 2009. "Parents and Children across Borders: Legal Instability and Intergenerational Relations in Guatemalan and Salvadoran Families," pp. 160–89 in N. Foner (ed.), *Across Generations: Immigrant Families in America*. New York: New York University Press.

Menjívar, Cecilia, and Cynthia Bejarano. 2004. "Latino Immigrants' Perceptions of Crime and Police Authorities in the United States: A Case Study from the Phoenix Metropolitan Area." *Ethnic and Racial Studies* 27(1): 120–48.

Merton, Robert K. 1949. *Social Theory and Social Structure*. New York: Free Press.

Meszaros, Eva. 2012. "Ethnic Foods: Flying High." Specialtyfood.com, July 1. Accessed at http://www.specialtyfood.com/news-trends/featured-articles/article/research-spotlight-ethnic-foods-flying-high/ on February 2, 2013.

Michels, Patrick. 2012. "Blowing the Whistle on El Paso's Crooked Schools." *Texas Observer*, December 18. Accessed at http://www.texasobserver.org/blowing-the-whistle-on-el-pasos-crooked-schools/ on April 14, 2014.

Michelson, Melissa R. 2005. "Meeting the Challenge of Latino Voter Mobilization." *The Annals of the American Academy of Political and Social Science* 601(1): 85-101.

Michelson, Melissa R. 2006. "Mobilizing Latino Voters." *Latino(a) Research Review* 6(1-2): 33-49.

Mills, C. Wright. 1956. *The Power Elite*. New York: Oxford University Press.

Milner, J. Richard and Tyrone C. Howard. 2013. "Counter-Narrative as Method: Race, Policy and Research for Teacher Education." *Race Ethnicity and Education* 16(4): 536-61.

Miniño, Arialdi M., Melonie P. Heron, Sherry L. Murphy, and Kenneth D. Kochanek. 2007. "Deaths: Final Data for 2004." *National Vital Statistics Reports* 55(19). Hyattsville, MD: National Center for Health Statistics.

Miniño, Arialdi M., Sherry L. Murphy, Jiaquan Xu, and Kenneth D. Kochanek. 2011. "Deaths: Final Data for 2008." *National Vital Statistics Reports* 59(10). Hyattsville, MD: National Center for Health Statistics.

Mirande, Alfredo. 1987. *Gringo Justice*. Notre Dame, IN: University of Notre Dame Press.

Mirande, Alfredo. 1997. *Hombres y Machos: Masculinity and Latino Culture*. Boulder, CO: Westview Press.

Model, Suzanne. 1993. "The Ethnic Niche and the Structure of Opportunity: Immigrants and Minorities in New York City," pp. 161-93 in M. Katz (ed.), *The "Underclass" Debate: Views from History*. Princeton, NJ: Princeton University Press.

Monk-Tanner, Elizabeth, Mary Heiserman, Crystle Johnson, Vanity Cotton, and Manny Jackson. 2010. "The Portrayal of Racial Minorities on Prime Time Television: A Replication of the Masto and Greenberg Study a Decade Later." *Studies in Popular Culture* 32(2): 101-14.

Montejano, David. 1987. *Anglos and Mexicans in the Making of Texas, 1836-1986*. Austin, TX: University of Texas Press.

Montejano, David. 1999. "On the Question of Inclusion," pp. xi-xxvi in David Montejano (ed.), *Chicano Politics and Society in the Late Twentieth Century*. Austin, TX: University of Texas Press.

Montejano, David. 2010. *Quixote's Soldiers: A Local History of the Chicano Movement, 1966-1981*. Austin, TX: University of Texas Press.

Montes, Segundo. 1987. *El Compadrazgo: Una Estructura de Poder en los Estados Unidos*. San Salvador, El Salvador: UCA Editores.

Montes de Oca, Verónica, Rogelio Sáenz, and Ahtziri Molina. 2012. "Caring for the Elderly: A Binational Task," pp. 293-315 in J.L. Angel, F. Torres-Gill, and K. Markides (eds.), *Aging, Health, and Longevity in the Mexican-Origin Population*. New York: Springer.

Monteverde, Malena, Kenya Noronha, Alberto Palloni, and Beatriz Novak. 2010. "Obesity and Excess Mortality among the Elderly in the United States and Mexico." *Demography* 47(1): 79-96.

Montgomery, Tommie Sue. 1982. *Revolution in El Salvador: Origins and Evolution*. Boulder, CO: Westview Press.

Montoya, Margaret E. 1994. "Mascaras, Trenzas, y Greñas: Un/masking the Self While Un/braiding Latina Stories and Legal Discourse." *Chicano-Latino L. Rev* 15: 1.

Moore, Joan W. with Alfredo B. Cuéllar. 1970. *Mexican Americans*. Englewood Cliffs, NJ: Prentice-Hall.

Mora, Marie T. and Alberto Davila. 2006a. "Hispanic Ethnicity, Gender, and the Change in the LEP-Earnings Penalty in the United States during the 1990s." *Social Science Quarterly* 87(Supp. 1): 1295-318.

Mora, Marie T. and Alberto Davila. 2006b. "A Note on the Changes in the Relative Wages of LEP Hispanic Men between 1980 and 2000." *Industrial Relations* 45(2): 169-72.

Morales, Maria Cristina. 2008a. "The Ethnic Niche as an Economic Pathway for the Dark Skinned: Labor Market Incorporation of Latina/o Workers." *Hispanic Journal of Behavioral Sciences* 30(3): 280-98.

Morales, Maria Cristina. 2008b. "Immigrant Movements and the Struggle for Diverse Representations of Citizenship," pp. 62-72 in D. Dentice and J.L. Williams (eds.), *Social Movements: Contemporary Perspectives*. Newcastle: Cambridge Scholars Publishing.

Morales, Maria Cristina. 2009. "Ethnic-Controlled Economy or Segregation? Exploring Inequality in Latina/o Co-Ethnic Jobsites." *Sociological Forum* 24: 589–610.

Morales, Maria Cristina. 2011. "Latina/o Immigrant Construction Workers and Gendered Patterns of Exploitation and Resistance in Sin City." Paper presented at the annual meeting of the American Sociological Association.

Morales, Maria Cristina and Cynthia Bejarano. 2008. "Border Sexual Conquest: A Framework for Gendered and Racial Sexual Violence," pp. 181–98 in Angela Hattery, David Embrick, and Earl Smith (eds), *Globalization in America: Race, Human Rights and Inequality*. Lanham, MD: Rowman & Littlefield.

Morales, Maria Cristina and Cynthia Bejarano. 2009. "Transnational Sexual and Gendered Violence: An Application of Border Sexual Conquest at a Mexico–US Border." *Global Networks* 9(3): 420–39.

Morales, Maria Cristina and Rogelio Sáenz. 2007. "Correlates of Mexican American Students' Standardized Test Scores: An Integrated Model Approach." *Hispanic Journal of Behavioral Science* 29: 349–65.

Morales, Maria Cristina, Oscar Morales, Angelica C. Menchaca and Adam Sebastian. 2013a. "The Mexican Drug War and the Consequent Population Exodus: Transnational Movement at the US–Mexican Border." *Societies* 3: 80–103.

Morales, Maria Cristina, Aurelia Lorena Murga and Marisa E. Sanchez. 2013b. "Immigrant Mobilizations and Intra-Ethnic Political Cleavages: An Example of the Racial- and Citizenship-Divide." *Sociological Inquiry* 83: 32–54.

Morris, Aldon D. 1984. *The Origins of the Civil Rights Movement: Black Communities Organizing for Change*. New York: Free Press.

Moss, Philip and Chris Tilly. 1996. "'Soft' Skills and Race: An Investigation of Black Men's Employment Problems." *Work and Occupations* 23: 252–76.

Moynihan, Daniel Patrick. 1965. *The Negro Family: The Case for National Action*. Washington, DC: Office of Policy Planning and Research, US Department of Labor.

Mungin, Lateef and Mark Davis. 2003. "Gangs Put Their Mark on Gwinnett." *Atlanta Journal-Constitution*, April 13: 1A.

Murguia, Edward and Edward E. Telles. 1996. "Phenotype and Schooling among Mexican Americans." *Sociology of Education* 69(4): 276–89.

Murphy, Kate. 2008. "Mexican Robin Hood Figure Gains a Kind of Notoriety in US." *New York Times*, November 8. Accessed at http://www.nytimes.com/2008/02/08/us/08narcosaint.html?_r=0 on October 30, 2014.

Murphy, Sherry L., Jiaquan Xu, and Kenneth D. Kochanek. 2013. "Deaths: Final Data for 2010." *National Vital Statistics Reports* 61(4). Hyattsville, MD: National Center for Health Statistics.

Myrdal, Gunnar. 1957. *Rich Lands and Poor*. New York: Harper and Row.

Nam, Charles B. 1995. "Another Look at Mortality Crossovers." *Social Biology* 42(1–2): 133–42.

National Center for Health Statistics. 2013. *Health, United States, 2012: With Special Feature on Emergency Care*. Hyattsville, MD: National Center for Health Statistics.

National Council of La Raza. 2009. *Children Living in Mixed-Status Families: By the Numbers*. Washington, DC: National Council of La Raza.

National Hispanic Caucus of State Legislators. 2010. *Hispanic Obesity: A National Crisis*. Washington, DC: National Hispanic Caucus of State Legislators.

National Longitudinal Study of Adolescent Health (Add Health). 2008. *National Longitudinal Study of Adolescent Health (Add Health), 1994–2008 Core Files*. Chapel Hill, NC: University of North Carolina at Chapel Hill.

Nazario, Sonia. 2007. *Enrique's Journey*. New York: Random House.

Newman, Andrew Adam. 2012. "Rolling Stone Pages Aimed at Latinos, Even the Ads." *New York Times*, November 6. Accessed at http://www.nytimes.com/2012/11/07/business/media/rolling-stone-section-is-aimed-at-latinos-even-the-ads.html?_r=0 on February 2, 2013.

Ngai, Mae. 2004. *Impossible Subjects: Illegal Aliens and the Making of Modern America*. Princeton, NJ: Princeton University Press.

Nielsen, Carolyn. 2013. "Wise Latina: Framing Sonia Sotomayor in the General-Market and Latina/o-Oriented Prestige Press." *The Howard Journal of Communications* 24: 117–33.

Noguera, Pedro A. 1995. "Educational Rights and Latinos: Tracking as a Form of Second Generation Discrimination." *La Raza Law Journal* 8(1): 25–41.

Noorani, Ali. 2014. "Immigration Reform and Other Hispanic Legislative Priorities for the Second Session of the 113th Congress." Presentation at the Hispanic Association of Colleges and Universities 20th Annual National Capitol Forum on Hispanic Higher Education, April 8. Washington, DC.

O'Brien, Soledad. 2009. *Latino in America*. Atlanta: CNN. Accessed at http://www.cnn.com/SPECIALS/2009/latino.in.america/ on March 16, 2014.

O'Neil, Shannon K. 2013. *Two Nations Indivisible: Mexico, the United States, and the Road Ahead*. New York: Oxford University Press.

O'Neill, Molly. 1992. "New Mainstream: Hot Dogs, Apple Pie and Salsa." *New York Times*, March 11. Accessed at http://www.nytimes.com/1992/03/11/garden/new-mainstream-hot-dogs-apple-pie-and-salsa.html on February 2, 2013.

Ochoa, Gilda. 2004. *Becoming Neighbors in a Mexican American Community: Power, Conflict, and Solidarity*. Austin, TX: University of Texas Press.

Odem, Mary E. 2004. "Our Lady of Guadalupe in the New South: Latino Immigrants and the Politics of Integration in the Catholic Church." *Journal of American Ethnic History* 24: 26–57.

Ogbu, John U. 1991. "Minority Coping Responses and School Experience." *The Journal of Psychohistory* 18(4): 433–56.

Oktavec, Eileen. 1995. *Answered Prayers: Miracles and Milagros Along the Border*. Tucson, AZ: University of Arizona Press.

Olmos, Edward J., Lea Ybarra, and Manuel Monterrey (eds.). 1999. *Americanos*. Boston, MA: Little, Brown.

Omi, Michael and Howard Winant. 1994. *Racial Formation in the United States: From the 1960s to the 1980s*. New York: Routledge and Kegan Paul.

Orfield, Gary and Susan E. Eaton. 1996. *Dismantling Desegregation: The Quiet Reversal of Brown v. Board of Education*. New York: New Press.

Orfield, Gary and Chungmei Lee. 2007. *Historic Reversals, Accelerating Resegregation, and the Need for New Integration Strategies*. Los Angeles, CA: The Civil Rights Project, Proyecto Derechos Civiles.

Orozco, Manuel. 2002. "Globalization and Migration: The Impact of Family Remittances in Latin America." *Latin American Politics and Society* 44(2): 41–66.

Orozco, Manuel. 2012. "Future Trends in Remittances to Latin America and the Caribbean." Inter-American Dialogue Report. Washington, DC: Inter-American Dialogue.

Orrenius, Pia M. and Madeline Zavodny. 2009. "Do Immigrants Work in Riskier Jobs?" *Demography* 46(3): 535–51.

Osypuk, Theresa L., Lisa M. Bates, and Dolores Acevedo-Garcia. 2010. "Another Mexican Birthweight Paradox? The Role of Residential Enclaves and Neighborhood Poverty in the Birthweight of Mexican-Origin Infants." *Social Science & Medicine* 70: 550–60.

Ousey, Graham and Charis Kubrin. 2009. "Exploring the Connection between Immigration and Violent Crime Rates in US Cities, 1980–2000." *Social Problems* 56(3): 447–73.

Pablos-Mendez, Ariel. 1994. "Mortality among Hispanics." *Journal of the American Medical Association* 271(16): 1237–8.

Padilla, Felix. 1985. *Latino Ethnic Consciousness: The Case of Mexican Americans and Puerto Ricans in Chicago*. Notre Dame, IN: University of Notre Dame Press.

Palloni, Alberto and Elizabeth Arias. 2004. "Paradox Lost: Explaining the Hispanic Adult Mortality Advantage." *Demography* 41(3): 385–415.

Palloni, Alberto and Jeffrey D. Morenoff. 2001. "Interpreting the Paradoxical in the Hispanic Paradox." *Annals of the New York Academy of Science* 954: 140–74.

Palmer-Boyes, Ashley. 2010. "The Latino Catholic Parish as a Specialist Organization: Distinguishing Characteristics." *Review of Religious Research* 51(3): 302–23.

Park, Robert E. 1950. *Race and Culture*. Glencoe, IL: The Free Press.
Passel, Jeffrey S. and D'Vera Cohn. 2012. *Unauthorized Immigrants: 11 Million in 2011*. Washington, DC: Pew Research Center's Hispanic Trends Project.
Passel, Jeffrey S., D'Vera Cohn, and Ana Gonzalez-Barrera. 2012. *Net Migration from Mexico Falls to Zero – And Perhaps Less*. Washington, DC: Pew Research Center's Hispanic Trends Project.
Passel, Jeffrey S., D'Vera Cohn, and Ana Gonzalez-Barrera. 2013. *Population Decline of Unauthorized Immigrants Stalls, May Have Reversed*. Washington, DC: Pew Research Center's Hispanic Trends Project.
Patel, Kushang V., Karl Eschbach, Laura L. Rudkin, M. Kristen Peek, and Kyriakos S. Markides. 2003. "Neighborhood Context and Self-Rated Health in Older Mexican Americans." *Annals of Epidemiology* 13(9): 620–8.
Patterson, Orlando. 1982. *Slavery and Social Death: A Comparative Study*. Boston, MA: Harvard University Press.
PBS NewsHour. 2006. "The Spanish Media Organize their Listeners to React to the Immigration Bill." PBS NewsHour, April 11. Accessed at http://www.pbs.org/newshour/bb/latin_america-jan-june06-immigration_4-11/ on March 22, 2014.
Pérez, Eliseo J., Amelie Ramirez, Roberto Villareal, Gregory A. Talavara, Edward Trapido, Lucina Suarez, José Marti, and Alfred McAlister. 2001. "Cigarette Smoking Behavior among US Latino Men and Women from Different Countries of Origin." *American Journal of Public Health* 91(9): 1424–30.
Perlman, Joel. 2005. *Italians Then, Mexicans Now: Immigrant Origins and Second-Generation Progress, 1890–2000*. New York: Russell Sage Foundation.
Pew Research Center's Hispanic Trends Project. 2007a. *Changing Faiths: Latinos and the Transformation of American Religion*. Washington, DC: Pew Research Center's Hispanic Trends Project.
Pew Research Center's Hispanic Trends Project. 2007b. *Changing Faiths: Latinos and the Transformation of American Religion*. [2006 Hispanic Religion Survey.] Downloadable Dataset. Washington, DC: Pew Research Center's Hispanic Trends Project. Downloaded from http://www.pewhispanic.org/category/datasets/2007/ on January 3, 2014.
Pew Research Center's Hispanic Trends Project. 2008. *2008 National Survey of Latinos*. Washington, DC: Pew Research Center's Hispanic Trends Project.
Pew Research Center's Hispanic Trends Project. 2011. *2011 National Survey of Latinos*. Washington, DC: Pew Research Center's Hispanic Trends Project.
Pew Research Center's Hispanic Trends Project. 2013. *A Nation of Immigrants: A Portrait of 40 Million, Including 11 Million Unauthorized*. Washington, DC: Pew Research Center's Hispanic Trends Project.
Pfeffer, Max J. and Pilar A. Parra. 2009. "Strong Ties, Weak Ties, and Human Capital: Latino Employment Outside the Enclave." *Rural Sociology* 74(2): 241–69.
Phillips, Julie A. and Douglas S. Massey. 1999. "The New Labor Market: Immigrants and Wages after IRCA." *Demography* 36(2): 233–46.
Piore, Michael J. 1979. *Birds of Passage: Migrant Labor in Industrial Societies*. Cambridge: Cambridge University Press.
Plunkett, Scott W. and Mayra Y. Bamaca-Gomez. 2003. "The Relationship between Parenting, Acculturation, and Adolescent Academics in Mexican-Origin Immigrant Families in Los Angeles." *Hispanic Journal of Behavioral Sciences* 25: 222–39.
Population Reference Bureau. 2010. *2010 World Population Data Sheet*. Washington, DC: Population Reference Bureau.
Portales, Marco. 2000. *Crowding Out Latinos: Mexican Americans in the Public Consciousness*. Philadelphia, PA: Temple University Press.
Portes, Alejandro and Robert L. Bach. 1985. *Latin Journey: Cuban and Mexican Immigrants in the United States*. Berkeley, CA: University of California Press.
Portes, Alejandro and Min Zhou. 1993. "The New Second Generation: Segmented Assimilation and its Variants." *The Annals of the American Academy of Political and Social Science* 530(1): 74–96.

Poston, Dudley L., Jr. and Leon F. Bouvier. 2010. *Population and Society: An Introduction to Demography*. Cambridge: Cambridge University Press.

Poston, Dudley L., Jr., David Alvirez, and Marta Tienda. 1976. "Earnings Differences between Anglo and Mexican American Male Workers in 1960 and 1970: Changes in the 'Cost' of Being Mexican American." *Social Science Quarterly* 57: 618-31.

Powell, John. 2005. *Encyclopedia of North American Immigration*. New York: Facts on File.

Poyo, Gerald E. 2010. "Latino American Religion: Catholics, Twentieth Century," in C.H. Lippy and P.W. Williams (eds.), *Encyclopedia of Religion in America*. Washington, DC: CQ Press.

Preston, Samuel H., Irma T. Elo, Ira Rosenwaike, and Mark Hill. 1996. "African-American Mortality at Older Ages: Results of a Mortality Study." *Demography* 33(2): 193-209.

Pro English. 2014. *Official English Map*. Arlington, VA: Pro English. Accessed at https://www.proenglish.org/official-english/state-profiles on March 14, 2014.

Putnam, Robert D. 2000. *Bowling Alone: The Collapse and Revival of American Community*. New York: Simon and Schuster.

Putnam, Robert D. and David E. Campbell. 2010. *American Grace: How Religion Divides and Unites Us*. New York: Simon and Schuster.

Rai, Saritha. 2004. "Short on Priests, US Catholics Outsource Prayers to Indian Clergy." *New York Times*, June 13. Accessed at http://www.nytimes.com/2004/06/13/world/short-on-priests-us-catholics-outsource-prayers-to-indian-clergy.html on February 11, 2014.

Ramakrishnan, S. Karthick and Mark Baldassare. 2003. "Beyond the Ballot Box: Political Participation and Racial Inequality in California." Paper presented at the annual meeting of the Western Political Science Association, Denver, CO.

Ramirez, Oscar. 1990. "Mexican American Children and Adolescents," pp. 224-50 in J.T. Gibbs and L.N. Huang (eds.), *Children of Color*. San Francisco, CA: Jossey-Bass.

Ramos, Jorge. 2004. *The Latino Wave: How Hispanics Will Elect the Next American President*. New York: Rayo.

Reichman, Nancy E., Erin R. Hamilton, Robert A. Hummer, and Yolanda C. Padilla. 2008. "Racial and Ethnic Disparities in Low Birthweight among Urban Unmarried Mothers." *Maternal and Child Health Journal* 12: 204-15.

Reimers, David M. 1983. "An Unintended Reform: The 1965 Immigration Act and Third World Immigration to the United States." *Journal of American Ethnic History* 3(1): 9-28.

Reno, Jamie. 2012. "Why Don't We Have More Hispanic Talking Heads?" *The Daily Beast*, November 11. Accessed at http://www.thedailybeast.com/articles/2012/11/10/why-don-t-we-have-more-hispanic-talking-heads.html on March 10, 2014.

Revilla, Anita. 2006. "Student and Community Activism in Nevada on Behalf of Immigrants." Paper presented at the annual Latina/o Critical Theory Conference. Las Vegas, NV.

Ricourt, Milagros and Ruby Danta. 2003. *Hispanas de Queens: Latino Panethnicity in a New York City Neighborhood*. Ithaca, NY: Cornell University Press.

Rios, Victor M. 2011. *Punished: Policing the Lives of Black and Latino Boys*. New York: New York University Press.

Riosmena, Fernando. 2010. "Policy Shocks: On the Legal Auspices of Latin American Migration to the United States." *The Annals of the American Academy of Political and Social Research* 630: 270-93.

Robles, Arodys and Susan Cotts Watkins. 1993. "Immigration and the Family Separation in the United States at the Turn of the 20th Century." *Journal of Family History* 18: 191-211.

Rodríguez, Clara E. 2000. *Changing Race: Latinos, the Census, and the History of Ethnicity in the United States*. New York: New York University Press.

Rodríguez, Clara E. 2008. *Heroes, Lovers, and Others: The Story of Latinos in Hollywood*. New York: Oxford University Press.

Rodriguez, Fernando S., Theodore R. Curry, and Gang Lee. 2006. "Gender Differences in Criminal Sentencing: Do Effects Vary across Violent, Property, and Drug Offenses?" *Social Science Quarterly* 87(2): 318-39.

Rodriguez, Gregory. 2012. "Why Arizona Banned Ethnic Studies." *Los Angeles Times*, February

20. Accessed at http://articles.latimes.com/2012/feb/20/opinion/la-oe-rodriguez-ethnic-studies-20120220 on April 14, 2014.

Rodriguez, Jeanette. 1994. *Our Lady of Guadalupe: Faith and Empowerment among Mexican-American Women*. Austin, TX: University of Texas Press.

Rodriguez, Louie F., Eduardo Mosqueda, Pedro E. Nava, and Gilberto Conchas. 2013. "Reflecting on the Institutional Processes for College Success: The Experiences of Four Chicanos in the Context of Inequality." *Latino Studies* 11: 411-27.

Roediger, David R. 2005. *Working Toward Whiteness: The Strange Journey from Ellis Island to the Suburbs*. New York: Basic Books.

Rogers, Richard G., Robert A. Hummer, and Charles B. Nam. 2000. *Living and Dying in the USA: Behavioral, Health, and Social Differentials of Adult Mortality*. San Diego, CA: Academic Press.

Romero, Simon. 2013. "On Election Day, Latin America Willingly Trades Machismo for Female Clout." *New York Times*, December 15. Accessed at http://nytimes.com/2013/12/15/world/americas/on-election-day-latin-america-willingly-trades-machismo-for-female-clout.html on January 28, 2014.

Romo, David. 2010. "My Tío, the Saint." *Texas Monthly*, November. Accessed at http://www.texasmonthly.com/story/my-t%C3%ADo-saint on October 1, 2014.

Romo, Harriett D. and Toni Falbo. 1996. *Latino High School Graduation: Defying the Odds*. Austin, TX: University of Texas Press.

Rosaldo, Renato. 1994. "Cultural Citizenship and Educational Democracy." *Cultural Anthropology* 9: 402-11.

Ross, Catherine E. and Chia-Ling Wu. 1996. "Education, Age, and the Cumulative Advantage in Health." *Journal of Health and Social Behavior* 37: 104-20.

Rowan, Helen. 1967. "A Minority Nobody Knows." *The Atlantic* 219: 47-52.

Ruggles, Steven, Matthew Sobek, Trent Alexander, Catherine A. Fitch, Ronald Goeken, Patricia Kelly Hall, Miriam King, and Chad Ronnander. 2010. *Integrated Public Use Microdata Series: Version 4.0* [Machine-readable database]. Minneapolis, MN: Minnesota Population Center.

Sáenz, Rogelio. 1997. "Ethnic Concentration and Chicano Poverty: A Comparative Approach." *Social Science Research* 26: 205-28.

Sáenz, Rogelio. 2005. "The Changing Demographics of Roman Catholics." *Population Reference Bureau*. Accessed at http://www.prb.org/Publications/Articles/2005/TheChangingDemographicsofRomanCatholics.aspx on February 11, 2014.

Sáenz, Rogelio. 2008. "US Employment Instability on the Margins." *Population Reference Bureau*. Accessed at http://www.prb.org/Articles/2008/employmentinstability.aspx on September 2, 2013.

Sáenz, Rogelio. 2010. "Latinos in the United States 2010." *Population Reference Bureau Bulletin Update*. Accessed at http://www.prb.org/pdf10/latinos-update2010.pdf on January 12, 2015.

Sáenz, Rogelio. 2012a. "Changing Demography, Eroding Democracy." *La Voz de Esperanza* 25(7): 5-6.

Sáenz, Rogelio. 2012b. "Rural Race and Ethnicity," pp. 207-23 in L.J. Kulcsár and K.J. Curtis (eds.), *International Handbook of Rural Demography*. New York: Springer.

Sáenz, Rogelio. 2014a. *CCF Civil Rights Symposium: The State of Latino Children*. Chicago, IL: Council on Contemporary Children. Accessed at http://www.contemporaryfamilies.org/state-of-latino-children/ on April 1, 2014.

Sáenz, Rogelio. 2014b. "Fifty Years of the Deferment of the Dream for Racial Justice," pp. 119-24 in K.J. Fasching-Varner, A. Dixon, R. Reynolds, and K. Albert (eds.), *Trayvon Martin, Race, and "American Justice": Writing Wrong*. Rotterdam: Sense Publishers.

Sáenz, Rogelio and Maria Cristina Morales. 2005. "Demography of Race and Ethnicity," pp. 169-208 in D.L. Poston, Jr. and M. Micklin (eds.), *The Handbook of Population*. New York: Kluwer Academic/Plenum Publishers.

Sáenz, Rogelio and Trinidad Morales. 2012. "The Latino Paradox," pp. 47-73 in R.R. Verdugo (ed.), *The Demography of the Hispanic Population: Selected Essays*. Charlotte, NC: Information Age Publishing.

Sáenz, Rogelio and Aurelia Lorena Murga. 2011. *Latino Issues: A Reference Handbook*. Santa Barbara, CA: ABC-CLIO.

Sáenz, Rogelio and Carlos Siordia. 2012. "The Inter-Cohort Reproduction of Mexican American Dropouts." *Race and Social Problems* 4(1): 68-81.

Sáenz, Rogelio, Karen Manges Douglas, David Geronimo Embrick, and Gideon Sjoberg. 2007a. "Pathways to Downward Mobility: The Impact of Schools, Welfare, and Prisons on People of Color," pp. 373-409 in H. Vera and J.R. Feagin (eds.), *Handbook of the Study of Racial and Ethnic Relations*. New York: Springer.

Sáenz, Rogelio, Janic Filoteo, and Aurelia Lorena Murga. 2007b. "Are Mexicans in the United States a Threat to the American Way of Life? A Response to Huntington." *Du Bois Review* 4: 375-93.

Sáenz, Rogelio, Cecilia Menjivar, and San Juanita Edilia Garcia. 2011. "Arizona's SB 1070: Setting Conditions for Violations of Human Rights Here and Beyond," pp. 155-78 in J. Blau and M. Frezzo (eds.), *Sociology and Human Rights: A Bill of Rights in the Twenty-First Century*. Newbury Park, CA: Pine Forge Press.

Sáenz, Rogelio, Karen Manges Douglas, and Maria Cristina Morales. 2013. "Latina/o Sociology," pp. 59-68 in D.L. Brunsma, K.E. Iyall Smith, and B.K. Gran (eds.), *Handbook of Sociology and Human Rights*. Boulder, CO: Paradigm Publishers.

Sáenz, Victor and Luis Ponjuan. 2008. "The Vanishing Latino Male in Higher Education." *Journal of Hispanic Higher Education* 8(1): 54-89.

Salazar, Rubén. 1969. "The Mexican-American Newsbeat – Past Practices and New Concepts," pp. 33-38 in US Department of Justice, Community Relations Service (ed.), *Southwest Texas Conference on Mass Media and Mexican-Americans*. San Antonio, TX: St. Mary's University.

Sampson, Robert J. 1985. "Race and Criminal Violence: A Demographically Disaggregated Analysis of Urban Homicide." *Crime and Delinquency* 31(1): 47-82.

Sampson, Robert J. 2008. "Rethinking Crime and Immigration." *Contexts* 7(1): 28-33.

Sampson, Robert J. and Lydia Bean. 2006. "Cultural Mechanisms and Killing Fields: A Revised Theory of Community-level Racial Inequality," pp. 8-38 in R.D. Peterson, L.J. Krivo, and J. Hagan (eds.), *The Many Colors of Crime: Inequalities of Race Ethnicity and Crime in America*. New York: New York University Press.

Sampson, Robert J. and William Julius Wilson. 1995. "Toward a Theory of Race, Crime, and Urban Inequality," pp. 37-54 in J. Hagan and R.D. Peterson (eds.), *Crime and Inequality*. Stanford, CA: Stanford University Press.

Sanches, L. 1999. "Olmos Touts Latinos' Contributions." *San Diego Union Tribune*, April 17: B1.

Sanchez, Gabriel R. and Natalie Masuoka. 2010. "Brown-Utility Heuristic? The Presence and Contributing Factors of Latino Linked Fate." *Hispanic Journal of Behavioral Sciences* 32(4): 519-31.

Sánchez Walsh, Arlene M. 2010. "Latino American Religion: Pentecostals," in C.H. Lippy and P.W. Williams (eds.), *Encyclopedia of Religion in America*. Washington, DC: CQ Press.

Santa Ana, Otto. 2002. *Brown Tide Rising: Metaphors of Latinos in Contemporary American Public Discourse*. Austin, TX: University of Texas Press.

Santa Ana, Otto. 2013. *Juan in a Hundred: The Representation of Latinos on Network News*. Austin, TX: University of Texas Press.

Santos, Fernanda and Rebekah Zemansky. 2013. "Arizona Desert Swallows Migrants on Riskier Paths." *New York Times*, May 20. Accessed at http://www.nytimes.com/2013/05/21/us/immigrant-death-rate-rises-on-illegal-crossings.html on June 21, 2013.

Sarkisian, Natalie, Mariana Gerena, and Naomi Gerstel. 2006. "Extended Family Ties among Mexicans, Puerto Ricans, and Whites: Superintegration or Disintegration?" *Family Relations* 55: 331-44.

Saucedo, Leticia and Maria Cristina Morales. 2010. "Masculinities, Narratives and Latino Immigrant Workers: A Case Study of the Las Vegas Residential Construction Trades." *Harvard Journal of Law and Gender* 33: 625-59.

Schirmer, Jennifer. 1993. "The Seeking of Truth and the Gendering of Consciousness: The Comadres of El Salvador and the Conavigua Widows of Guatemala," pp. 30-64 in S. A. Radcliffe and S. Westwood (eds.), *'ViVa': Women and Popular Protest in Latin America*. New York: Routledge.

Schlosser, Eric. 2001. "The Most Dangerous Jobs in America." *Mother Jones*, July/August. Accessed at http://www.motherjones.com/politics/2001/07/dangerous-meatpacking-jobs-eric-schlosser on December 24, 2013.

Schmalzbauer, Leah. 2005. *Striving and Surviving: A Daily Life Analysis of Honduran Transnational Families*. New York: Routledge.

Seid, Michael, Donna Castañeda, Ronald Mize, Mirjana Zivkovic, and James W. Varni. 2003. "Crossing the Border for Health Care: Access and Primary Care Characteristics for Young Children of Latino Farm Workers along the US–Mexico Border." *Ambulatory Pediatrics* 3(3): 121–30.

Selig Center for Economic Growth. 2012. *Hispanic Consumer Market in the US is Larger than the Entire Economies of All but 13 Countries in the World, According to Annual UGA Selig Center Multicultural Economy Study*. Athens, GA: University of Georgia, Selig Center for Economic Growth.

Sharp, Gregory and John Iceland. 2013. "The Residential Segregation Patterns of Whites by Socioeconomic Status, 2000–2011." *Social Science Research* 42: 1046–60.

Shaw, Clifford R. and Henry D. McKay. 1942. *Juvenile Delinquency and Urban Areas*. Chicago, IL: University of Chicago Press.

Sherkat, Darren E. and Christopher G. Ellison. 1999. "Recent Developments and Current Controversies in the Sociology of Religion." *Annual Review of Sociology* 25: 363–94.

Shin, Hyoung-jin and Richard Alba. 2009. "The Economic Value of Bilingualism for Asians and Hispanics." *Sociological Forum* 24(2): 254–75.

Sierra, J.A. 2014. "Fulgencio Batista." Accessed at http://historyofcuba.com/history/funfacts/batist.htm on March 31, 2014.

Siskin, Alison. 2007. *Immigration-Related Detention: Current Legislative Issues*. Congressional Research Service Report for Congress. Order Code RL32369. Washington, DC: Congressional Research Service. Accessed at http://www.ilw.com/immigdaily/news/2007,0406-crs.pdf on April 22, 2014.

Siskin, Alison. 2012. *Immigration-Related Detention: Current Legislative Issues*. Congressional Research Service Report for Congress. Order Code RL 32369. Washington, DC: Congressional Research Service. Accessed at http://www.fas.org/irp/crs/RL32369.pdf on April 22, 2014.

Sjoberg, Gideon, Richard A. Brymer, and Buford Farris. 1966. "Bureaucracy and the Lower Class." *Sociology and Social Research* 50: 325–37.

Skirrbekk, Vegard, Erik Kaufmann, and Anne Goujon. 2010. "Secularism, Fundamentalism, or Catholicism? The Religious Composition of the United States to 2043." *Journal for the Scientific Study of Religion* 49(2): 293–310.

Smith-Morris, Carolyn, Daisy Morales-Campos, Edith Alejandra Castañeda Alvarez, and Matthew Turner. 2012. "An Anthropology of *Familismo*: On Narratives and Description of Mexican/Immigrants." *Hispanic Journal of Behavioral Science* 35(1): 35–60.

Smock, Pamela J. 2000. "Cohabitation in the United States: An Appraisal of Research Themes, Findings, and Implications." *Annual Review of Sociology* 26: 1–20.

Stanzione, Vincent. 2003. *Rituals of Sacrifice: Walking the Face of the Earth on the Sacred Path of the Sun*. Albuquerque, NM: University of New Mexico Press.

Stevens-Arroyo, Anthony M. 2010. "Latino American Religion: Struggles for Justice," in C.H. Lippy and P.W. Williams (eds.), *Encyclopedia of Religion in America*. Washington, DC: CQ Press.

Stewart, Craig O., Margaret J. Pitts, and Helena Osborne. 2011. "Mediated Intergroup Conflict: The Discursive Construction of 'Illegal Immigrants' in a Regional US Newspaper." *Journal of Language and Social Psychology* 30(1): 8–27.

Stowell, Jacob I. 2007. *Immigration and Crime: The Effects of Immigration on Criminal Behavior*. New York: LFB Scholarly Publishing.

Stowell, Jacob I., Steven F. Messner, Kelly F. McGeever, and Lawrence E. Raffalovich. 2009. "Immigration and the Recent Violent Crime Drop in the United States: A Pooled, Cross-Sectional Time-Series Analysis of Metropolitan Areas." *Criminology* 47(3): 889–928.

Strawbridge, William A., Richard D. Cohen, Sarah J. Shema, and George A. Kaplan. 1997. "Frequent Attendance at Religious Services and Mortality Over 28 Years." *American Journal of Public Health* 87(6): 957–61.

Suárez-Orozco, Cerola, Irina L.G. Todorova, and Josephine Louie. 2002. "Making Up For Lost Time: The Experience of Separation and Reunification among Immigrant Families." *Family Process* 41(4): 625–43.

Sullivan, Kathleen. 2000. "St. Catherine's Catholic Church: One Church, Parallel Congregations," pp. 255-89 in H. Ebaugh and J. Chafetz (eds.), *Religion and the New Immigrants*. Walnut Creek, CA: AltaMira Press.

Sussner, Katarina M., Ana C. Lindsay, and Karen E. Peterson. 2008. "The Influence of Acculturation on Breast-Feeding Initiation and Duration in Low-Income Women in the US." *Journal of Biosocial Science* 40: 673-96.

Swidler, Ann. 1986. "Culture in Action: Symbols and Strategies." *American Sociological Review* 51: 273-86.

Tamis-LeMonda, Catherine S., Ronit Kahana-Kalman and Hirokazu Yoshikawa. 2009. "Father Involvement in Immigrant and Ethnically Diverse Families from the Prenatal Period to the Second Year: Prediction and Mediating Mechanisms." *Sex Roles* 60: 496-509.

Taylor, J. Edward, Philip L. Martin, and Michael Fix. 1997. *Poverty Amid Prosperity: Immigration and the Changing Face of Rural California*. Washington, DC: Urban Institute.

Taylor, Nikki M. 2005. *Frontiers of Freedom: Cincinnati's Black Community, 1802-1868*. Athens, OH: Ohio University Press.

Taylor, Paul and Mark Hugo Lopez. 2010. *National Latino Leader? The Job is Open*. Washington, DC: Pew Research Center's Hispanic Trends Program.

Taylor, Paul, Ana Gonzalez-Barrera, Jeffrey Passel, and Mark Hugo Lopez. 2012a. *An Awakened Giant: The Hispanic Electorate is Likely to Double by 2030*. Washington, DC: Pew Research Center's Hispanic Trends Project.

Taylor, Paul, Mark Hugo Lopez, Jessica Hamar Martinez, and Gabriel Velasco. 2012b. *When Labels Don't Fit: Hispanics and Their Views of Identity*. Washington, DC: Pew Research Center's Hispanic Trends Project.

Taylor, Paul, Mark Hugo Lopez, Gabriel Velasco, and Seth Motel. 2012c. *Hispanics Say They Have the Worst of a Bad Economy*. Washington, DC: Pew Research Center's Hispanic Trends Project.

Teller, Charles H. and Steve Clyburn. 1974. "Trends in Infant Mortality." *Texas Business Review* 48: 240-6.

Telles, Edward E. 2006. *Race in Another America: The Significance of Skin Color in Brazil*. Princeton, NJ: Princeton University Press.

Telles, Edward E. and Vilma Ortiz. 2008. *Generations of Exclusion: Mexican Americans, Assimilation, and Race*. New York: Russell Sage Foundation.

Texas Tribune, The. 2010. *Public School Explorer*. Accessed at http://www.texastribune.org/publiced/explore/ on April 7, 2013.

Thomas, Pedro M. 2011. "Theoretical Articulation on Immigration and Crime." *Homicide Studies* 15(4): 382-403.

Thornton, Arland. 2005. *Reading History Sideways: The Fallacy and Enduring Impact of the Developmental Paradigm on Family Life*. Chicago, IL: University of Chicago Press.

Tienda, Marta and Ronald Angel. 1982. "Headship and Household Composition among Blacks, Hispanics, and Other Whites." *Social Forces* 61: 508-31.

Time. 1967. "Minorities: Pocho's Progress." *Time* 89: 24-25.

Toldson, Ivory A. and Brianna P. Lemmons. 2013. "Social Demographics, the School Environment, and Parenting Practices Associated with Parents' Participation in Schools and Academic Success among Black, Hispanic, and White Students." *Journal of Human Behavior in the Social Environment* 23(2): 237-55.

Treviño, Robert R. 2006. *The Church in the Barrio: Mexican American Ethno-Catholicism in Houston*. Chapel Hill, NC: University of North Carolina Press.

Trueba, Enrique (Henry) T. 1999. *Latinos Unidos from Cultural Diversity to the Politics of Solidarity*. Lanham, MD: Rowman and Littlefield.

Tuttle, William M. 1996. *Race Riot: Chicago in the Red Summer of 1919*. Urbana, IL: University of Illinois Press.

Ulmer, Jeffery T., Casey T. Harris, and Darrell Steffensmeier. 2012. "Racial and Ethnic Disparities in Structural Disadvantage and Crime: White, Black, and Hispanic Comparisons." *Social Science Quarterly* 93: 799-819.

United Nations. 1993. *Report of the UN Truth Commission on El Salvador*. New York: United Nations, Security Council. Accessed at http://www.derechos.org/nizkor/salvador/informes/truth.html on March 2, 2013.

US Census Bureau. 2013a. *2000 SF1 100% Data*. American Factfinder webpage. Washington, DC: US Census Bureau. Accessed at http://factfinder2.census.gov/faces/nav/jsf/pages/searchresults.xhtml?refresh=t on March 23, 2013.

US Census Bureau. 2013b. *2010 American Community Survey 1-Year Estimates*. Washington, DC: US Census Bureau. Accessed at http://factfinder2.census.gov/faces/tableservices/jsf/pages/productview.xhtml?pid=ACS_10_1YR_C16001&prodType=table and http://factfinder2.census.gov/faces/tableservices/jsf/pages/productview.xhtml?pid=ACS_10_1YR_C16006&prodType=table on February 2, 2013.

US Census Bureau. 2013c. *2010 SF1 100% Data*. American Factfinder webpage. Washington, DC: US Census Bureau. Accessed at http://factfinder2.census.gov/faces/tableservices/jsf/pages/productview.xhtml?fpt=table on March 14, 2013.

US Census Bureau. 2013d. *2011 American Community Survey 5-Year Estimates*. American Factfinder webpage. Accessed at http://factfinder2.census.gov/faces/nav/jsf/pages/searchresults.xhtml?refresh=t#none on March 24, 2013.

US Census Bureau. 2013e. *2012 National Population Projections: Summary Tables*. Washington, DC: US Census Bureau. Accessed at http://www.census.gov/population/projections/data/national/2012/summarytables.html on March 20, 2013.

US Census Bureau. 2013f. *Methodology and Assumptions for the 2012 National Projections*. Washington, DC: US Census Bureau. Accessed at http://www.census.gov/population/projections/files/methodology/methodstatement12.pdf on March 21, 2013.

US Census Bureau. 2014. "Census Bureau Highlights Young Noncitizen Population in the US." Accessed at http://www.census.gov/newsroom/releases/archives/american_community_survey_acs/cb14-34.html on March 7, 2014.

US Department of Homeland Security. 2012. *2011 Yearbook of Immigration Statistics*. Washington, DC: US Department of Homeland Security, Office of Immigration Statistics. Accessed at http://www.dhs.gov/sites/default/files/publications/immigration-statistics/yearbook/2011/ois_yb_2011.pdf on March 1, 2013.

US Department of Homeland Security. 2013. *Yearbook of Immigration Statistics: 2012 Legal Permanent Residents*. Washington, DC: US Department of Homeland Statistics, Office of Immigration Statistics. Accessed at http://www.dhs.gov/yearbook-immigration-statistics-2012-legal-permanent-residents on April 22, 2014.

US Department of Homeland Security. 2014. "Number of I-821D, Consideration for Deferred Action for Childhood Arrivals by Fiscal Year, Quarter, Intake, Biometrics and Case Status: 2012–2014 First Quarter." Accessed at http://www.uscis.gov/sites/default/files/USCIS/Resources/Reports%20and%20Studies/Immigration%20Forms%20Data/All%20Form%20Types/DACA/DACA-06-02-14.pdf on April 24, 2014.

US Department of Labor. 2014a. *History of Federal Minimum Wage Rates Under the Federal Labor Standards Act, 1938–2009*. Washington, DC: US Department of Labor. Accessed at http://www.dol.gov/whd/minwage/chart.htm on April 11, 2014.

US Department of Labor. 2014b. *Minimum Wage Laws in the States – January 1, 2014*. Washington, DC: US Department of Labor. Accessed at http://www.dol.gov/whd/minwage/america.htm on April 11, 2014.

US Government Accountability Office. 2006. *Border-Crossing Deaths Have Doubled Since 1995; Border Patrol's Efforts to Prevent Deaths Have Not Been Fully Evaluated*. Washington, DC: US Government Accountability Office. Accessed at http://www.gao.gov/new.items/d06770.pdf on June 21, 2013.

US Immigration and Customs Enforcement. 2014. *FY 2014 ICE Immigration Removals*. Washington, DC: US Immigration and Customs Enforcement. Accessed at https://www.ice.gov/removal-statistics/ on January 13, 2015.

US Immigration and Customs Enforcement. 2015. Secure Communities. Washington, DC: US

Immigration and Customs Enforcement. Accessed at http://www.ice.gov/secure-communities on January 12, 2015.

US Immigration and Naturalization Service. 1948. *Annual Report of the Immigration and Naturalization Service for the Fiscal Year Ending 1948*. Washington, DC: Immigration and Naturalization Service.

Valdés, Guadalupe. 1996. *Con Respeto: Bridging the Distances between Culturally Diverse Families and Schools: An Ethnographic Portrait*. Amsterdam Avenue, NY: Teaching College Press.

Valdez, Zulema. 2011. *The New Entrepreneurs: How Race, Class, and Gender Shape American Enterprise*. Stanford, CA: University of Stanford Press.

Valenzuela, Angela. 1999. *Subtractive Schooling US-Mexican Youth and the Politics of Caring*. Albany, NY: State University of New York Press.

Valenzuela, Angela, and Sanford M. Dornbusch. 1994. "Familism and Social Capital in the Academic Achievement of Mexican Origin and Anglo Adolescents." *Social Science Quarterly* 75: 18-36.

Valverde, Sylvia A. 1987. "A Comparative Study of Hispanic High School Dropouts and Graduates. Why Do Some Leave School Early and Some Finish?" *Education and Urban Society* 19(3): 320-9.

Van Dijk, Teun A. 1991. *Racism in the Press*. London: Routledge.

Vega, William A. 1995. "The Study of Latino Families," pp. 3-17 in R.E. Zambrana (ed.), *Understanding Latino Families: Scholarship, Policy and Practice*. Thousand Oaks, CA: Sage.

Vélez, William. 2008. "The Educational Experiences of Latinos in the United States," pp. 129-48 in H. Rodríguez, R. Sáenz, and C. Menjívar (eds.), *Latina/os in the United States: Changing the Face of América*. New York: Springer.

Verba, Sidney, Kay Lehman Schlozman, and Henry E. Brady. 1995. *Voice and Equality: Civic Voluntarism in American Politics*. Cambridge, MA: Harvard University Press.

Verdeja, Ernesto. 2002. "Law, Terrorism, and the Plenary Power Doctrine: Limiting Alien Rights." *Constellations* 9(1): 89-97.

Videla, Nancy Plankey. 2008. "Maquiladoras," pp. 591-4 in W.A. Darity, Jr. (ed.), *International Encyclopedia of the Social Sciences*. Vol. 4, 2nd edn. Detroit, MI: Macmillan Reference USA. Accessed at http://www.encyclopedia.com/topic/Offshore_assembly_industry.aspx on May 17, 2013.

Voces Oral History. 2014. *Voces Oral History*. Accessed at http://www.lib.utexas.edu/voces/ on April 12, 2014.

Wade, Peter. 1997. *Race and Ethnicity in Latin America*. London: Pluto Press.

Waldinger, Roger. 1996. *Still the Promised City? African-Americans and New Immigrants in Postindustrial New York*. Cambridge, MA: Harvard University Press.

Wallace, Steven P., Carolyn Mendez-Luck, and Xóchitl Castañeda. 2009. "Heading South: Why Mexican Immigrants in California Seek Health Services in Mexico." *Medical Care* 47(6): 662-9.

Wallerstein, Immanuel. 1974. *The Modern World System, Capitalist Agriculture and the Origins of the European World Economy in the Sixteenth Century*. New York: Academic Press.

Warner, R. Stephen and Judith G. Wittner. 1998. *Gatherings in Diaspora: Religious Communities and the New Immigration*. Philadelphia, PA: Temple University Press.

Waterman, Stephanie J. 2013. "Using Theory to Tell It Like It Is." *Urban Review* 45: 335-54.

Weimann, Gabriel. 2000. *Communicating Unreality: Modern Media and the Reconstruction of Reality*. Thousand Oaks, CA: Sage.

Weitzer, Ronald and Steven A. Tuch. 2005. "Determinants of Public Satisfaction with the Police." *Police Quarterly* 8(3): 279-97.

White, Christopher M. 2009. *The History of El Salvador*. Westport, CT: Greenwood Press.

Wikipedia. 2013. *List of English Words of Spanish Origin*. Accessed at http://en.wikipedia.org/wiki/List_of_English_words_of_Spanish_origin on February 1, 2013.

Wikipedia. 2014. *Political Status of Puerto Rico*. Accessed at http://en.wikipedia.org/wiki/Political_status_of_Puerto_Rico on March 31, 2014.

Williams, David R. 1999. "Race, Socioeconomic Status, and Health: The Added Effects of Racism and Discrimination." *Annals of the New York Academy of Sciences* 896(1): 173-88.

Williams, David R. and Pamela Braboy Jackson. 2005. "Social Sources of Racial Disparities in Health." *Health Affairs* 24(2): 325-34.

Williams, Johnny E. 2003. *African-American Religion and the Civil Rights Movement in Arkansas*. Jackson, MS: University of Mississippi Press.

Williams, Philip J. and Patricia Fortuny Loret de Mola. 2007. "Religion and Social Capital among Mexican Immigrants in Southwest Florida." *Latino Studies* 5: 233–53.

Wilson, William Julius. 1987. *The Truly Disadvantaged: The Inner City, the Underclass, and Public Policy*. Chicago, IL: University of Chicago Press.

Wilson, William Julius. 1997. *When Work Disappears: The World of the New Urban Poor*. New York: Vintage.

World Health Organization. 2000. *Obesity: Preventing and Managing the Global Epidemic*. Technical Report Series 894. Geneva: World Health Organization.

Xi, Juan, Sean-Shong Hwang, and Yue Cao. 2010. "Ecological Context and Immigrants' Earnings: English Ability as a Mediator." *Social Science Research* 39: 652–61.

Xu, Qingwen and Kalina Brabeck. 2012. "Service Utilization for Latino Children in Mixed-Status Families." *Social Work Research* 36(3): 209–21.

Yu, Roger. 2010. "Boycotts of Arizona Immigration Law Add Up." *USA Today*, April 27. Accessed at http://usatoday30.usatoday.com/travel/news/2010-04-27-arizonaboycott27_ST_N.htm?csp= on March 27, 2014.

Zambrana, Ruth E. 2011. *Latinos in American Society: Families and Communities in Transition*. Ithaca, NY: Cornell University Press.

Zambrana, Ruth E., C.M. Scrimshaw, Nancy L. Collins, and Christine Dunkel-Schetter. 1997. "Prenatal Health Behaviors and Psychosocial Risk Factors in Pregnant Women of Mexican Origin: The Role of Acculturation." *American Journal of Public Health* 87(6): 1022–6.

Zamudio, Margaret M. and Michael I. Lichter. 2008. "Bad Attitudes and Good Soldiers: Soft Skills as a Code for Tractability: Immigrant Latina/os over Native Blacks in the Hotel Industry." *Social Problems* 55(4): 573–89.

Zúñiga, Víctor and Rubén Hernández-León (eds.). 2006. *New Destinations: Mexican Immigration in the United States*. New York: Russell Sage Foundation.

Index

Affordable Care Act (Obamacare) 174, 176–7
  see also Obamacare
age divide 54
age-sex pyramid 52–3
American Civil Liberties Union (ACLU) 77, 180
Americanos: Latino Life in the US/La Vida Latina en los Estados Unidos (*Americanos*) 209–11
assimilation perspective 89–90, 122, 210, 218, 221

bandido (bandit) 181, 185, 195
bicultural education 71, 76, 84, 97
  see also bilingual education
bilingual education 71, 75–6, 84, 97, 99
  see also bicultural education
biological determinism 88
bi-racial framework 219, 231
  see also tri-racial framework
blaming the victim 88, 98, 122
Border Industrialization Program 9, 28, 36, 39
border sexual conquest thesis 193–4
Bracero Program 9, 32–4, 36–7, 39
Brown v Board of Education 75, 222

Castro, Fidel 3, 11, 14, 21
Chávez, César 74, 215
Chicano Movement 74–5, 84, 155
citizenship, US 8–10, 12–13, 19, 37–8, 69–70, 73–4, 76–7, 82–4, 87, 116–18, 138, 160, 173–4, 178, 206, 221, 223–5
  see also rights claiming
civil rights (social and cultural citizenship) 37, 70–1, 73, 76, 82–5, 96–7, 149, 182–3, 200, 219, 222–3
  see also human rights; immigrant rights; labor rights
collective black 220, 224
colonized group 10–11, 100
  see also colonized minority

colonized minority 13, 15
  see also colonized group
colorblind 207, 209–10, 219, 223
Corrections Corporation of America (CCA) 42, 184
counterframe 201, 207
  see also counterimage, counternarrative, and counterstory
counterimage 201, 207–8
  see also counterframe, counternarrative, and counterstory
counternarrative 197, 200–2, 204, 207, 216
  see also counterframe, counterimage, and counterstory
counterstory 200–1
  see also counterframe, counterimage, and counternarrative
criminalization of immigrants 32, 41, 69, 82, 181, 184
  see also criminalization of Latinos; HR 4437 (Border Protection Anti-Terrorism and Illegal Immigration Control Act of 2005, Sensenbrenner Bill)
criminalization of Latinos 180–6, 195
  see also criminalization of immigrants; HR 4437 (Border Protection Anti-Terrorism and Illegal Immigration Control Act of 2005, Sensenbrenner Bill)
critical race theory (CRT) 198, 200, 206–7
cultural capital 90
cultural citizenship 74
cultural explanations 88–90, 121–3
culture of poverty 88–9, 121, 138, 185
cumulative advantages/disadvantages 159–60
cumulative causation 30, 33, 36
Curb Your Enthusiasm 212

Deferred Action for Childhood Arrivals (DACA) 84, 87
denominational affiliation 140, 144, 149, 151–2, 157

Department of Homeland Security 19, 21-2, 40, 42, 44-5, 84, 136, 182
  see also militarization of the US-Mexico border; US-Mexico border security
deportation 32, 34-5, 41-2, 80, 82, 121, 136-7, 177, 184, 187, 189-91, 195
detention centers 42, 184, 225
diabetes 57, 158, 161, 164, 166-7, 172, 178, 230
Diego, Juan 141-2
disability 145, 158, 160, 166, 169-72, 177, 230
discouraged workers 106
DREAM (Development Relief and Education for Alien Minors) Act 87
Dreamers, The 84, 87
dual labor market theory 26-7

elite model of power 71
English as official language 76, 200
English-only policies 75-7, 98
epidemiological paradox 57, 158, 161, 179-80
  see also Latino paradox; other side of paradox
erasure of memory 97, 99
ethnic studies 97, 99

familism 123-4, 165
  see also familismo
familismo 123-5
  see also familism
fertility 25, 27, 47, 49, 51, 54, 56-7, 68, 150, 216
food 2, 178
Foraker Act 12
framing of Latinos 197-201, 203-7, 215-16

GEO group 42
Ghost 212
golden exiles 3, 11
group size perspective 103, 199
  see also power threat perspective
Gutiérrez, José Ángel 75

Hazelton, Pennsylvania 183
health insurance 57, 107-9, 158, 160, 173-7, 179, 209, 225-6, 230
honorary whites 220, 224
HR 4437 (Border Protection Anti-Terrorism and Illegal Immigration Control Act of 2005, Sensenbrenner Bill) 82, 203
  see also criminalization of immigrants; criminalization of Latinos

human capital 30-1, 101-4, 106, 113
human capital perspective 101
human rights 30, 70, 74, 149, 156, 184, 194-5, 225
  see also civil rights; immigrant rights; labor rights
Huntington, Samuel 47, 207, 225

Illegal Immigration Reform and Immigrant Responsibility Act (IIRIRA) 41-2, 136
immigrant jobs 31, 107-8, 233-4
  see also immigrant niche
immigrant niche 104, 109, 227
  see also immigrant jobs
immigrant revitalization theory 187
immigrant rights 41, 69-70, 73, 81-5, 149, 224-5
  Immigrant rights marches 83, 203, 215, 224
  Immigrant Rights Movement 80-5
  see also civil rights; human rights; labor rights
Immigration and Nationality Act of 1965 (Hart-Celler Act) 37-8, 43
immigration-industrial complex 42, 184
immigration integration 146-9
immigration reform 81, 84, 89, 116-17, 149, 178, 184, 194, 203, 224-5
Immigration Reform and Control Act of 1986 (IRCA, Simpson-Mazzoli Act of 1986) 38-9, 182, 224
index of dissimilarity (D) 63-4
indigenous 3, 4, 7, 15-16, 40, 47, 69, 139-42, 219, 221
institutional corruption 95, 98
institutional theory 29-30
intermarriage 103, 125, 127-30, 221
involuntary minorities 89

Jones Act 12

La Matanza (The Massacre) 16-17
La Violencia (The Violence) 22
labeling hype 185
labeling theory 185
labor rights 20, 70, 75, 225
  see also civil rights; human rights; immigrant rights
labor unions 16-17, 20-1, 65, 70, 74, 82, 210
Latino in America 209-11
Latino immigrant crime paradox 180-1, 184, 186-7, 195
Latino paradox 158, 161-6, 179
  see also epidemiological paradox; other side of paradox

Latino purchasing power 208–9, 216, 229
Latino spin 207–9, 217
Latino threat narrative 198
life expectancy 57–8, 158–9, 161, 163, 177, 230
linked fate 72–3, 77, 84

machismo 122–3
manifest destiny 7–8
maquiladora 36
marianismo 122
Marielitos 11
Martin, Trayvon 199
Mayan 20, 142, 146–7
metonym 205
Mexican–American War 1, 9, 47, 181, 195
  see also US–Mexico War
militarization of the US–Mexico border 40–1, 47, 177, 182, 184, 193–5, 225
  see also Department of Homeland Security; US–Mexico border security
minimum wage 227
mixed-status families (households) 82, 121, 137
mortality 49, 51, 57–60, 158–61, 165–6, 169, 173, 179, 230
mortality crossover 160

narco violence 10, 177
natural increase (decrease) 59–60
neoclassical economics perspective 25–6
network theory 29, 36
new-destination areas (states) 39–40, 64–8, 140, 154, 183, 205–6, 216
new economics of migration perspective 26
New York Times, The 200, 206–7, 213–14
North American Free Trade Agreement (NAFTA) 9, 28, 36, 39–41

Obamacare 174, 179
  see also Affordable Care Act
obesity 57, 158, 167–9, 172, 177–8, 230
Operation Bootstrap 12, 28
opportunity structure 104, 185
oppositional culture (behavior) 89
other side of the paradox 158, 166, 179, 230
  see also epidemiological paradox; Latino paradox
Our Lady of Guadalupe 139, 141–2
  see also Virgin of Guadalupe

pan-ethnic 4, 72–3, 81, 84
passport 15, 30

  see also political asylum; political refugees
people of color 70, 88, 90, 97, 121, 127, 138, 148, 159–60, 180–1, 184, 195, 197–8, 200–1, 204, 207, 227–8, 231
pluralist model of power 71
political asylum 10, 19
  see also political refugees
political party affiliation 71–3, 77, 153, 224
political refugees 11, 19, 21, 38
  see also political asylum
Pope Francis 154, 156–7
population projections 1, 49, 60–1, 81, 100, 140, 215, 228–30
power threat perspective 198–200
  see also group size perspective

race, biological perceptions 4
racial census identification 3–4
racial formation perspective 198–9
racial identity 4–6
racial invariance thesis 186
racial profiling 83, 97, 180, 183, 185–6
racialized racial system 91
racism 32, 74, 89, 91, 97, 181–2, 186, 200, 207, 219, 222
Ramos, Jorge 208, 215
religion as social capital 143–6
religious conversion 140–2, 150–1, 156–7, 231
religious marketplace 140, 149–50
religious syncretism 141–2
remittances 26, 30, 136, 147
Repatriation Program 3, 32, 203
residential segregation 103–4
rights claiming 70, 73–4, 203, 215, 224
  League of United Latin American Citizens (LULAC) 75
  Mexican American Legal Defense and Education Fund (MALDEF) 75–6
  National Council of La Raza (NCLR) 75, 82, 137
  Puerto Rican Legal Defense Education Fund (PRLDEF) 209
  see also civil rights; human rights; immigrant rights; labor rights; labor unions

Salazar, Rubén 202
same-sex couples (cohabitation) 121, 125, 130–2, 137–8
SB 1070 83, 97, 183
SB 2211 97
school segregation 69, 75, 86–7, 95, 222
secularization 151–4, 156–7

Secure Communities 183-4, 189
segmented assimilation 89
Seinfeld 212
sex ratio 62, 68, 152-3
skin color 3-4, 11, 15, 21, 109, 113-14, 219-21, 231
social capital 25, 29-30, 36, 143-5, 156
    see also social networks
social construction of race 4
social disorganization theory 186-7
social incapacities 195
social networks 24-5, 29, 36, 63, 102-3, 107, 137, 143, 147, 165
    see also social capital; weak ties
soft skills 101-2
Sotomayor, Sonia 206-7, 215
Spanish-American War 11-12
Spanish-language media 197, 201-4, 206, 208, 215-17
spatial mismatch 104
stratification 4, 10, 13, 90, 159, 218, 220-2, 224, 231
structural criminalization 183
structural explanations 87-8, 90-1, 98, 101, 103-4, 121-5, 138, 181, 185-6, 221-4, 231
structural violence 193, 195
subculture of violence 185
subtractive education 90

Telemundo 203
Teller Act 10-11
temporary protected status (TPS) 19
Tijerina, Reis López 75
transnational/transnationalism 121, 135, 147, 177
    see also transnational families
transnational families 135-6
    see also transnational/transnationalism
Treaty of Guadalupe Hidalgo 1, 9-10, 47, 203, 231
Treaty of Paris 10-11
tri-racial framework 219-20, 224, 231
    see also bi-racial framework

undocumented (unauthorized) 19, 21, 30-5, 38-42, 46, 70, 73, 81-2, 87, 97, 102, 106, 118, 137-8, 158, 172-4, 177-9, 182-5, 198-200, 203, 205, 223-5
unequal funding of education 86-7
United Fruit Company (UFCO) 19-21
Univision 203, 208, 215-16
US-Mexico border 8-9, 31-9, 95, 100, 174, 177-8, 180-3
    see also Treaty of Guadalupe Hidalgo
US-Mexico border operations 34-6, 40, 182, 203
    see also Department of Homeland Security; militarization of US-Mexico border; US-Mexico border security
US-Mexico border security (national security) 34, 41, 47, 117, 95, 177-8, 182, 184, 194, 225
    see also Department of Homeland Security; militarization of US-Mexico border; Secure Communities; US-Mexico border operations
US-Mexico War 231
    see also Mexican-American War
USA PATRIOT Act of 2001 42

Virgin of Guadalupe 139, 141-2, 145, 147, 156-7
    see also Our Lady of Guadalupe
voter mobilization 81, 85
Voting Rights Act (VRA) 75-7

weak ties 102-3
    see also social networks
white hegemony 183, 199
white privilege 4, 69, 199, 220-1
white supremacy 219, 226, 231
world system theory 7, 27-8, 36, 39

youth control complex 181

zoot suit 182, 195, 202

CPSIA information can be obtained
at www.ICGtesting.com
Printed in the USA
BVHW011415301220
596012BV00025B/108